INTERNATIONAL TRADE, INVESTMENT, AND THE SUSTAINABLE DEVELOPMENT GOALS

||||| ||| ||||||| ||| |||||| |||
T0371253

In September 2015, world leaders adopted the 2030 Agenda for Sustainable Development. The Sustainable Development Goals (SDGs) represent a distinctive approach to development that moves away from a narrow perspective on economic development to an integrative agenda that simultaneously pursues ecological, social and economic goals. Trade and foreign investment are important economic vectors through which many of these goals can be achieved. Much depends, however, on whether and how SDGs are incorporated in international trade and investment agreements, and in private or public sector initiatives. Policymakers are also confronted with the interdependence of the SDGs which raises difficult trade-offs between various Goals. The contributions in this book explore the penetration and trade-offs of the SDGs, drawing on a multidisciplinary approach incorporating insights from economists, lawyers and political scientists. The book offers a valuable guide for scholars and policymakers in identifying and evaluating the complex challenges related to sustainable development.

COSIMO BEVERELLI is a research economist at the World Trade Organization and programme associate in the Global Governance Programme, European University Institute. He has published in peer-reviewed journals, including the *Journal of International Economics*, on the effects of international fragmentation of production, the impact of services trade policies on manufacturing, trade facilitation, trade policy substitution, and international migration.

JÜRGEN KURTZ is Professor of International Economic Law at the European University Institute. His most recent book is *The WTO and International Investment Law: Converging Systems* (2016). Professor Kurtz has acted as an International Centre for the Settlement of Investment Disputes arbitrator and serves on the editorial boards of *Journal of International Dispute Settlement* and *Journal of World Investment and Trade*.

DAMIAN RAESS is Assistant Professor of Political Science, funded by the Swiss National Science Foundation, at the World Trade Institute, University of Bern, specialising in international political economy. He is the co-author of the Labor Provisions in Trade Agreements (LABPTA) dataset, which provides detailed information that documents key features of labour provisions across preferential trade agreements signed from 1990 onwards.

INTERNATIONAL TRADE, INVESTMENT, AND THE SUSTAINABLE DEVELOPMENT GOALS

World Trade Forum

Edited by

COSIMO BEVERELLI

World Trade Organization

JÜRGEN KURTZ

European University Institute

DAMIAN RAESS

World Trade Institute, University of Bern

CAMBRIDGE
UNIVERSITY PRESS

CAMBRIDGE
UNIVERSITY PRESS

University Printing House, Cambridge CB2 8BS, United Kingdom

One Liberty Plaza, 20th Floor, New York, NY 10006, USA

477 Williamstown Road, Port Melbourne, VIC 3207, Australia

314-321, 3rd Floor, Plot 3, Splendor Forum, Jasola District Centre, New Delhi - 110025, India

103 Penang Road, #05-06/07, Visioncrest Commercial, Singapore 238467

Cambridge University Press is part of the University of Cambridge.

It furthers the University's mission by disseminating knowledge in the pursuit of education, learning and research at the highest international levels of excellence.

www.cambridge.org
Information on this title: www.cambridge.org/9781108744119
DOI: 10.1017/9781108881364

© Cambridge University Press 2020

First published 2020
First paperback edition 2022

A catalogue record for this publication is available from the British Library

Library of Congress Cataloging in Publication data
Names: World Trade Forum (2018 : Florence, Italy), author. | Beverelli, Cosimo, editor. | Kurtz, Jürgen, editor. | Raess, Damian, editor.
Title: International trade, investment, and the sustainable development goals : World Trade Forum / edited by Cosimo Beverelli, World Trade Organization; Jürgen Kurtz, European University Institute; Damian Raess, World Trade Institute, University of Bern.
Description: Cambridge, United Kingdom ; New York, NY : Cambridge University Press, [2020] | Includes bibliographical references and index.
Identifiers: LCCN 2020018639 | ISBN 9781108840880 (hardback) | ISBN 9781108881364 (ebook)
Subjects: LCSH: Foreign trade regulation–Congresses. | Investments, Foreign (International law)–Congresses. | Sustainable development–Law and legislation–Congresses. | International trade–Congresses. | Commercial policy–Congresses.
Classification: LCC K4600.A6 W67 2018 | DDC 332.67/3–dc23
LC record available at https://lccn.loc.gov/2020018639

ISBN 978-1-108-84088-0 Hardback
ISBN 978-1-108-74411-9 Paperback

CONTENTS

FIGURES

TABLES

CONTRIBUTORS

GIOVANNA ADINOLFI is a professor of international law at the University of Milan, where she teaches public international law and international economic law. Her areas of expertise include international trade law and international monetary and financial law, and she has authored several publications on these topics. In more recent times, she has expanded her research activities to sustainable development issues, in particular on the relationship between international trade agreements and multilateral environmental agreements. She is a member of the International Law Association Committee on Sustainable Development and the Green Economy in International Trade Law, where she coordinates the working group on mutual supportiveness between trade and environmental measures. She was involved as a consultant for a research on "Trade and Natural Disasters" commissioned by the Secretariat of the World Trade Organization.

KOSSIVI BALEMA is an economist and statistician and currently holds the position of Group Evaluation Officer at the African Guarantee Fund. Previously, he was a research analyst at the United Nations International Fund for Agricultural Development in Rome. Prior to that, he worked as young professional in the Agriculture and Commodities Division of the World Trade Organization, and in various international NGOs and multilateral financial institutions including Premiere Urgence Internationale (Mali) and the African Export-Import Bank (Egypt). Passionate about agricultural and rural development related aspects, he has been involved over the past five years in many development projects with a view to improve rural people's lives and livelihoods. Mr Balema holds an MSc in applied development economics at the African School of Economics (Centre of Excellence in Africa) and a BSc in statistics from the National School of Statistics and Economic Analysis (ENSAE) in Dakar.

J. ROBERT BASEDOW is an assistant professor of international political economy at the London School of Economics and Political Science (LSE). His research focuses on EU trade and investment policy and international regulatory cooperation. Before joining the LSE, he was a Max Weber Fellow at the European University Institute, worked as an official at the Organisation for Economic Co-Operation and Development (OECD) in Paris, and taught international political economy at Sciences Po Paris and the College of Europe. He has advised the institutions of the EU, the German government, and the House of Commons on matters of trade and investment policy. Robert studied political science and political economy at the LSE, Sciences Po Paris, the University of St Gallen, and the Moscow State Institute for International Relations (MGIMO).

SARAH BAUERLE DANZMAN is an assistant professor of international studies at Indiana University Bloomington. Her research focus is international political economy, particularly the politics of foreign investment regulation. She received her PhD in political science from the University of North Carolina, Chapel Hill. In 2014–2015, she was a postdoctoral research fellow at the Niehaus Center for Globalization and Governance at Princeton University's Woodrow Wilson School of Public and International Affairs. She has published in various outlets including *International Relations Quarterly* and *Perspectives on Politics.* Her book *Merging Interests: When Domestic Firms Shape FDI Policy* was published by Cambridge University Press in 2019. She consults regularly with international organisations including the World Association of Investment Promotion Agencies and the World Bank Group on investment promotion policy. Prior to graduate school, she was a technical analyst for Citigroup Smith Barney.

AXEL BERGER is a senior researcher at the German Development Institute/Deutsches Institut für Entwicklungspolitik (DIE), Programme Transformation of Economic and Social Systems. He heads the G20 Policy Research Group at DIE and led the T20 Task Force on Trade, Investment and Tax in 2017, 2018, and 2019. Axel holds a doctorate in political science from the University of Duisburg-Essen and a master's degree in political science, economics, and modern history from the Munich Ludwig-Maximilians-University. He works on the design, effects, and diffusion patterns of international trade and investment agreements, with a focus on emerging markets and developing countries. Other areas of current research include the impact of free trade agreements on upgrading within global value chains and the role of the G20 in global governance. He teaches international political economy at the University of Bonn and regularly advises developing countries, development agencies, and international organisations on trade and investment matters.

COSIMO BEVERELLI is a research economist in the Economic Research and Statistics Division of the World Trade Organization and programme associate in the Global Governance Programme, Robert Schuman Centre for Advanced Studies, European University Institute. He has worked on topics such as international fragmentation of production, services trade policies, trade facilitation, trade policy substitution, and international migration. His work has been published in several economic journals, including the *Journal of International Economics*, *Regional Science and Urban Economics*, the *Review of World Economics*, *The World Economy*, and *World Development*. He is currently working on the effects of country-level characteristics on bilateral trade and migration flows, on the impact of aid for trade, on the impact of trade facilitation on tariff evasion, and on the relation between illicit animal trade and the spread of diseases. Cosimo Beverelli held teaching positions at the Geneva School of Economics and Management, University of Geneva, between 2009 and 2016. During the academic year 2018–2019 he was Jean Monnet Fellow at the Robert Schuman Centre for Advanced Studies, European University Institute, where he conducted research on the impact of globalisation versus technology on labour markets. He holds a PhD in international economics from the Graduate Institute, Geneva. In his capacity as a co-editor of this scholarly volume, he is not expressing any WTO official positions.

CLARA BRANDI is a senior researcher at the German Development Institute/Deutsches Institut für Entwicklungspolitik (DIE), Programme Transformation of Economic and Social Systems. Clara holds a PhD from the European University Institute, a master's degree from the University of Oxford (MPhil in Politics), and a master's degree in economics from the University of Freiburg, where she received the Hayek Award. She works on global governance and sustainable development, with a focus on the interplay between trade and the environment, paying particular attention to developing countries and emerging markets. Her current research includes a focus on the drivers and effects of including non-economic issues in international trade agreements. Clara provides policy advice at the national and the international level. She teaches global governance and development at the University of Duisburg-Essen.

ALISA DICAPRIO is the head of the Trade and Supply Chain at R3 in New York City. Her primary focus is building blockchain capability and infrastructure into the global trade ecosystem. Prior to R3, Alisa was a senior economist at Asian Development Bank working on digital trade, trade finance, and innovation. She has also worked in both the public and private sectors on export promotion, trade negotiations, and labour issues. She co-chairs the BAFT Innovation Council, sits on the US Department of Commerce Trade Finance Advisory Council, and is a member of the ICC Digitalization working group. She has worked in Cambodia, Chile, Finland, Japan, the Philippines, Thailand, and the United States. Her PhD is from MIT, and she holds a BA and MA from Johns Hopkins University.

ILARIA ESPA is an assistant professor of international economic law at Università della Svizzera italiana, a senior research fellow at the World Trade Institute (WTI), and an adjunct professor at the University of Milan. Formerly awarded a Marie Curie Fellowship from the European Commission for her post-doctoral studies (2013–2015), Ilaria was a member of the WTI-based National Centres of Competence in Research (NCCR) Programme in 'Trade Regulation: From Fragmentation to Coherence' until its expiration in 2017 in addition to acting as scientific coordinator of the WTI doctoral programme (2015–2017). Ilaria holds a PhD in international law and economics from the Department of Legal Studies of Bocconi University and was a visiting scholar at Columbia Law School in 2012. She has published extensively in leading international journals on issues at the intersection of trade and sustainability, mainly in the areas of climate change, energy, and commodities, as well as on the law governing the sustainable management of natural resources, always from a multilayered governance perspective. She is an elected member of the International Law Association (ILA) Committee on The Role of International Law in Sustainable Natural Resources Management for Development.

MATTEO FIORINI is a research fellow in global economics at the Robert Schuman Centre for Advanced Studies of the European University Institute in Florence, Italy. His research focuses on international trade, trade policy, and development. He holds a PhD in economics from the European University Institute and a master's degree in economics and social sciences from Bocconi University. Prior to joining the Schuman Centre, he worked as a researcher at the Migration Policy Centre (EUI) and the World Trade Organization.

GEOFFREY GERTZ is a fellow in the Global Economy and Development program at the Brookings Institution and a Research Associate at the Global Economic Governance Programme at the University of Oxford. His research focuses on international political economy, including the politics of trade and foreign investment, investor–state dispute settlement, commercial diplomacy, and private sector development in fragile states. He has published on these topics in both academic and policy outlets, and frequently briefs American and European policymakers on international trade and investment policy. Originally from Ottawa, Canada, he received an MPhil and DPhil in international relations from the University of Oxford and a BA in economics from DePauw University.

HINNERK GNUTZMANN is an economist with a research focus in the area of industrial organisation and international trade. He holds a PhD in economics from the European University Institute, as well as degrees from University of Utrecht and Cambridge University. Hinnerk has previously held positions at the Leibniz Universität Hannover and Universita Cattolica di Milano.

AREVIK GNUTZMANN-MKRTCHYAN is a junior professor at Leibniz University of Hannover. She obtained PhD in economics from European University Institute and holds degrees from Universidad Autonoma de Barcelona, Université Paris-1 Panthéon-Sorbonne, and Bauman Moscow State Technical University. She is also a research fellow at Belarusian Economic Research and Outreach Center and CESifo Affiliate and has previously held positions at the World Trade Organization. Arevik's research is in the area of international trade and globalisation.

BERNARD HOEKMAN is a professor and director of global economics at the Robert Schuman Centre for Advanced Studies, European University

Institute in Florence, Italy. Prior positions include director of the International Trade Department and research manager in the Development Research Group of the World Bank. He has been an economist in the General Agreement on Tariffs and Trade (GATT) Secretariat and held visiting positions at Sciences Po, Paris. A graduate of the Erasmus University Rotterdam, he obtained his PhD in economics from the University of Michigan. He is a Center for Economic and Policy Research (CEPR) research fellow, where he also co-directs the Trade Policy Research Network; a senior associate of the Economic Research Forum for the Arab countries, Turkey and Iran; and a member of the World Economic Forum Global Action Council on Logistics and Supply Chains.

LEE ANN JACKSON is the head of the Agro-Food Trade and Markets Division in the Trade and Agriculture Directorate (TAD) at the OECD. She joined the OECD in 2020 after sixteen years at the WTO, where her most recent position was as Counselor of Food and Agricultural Policy Research in the Economic Research and Statistics Division. She was previously the secretary to the WTO's Committee on Agriculture in the Agriculture and Commodities Division, where her responsibilities included the implementation and monitoring of WTO rules on agriculture and multilateral agriculture negotiations. Prior to the WTO, Dr. Jackson held various research roles including as a research fellow in the School of Economics at the University of Adelaide in South Australia and a researcher in the Environment Division of the International Food Policy Research Institute in Washington, DC. Dr. Jackson completed her PhD in applied economics at the University of Minnesota; she has joint master's degrees in public and private management and environmental studies from Yale University.

HYE-SUNG KIM is an assistant professor in the Department of Political Science at Winthrop University. Her research interests include the political economy of development in Africa, public opinion, and experimental research. Dr. Kim received her PhD in political science from the University of Rochester.

JÜRGEN KURTZ is a professor of international economic law jointly in the Robert Schuman Center for Advanced Studies and the Department of Law at the European University Institute. He is on leave from his position as professor and director of international economic law studies at the University of Melbourne Law School in Australia, where he has taught since 2003. Jürgen researches and teaches in the various strands of international economic law including the World Trade Organization and international investment law. His most recent book is *The WTO and International Investment Law: Converging Systems* (Cambridge University Press, 2016). His other research interests engage legal hermeneutics, jurisprudential borrowing in public international law, political economy, and development theory. Jürgen has acted as a party-nominated arbitrator in International Centre for Settlement of Investment Disputes (ICSID) proceedings and as expert consultant to the World Bank, the European Union, the Association of Southeast Asian Nations (ASEAN) Secretariat, United Nations Development Programme (UNDP), and United Nations Conference on Trade and Development (UNCTAD). He currently serves on the editorial boards of the *Journal of International Dispute Settlement* and the *Journal of World Investment and Trade*.

YOUNGCHAE LEE is a project assistant in the Department of Political Science at the University of Rochester. She received a PhD in political science from the University of Rochester and a BA (summa cum laude) in international relations and economics from New York University. Her research focuses on foreign direct investment, international trade, and the political economy of developing nations.

CHRISTINE MCDANIEL is a senior research fellow at the Mercatus Center. Her research focuses on international trade, globalisation, and intellectual property rights. McDaniel previously worked at Sidley Austin, LLP, a global law firm, where she was a senior economist. She has held several positions in the US government, including deputy assistant secretary at the Treasury Department and senior trade economist in the White House Council of Economic Advisers, and has worked in the economic offices of the US Department of Commerce, US Trade Representative, and US. International Trade Commission. Christine spent three years in Australia as deputy chief economist in Australia's patent office. She has published in the areas of international trade, intellectual property, and empirical trade analysis and modelling. She holds a PhD in economics from the University of Colorado and received her BA in economics and Japanese studies from the University of Illinois at Urbana-Champaign.

JEAN-FRÉDÉRIC MORIN is an associate professor at Laval University (Québec, Canada), where he holds the Canada Research Chair in International Political Economy. Before being invited to hold this research chair, he was professor of international relation at Université libre de Bruxelles from 2008 to 2014 and post-doctoral researcher at McGill University from 2006 to 2008. His most recent research projects look at institutional interactions and regime complexity in the fields of trade, intellectual property, and the environment. His publications have appeared in journals such as *International Studies Quarterly*, *Global Environmental Politics*, *European Journal of International Relations*, and *Review of International Political Economy*. His current working papers can be downloaded from www.chaire-epi.ulaval.ca/en.

BADRI GOPALAKRISHNAN NARAYANAN is an economist, affiliated with University of Washington Seattle. He co-founded Infinite-Sum Modeling Inc., with offices in Canada, the United States, India, and China. His broad expertise lies in the analysis for business strategy and trade policy, employing a variety of quantitative models. Recently, apart from his more than seventeen years of applied economic research experience in trade, energy/environment, and development issues for several international and national organisations including the United Nations, World Bank, International Monetary Fund, etc., he has been working on several other issues such as business economics of new technologies, including AI, blockchain, internet of things, cloud, 3-d printing, robotics, drones, etc., advising several start-ups in these sectors. He has written more than seventy-five research papers and presented his work in twenty-four countries, with thousands of researchers citing his research.

HANNA C. NORBERG is an independent trade policy advisor, founder of Trade Economista, co-director of DigitalTradePolicy.com, and a #TradeExperettes Instigator. She holds a PhD in international economics from Lund University, Sweden, with the thesis largely written during an extended study visit to Columbia University and the National Bureau of Economic Research office in New York. Her primary academic research interests are trade, trade policy, economic integration, and development. Apart from her work as university lecturer and researcher, Hanna has substantial experience in applied economics, conducting numerous trade policy impact assessment projects for the European Commission (free trade agreements [FTAs] covering major parts of the world, e.g. Transatlantic Trade and Investment Partnership, Japan, Association of Southeast Asian Nations, Korea, various Middle East and North Africa countries, Mercosur), Economic and Financial Affairs of the European Commission, Organisation for Economic Co-operation and Development, World Trade Organization, and national governments. She has considerable practical experience, working on implementing FTAs, surveying exporting small and medium-sized enterprises, and economic development through private–public partnerships. She is currently involved in projects on digital protectionism, cross-border data flows, and the effects of blockchain on trade.

DAMIAN RAESS SPECIALIZES in the international political economy of labour. He is the project leader of the collaborative research projects A Social Clause through the Back Door: Labor Provisions in Preferential Trade Agreements (2014–2016), which examines the causes and effects of the inclusion of labour provisions in preferential trade agreements, and BRICS Globalization and Labor Protections in Advanced and Emerging Economies (2017–2020), which investigates the conditions under which BRICS outward foreign direct investment improves labour standards in Europe and the BRICS economies (in particular Brazil and China). He is the co-author of two datasets on the content of labour provisions in trade agreements, including the state-of-the-art Labor Provisions in Trade Agreements (LABPTA) dataset. He has provided scientific expertise on trade–labour linkages to the European Free Trade Association, the European Parliament, and the World Bank, among others. He has published articles in distinguished political science and labour relations journals such as *Annual Review of Political Science, British Journal of Industrial Relations, International Studies Quarterly, Socio-Economic Review, Review of International Organizations,* and *Review of International Political Economy.* Damian Raess is Swiss National Science Foundation Assistant Professor in political science at the World Trade Institute, University of Bern. He holds a PhD in social sciences from the University of Amsterdam.

JAKOB SCHWAB is an economist and post-doctoral researcher in the research programme Transformation of Economic and Social Systems at the German Development Institute (Deutsches Institut für Entwicklungspolitik, DIE) and a member of the Global Justice Program at Yale University. He received his PhD from the Gutenberg University of

Mainz/GSEFM Frankfurt, where he has also been a member of the Gutenberg Academy. His research interests lie in the economic interaction between developed and developing countries, with a particular focus on drivers and effects of capital flows and the global production structure and their effects on growth in developing countries.

PREFACE

International trade and foreign investment are important pathways to realise the ambitious set of Sustainable Development Goals (SDGs) finalised as part of the United Nations' 2030 Agenda for Sustainable Development. To evaluate the promises and limits of these vectors, we invited leading scholars from political science, law, and economics to Florence to participate in the World Trade Forum in September 2018. The focus of our attention was the manner in which the SDGs have found their way into international trade and investment agreements, together with the problem of interactions and trade-offs across Goals. We hope this volume will offer a valuable guide for scholars and policymakers in identifying and evaluating the complex challenges related to sustainable development.

We benefited greatly from the exchange among the participants and wish to thank all of them for their contributions, which resulted in this volume. This volume would not have been possible without the support of the Robert Schuman Centre for Advanced Studies at the European University Institute (EUI) and the World Trade Institute (WTI) at the University of Bern, and of Manfred Elsig and Bernard Hoekman in particular. We wish to thank the EUI for financial support and for hosting the World Trade Forum conference that provided the basis for this book. We are also grateful for the financial support of the Bertelsmann Stiftung, the CEPR Trade Policy Research Network, the WTI, and the European Horizon 2020 Research and Innovation Program under Grant Agreement No. 770680 (RESPECT). Damian Raess acknowledges the support of the Swiss National Science Foundation under Grant Agreement No. PP00P1_163745. We further wish to thank Maria Fanou of the EUI for her excellent editorial support, as well as Marianne Nield and Finola O'Sullivan from Cambridge University Press for their guidance throughout the entire process and continued support for the World Trade Forum.

~

Introduction

COSIMO BEVERELLI, JÜRGEN KURTZ,
AND DAMIAN RAESS

In September 2015, world leaders adopted the 2030 Agenda for Sustainable Development, a global effort under the auspices of the United Nations (UN) to tackle poverty, climate change and violence while promoting more equal, inclusive and prosperous societies. They agreed on 17 Sustainable Development Goals (SDGs) and 169 ambitious SDG targets covering all areas of human development and the environment to guide development efforts through the 2030 time horizon. The SDGs represent a fundamentally distinctive approach to development that moves away from a narrow perspective on economic development to an integrative agenda that simultaneously pursues ecological, social and economic goals (Stevens and Kanie 2016). By aiming to create social floors and to ensure that the human impact on the environment does not exceed planetary boundaries, the SDGs encapsulate the seeds of substantive transformation toward *sustainable* development. The effective implementation of the SDGs requires national action and international cooperation, as well as the involvement of a wide variety of both state and non-state actors.

Illustrative of this holistic development approach, the promotion of international trade and investment is not per se an objective of the SDGs. Instead, trade, foreign investment and related domestic and international policies are seen as important vectors though which many of the core goals and targets can be achieved. To that end, some of the SDGs explicitly call for the active use of trade measures, in particular when meeting compelling public policy goals. Goal 2 (Zero Hunger) includes a call to correct and prevent trade restrictions and distortions in world agricultural markets, while Goal 14 (Life Below Water) points to the need to reduce fishery subsidies to avoid overcapacity and overfishing. Trade benefits for poorer states are also explicitly raised in Goal 17 (Partnership for the Goals), through commitments to improve market access for least developing countries (via, among other tools, increased aid for trade support, duty-free and quota-free market access) with the objective of doubling their export market share. From a broader economic perspective, general economic growth remains the most important channel through which trade can support the SDGs (Helble and Shepherd 2017b; Hoekman 2017). Indeed, the valuable benefits to individuals that can flow from inclusive and sustained economic growth are explicitly recognised in Goal 8 (Decent Work and Economic Growth).

That broader vision requires careful attention to a variety of economic pathways to the achievement of the SDGs beyond trade policy. Domestic and foreign investment is especially vital and, not surprisingly, occupies a central place in the normative vision of the SDGs. The 2030 Agenda for Sustainable Development openly frames 'private business activity, investment and innovation [as] major drivers of productivity, inclusive economic growth and job creation' (United Nations 2015, p. 29). According to the 2030 Agenda, increased investment in rural infrastructure, agricultural research and extension services, technology development and plant and livestock gene banks is instrumental to enhance agricultural productive capacity, in particular in least developed countries, in the framework of Goal 2 (Zero Hunger). Investment in energy infrastructure and clean energy technology is centrally positioned within Goal 7 (Sustainable and Modern Energy). Moreover, official development assistance and financial flows, including foreign direct investment, should be encouraged in the framework of Goal 10 (Reduce Inequality Within and Among Countries). And the adoption and implementation of investment promotion regimes for least developed countries should be encouraged in the framework of Goal 17 (Global Partnership for Sustainable Development). Against this backdrop, this edited volume focuses on various channels through which both international trade and investment can help contribute to the realisation of the SDGs. We are particularly interested in two sets of questions that are explored through a range of methodologies – including legal and statistical analysis as well as case studies – incorporating insights from law, economics and political science.

First, we explore the channels through which the Agenda for Sustainable Development has found its way into international trade and investment agreements, and related public and/or private initiatives. One can conceive of this inquiry on a vertical plane. Beginning from the international/supranational level, there is the vital mapping question of whether treaty design features of recent international trade and investment agreements incorporate substantive commitments on states parties to contribute towards sustainable development. Yet those treaty commitments require engagement by both public bodies and private entities to internalise and realise these goals. The importance of investigating the multiplicity of channels thorough which various public and private actors are involved in sustainable development is evident when one considers the sizeable challenge of achieving the SDGs by 2030 (United Nations 2019). For one, efforts by governments alone will not suffice. Many developing countries in particular have only limited financial and human resources at their disposal. While civil society organisations (including non-governmental organisations and social partners) and international organisations have a crucial role to play, business as the main economic actor in trade and investment (and innovation) occupies a place of choice without which the 2030 Agenda cannot be achieved (van Zanten and van Tulder 2018).

The second set of questions occupying the book concerns trade-offs between SDGs. Does progress toward any one of the SDGs or targets affect the likelihood to achieve any other Goal or target? Specifically, when and how does pursuing one SDG and its related targets lead to positive synergies for reaching other SDGs and under what conditions does it lead to trade-offs? While interdependence is inherent in the DNA of the SDGs, difficult trade-offs between the various Goals seem inevitable in view of the all-encompassing nature of the 2030 Agenda (Nilsson et al. 2016). Interactions and possible trade-offs across Goals are at the core of several contributions to this volume. The analysis of such interactions and possible trade-offs can be a valuable guide for scholars and policymakers in identifying and evaluating the complex challenges related to sustainable development.

Our approach does not track each of the 17 SDGs in chronological order. Instead, we have structured the contributions of the various authors to this edited collection in three substantive parts. Part I explores patterns of penetration and diffusion of the SDGs, principally through international commitments such as preferential trade agreements (PTAs) and the World Trade Organization (WTO). Part II shifts direction to focus on the role of key public bodies (including entities such as investment promotion agencies) in shaping SDG-related outcomes and trade-offs. Part III contrasts with exploration of the private sector initiatives (such as voluntary sustainability standards and new technologies like blockchain) that have important potential to shape the SDG agenda while raising the ever-present policy question of managing trade-offs.

We are certainly not the first to explore the links between international trade, investment and sustainable development. The question of how trade in particular can contribute to sustainable development is at the core of extensive literature. The recent volume by Helble and Shepherd (2017a) offers a more targeted view of the relationship between trade and the SDGs from the perspective of economic analysis. Our focus too is directed principally at the SDGs, but we seek to explore the potential of *both* trade and investment in the achievement of SDGs. The present volume also adds a multidisciplinary approach incorporating insights from economists, lawyers and political scientists. Given the simultaneous focus of the SDGs on the environment, the society, and the economy, this more holistic approach is much-needed and arguably better equipped to uncover potential trade-offs.

Chapters Overview

Part 1 of the book includes three chapters that explore the penetration and diffusion of sustainability provisions through various international agreements. The contributions here are organised in line with recency and vibrancy of international law-making engaging the SDGs. We thus begin with Adinolfi's exploration of SDG-related provisions in recent PTAs concluded by the European Union (EU). Sustainable development has long been a central policy objective of the EU, enshrined in its treaties since 1997. Aside from its internal manifestations, the EU is a central player in the external projection of the SDGs through various channels. The EU has a set of comparative advantages in acting as a norm entrepreneur for the SDGs, not least strong welfare systems, public investment in research and innovation and high labour and environmental standards. But like many other actors and states, it faces complex and interlinked challenges (engaging trade-offs between SDGs) relating to, for example, climate change, demographic shifts, inequality and social cohesion. Adinolfi explores the EU's role in promoting the SDGs globally to select counterparties through its growing network of PTAs. She does so naturally against the backdrop of stasis in the WTO, particularly the stalled Doha 'development' round of negotiations. Adinolfi offers a legal analysis of the trade and sustainable development (TSD) chapters inserted in recent PTAs concluded by the EU. Her main objective is to assess the extent to which these TSD chapters offer viable mechanisms for the attainment of the SDGs. After an introduction on relevant EU primary law, the chapter is structured in three sections covering the relationship between EU PTAs and multilateral environmental agreements, the recognition of the parties' rights to regulate in environmental matters, and the enforcement and dispute settlement mechanisms enshrined in TSD chapters.

The framing of Adinolfi's contribution ultimately suggests an optimistic account of the role of trade agreements to externally project preferences about the SDGs. By contrast, in Chapter 2 Basedow injects a note of caution for the reader, at least in understanding the complex political economy behind the inclusion of SDG-linked provisions in external treaties. His chapter adopts a more targeted focus exploring whether the EU's recent empowerment to conclude international investment agreements (IIAs) has made these agreements more development-friendly. Focusing on the EU's choice of partner countries, substantive protection and treatment provisions as well as procedural provisions on investor-to-state dispute settlement, the chapter explores whether the EU's IIAs have indeed become more development-friendly in comparison to the international investment agreements of individual EU member states (where in the latter, typically, there is little consideration of developmental goals). Interestingly, the chapter goes on to test whether policy changes are due to European law obligations applying to EU IIAs, increased politicisation of IIA policymaking in the context of EU's Common Commercial Policy or simply the aggregation of diverse member state preferences into a common European approach.

Of course, regional trade agreements are not the only international vector through which the SDGs can be promoted or constrained. The law and practice of the WTO remain a vital multilateral script to set the rules of economic globalisation and to manage its downside effects. That said, most of the rules of the WTO predate the September 2015 adoption of the UN 2030 Agenda for Sustainable Development and the 17 Sustainable Development Goals. But the WTO legal system has proven itself (particularly through adjudication) to be reasonably elastic in the incorporation of contemporary values and needs of its membership. Chapter 3 by Espa explores this dynamic when assessing whether the law and practice of the WTO are sufficiently aligned with the international law principle of sustainable use of natural resources as enshrined in the SDGs. Focusing specifically on WTO dispute settlement (in cases involving the notion of 'conservation' under Article XX(g) of the General Agreement on Tariffs and Trade and Article 2 of the Agreement on Technical Barriers to Trade), she analyses whether such provisions have been interpreted by WTO adjudicators so as to preserve sufficient flexibility for WTO members to pursue sustainable natural resource management goals through trade-related policy instruments (including, provocatively, those that are unilateral measures with extraterritorial reach).

Part II of the book then turns to a series of chapters exploring the impact of select public (both governmental and intergovernmental) interventions on SDG-related outcomes and trade-offs. As the chapter by Adinolfi demonstrates, the inclusion of social and environmental provisions in PTAs has become a tool of choice for developed country governments to promote compliance with internationally recognised labour, human rights and environmental standards. While the jury is still out on the effectiveness of trade linkage strategies to achieve social and environmental goals – among others because the incentives to take costly enforcement action again non-complying partners is low – many developing countries are also inclined to view such provisions as amounting to protectionism in disguise (Beattie 2019). Surprisingly, we still know very little about the economic impact of social and environmental provisions in PTAs. One reason is that data on the inclusion of non-trade issues in PTAs has long been missing. This has now changed as detailed datasets on the design of environmental and labour provisions in PTAs have recently been made available (e.g., Trade and Environment Database [TREND], Morin et al. 2018; Labor Provisions in Trade Agreements [LABPTA], Raess and Sari 2018). Using the TREND dataset, Chapter 4 by Berger, Brandi, Morin and Schwab investigates the impact of the introduction of environmental provisions in PTAs on bilateral trade flows. In line with the protectionism in disguise argument, the authors hypothesise that such provisions will reduce bilateral trade flows, particularly Southern exports into Northern markets. This contribution is long overdue. To our knowledge, it is the first study that systematically examines the trade flow effect of environmental provisions in PTAs.

No doubt, achieving the SDGs will require significant private financial investment. In the global race to attract and retain foreign direct investment (FDI), almost every country in the world has established its own investment promotion agencies (IPAs). As domestic institutions embodied with particular mandates that prioritise certain goals over others, IPAs provide a country-led means of both catalysing new foreign investment and targeting certain types of investment – perhaps promoting some type of investment while discouraging other types. This tension inherent in the dual nature of IPAs, as agents of government and advocates for foreign firms, is at the core of our next contribution. In Chapter 5 Bauerle Danzman and Gertz ask whether and how the governance structures of IPAs, by reflecting particular interests and ideas, influence their potential contribution to sustainable development. The chapter has a rich empirical base that combines quantitative and qualitative data, including World Bank surveys of IPA officials and a case study of Costa Rica's IPA on the basis of a 'before-and-after' research design. Both contributions draw our attention to the important question of trade-offs. While Berger et al. focus on possible trade-off between economic and environmental goals, Bauerle Danzman and Gertz more broadly tackle potential trade-offs between economic goals and general development goals.

Lastly, Part III of the book analyses 'bottom-up' private initiatives that have potential to drive outcomes on the SDGs. The UN Secretary General recently forcefully reiterated the need of private sector involvement to make progress towards the attainment of SDGs (Guterres 2019). There are several dimensions of private sector participation in activities that might be relevant for the achievement of SDGs. One of them is private finance. As reported by Bauerle Danzman and Gertz, the UN has estimated that an additional US$2.5 trillion in annual public and private finance will be needed to meet the SDG targets. Another relevant dimension relates to the private sector as standard setter, in particular in the domain of so-called voluntary sustainability standards (VSS). These are defined by the United Nations Forum on Sustainability Standards as 'rules that producers, traders, manufacturers, retailers or service providers may be asked to follow so that the things they make, grow or do don't hurt people and the environment' (UNFSS, unfss.org). The involvement of firms is essential because, by their very nature, such standards are not compulsory standards set by the government. VSS can, in principle, impact SDGs because they help keep workers healthy and safe, protect communities and land and uphold human rights, as well as moderating the environmental impacts of production and consumption. In Chapter 6 Fiorini, Gnutzmann, Gnutzmann-Mkrtchyan and Hoekman discuss the channels through which the adoption of VSS can impact different SDGs. The authors draw on and complement the mapping proposed by UNFSS (2018), according to which VSS have a direct impact on sustainable development (because they strengthen sustainability in the economic activity to which they are directed) and an indirect one, through their trade effects. The chapter argues that the impact of VSS on SDGs can be categorised based on five economic channels: pricing, supply chain competitiveness, certificate design, production process and public goods. A distinction is introduced between Fair Trade VSS developed by non-governmental organisations and corporate-backed private VSS, which the theoretical and empirical literature carefully surveyed in the chapter has shown to have distinct effects on the five channels above. Finally, the chapter discusses the existence of trade-offs between different dimensions of sustainability, which should be considered to identify the most appropriate design of VSS.

What are the determinants of VSS adoption in the first place? Chapter 7 by Jackson and Balema uses survey data on cocoa producing households in Côte d'Ivoire to address this question. Côte d'Ivoire is the largest cocoa producing country. With almost 2.7 million hectares dedicated to cocoa production, it accounted for 40 per cent of the world production of cocoa in 2017. Between 2011 and 2015, the number of producers of certified cocoa increased from 55,387 to 225,938. Such four-fold increase in the number of certified farmers most likely implies that the livelihood of farmers is affected in very significant ways by joining certification schemes. The chapter shows that farmers' motivation to become certified relates to a combination of socio-demographic characteristics and farm-specific features. The chapter further tests empirically the public goods channel identified by Fiorini et al., asking whether the adoption of practices such as water conservation, soil management, integrated waste management and ecosystem conservation increased for farmers who joined a certification program, and whether the price premia received by certified farmers' organisations helped finance local public goods such as health care, education and clean water.

Another broad vector through which SDGs are affected is technology. Throughout history, technological innovations have significantly reduced the costs of trading and transformed the way we communicate, consume, produce and exchange goods and services. In the current digital era, a series of innovations that leverage the internet – such as the Internet of Things, artificial intelligence, 3D printing or blockchain – is having and will continue to have profound implications for international trade and investment. In Chapter 8 DiCaprio, McDaniel, Narayanan and Norberg focus on one particular digital technology: blockchain. They ask whether the adoption of blockchain can indirectly affect SDGs through the various impacts of blockchain on international trade. They identify three areas where blockchain technology can greatly reduce trade frictions, lowering the threshold for firms, including small and medium-sized enterprises, to enter global markets: streamlining customs and border measures, increasing access to trade finance and increasing utilisation rates of tariff preferences. The chapter presents an empirical application based on a computable general equilibrium model, showing the potential effects on world trade and world gross domestic product of blockchain-induced reduction in trade costs and in preference utilisation gaps.

Lastly, the long-term feasibility of sustainable-development initiatives and policies depends significantly on the support of the public at large. Individuals play an indirect political role as consumers by purchasing (or not) goods and services produced under 'ethical' conditions, as those generated under VSS. Citizens also interact with their governments through the expression of their (public) opinion, including at the ballot-box. Because of electoral accountability in democracies there is a fair amount of consistency between public opinion and public policy in the medium to long term. Accordingly, it is essential to understand how individuals think about possible trade-offs in charting potential policy choices. The final contribution to this volume, Chapter 9 by Kim and Lee, examines whether concerns about potential negative environmental effects associated with international investment has any bearing on individual attitudes towards FDI, and whether those views differ between developed and developing countries. The authors revisit an old but important debate – namely whether environmental quality is a luxury affordable only by those who live in affluent societies – with survey experiments in the United States and in India, employing state-of-the-art research methodology which arguably avoids some of the pitfalls of survey data.

Science is called upon to play its role in contributing to the realisation of the SDGs (Independent Group of Scientists appointed by the Secretary-General 2019). This volume aims to contribute by outlining the state of play regarding the penetration and diffusion of the SDGs in select international fora pertaining to global economic governance, and by producing new evidence on possible trade-offs relating to the contribution of the trade and investment levers to achieving the SDGs. The size of challenge before policymakers remains formidable. There are significant knowledge gaps as to our understanding of all possible target/Goal-level interactions (Independent Group of Scientists appointed by the Secretary-General 2019: Box 1–2), and as we are currently just under one third into the process, the world is seriously off-track to reach the SDGs by 2030 (Guterres 2019). Sustained scholarly attention to the SDGs is much needed and timely. With this volume, we hope to make a modest scientific contribution to help countries navigate some of the difficult trade-offs involved in sustainable development.

References

Beattie, A. (2019). 'Is the EU's Green Policy Protecting the Planet or European Industry?' *Financial Times*, 12 December.

Guterres, A. (2019). 'Progress Toward Sustainable Development Is Seriously Off-track'. *Financial Times*, 4 November.

Helble, M., and Shepherd, B., eds. (2017a). *Win-Win: How International Trade Can Help Meet the Sustainable Development Goals*. Tokyo, Japan: Asian Development Bank Institute.

Helble, M. and Shepherd, B. (2017b). Introduction. In Matthias Helble and Ben Shepherd (eds.), *Win-Win: How International Trade Can Help Meet the Sustainable Development Goals*. Tokyo, Japan: Asian Development Bank Institute, pp. 1–8.

Hoekman, Bernard (2017). 'Trade and the Post-2015 Development Agenda'. In Matthias Helble and Ben Shepherd (eds.), *Win-Win: How International Trade Can Help Meet the Sustainable Development Goals*. Tokyo, Japan: Asian Development Bank Institute, pp. 32–58.

Independent Group of Scientists appointed by the Secretary-General (2019). *Global Sustainable Development Report 2019: The Future Is Now – Science for Achieving Sustainable Development*. New York: United Nations.

Morin, J.-F., Dür, A. and Lechner, L. (2018). 'Mapping the Trade and Environment Nexus: Insights from a New Data Set'. *Global Environmental Politics* 18: 122–139.

Nilsson, M., Griggs, D. and Visbeck, M. (2016). 'Policy: Map the Interactions Between Sustainable Development Goals'. *Nature* 534: 320–322.

Raess, D. and Sari, D. (2018). 'Labor Provisions in Trade Agreements (LABPTA): Introducing a New Dataset'. *Global Policy* 9(4): 451–466.

Stevens, C. and Kanie, N. (2016). 'The Transformative Potential of the Sustainable Development Goals (SDGs)'. *International Environmental Agreements: Politics, Law and Economics* 16: 393–396.

United Nations. (2015). *Transforming Our World: The 2030 Agenda for Sustainable Development*. A/RES/70/1. New York: United Nations.

United Nations. (2019). *The Sustainable Development Goals Report 2019*. New York: United Nations.

United Nations Forum on Sustainability Standards (UNFSS) (2018). *Voluntary Sustainability Standards, Trade and Sustainable Development*. Third Flagship Report of the UNFSS. New York: United Nations.

van Zanten, J. A. and van Tulder, R. (2018). 'Multinational Enterprises and the Sustainable Development Goals: An Institutional Approach to Corporate Engagement'. *Journal of International Business Policy* 1: 208–233.

PART I

Penetration and Diffusion of the Sustainable Development Goals

A Cross-Cutting Legal Analysis of the European Union Preferential Trade Agreements' Chapters on Sustainable Development

Further Steps Towards the Attainment of the Sustainable Development Goals?

GIOVANNA ADINOLFI

1.1 Setting the Scene

The concept of 'sustainable development' was officially used for the first time in 1987 by the United Nations World Commission on Environment and Development in its report 'Our Common Future'.[1] Since then, it has been going through a process of progressive refinement, with the 2030 Agenda for Sustainable Development being the latest step (United Nations 2015). Conceptually, in its text the United Nations General Assembly espouses the notion of sustainable development already affirmed in 2002 at the Johannesburg Summit (United Nations 2002), articulated along three integrated dimensions: economic development, social development (including the promotion of human and labour rights) and environmental protection (United Nations 2015, paras. 2, 5).

As stated by the Assembly, sustainable development would be achieved by the progressive attainment of 17 Sustainable Development Goals (SDGs), to be measured according to 169 different targets. Within this general and complex architecture, trade is recognised as prominent. Indeed, the Agenda affirms that 'international trade is an engine for

The author is grateful to Cosimo Beverelli, Jürgen Kurtz, Damien Raess and all the participants in the 2018 World Trade Forum for their comments on a previous draft of this paper. She also wishes to thank Mary Footer and the other members of the International Law Association Committee on Sustainable Development and the Green Economy in International Trade Law for the enlightening discussions during the Committee's meeting.

[1] See the annex to UN doc. A/42/427, 4 August 1987, p. 54, para. 1: 'Sustainable development is development that meets the needs of the present without compromising the ability of future generations to meet their own needs.'

inclusive economic growth and poverty reduction, and contributes to the promotion of sustainable development' (United Nations 2015, para. 68). Accordingly, Goal 17 acknowledges the decisive role of the universal rule-based system of the World Trade Organization (WTO).[2] In more specific terms, the multilateral trading system is considered pivotal for the pursuit of the SDGs on ending hunger, ensuring healthy lives, promoting decent work, reducing inequalities and regulating fisheries subsidies (goals 2, 3, 8, 10 and 14) (Hoekman 2017, p. 32; WTO 2018).

When exploring relevant trade regimes that could enhance progress towards sustainable development, the UN General Assembly considers exclusively the role of the WTO, without any reference to other international agreements. In this way, significant evolutions in the international trade agenda are overlooked, in particular, the deep crisis the WTO was already going through in 2015 and the remedies undertaken by states to tackle it. Indeed, because of the stalemate of the WTO multilateral trade negotiations launched in 2001, states have been putting growing efforts towards the conclusion of trade liberalisation deals on a preferential basis. One of the distinctive features of these negotiations is the emergence of a common will to reach an agreement also on sustainable development issues. As a result, most recent preferential trade agreements (PTAs) usually include a chapter on trade and sustainable development (TSD chapter) covering both the promotion of labour rights and the protection of the environment.

This development does not in itself represent a 'Copernican revolution'. In 1993, the North American Free Trade Agreement was finalised only once two side agreements were agreed on, precisely addressing the trade-and-labour and the trade-and-environment linkages (Charnovitz 1994). More recent PTAs are built on those first steps, and they find further support in the policy and legal discourse prompted by the United Nations.

In view of these evolutions, the question arises as to whether and to what extent the PTAs contribute to the attainment of the SDGs set in the 2030 Agenda. In this regard, this chapter offers a legal appraisal of the environmental provisions included in the TSD chapters of the latest PTAs concluded by the European Union (EU) (Durá et al. 2012; Jinnah et al. 2013; Douma 2017; Hradilova et al. 2018).

The attention to environmental issues is justified by the relevance they have gained within the multilateral trading system. As for trade-and-labour

---

[2] Agreement Establishing the World Trade Organization, Marrakesh, 15 April 1994, in force 1 January 1995, 1867 UNTS 154 (hereinafter 'Marrakesh Agreement').

issues, no dispute has ever arisen out before the WTO adjudicatory bodies, and as early as 1996 the members agreed that the International Labour Organization (ILO) is the competent body for dealing with core labour standards (WTO 1996, para. 4). On the contrary, since 1995 the relationship between trade and environmental policies has been the object of an intricate debate within the WTO, anchored in the preamble of the Marrakesh Agreement, where the purpose is also set to allow 'the optimal use of world's resources in accordance with the principle of sustainable development'.

The WTO has tackled the issue focusing on the members' margin of manoeuvre in determining the content of their environmental policies and on the relationship between the multilateral trading system and the multilateral environmental agreements (MEAs). The core question is whether members may derogate from WTO law for the purpose of implementing discriminatory or trade restrictive environmental measures. The topic has been addressed by the WTO dispute settlement bodies in highly contentious cases. In parallel, it has also been put on the agenda of the Committee on Trade and Development and of the Doha Development Round (WTO 1994, 2001, para. 31). The more recent PTAs fit into this debate, trying to find a possible solution to the fruitless WTO negotiations started in 2001.

Furthermore, the choice to focus the following analysis on the EU PTAs does not intend to disregard similar developments occurring within other regions (Akiko 2014; Jinnah et al. 2016; Berger et al. 2017; Allen 2018). This approach is rather driven by the following considerations: the leading role played by the EU in the creation of the current global network of PTAs (Pauwelyn et al. 2015), its active stance in the negotiations for MEAs, as in the case of the 2015 Paris Agreement on Climate Change, and the emphasis it has been laying on the inclusion of environment-related provisions in its PTAs since the publication of the 'Global Europe' communication in 2006 (European Commission 2006). In particular, the purpose to promote a value-based trade and investment policy (European Commission 2015) has prompted the development of a strategy consistent with the ideals enshrined in the EU Treaties. This course has been followed by the EU irrespective of the geographical location, the economic size or the level of economic development of its partners. As an outcome, the aims set in the preamble of the more recent EU PTAs have been expanded to cover also issues pertaining to environmental protection, and TSD chapters have been included in the main text of the agreements. In particular, the first TSD chapter was agreed upon for the 2008 Economic Partnership Agreement with the CARIFORUM

States;[3] in the 2010 agreement with the Republic of Korea,[4] a model has been drawn up with the ultimate purpose of replicating it in the next agreements. To a large extent, the overall purpose of the EU seems to be in playing a twofold role as both a market player and a rule generator, offering access to its internal market as a lever in order to obtain the consensus on the inclusion of new legal provisions on the trade-and-environment nexus (Cremona 2004). The present chapter investigates the legal outcomes achieved so far.[5]

The following analysis will not focus on one or more specific SDGs. As their trade components mostly reflect the needs of developing and least-developed countries, they may not always find a corresponding legal regime under EU PTAs, in particular when concluded with advanced economies (i.e. Canada, Japan, Republic of Korea and Singapore). Rather, this contribution aims at assessing the weight environmental concerns have been acknowledged in PTAs, in order to ascertain to what extent the environmental dimension of sustainable development is pursued in treaties envisaging strict obligations for the liberalisation of trade flows (and for the promotion and protection of foreign investments). The following analysis is focused on the interaction between environmental protection and trade liberalisation. The investment component of EU PTAs is considered when germane. However, it offers interesting inputs for analysis, that would deserve further analysis, which is beyond the purpose of this chapter.

Against this backdrop, Section 1.2 of this chapter will focus on the EU Treaties in order to ascertain on which bases they require the EU to pursue a foreign trade policy consistent with the environmental goals set under its own legal order. Building on these premises, the subsequent sections (Sections 1.3–1.5) will provide a cross-cutting legal analysis of the TSD chapters of the more recent EU PTAs (Morin et al. 2018, p. 122; for an account of more recent EU PTAs, De Micco 2014; Harrison 2014; Segura Serrano 2016; Van der Loo 2016; Hoekman 2016),[6] in particular the Cotonou agreement with the Africa-

[3] OJ 2008 No. L289/3 (hereinafter 'EU-Cariforum').
[4] OJ 2011 No. L127/6 (in force 13 December 2015, hereinafter 'EU-Korea').
[5] For an analysis of the (positive) trade impact of PTAs' environmental provision, see Chapter 4 by Axel Berger et al. in this volume.
[6] The basic information over the content of the TSD chapters have been inferred from TREND Trade and Environment Database, available at www.chaire-epi.ulaval.ca/en/trend.

Caribbean-Pacific countries[7] and the agreements that have already entered into force with the CARIFORUM States, Korea, Moldova,[8] Georgia,[9] Ukraine[10] and Japan.[11] Furthermore, reference will be made to the agreements applied on a provisional basis with a group of Central American States,[12] Peru, Colombia and Ecuador[13] and, finally, with Canada.[14] Relevant texts are also offered by the trade and investment agreements with Singapore[15] and Vietnam,[16] even though at the time of writing they have not yet entered into force, not even on a provisional basis.

The scope of the TSD provisions included in these agreements extends to a wide range of topics, covering specific environmental concerns (e.g. climate change, biodiversity, management of forests) or specific trade-related environmental issues (for instance, renewable energy or fishing subsidies, trade in timber and in fish products or in environmental goods and services). They also pay special attention to public participation in environmental decision-making and in monitoring the implementation of the PTAs themselves. However, this chapter focuses on three general issues at the core of the debate over the trade-and-environment nexus. The first concerns the relationship between the EU PTAs and MEAs, in light of the principle of mutual supportiveness (Section 1.3) This issue is under scrutiny also within the WTO. However, no common understanding has been reached so far and, in view of the deadlock of the Doha Development Round, it will be hardly settled in the near future. The analysis of the EU PTAs will allow ascertaining the degree and the manner in which the parties are allowed to derogate from their trade

---

[7] OJ 2000 No. L317/3.

[8] OJ 2014 No. L260/4 (in force 1 July 2016, hereinafter 'EU-Moldova').

[9] OJ 2014 No. L261/4 (in force 1 July 2016, hereinafter 'EU-Georgia').

[10] OJ 2014 No. L161/33 (in force 1 September 2017, hereinafter 'EU-Ukraine').

[11] OJ 2018 No. L330/3 (in force 1 February 2019, hereinafter 'EU-Japan').

[12] OJ 2012 No. L346/3 (hereinafter EU-Central America). Its trade part is provisionally applied since end 2013.

[13] OJ 2012 No. L354/3 (hereinafter EU-Andean Community). The agreement is provisionally applied with Peru and Colombia since 2013 (OJ 2013 No. L201/7), and with Ecuador since 2017 (OJ 2016 No. L358/1).

[14] OJ 2017 No. L11/3 (hereinafter CETA). Its trade chapters are provisionally applied as from 1 September 2017.

[15] Signed on 19 October 2018. The Free Trade Agreement and the Investment Protection Agreement (hereinafter, respectively 'EU-Singapore (Trade)' and 'EU-Singapore (Investment)') are available at http://trade.ec.europa.eu/doclib/press/index.cfm?id=961.

[16] In July 2018, the EU and Vietnam agreed on the final texts of the trade agreement (hereinafter 'EU-Vietnam (Trade)') and of the agreement on investment protection (hereinafter 'EU-Vietnam (Investment)'). Both have not yet been signed; their text is available at http://trade.ec.europa.eu/doclib/press/index.cfm?id=1437.

liberalisation obligations in view of implementing commitments accepted under international agreements on environmental protection.

Section 1.4 is devoted to the PTAs' provisions addressing the parties' right to regulate, in particular, their discretion in determining the domestic level of environmental protection according to their laws and regulations. In this regard, the purpose is to ascertain the equilibrium set in the EU PTAs between the preservation of regulatory autonomy and the promotion of 'fair' trade relationships, and to assess whether it departs from the solutions reached so far within the WTO[17] or in other PTAs.

Section 1.5 concerns the dispute settlement mechanisms envisaged by the EU PTAs' TSD chapters, replacing the general adjudicatory mechanism with a consultation and conciliatory procedure. In this respect, the EU's practice markedly differs from the PTAs concluded by the United States, where the enforcement of the substantive obligations on trade-related aspects of environmental protection comes under the scope of an arbitral procedure and may lead to the adoption of trade countermeasures. The EU has chosen to follow a non-confrontational approach, and its effectiveness will be assessed according to the relevant (albeit limited) practice.

Some final remarks will close the chapter (Section 1.6).

1.2 Sustainable Development Under EU Primary Law

The entry into force of the Treaty of Lisbon[18] has led to a potential strengthening of the EU's role as an exporter of values and rules in the field of environmental protection according to the principle of sustainable development. Indeed, in the Preamble of the Treaty on the European Union (TEU)[19] EU members express the desire 'to promote economic and social progress of their peoples, taking into account the principle of *sustainable development . . . '*: the ambition is proposed to make sustainable development an overarching principle on whose basis EU institutions will foster the progress of Members' national communities. In general terms, according to Article 3(5) TEU, one of the overall objectives of the Union is to 'contribute to . . . the *sustainable development* of the Earth'. More specifically on the environmental dimension, Article 11 of the Treaty on the Functioning of the European Union (TFEU)[20]

---

[17] In this regard, see Chapter 3 by Ilaria Espa in this volume.
[18] OJ 2007 No. C306.
[19] OJ 2012 No. C326/13.
[20] Ibid., p. 47.

envisages that '[e]nvironmental protection requirements must be integrated into the definition and implementation of the Union's policies and activities, in particular with a view to promoting *sustainable development*' (Durán et al. 2012, p. 25). Accordingly, the action by the EU for the protection of the environment is not constrained within the boundaries of its environmental policy (Articles 191–193 TFEU). The promotion of sustainable development, and in particular of a living space for individuals and communities, is deemed to be of primary importance and, therefore, meant to inform all EU policies and activities.

As far as the external action is concerned, its cornerstone is set in Article 21 TEU, establishing its principles and objectives. Among the latter, fostering 'the sustainable, economic, social and environmental protection of developing countries, with the primary aim of eradicating poverty' (Article 21(2)(d)) is included, directing primarily the EU policy on development cooperation (Articles 208–211 TFEU). At the same time, under a more comprehensive approach, the purpose is also set to 'help develop international measures to preserve and improve the quality of the environment and the sustainable management of global natural resources, in order to ensure *sustainable development*' (Article 21(2)(f) TEU). The prominence of this provision is strengthened by Article 205 TFEU, the opening clause of the Functioning Treaty's provisions on the external action, whereby '[t]he Union's action on the international sphere ... shall be guided by the principles, pursue the objectives and be conducted in accordance with the general provisions' laid down in Article 21 TEU. Most importantly, Article 207 TFEU prescribes that 'the common commercial policy shall be conducted in the context of the principles and objectives of the Union's external action'.

It is against this background that the EU Court of Justice has affirmed that the objective of sustainable development 'forms an integral part of the common commercial policy'[21] and that, accordingly, the sustainable development chapters come under the scope of the EU exclusive competence on trade and investment matters referred to in Article 3(1)(e) TFEU.[22]

At the policy level, the 2006 and 2015 communications by the European Commission on commercial policy highlight how the Union may use trade policy to promote the social and environmental pillars of sustainable development (European Commission 2006; European

---

[21] Opinion 2/15 of the Court (Full Court), 16 May 2017, ECLI:EU:C:2017:376, para. 162.
[22] Ibid., para. 167.

Commission 2015). In 2017, the Commission acknowledged that 'trade policy has an important role in harnessing globalisation to ensure its economic, social and environmental effects are positive for people and businesses in Europe and beyond' (European Commission 2017b, p. 3). It also gave voice to the intent of using 'trade policy instruments to promote around the world the high European standards of environmental, consumer, social and labour protection, in line with the Sustainable Development Goals' (European Commission 2017b, p. 4). Ultimately, the EU places itself into the wider context of the 2030 Agenda, and its commercial policy is deemed to serve the diffusion of a 'EU way' to sustainable development, without at the same time ignoring its 'internal' interests (to promote EU exports on world markets, to support fair conditions of trade competition, to preserve members' rights to regulate in environmental matters) (Morin et al. 2017).[23]

1.3   Mutual Supportiveness and the Relationship with MEAs

All EU PTAs incorporate or reproduce Article XX of the General Agreement on Tariffs and Trade (GATT) 1994 on 'general exceptions', which has been usually invoked under the WTO to justify the adoption of unlawful trade-related environmental measures. A consistent body of WTO case law has clarified that these measures are permitted to the extent they satisfy three requirements (Van den Bossche et al. 2018, p. 544). First, their objective has to be among those expressly envisaged in Article XX. For environmental measures, the common practice is to bring them under the scope of Article XX(b) or (g), respectively addressing the safeguard of human, animal and plant life and health and the preservation of exhaustible natural resources. In addition, in the more recent practice the protection of public morals under Article XX(a) has also been affirmed as a proper justification of policies addressing the SDGs, to the extent their fulfilment is a public moral imperative for the member concerned 'in its particular context' (Moon 2018).[24] Second, measures justified under Article XX must be 'necessary' or 'relating to' the achievement of their stated purpose. Finally, according to the chapeau of Article XX, they must not be applied so as to constitute a disguised restriction on trade or an arbitrary or unjustifiable discrimination between states where the same conditions prevail.

---

[23] See Chapter 2 by J. Robert Basedow in this volume.
[24] *Brazil –Taxation*, Panel Report, para. 7.567 (not appealed).

Even though the general exceptions clause does not specifically address the implementation of MEAs, it is beyond any doubt that this circumstance may well come under its scope. Therefore, the parties to an EU PTAs may invoke it to uphold the legitimacy of trade-related measures adopted consistently with the MEAs they have accepted. This approach is expressly followed under the Comprehensive Economic and Trade Agreement (CETA). Indeed, Article 24.4(4) therein provides that the general exceptions clause set in Article 28.3 may be used 'in relation to environmental measures, including those pursuant to the multilateral environmental agreements to which they are parties'.

However, the legal discipline on trade-and-environment linkage is not confined to the incorporation of GATT's general exceptions. In fact, it is further elaborated in the TSD chapters whose overall purpose is to establish the normative content of the principle of mutually supportiveness usually recalled in the PTAs' preamble.

As well known, mutual supportiveness has been first envisaged in the preamble of MEAs, such as the 1998 Rotterdam Convention on Prior Informed Consent,[25] the 2000 Cartagena Protocol to the Convention on Biological Diversity,[26] the 2001 Stockholm Convention on Persistent Organic Pollutants,[27] or the 2010 Nagoya Protocol to the Convention on Biological Diversity (United Nations 2010). In their texts, mutual supportiveness is set between trade and environmental national policies or international agreements, emphasizing a growing awareness that the conclusion of environmental treaties potentially affects the states' trade obligations. Therefore, the wish is expressed that apparently conflicting regimes support each other, also with a view to achieving sustainable development.

However, the legal significance of mutual supportiveness can be questioned in light of other clauses that usually go along with it. In this regard, the 2010 Nagoya Protocol stands out as a striking example of a masterpiece of ambiguity (Pavoni 2013). Indeed, in its Article 4, mutual supportiveness with other regimes (para. 3) comes together with clauses both establishing the priority of other treaties over the Protocol (para. 1) and prohibiting the

---

[25] Rotterdam Convention on the Prior Informed Consent Procedure for Certain Hazardous Chemicals and Pesticides in International Trade, 10 September 1998, in force 24 February 2004, 2244 UNTS 337.

[26] Cartagena Protocol on Biosafety to the Convention on Biological Diversity, 29 January 2000, in force 11 September 2003, 2226 UNTS 208.

[27] Stockholm Convention on Persistent Organic Pollutants, 22 May 2001, in force 17 May 2004, 2256 UNTS 119.

contracting parties from developing and implementing other agreements in a manner contrary to the Protocol's objectives (para. 2).

The TSD chapters included in the more recent EU's preferential trade agreements help to shed some new light over the relationship between regimes addressing trade liberalisation and environmental protection. Indeed, in this case, mutual supportiveness is envisaged in agreements clearly pursuing the liberalisation of trade flows between the contracting parties. The aim does not appear to be merely to acknowledge the existence of competing (environmental) concerns and their related international regimes and, therefore, to mould on their basis the interpretation of trade provisions. Rather, the objective pursued in EU PTAs is to incorporate environmental considerations within a regime based on the establishment of a free trade area, with the result that environmental issues are meant to become an integral part of trade policies. The trade-and-environment link is no longer perceived in terms of a confrontation between clashing and competing concerns (trade liberalisation or environmental protection). On the contrary, the overall approach is to recognise the legitimate interest of the parties to pursue coherent and effectively mutually supportive trade and environmental policies (trade liberalisation consistent with environmental protection, and vice versa).

Accordingly, most of the agreements under consideration recall the principle of *sustainable development* in their preamble and/or in the operative text. The language used may vary, as reference is made to the parties' commitment to sustainable development,[28] to promote it,[29] to work towards its achievement,[30] to develop trade relations in such a way as to contribute to it[31] or to implement the PTAs in accordance with it.[32] In general terms, the accepted notion of sustainable development is explicitly shaped according to the interdependent and mutually reinforcing components of economic development, social development and environmental protection, supported by a reference to the 2000 UN Millennium Development Goals[33] and, in the most recent PTAs, the 2030 Agenda for Sustainable Development.[34] The overall idea is that

---

[28] EU-Korea, Preamble, fifth paragraph.
[29] EU-Central America, Preamble, tenth paragraph; CETA, Preamble, ninth paragraph; EU-Vietnam (Trade), Preamble, fourth paragraph.
[30] EPA-Cariforum, Preamble, sixth paragraph.
[31] EU-Korea, Art. 1(1); EU-Andean Community, Art. 4(j).
[32] EU-Korea, Preamble, eleventh paragraph.
[33] EU-Andean Community, Art. 267(1).
[34] EU-Vietnam (Trade), Art. 13.1(2) and EU-Japan, Art. 16(1).

trade liberalisation is also conducive to the achievement of sustainable development and, at the same time, has to be pursued without disregarding its potential impact over social and environmental concerns.

As for *mutual supportiveness*, it forms part of the operative text of the agreements, but it is applied to the very general relationship between 'trade and environment'.[35] In some PTAs a more concrete approach has been preferred, as the parties decided to stress the need to enhance mutual supportiveness between trade and environmental *policies* (in CETA and in the treaty with Singapore, also between trade and environmental *rules and measures*).[36]

At first sight, it may seem that the EU PTAs do not innovate in comparison with existing international agreements. Sustainable development is referred to in terms similar to those under the preamble to the WTO Agreement; as for mutual supportiveness, the EU PTAs seem rather to mark a step backwards compared to those MEAs, where it is expressly acknowledged with respect to *trade agreements*. However, this preliminary consideration needs to be confronted with the other provisions included in the TSD chapters addressing the relationship with environmental treaties. As will be clear, they mark an improvement with respect to this practice.

Indeed, in their preamble, EU PTAs usually declare that they are built upon the existing treaties effective for the contracting parties;[37] accordingly, rights and obligations under these other treaties are 'reaffirmed'. In particular, in a recurring clause, the parties reiterate 'their commitments to the effective implementation in their respective laws and practices of the multilateral environmental agreements to which they are party'.[38] The PTAs with the Central and Latin American countries[39] and the three deep and comprehensive free trade agreements with Moldova, Georgia and Ukraine[40] supplement these provisions by enumerating the relevant MEAs the parties commit to implementing at the domestic level and envisaging the ratification of further environmental treaties, which have

[35] 2000 Cotonou Agreement, Art. 49(2); EU-Central America, Art. 287(1); EU-Andean Community, Art. 270(1); EU-Vietnam (Trade), Art. 4.1; EU-Singapore (Trade), Art. 13.6(1); EU-Japan, Art. 16.4(1).
[36] CETA, Art. 24.4(1); EU-Georgia, Art. 230(1); EU-Moldova, Art. 366(1); EU-Singapore (Trade), Art. 12.6(1); EU-Ukraine, Art. 289(2).
[37] Among the others, see the preambles of the agreements with Canada and Japan and of the trade agreements with Singapore and Vietnam.
[38] For instance, see Art. 13.5(2) of the EU-Korea PTA.
[39] EU-Central America, Art. 287(2) and EU-Andean Community, Art. 270(2).
[40] EU-Moldova, Art. 366(4); EU-Georgia, Art. 230(4)); EU-Ukraine, Annex XXXI.

not yet been accepted.[41] Some PTAs also provide for the exchange of information on the implementation of MEAs, the participation in new environmental negotiations and the views on becoming a party to an additional MEA.[42]

The adoption of trade or trade-related measures is expressly envisaged, in particular where it is affirmed that

> [n]othing in this Agreement prevents a Party from adopting or maintain-
> ing measures to implement the multilateral environmental agreements to
> which it is party, provided that such measures are not applied in a manner
> that would constitute a means of arbitrary or unjustifiable discrimination
> against the other Party or a disguised restriction on trade.[43]

The significance of this PTA-MEAs clause may be better appreciated comparing the EU PTAs with some similar agreements concluded by other states. For instance, the 2018 Comprehensive and Progressive Agreement for Trans-Pacific Partnership (CPTPP)[44] merely reaffirms the parties' commitments under MEAs (Article 20.4(2)), without any further clarification over the legitimacy of trade-related measures adopted with the purpose of implementing them. The Environmental Cooperation Agreement attached to the 2018 Canada–United States–Mexico Agreement (CUSMA) simply envisions strengthened cooperation among the parties in 'addressing issues of mutual interests related to multilateral environmental agreements' (Article 10(2)(b)). Other trade agreements concluded by Canada include a provision establishing the prevalence of MEAs, but their scope is limited to the rights and obligations arising under their chapters on the environment and not under the PTA as a whole.[45] Finally, similar provisions are not included in the free trade agreements concluded by the ASEAN (Association of Southeast

---

[41] For instance, see EU-Central America, Art. 287(3) and (4).
[42] See EU-Moldova, Art. 366(3); EU-Georgia, Art. 230(3); CETA, Art. 24.4(3); EU-Vietnam
     (Trade), Art. 13.5(3); EU-Japan, Art. 16.4(3).
[43] EU-Japan, Art. 16.4(5). See also EU-Andean Community, Art. 270(4); EU-Georgia, Art.
     230(5); EU-Moldova, Art. 366(5); EU-Ukraine, Art. 292(3); EU-Singapore (Trade), Art.
     12.6(4); EU-Vietnam (Trade), Art. 13.5(4).
[44] Signed 8 March 2018, entered into force 30 December 2018. As of May 2019, parties to the
     CPTPP are Australia, Canada, Japan Mexico, New Zealand, Singapore and Vietnam.
[45] For instance, see Art. 12.10 of the 2016 FTA with Ukraine, Art. 23 of the 2010 Canada-
     Panama environment agreement, or Art. 23 of the 2013 Agreement of environmental
     cooperation with Honduras. The text of these agreements is available at www.international
     .gc.ca/trade-commerce/trade-agreements-accords-commerciaux/agr-acc/index.aspx?
     lang=eng.

Asian Nations) with a number of trade partners[46] or in the 2018 Agreement Establishing the African Continent Free Trade Area.[47]

1.3.1 The Legal Implications

In the legal literature, the status of mutual supportiveness as enshrined in MEAs has been extensively debated and different positions have been voiced. Indeed, it has been variously qualified as a mere policy statement devoid of any legal effect, as an interpretative guideline or principle (Boisson de Chazournes 2007; Pavoni 2010), as a law-making principle implying a duty to pursue good faith negotiations aiming at clarifying the relationship between competing treaty regimes (Pavoni 2010), or as a conflict clause establishing hierarchy in favour of non-environmental regimes (Safrin 2002). When determining its interpretative value, it is almost automatic to read in mutual supportiveness a recall to Article 31(3)(c) of the 1969 Vienna Convention on the Law of Treaties (VCLT),[48] whereby treaty interpretation shall take into account 'any relevant rules of international law applicable in the relations between the parties'. Therefore, MEAs provisions need to be interpreted also in light of the commitments accepted by their parties under trade liberalisation agreements, in view of achieving a harmonious interpretation of apparently conflicting obligations: 'when several norms bear on a single issue, they should, to the extent possible, be interpreted so as to give rise to a single set of compatible obligations' (ILC 2006, p. 178).

Some authors offer a different approach. In their opinion, the interpretative value of mutual supportiveness can be better ascertained under Article 31(1) VCLT. As a result, two apparently conflicting agreements 'should take into account and support each other *right from the beginning of interpretation*, when the terms of the treaty are interpreted in their context and *in the light of the object and purpose of either*' (Kuijper 2010, p. 15 [emphasis added]).

---

[46] These agreements have been concluded with Australia and New Zealand, China, India, Japan and South Korea. They constitute the basis for the ongoing negotiations on the Regional Comprehensive Economic Partnership, establishing a free trade area among these countries. Relevant texts are available at https://asean.org/asean-economic-community/free-trade-agreements-with-dialogue-partners/.

[47] Available at https://au.int/en/treaties/agreement-establishing-african-continental-free-trade-area.

[48] Vienna Convention on the Law of Treaties, Vienna, 23 May 1969, in force 27 January 1980, 1155 UNTS 331.

The determination of the relationship with other treaties becomes even more complex when the aforementioned contradictory conflict clauses included in the MEAs are taken into account. In an attempt to find their rationale, authors have expressed the view that the MEAs suggest that the environmental treaty *'ne saurait être écarté ni de jure ni de facto du processus d'interpretation'* of other relevant rules of international law (Boisson de Chazournes 2007, p. 855).

The EU practice tries to sort out this complex and rather obscure legal architecture. First, its PTAs usually derive from mutual supportiveness the common will of the parties to cooperate in view of making their respective trade and environmental policies mutually reinforcing and strengthening cooperation on these matters. Therefore, institutional mechanisms are established wherein exchange of views and information might occur, and consultations may be held on trade-related environmental matters of mutual interest.

Furthermore, mutual supportiveness is mentioned along with provisions addressing the relationship with MEAs, which are not worded in terms of hierarchy or subordination, even if only to exclude both. The content of these provisions has been questioned and, in particular, the impact in terms of the legal obligation of the 'reaffirmation' of commitments undertaken under multilateral environmental agreements (Bartels 2013, p. 307). It is beyond any doubt that substantively nothing new is added, since the obligations on environmental protection remain unaltered in their scope and content. However, they become an integral part of a trade liberalisation regime, whose implementation may not compel the parties to act at variance with them.

This conclusion is supported by the clause quoted earlier recognizing that participation in the PTAs does not prevent their parties from adopting or maintaining measures implementing the MEAs they have accepted. A reading of this text supports the idea that an exception is envisaged. Indeed, it is opened by the phrase 'nothing in this Agreement', i.e., the treaty language commonly used in international agreements to permit the parties to adopt an otherwise unlawful conduct. As a result, this provision does not differ from the clause on general exceptions usually included in the PTA of reference.

On these bases, the issue arises as to whether measures adopted in view of implementing MEAs come also under the scope of these general exceptions provision. In this regard, it has to be considered that the PTA-MEAs clause establishes to what extent the environmental concerns as covered by the MEAs may be pursued by the PTA's parties notwithstanding the commitments they have accepted thereunder. It could be understood as a special provision expressly addressing one category of measures that come under the purview of the general exceptions clause (i.e., trade measures adopted in accordance with MEAs), setting ad hoc, less stringent substantive requirements. Indeed, as mentioned earlier, the common general exceptions rule applies to the extent relevant measures may be deemed as 'necessary' or 'relating to' environmental concerns; on the contrary, the PTA-MEAs provision legitimises measures 'implementing' MEAs, and not 'necessary' to or 'relating to' the implementation of MEAs. Eventually, a favour is acknowledged to trade-related measures under MEAs, which does not also extend to measures adopted unilaterally.

This would be justified by the fact that PTAs are built upon already existing MEAs. The clauses on mutual supportiveness are introduced by an almost standard language whereby the parties 'recognise the value of international environmental governance and agreements as a response of the international community to global or regional environmental problems'[49]; furthermore, those same clauses are complemented by the reaffirmation of the commitment accepted under the MEAs. It is all the more evident that, during the negotiations for the establishment of a preferential trade regime, the contracting parties were fully aware of the existence of international environmental obligations, and it is against this background that they have agreed on including them in the PTA submitting their implementation under a more flexible regime.

Building on these premises, some further considerations may be developed according to the variations in the scope and content of MEAs. Indeed, the PTA-MEAs clause undoubtedly covers the environmental treaties regulating international trade flows that may pose a risk to the protection of the environment, with the purpose of prohibiting them (for instance, under the 1973 Convention on International Trade of Endangered Species of Wild Flora and Fauna)[50] or of subjecting them to compliance with specific requirements (as according to the 1989 Basel Convention on the Control of Transboundary Movements of Hazardous Wastes and their Disposal).[51] The obligation to adopt trade restrictions is also envisaged in a second typology of MEAs, whose scope is wider than

---

[49] For instance, EU–Singapore (Trade), Art. 12.6(1).

[50] Convention on International Trade of Endangered Species of Wild Flora and Fauna, Washington, 3 March 1973, in force 1 July 1975, 993 UNTS 243.

[51] Basle Convention on the Control of Transboundary Movements of Hazardous Wastes and their Disposal, Basel, 22 March 1989, in force 5 May 1992, 1673 UNTS 57.

trade, but whereby the attainment of the stated objective, e.g., the reduction or removal of emissions or the use of hazardous substances, is also
pursued through a commitment to adopt import and export restrictions
(for instance, the 1987 Montreal Protocol on Substances that Deplete the
Ozone Layer).[52]

A third category of MEAs raises some more complex issues, as they do
not expressly require recourse to trade measures. In this regard, reference
could be made to the 1997 Kyoto Protocol[53] or to the 2015 Paris
Agreement[54] on climate change. The two texts follow considerably different normative approaches on climate change mitigation (Maljean-
Dubois 2016). However, they share a common characteristic, as neither
of them compels the adoption of predetermined measures; when specific
means of implementation area envisioned (e.g., the so-called flexibility
mechanisms under the Kyoto Protocol), a legal entitlement arises to
adopt them, not a legal obligation. However, within the margin of
discretion yielded in deciding how to address domestic efforts, the parties
may resort to measures likely to have an impact on trade flows. For
instance, also in view of implementing the obligations under the climate
change regime, a number of EU directives and regulations set the quality
of the products that may be placed on the internal market,[55] establish
some characteristics of their production method,[56] or condition their
marketing upon the fulfilment of licensing or certification schemes.[57]

Their legitimacy under the PTAs depends on compliance with the sole
substantive requirements provided for in the PTA-MEAs clause, namely
that measures implementing MEAs must not be applied 'in a manner that
would constitute a means of arbitrary or unjustifiable discrimination
between the parties or a disguised restriction on trade'. The evident
source of inspiration of this provision is to be found in the chapeau of
Article XX of GATT 1994, whose language is used in this case to give

[52] Montreal Protocol on Substances that Deplete the Ozone Layer, Montreal, 16 September 1987, in force 1 January 1989, 1522 UNTS 3.
[53] Kyoto Protocol to the United Nations Framework Convention on Climate Change, Kyoto, 11 December 1997, in force 16 February 2005, 2303 UNTS 162.
[54] Available https://unfccc.int/process-and-meetings/the-paris-agreement/the-paris-agreement.
[55] For example, Council and European Parliament Directive 98/70/EC of 13 October 1998, OJ 1998 No. L350/58 (as subsequently amended).
[56] See the recent European Parliament and Council Directive 2018/2001 of 11 December 2018 on energy from renewable sources (OJ 2018 No. L328/82).
[57] For instance, see the EU Timber Regulation (European Parliament and Council Regulation 995/2010 of 20 October 2010, OJ 2010 No. L295/23).

a normative content to the principle of mutual supportiveness. If trade and environment, or their related policies, have to be mutually support-ive, then measures implementing MEAs are legitimate to the extent they are not applied so as merely to hamper market access or to discriminate against the foreign products. The chapeau of Article XX GATT 1994 has been interpreted by the WTO Appellate Body as 'one expression of the principle of good faith'.[58] It clarified that

> [o]ne application of this general principle, the application widely known as the doctrine of *abus de droit*, prohibits the abusive exercise of a state's rights and enjoins that whenever the assertion of right 'impinges on the field covered by a treaty obligation, it must be exercised bona fide, that is to say, reasonably.[59]

As for the MEAs prescribing the adoption of trade measures, an abusive exercise of the right to implement them would be hard to prove under the PTA-MEAs clause, insofar as the disputed measure is set as required under the relevant environmental treaty. On the contrary, the issue may raise a number of controversies when the MEA leaves the determination of its means of implementation to the discretion of the parties. In these circumstances, their non-discriminatory and non-protectionist applica-tion would have to be ascertained according to the specific circumstances of the case.

However, since measures implementing MEAs are removed from the orbit of the PTAs' general exceptions, their inconsistency with the 'chap-eau-style' provision can be raised under the ad hoc consultation and conciliation mechanism envisaged in the TSD chapters, derogating the general adjudicatory procedure envisaged in the PTAs themselves, as shown in the text that follows[60]: the dialogue between the parties will be the primary means for settling any potential dispute, and a determination of non-compliance by an independent panel would not entail any obli-gation upon the interested party. Accordingly, even acknowledging the need to find a proper balance between, on the one hand, compliance with legal commitments on trade liberalisation and, on the other hand, the implementation of MEAs, the approach has prevailed to reserve the disputes in this regard to diplomatic channels, in view of the widest implications they may have on the parties' commitments under environ-mental agreements and governance mechanisms 'responding to global or

---

[58] *US – Shrimp*, Appellate Body Report, para. 158.
[59] Ibid.
[60] See Section 1.5.

regional environmental concerns'. In this regard, the CETA follows a different approach. Indeed, it does not include a specific PTA-MEAs provision, but rather places the implementation MEAs under the scope of the general exceptions clause, as mentioned earlier. By implication, any claim about the violation of the chapeau requirements come under the purview of the general arbitration procedure, which may result in the adoption of countermeasures in case of non-compliance.

1.4   Parties' Right to Regulate and No-Retrogression Clauses

TSD chapters go well beyond addressing the implementation of MEAs. Indeed, they address the domestic environmental policies in more general terms, trying to set a balance between the competing interests of supporting policies pursuing high levels of environmental protection, avoiding that these policies disguise protectionist and/or discriminatory intents, and condemning a 'race to the bottom' whereby more favourable competitive conditions on international markets are achieved by deregulation.

In this regard, the premise of EU PTAs is the recognition of the right of the parties to establish their own level of environmental protection and, therefore, to adopt and modify domestic laws and regulations.[61] Consistently with the WTO jurisprudence,[62] decisions over the domestic level of environmental protection are left to the parties, in view of their own priorities and through the preferred means of implementation.

To some extent, the recognition of this autonomy mirrors the provisions included in other PTAs' chapters on trade in goods and investments. Specifically, the chapters on the technical barriers to trade incorporate large parts of the relevant agreement annexed to the Marrakesh Agreement, in particular its Article 2 whereby the WTO members may introduce technical regulations (i.e. documents laying down product characteristics or their related process and production methods) for the purpose of pursuing legitimate objectives, including the protection of the environment, provided they are non-discriminatory and not prepared, adopted or applied 'with a view to or with the effect of creating unnecessary obstacles to trade'. A corresponding provision may

---

[61] EU-Cariforum, Art. 184(1); EU-Korea, Art. 13.3; EU-Central America, Art. 285(1); EU-Andean Community, Art. 268; EU-Moldova, Art. 364(1); EU-Georgia, Art. 228(1); EU-Ukraine, Art. 290(1); EU-Singapore (Trade), Art. 12.2(1); CETA, Art. 24.3; EU-Vietnam (Trade), Art. 13.2(1); EU-Japan, Art. 16.2(1).
[62] See *EC – Asbestos*, Appellate Body Report, para. 168.

also be found in the PTAs' chapters on sanitary and phytosanitary (SPS) measures, where the rights and obligations under the WTO SPS agreement are reaffirmed. Broadly speaking, the parties are allowed to take SPS measures necessary for the protection of human, animal and plant life or health on condition that they are based on scientific evidence and are not applied in a discriminatory or protectionist manner.

Likewise, the investment regime offered by EU PTAs envisages similar provisions aiming at setting a balance between, on the one side, the effective protection of foreign investments and, on the other side, the parties' power to regulate. The CETA (and the agreements with Singapore and Vietnam) directly addresses this issue, reaffirming the right of the parties to regulate within their territories in order to achieve legitimate policy objectives (such as the protection of the environment) and, at the same time, excluding that a violation of the obligations on expropriation and fair and equitable treatment may be affirmed merely on the basis that a domestic regulation has negatively affected a foreign investment or interfered with a foreign investor's expectations.[63] On expropriation, Annex 8-A further states that 'except in the rare circumstance when the impact of a measure . . . is so severe in light of its purpose that in appears manifestly excessive, non-discriminatory measures of a Party that are designed and applied to protect legitimate public welfare objectives, such as . . . the environment do not constitute indirect expropriations' (para. 3).[64] It is worth highlighting that the combination of investors' individual interests with collective policy objectives is felt like a relevant topic also within the framework of PTAs concluded in other geographical areas: for instance, both the CPTPP and the CUSMA include provisions analogous to those just mentioned,[65] allowing their parties a given leeway in pursuing environmental policies notwithstanding their potential harmful impact for foreign investors.

However, these provisions raise a number of interpretative uncertainties. As for EU PTAs, they concern for instance the 'manifest arbitrariness' required for a regulatory measure to be qualified as tantamount to a violation of the fair and equitable treatment, or the content of the non-proportionality prerequisites imposed to establish the existence of an

---

[63] CETA, Art. 8.9(1) and (2); EU-Singapore (Investment), Art. 2.2(1) and (2); EU-Vietnam (Investment), Art. 2.2(1).

[64] See also EU-Singapore (Investment), Annex 1, para. 2; EU-Vietnam (Investment), Annex 4, para. 3.

[65] See CUSMA, Arts. 16.6(4), 14.16 and Annex 14-B, para. (3)(b); CPTPP, Arts. 9.6(4), 9.16 and Annex 9-B, para. (3)(b).

indirect expropriation. Nevertheless, similarly to the clauses in the TSD chapters on the parties' right to determine their own environmental policies, they highlight the need to preserve the domestic regulatory autonomy, offering legal benchmarks and guidelines over the judicial interpretation of the provisions on investment protection.

Once acknowledged the regulatory discretion, some restraints are introduced to its exercise. Most EU PTAs do not go beyond requiring to 'seek to ensure' that domestic laws and regulations 'provide for and encourage high levels of environmental protection and shall strive to ensure to continue to improve such laws and policies and their under-lying levels of protection'.[66] While formulated in terms of a duty ('each Party *shall*') to abide by in the determination of the level of environmen-tal protection (irrespective of its impact on trade and investment flows), these provisions merely introduce a best endeavour obligation, whose concrete binding force is limited. In the PTAs concluded with developing countries, a further qualification is added, recognising that different efforts may be expected from the parties in view of their respective level of economic development.[67]

The agreements concluded with the three Republics of the former Soviet Union depart from this model. The close geographical proximity and the overall purpose of the EU neighbourhood policy explain the creation of a 'deep and comprehensive free trade agreement', grounded not only on the elimination of customs obstacles to trade (in accordance with the aim of establishing a free trade area) but also on a 'far-reaching regulatory approximation'. In the environmental field, this intent is expressed by the obligation binding upon Georgia, Moldova and Ukraine to implement within a given timeframe some EU directives concerning the protection of the environment and climate change.[68]

Other PTAs include specific provisions clearly excluding that the purpose of their TSD chapters is to harmonise the parties' domestic laws and regulations on environmental protection, and in particular their environmental standards.[69] A close coordination is rather envisaged on these topics, carried out within the Committee on Sustainable

---

[66] CETA, Art. 24.3. Similar provisions are included in the other EU PTAs here under consideration.
[67] For instance, EU-Central America, Art. 285
[68] For instance, EU-Moldova, Arts. 91 and 97.
[69] EU-South Korea, Art. 13.1(3); EU-Singapore (Trade), Art. 12.1(4); EU-Japan, Art. 16.1(2).

Development and according to the procedures envisaged on the different chapter on 'regulatory cooperation'.

The agreement on an overall effort to improve the level of environ-mental protection under domestic legislation usually comes along with clauses referring to its impact on trade relations. The more recent EU PTAs with Vietnam and Japan prohibit applying or using domestic environmental laws 'in a manner that would constitute a means of arbitrary or unjustifiable discrimination between the Parties or a disguised restriction on trade'.[70] Similarly to what is established under the PTA-MEAs clauses, notwithstanding the importance acknow-ledged to the adoption of domestic laws and regulations pursuing a high level of environmental protection, there again the concern is expressed that those same laws and regulations could conceal interests at variance with the trade liberalisation and non-discrimination.

An additional rule included in the PTAs is the so-called 'non-retrogression clause'. For instance, according to Article 13.7 of the EU-Korea PTA,

1. A Party shall *not fail to enforce its environmental . . . laws*, through a sustained or recurring course of action or inaction, in a manner affecting trade or investment between the Parties.
2. A Party shall *not weaken or reduce the environmental . . . protections afforded in its laws* to encourage trade or investment, by waiving or otherwise derogating from, or offering to waive or otherwise derogate from, its laws, regulations or standards, in a manner affecting trade or investment between the Parties. (emphasis added)

The minimum level of domestic environmental standards is not set. The only prohibition is to lower and to fail to enforce them in order to gain an unfair competitive trade advantage (or to attract foreign investments). Therefore, the race-to-bottom on environmental laws for competitive purposes is outlawed, both in the law-making activity and in the enforce-ment process.

However, the non-retrogression clause raises some interpretative issues. Non-compliance with the obligation on enforcement may be established only when a 'sustained or recurring course of action or inaction' has occurred. Even though in a different context, this notion has been understood as referring to the adoption of 'a repeated behaviour which displays sufficient similarity' or of 'a prolonged behaviour in which

---

[70] EU-Vietnam (Trade), Art. 13.3(4); EU-Japan, Art. 16.2(3).

there is sufficient consistency in sustained acts or omissions as to constitute a line of connected behaviour'.[71] Accordingly, a single failure to
effectively enforce environmental laws is not sufficient to substantiate
a violation of the non-retrogression clause. '[W]here there are isolated
instances of conduct with no apparent link among them other than the
fact that each such instance may be a failure to effectively enforce'
environmental laws 'there is no . . . "course" of action or inaction'. The
burden upon a claiming party results to be particularly heavy, since
adequate evidence has to be gathered about the existence of several not
isolated events, establishing an overall consistent practice: they should
'display sufficient similarity to one another and sufficient proximity in
time or place to one another to be treated as connected behaviour'.[72]

Furthermore, a second requisite is set; that is, the non-retrogression
over the content of domestic environmental laws and regulations and the
failure to enforce them must affect trade (and investment) between the
parties. Retrogression is not prohibited as such, in general and absolute
terms. Parties' behaviour must have had an influence, an impact over
trade flows in order to acknowledge its unlawfulness under the EU PTAs.
In the existing case law, this circumstance has been understood as
requiring that a waiver to environmental law or a failure to enforce it
has conferred 'a competitive advantage' in trade flows between the
parties,[73] in other words that the company or the industry enjoying the
waiver or benefiting the enforcement failure has attained cost savings
positively affecting its competitiveness.

Overall, the legal provisions addressing the right to regulate seem not
to innovate the already existing international legal framework. The
improvement in the domestic level of environmental protection is established under a mere best endeavour clause; the practice under the non-
retrogression clause, albeit limited, has evidenced its inherent limits and
the heavy burden of proof required to support a claim of infringement
(Araujo 2018, p. 288). Therefore, the question arises as to real impact of
the PTAs on domestic environmental policies.

---

[71] Dominican Republic-Central America-United States Free Trade Agreement, Arbitral
Panel established pursuant to Chapter Twenty, In the Matter of Guatemala – Issues
Relating to the Obligations Under Article 16.2.1(a) of the CAFTA-DR, Final Report of the
Panel, June 14, 2017, para. 152. The US claim dealt with the alleged violation by
Guatemala of the prohibition to fail to effectively enforce domestic labour law.
[72] Ibid., para. 433.
[73] Ibid., para. 190.

The issue could be better tackled according a more general approach. While the PTAs as such do not impose any strict commitment to increase the level of environmental protection, neither do they call upon the parties to adopt specific environmental measures, their positive impact may be ascertained from their negotiations. The conclusion of the agreement for establishing a free trade area, with all its relevant benefits in terms of increased volume of trade, is made conditional upon reaching a common understanding over environmental policies. Against this background, the parties may be persuaded to improve the domestic environmental policies and to ratify MEAs they have not yet accepted before the conclusion of the trade negotiations or with a view to PTAs' approval and entry into force (Vogt 2015).

This approach has been followed within the European Parliament with regard to trade agreement with Vietnam. Indeed, in September 2018 several members of the Parliament expressed the view that the agreement could be submitted for the approval by the Assembly only once Vietnam had done some concrete steps ahead in the protection of labour (and human) rights, including through the ratification of the ILO conventions on freedom of association, collective bargaining and the abolition of forced labour.[74] A following draft report by the Parliament's Committee on International Trade (European Parliament [INTA] 2018) bears witness to the political commitment expressed by the Vietnamese government to strengthen the labour legislation; it also welcomes the Vietnam's willingness to implement effectively multilateral environmental agreements. It is also on this basis that the proposal has been submitted for the conclusion of the trade agreement. In practice, similarly to the GSP+ scheme foreseen in the EU regulation, granting a special and differential tariff treatment on imports originating from developing countries which have ratified also some core environmental conventions,[75] in the case of the PTAs the effort could be placed on bringing the trade partner towards higher level of environmental (and labour rights) protection before the trade negotiations are concluded or the trade agreements are definitively approved.

---

[74] '32 MEPs send a joint letter to Mrs Mogherini and Commissioner Malmström to ask for more Human Rights progress in Vietnam' (17 September 2018), available at http://tremosa.cat/noticies/32-meps-send-joint-letter-mrs-mogherini-and-commissioner-malmstrom-ask-more-human-rights-progress-vietnam (accessed 1 February 2019).

[75] European Parliament and Council Regulation (EU) No. 978/2012 of 25 October 2012, OJ 2012 No. L303/1, as further amended.

As a final remark, it is worth mentioning Article 24.6 of the PTA between the EU and Canada, which expressly regulates the domestic enforcement procedures. In order to permit action and provide remedies in case of infringements of domestic environmental law, the parties are called upon to ensure that administrative or judicial proceedings be available to persons who maintain a right or a recognised legal interest. The reading of this text reveals a number of similarities with Article 9(3) and (4) of the 1998 Aarhus Convention on Access to Information, Public Participation in Decision-Making and Access to Justice in Environmental Matters.[76] In the case law, this provision has been considered as applicable to the judicial review of domestic measures of both individual scope and general application,[77] and to situations of a general failure by one of its contracting parties to implement and/or enforce environmental law.[78] Ultimately, the inclusion of Article 24.6 in the CETA acknowledges the importance attached by the parties to the issue of access to justice for the purposes of an effective enforcement of domestic environmental law, and this notwithstanding the fact that Canada is not a party to the 1998 Aarhus Convention and the several remarks raised by the Convention's Compliance Committee against the EU secondary law and the case law of its Court of Justice (Pirker 2017).[79]

1.5   Dispute Settlement and Enforcement

All EU PTAs envisage a dispute settlement mechanism based on the establishment of an arbitration panel, whose rulings are binding upon the parties. Failure to implement the panel report may lead the claiming party to request compensation from or, as an alternative, to suspend obligations raising under the PTAs in its relationships with the respondent. Both remedies are understood as temporary measures, since the

---

[76] Aarhus Convention on Access to Information, Public Participation in Decision-Making and Access to Justice in Environmental Matters, Aarhus, 25 June 1998, in force 30 October 2001, 2161 UNTS 447.

[77] See the *Findings and recommendations of the Compliance Committee with regard to communication ACCC/C/2008/32* (part II) *concerning compliance by the European Union* of the Meeting of the Parties to the Aarhus Convention, Un doc. ECE/MP/MP. PP/C.1/2017/7, 17 March 2017, paras. 50–51.

[78] See the *Findings and recommendations* of the Meeting of the Parties to the Aarhus Convention, UN doc. ECE/MP/MP.PP/C.1/20065/4/Add.1, 28 July 2006, para. 30(b).

[79] A full compilation of the findings by the Compliance Committee is available at www .unece.org/env/pp/pubcom.html (accessed 5 February 2019).

overall purpose of the dispute settlement and enforcement mechanism is to secure compliance with the concerned PTA.

However, this general dispute settlement procedure does not apply for the violations of the TSD chapters. In these circumstances, a special procedure is established, based on dialogue and excluding the adoption of countermeasures against the non-complying party. The following analysis is based on the CETA's provisions on the settlement of dispute under the TSD chapter (Arts. 24.14–24.16). Other PTAs foresee similar procedures, with only some minor differences. Only the agreement with the CARIFORUM States departs from this practice, as the general arbitral procedure applies. However, the peculiarities of the obligations under the TSD chapter have brought to exclude that their violation may be enforced through the suspension of trade concessions by the complaining party (Article 213).

Dispute settlement over the violation of the TSD chapter is articulated along three phases. First, any matter arising under the TSD chapter has to be brought to the attention of the other party; should the bilateral dialogue not be decisive, the issue is addressed in the Committee on Trade and Sustainable Development established under the PTAs.

In second phase, a panel of experts may be convened to examine a matter that has not been satisfactorily addressed through consultations. The panel is composed of three experts appointed on the basis of a list established by the Committee. They serve in their individual capacity, must not take instructions from any organisation or government and must have a specialised knowledge or expertise in environmental law, in the issues covered by the TSD chapter or in international dispute resolution. The mandate of the panel usually is to examine the matter referred to in the request for its establishment 'in the light of the relevant provisions' of the TSD chapter, and to deliver a report 'that makes recommendations for the resolution of the matter'. The final report by the panel of experts has to set out the findings of fact; the determinations on the matters, 'including as to whether the responding party has conformed with its obligations' under the TSD chapter; and the rationale behind its findings, determinations and recommendations.

Apparently, the applicable law to settle the dispute includes exclusively the TSD chapter. However, multilateral environmental agreements become relevant as long as they are recalled or reaffirmed under the TSD chapter. To facilitate the panels in the fulfilment of their mandate it is envisaged that they may seek views and information from the relevant bodies established under the MEAs, including any 'pertinent available interpretative guidance, findings, or decisions adopted by these bodies'. At the same time, it may not be disregarded that some of the provisions in the TSD chapters are modelled on international trade agreements, and especially on the WTO law. This is particularly the case where the parties are called to implement their commitments under MEAs or their domestic national legislations so as to constitute 'a means of arbitrary or unjustifiable discrimination between the parties or a disguised restriction on trade'. The interpretation to the chapeau of Article XX GATT 1994 given under WTO case law would inevitably be the primary reference for the assessment of the legitimacy of the complained measures.

The conciliatory nature of this procedure is evident in the provisions addressing the legal force of the panel's report. The panel has the power to enact mere recommendations that the parties are not bound implement. Rather, in case of non-compliance they are called to engage in discussions in order to 'endeavour to identify' an appropriate measure or to decide upon a 'mutually satisfactory action plan', taking into account the final report. The conciliatory procedure is mandatory, but the final settlement of the dispute does not have to be consistent with the panel's recommendations.

The closing of the panel procedure opens once again the dialogue between the parties. An obligation to negotiate arises, to be fulfilled in good faith and with the purpose of identifying a measure or an action plan suitable to put an end to the unlawful conduct. The PTAs do not give any indication over what may be considered as an 'appropriate' measure or the possible content of the 'plan of action'. However, they do not exclude that actions by both the respondent and the claimant may be agreed upon with the view of giving support and assistance to the implementation of the obligation on the protection of the environment. The enforcement of the panel determinations is strengthened by the involvement of the Committee on Trade and Sustainable Development, called to monitor the follow-up to the panel's report and recommendations.

This short illustration of the dispute settlement procedure highlights how a preference is expressed for a diplomatic solution of conflicts. Environmental policies are considered particularly crucial, as they involve and are based on more general policy choices over the preferred model of sustainable development and growth, with a cross-cutting impact on domestic societies. Consequently, in its trade agreements the

EU favours not subjecting environment-related disputes to the general arbitration mechanism and the sanction-based enforcement procedure.

In this regard, the EU model differs considerably from the approach prevailing in the United States' practice. Indeed, in the US PTAs the violation of the provisions of TSD chapters is subjected to an articulated consultation procedure. Should the parties be unable to find a solution, recourse to the general arbitration procedure is envisaged, and in case of non-compliance the withdrawal of concessions may be applied.

Both models are criticised, the EU approach for being largely rhetorical and lacking an effective enforcement mechanism. Evidence to that effect would be that, until very recently,[80] consultations and the dispute settlement procedures under TSD chapters have never been invoked. On the other hand, the US model is accused of being excessively time consuming and inefficient, as highlighted by the only claim raised under it, between the United States and Guatemala: the final report was published in 2017, six years after the establishment of the arbitral panel; notwithstanding the domestic labour laws were found not to be satisfactorily enforced by Guatemala, no violation of the non-retrogression clause was ascertained as, the panel affirmed, the United States had not submitted sufficient evidence that lack of enforcement had occurred as a consequence of a 'course' of action or inaction and that it had affected trade between the parties.

In order to meet the criticisms raised against the EU enforcement approach, in July 2017 the European Commission published a 'non-paper' (European Commission, 2017a), aiming at debating with interested stakeholders whether it could be strengthened by aligning it to the US model, as proposed also by some legal scholars (Krajewski and Hoffmann 2016; Stoll et al. 2018, p. 381) and advocated by the European Parliament (European Parliament 2016). This would have implied a significant turnaround of the previous practice. In a following non-paper of February 2018 (European Commission 2018), the Commission decided not to follow this path, primarily because of the lack of consensus that had emerged on it. Moreover, according to the

---

[80] See http://trade.ec.europa.eu/doclib/docs/2018/december/tradoc_157586.pdf (accessed January 2019) for the December 2018 EU's request for consultations with the Republic of Korea on alleged infringements of the obligations to promote and realise some fundamental labour rights and to make any effort to ratify some ILO labour conventions. For an account of other EU actions, see European Commission, 'Report on Implementation of EU Free Trade Agreement. 1 January 2017–31 December 2017' (Luxembourg: European Union, 2018), 39.

Commission, the adoption of the US jurisdictional approach would not be consistent with the rationale justifying the inclusion of TSD chapters in PTAs, while the adoption of sanctions would not generate a more effective improvement in domestic environmental legislation. Furthermore, it would also raise the highly contentious issue of finding a suitable methodology in order to quantify the economic damage to be remedied through the suspension of concessions. The European Parliament complained against this decision (European Parliament 2018, para. 46).

Following the 2018 non-paper, the economic partnership agreement with Japan has been concluded. The enforcement mechanism envisaged therein follows the traditional non-confrontational approach. However, a new provision has been added, with the seeming intent to improve the impartiality of the panel's determinations. Indeed, consistently with the rules on interpretation foreseen under the general arbitral procedure,[81] the panels of experts are called to interpret the TSD chapter in accordance with the customary rules of interpretation of public international law, including those codified in the 1969 Vienna Convention on the Law of Treaties (Article 16.18(2)). The dispute settlement mechanism maintains its conciliatory nature, but the role of the panellists has been strengthened with a view not only to a positive solution of the disputes but also to the adoption of an independent and legal approach in the exercise of their mandate.

1.6   Final Remarks

The adoption of the 2030 Agenda by the UN General Assembly has marked the formulation of a renewed universal consensus on the action for ending poverty, promoting social inclusion and improving environmental protection. If trade policies are meant to play a crucial role in this process, the establishment of stricter cooperation is essential, complemented by a modernisation of international trade agreements. A proper addressing of the environmental concerns requires finding a solution to specific contentious issues (some of which are also expressly mentioned in the 2030 Agenda), such as trade in environmental goods and services, fisheries subsidies, energy subsidies or carbon tax adjustment. At the same time, the determination of a more general new approach is needed, where the trade-and-environment linkage is not tackled in terms of

---

[81]   EU-Japan, Art. 21.16.

a confrontation between conflicting issues, but with the purpose of integrating the two components and enhancing the complementarities between them.

As a result of the stalemate in the WTO Doha Development Round, the debate over the relationship between trade and environmental policies has shifted away from the multilateral trade agenda to become part of the consultations on preferential trade agreements. Current PTAs offer an interesting laboratory. During negotiations, States are more aware than in the past that trade liberalisation can either promote or hinder environmental protection, and that the implementation of multilateral environmental agreements may require the adoption of trade measures. Those same issues arose also during past negotiations for MEAs. Nevertheless, they led to the drafting of conflict clauses whose interpretation and application raise a number of interpretative issues. Current consultations on PTAs follow a wider approach, where the complementarities between trade and environmental policies and related measures are explored in more detail.

The analysis proposed in this contribution investigates the trade-and-environment nexus from the perspective of the more recent preferential trade agreements concluded by the EU. This practice is relevant, in view of the role the EU has been playing in the setting of the current universal network of PTAs and in the negotiations for multilateral environmental agreements.

Against this background, this chapter covered three issues: the relationship between EU PTAs and multilateral environmental agreements, the recognition of the parties' rights to regulate in environmental matters and the enforcement and dispute settlement mechanisms. Overall, the model followed by the EU appears to be standardised. Irrespective of the level of economic development of its trade partners, the approach remains substantially unaltered, with only some minor variations.

Regarding the relationship with MEAs, the express codification of the principle of mutual supportiveness in the operative text of EU PTAs is followed by a reaffirmation of the parties' commitments under MEAs. Furthermore, a provision is included whereby nothing in the PTA prevents its parties from adopting or maintaining measures implementing the MEAs they are committed to. Far from establishing the subordination of the PTA to the MEAs, these clauses introduce an ad hoc exception to the trade liberalisation and non-discrimination commitments with regard of a specific typology of measures (i.e. measures adopted in accordance with MEAs having an impact on trade). Their legitimacy may be affirmed to the extent they comply with specific requirements, overtly inspired by the chapeau of Article XX GATT 1994, but at the same time also partially derogating from it, allowing the parties a wider leeway than under the WTO legal system. In this regard, the EU departs from the practice followed in other preferential agreements, lacking a clause expressly addressing their relationship with MEAs.

The focus on the trade impact of environmental measures typifies also the provisions on the right to regulate. Once the parties' rights to determine their preferred level of environmental protection and the best endeavour obligation to progressively raise it are established, the PTAs shift their attention to the possible harmful impact on trade of domestic environmental laws and regulations. The PTAs with Vietnam and Japan prohibit to use them in a manner which would constitute an arbitrary or unjustifiable discrimination or a disguised restriction on trade. Furthermore, as most PTAs concluded in the more recent years, all EU preferential trade agreements include a non-retrogression clause, with the key caveat that the prohibition to waive or derogate domestic environmental laws, or to effectively enforce them, applies only to the extent trade (and investment) flows are affected. Overall, the content of domestic environmental law and its means of implementation are not addressed as such, but in view of their impact on trade. Some interpretative issues arise, concerning the scope of the requirements of non-discrimination and non-restrictiveness and of the prohibition to affect trade and investment between the parties. A proper benchmark for the interpretation of the former may be given by the WTO case law on the chapeau of Article XX GATT 1994. For its part, the limited practice over the non-retrogression clause has proven how open is its interpretation and the difficulties in substantiating non-compliance with its requirements.

Overall, the purpose of avoiding a mutual harmful impact between trade and environmental policies is sought, laying on key provisions of the WTO agreements, such as the chapeau to Article XX GATT 1994. However, even though an effort has been made to fix a legal meaning of the rather vague principle of mutual supportiveness affirmed under MEAs, it rests on a provision whose interpretation in WTO case law has proved to be quite controversial (Bartels 2015; Howse et al. 2015, p. 117), and may support criticisms also against PTAs because of the allegedly undue constraints they would still impose on the parties' domestic regulatory autonomy.

Finally, as for the dispute settlement procedure, the practice under the EU PTAs fundamentally departs from the enforcement mechanism under the preferential trade agreements concluded by other countries, in particular the United States. The favour expressed by the European Commission during negotiations for a non-confrontational approach does not meet the support of other relevant stakeholders, the European Parliament first and foremost, but also scholars and the civil society organisations (ETUC 2017). It could also be claimed that a strengthening of the enforcement mechanisms could counterbalance the limited innovative character of the substantive provisions of the TSD chapters and trigger positive results not only in terms of the formal approval of environmental laws and regulations, but also in terms of their effective implementation and enforcement. A U-turn towards the model followed under US PTAs would also be significant in an effort to counter the criticisms that the EU is escaping its mandate to conduct a value-oriented trade policy.

However, the adjudicative model is questioned as well. Arbitration under the US PTAs has been initiated only in one case, which did not even tackle the improper enforcement of environmental legislation; besides, even though a number of enquiries have started before PTAs' institutional mechanism on the basis of submissions by citizens, in no case did they prompt the initiation of formal dispute settlement, which remains within the discretion of the states party to the trade agreement (Marx et al. 2017). Affirming the effectiveness of an adjudicative approach would require some counterfactual analysis, in order to ascertain to what extent, absent a hard enforcement procedure, domestic legislation would have pursued lower levels of environmental protection.

Undoubtedly, an advantage of an adjudicative system lies also in its potential promotional and deterrent effects, which may operate at different stages: during negotiations, as long hostility towards hard enforcement could put at risk the conclusion of the PTA or once the PTA has entered into force, when the threat of arbitration and sanctions or fines could put political pressure on the non-complying party to align itself to the commitments accepted under the TSD chapter.

Nevertheless, at present the EU is inclined to follow a different approach expressing a preference for a conciliation procedure and, within this framework, strengthening the impartiality of the panel of experts and the objectivity of their final determinations. This model borrows some elements from the non-compliance procedures established under the MEAs, whose purpose is not to sanction the party responsible for unlawful conduct, rather to support it in determining the causes of non-compliance and identifying the suitable measures to bring its environmental policies in line with the commitments undertaken (Dupuy et al. 2015, p. 185).

References

Akiko, Y. (2014). 'Environmental Provisions in Japanese Regional Trade Agreements with Developing Countries'. IDE Discussion Paper 2014-03-01. Institute of Developing Economies, Japan External Trade Organization.

Allen, L. (2018). 'Reassessing the 'Green' in NAFTA'. *Journal of World Trade* 52: 557–74.

Araujo, B. M. (2018). 'Labour Provisions in EU and US Mega-regional Trade Agreements: Rhetoric and Reality'. *International and Comparative Law Quarterly* 67: 233–253.

Bartels, L. (2013). 'Human Rights and Sustainable Development Obligations in EU Free Trade Agreements'. *Legal Issues of Economic Integration* 40: 297–313.

Bartels, L. (2015). 'The Chapeau of General Exceptions in the WTO GATT and GATS Agreements: A Reconstruction'. *American Journal of International Law* 109: 95–129.

Berger, A., Brandi, C., Bruhn D. and Chi, M. (2017). 'Towards "Greening" Trade? Tracking Environmental Provisions in the Preferential Trade Agreements of Emerging Markets', German Development Institute Discussion Paper 2/2017.

Boisson de Chazournes, L. and Moise Mbengue, M. (2007). 'A propos du soutien mutuel: les relations entre le Protocol de Cartagena et les accords de l'OMC'. *Revue Générale de Droit International Public* 4: 829–862.

Charnovitz S. (1994). 'The NAFTA Environmental Side Agreement: Implications for Environmental Cooperation, Trade Policy and American Treatymaking'. *Temple International and Comparative Law Journal* 8: 257–314.

Cremona, M. (2004). 'The Union as a Global Actor: Roles, Models and Identity'. *Common Market Law Review* 41: 553–573.

De Micco, P. (2014). 'The US and EU Free Trade Agreement with Peru and Colombia: A Comparison'. DG EXPO/B/PolDep/Note/2014_23 February 2014, PE 522.326.

Douma, Th. W. (2017). 'The Promotion of Sustainable Development Through EU Trade Instruments'. *European Business Law Review* 28: 197–216.

Dupuy, P.-M. and Viñuales, J. E., eds. (2015). *International Environmental Law*. Cambridge University Press.

European Commission. (2006). COM (2006) 567 Final, 'Global Europe: Competing in the World. A Contribution to the EU's Growth and Jobs Strategy', 4 October 2006.

European Commission. (2015). COM (2015) 497 Final, 'Trade for All. Towards a More Responsible Trade and Investment Policy', 14 October 2015.

European Commission. (2017a). Non-Report of the Commission Services, 'Trade and Sustainable development (TSD) Chapters in EU Free Trade Agreements (FTAs)', 11 July 2017.

European Commission. (2017b). COM (2017) 492 Final, 'A Balanced and Progressive Trade Policy to Harness Globalisation', 13 September 2017.

European Commission. (2018). 'Report on Implementation of EU Free Trade Agreement. 1 January 2017–31 December 2017'. Luxembourg: European Union.

European Parliament. (2016). Resolution of 5 July 2016 on Implementation of the 2010 Recommendations of Parliament on Social and Environmental Standards, Human Rights and Corporate Responsibility, P8_TA(2016)0298.

European Parliament. (2018). Resolution of 30 May 2018 on the Annual Report on the Implementation of the Common Commercial Policy, P8_TA (2018) 0230.

European Parliament (INTA). (2018). Draft Report Containing a Motion for a Non-legislative Resolution on the Proposal for a Council Decision on the Conclusion of the Free Trade Agreement between the European Union and the Socialist Republic of Viet Nam, 22 November 2018, 2018/0356 M(NLE).

European Trade Union Confederation. (2017). 'ETUC Submission on the Non-paper of the Commission services on Trade and Sustainable (TSD) Chapters in EU Free Trade Agreements (FTAs)', 11 October 2017. Available at www.etuc.org.

Harrison, J., ed. (2014). *The European Union and South Korea. The Legal Framework for Strengthening Trade, Economic and Political Relations.* Edinburgh University Press.

Hoekman, B. (2016). 'Deep and Comprehensive Free Trade Agreements'. EUI Working Paper RSCAS 2016/29.

Hoekman, B. (2017). 'Trade and the Post-2015 Development Agenda'. In Matthias Helble and Ben Shepherd (eds.), *Win-Win. How International Trade Can Meet the Sustainable Development Goals.* Asian Development Bank Institute, pp. 32–57.

Howse, R., Langille, J. and Sykes, K. (2015). 'Pluralism in Practice: Moral Legislation and the Law of the WTO after Seal Products'. *George Washington International Law Review* 82: 81–150.

Hradilova, K. and Svoboda O. (2018). 'Sustainable Development Chapters in the EU Free Trade Agreements: Searching for Effectiveness'. *Journal of World Trade* 52: 1019–1042.

ILC (International Law Commission). (2006). 'Conclusions of the Work of the Study Group on the Fragmentation of International Law: Difficulties Arising from the Diversification and Expansion of International Law'. *Yearbook of the International Law Commission*, vol. II, Part Two, p. 178.

Jinnah, S. and Lindsay, A. (2016). 'Diffusion Through Issue Linkage: Environmental Norms in US Trade Agreements'. *Global Environmental Politics* 16: 41–61.

Jinnah, S. and Morgera, E. (2013). 'Environmental Provisions in American and EU Free Trade Agreements: A Preliminary Comparison and Research Agenda'. *Review of European Community and International Environmental Law* 22: 324–339.

Krajewski, M. and Hoffmann, R. T. (2016). 'Alternative Model for a Sustainable Development Chapter and Related Provisions in the Transatlantic Trade and Investment Partnership (TTIP)'. Available at https://reinhardbuetikofer.eu/wp-content/uploads/2016/08/Model-SD-Chapter-TTIP-Second-Draft-July_final.pdf.

Kuijper, P. J. (2010). 'Conflicting Rules and Clashing Courts. The Case of Multilateral Environmental Agreements, Free Trade Agreements and the WTO'. ICTSD Issue Paper No. 10, Geneva, Switzerland.

Maljean-Dubois, S. (2016). 'The Paris Agreement: A New Step in the Gradual Evolution of Differential Treatment in the Climate Regime?' *Review of European Community and International Environmental Law* 25: 151–160.

Marín Durán, G. and Morgera, E. (2012). *Environmental Integration in EU's External Relations. Beyond Multilateral Dimension*. Hart Publishing.

Marx A., Ebert, F, Hachez, N. and Wouters, J. (2017). '*Dispute Settlement in the Trade and Sustainable Chapters of EU Trade Agreements*'. Leuven Centre for Global Governance Studies, 2017–01.

Moon, Gillian. (2018). 'A Fundamental Moral Imperative: Social Inclusion, the Sustainable Development Goals and International Trade Law after Brazil-Taxation'. *Journal of World Trade* 52: 995–1017.

Morin, J. F., Dür, A., Lechner, L. (2018). 'Mapping the Trade and Environment Nexus: Insights from a New Data Set'. *Global Environmental Politics* 18: 122–139.

Morin, J. F., and Mytiam R. (2017). 'Transatlantic Convergence of Preferential Trade Agreements Environmental Clauses'. *Business and Politics* 10: 621–658.

Pauwelyn, J. and Alschner, W. (2015). 'Forget About the WTO: The Network of Relations between Preferential Trade Agreements (PTAs) and Double PTAs'. In Andreas Dür and Elsig, Manfred (eds.), *Trade Cooperation: The Purpose, Design and Effects of Preferential Trade Agreements*. Cambridge University Press, pp. 497–532.

Pavoni, R. (2010). 'Mutual Supportiveness as a Principle of International and Law-Making: A Watershed for the "WTO-and-Competing-Regimes" Debate?' *European Journal of International Law* 21: 649–679.

Pavoni, R. (2013). 'The Nagoya Protocol and WTO Law'. In Elisa Morgera, Matthias Buck, and Elsa Tsioumani, (eds.), *The 2010 Nagoya Protocol on Access and Benefit-Sharing in Perspective: Implications for International Law and Implementation Challenges*. Martinus Nijhoff, pp. 185–216.

Pirker, B. (2017). 'Implementation of the Aarhus Convention by the EU – An Inconvenient Truth from the Compliance Committee' European Law Blog, 24 April 2017. Available at https://europeanlawblog.eu/tag/article-9-3-aarhus-convention.

Safrin, S. (2002). 'Treaties in Collision? The Biosafety Protocol and the World Trade Organization Agreements'. *American Journal of International Law* 96: 606–628.

Segura Serrano, A. (2016). 'From External Policy to Free Trade: The EU-Singapore Free Trade Agreement'. In Piet Eeckhout and Manuel Lopez-Escudero (eds.), *The European Union's External Action in Times of Crisis*. Hart Publishing, pp. 483–508.

Stoll, P.-T., Gött, H. and Abel, P. (2018). 'A Model Labour Chapter or Future EU Trade Agreements'. In G. Henner (ed.), *Labour Standards in International Economic Law*. Springer, pp. 381–430.

United Nations. (2002). *Johannesburg Declaration on Sustainable Development*, A/CONF.199/20, 4 September 2002.

United Nations. (2010). UN doc. UNEP/CBD/COP/DEC/X/1, 29 October 2010.

United Nations. (2015). *Transforming Our World: The 2030 Agenda for Sustainable Development*, A/RES/70/1, 25 September 2015.

Van den Bossche, P. and Zdouc, W. (2018). *The Law and Policy of the World Trade Organization. Text, Cases and Materials*. 4th ed. Cambridge University Press.

Van der Loo, G. (2016). *The EU-Ukraine Association Agreement and Deep and Comprehensive Free Trade Area*. Brill Nijhof.

Vogt, S. J. (2015). 'The Evolution of Labour Rights and Trade – A Transatlantic Comparison and Lessons for the Transatlantic Trade and Investment Partnership'. *Journal of International Economic Law* 18: 827–860.

World Trade Organization. (1996). *Singapore Ministerial Declaration*, WT/MIN (96)/DEC, 18 December 1996.

World Trade Organization. (2001). *Ministerial Declaration*, WT/MIN(01)/DEC/1, 20 November 2001.

World Trade Organization. (2018). *Mainstreaming Trade to Attain the Sustainable Development Goals*. Geneva, Switzerland: World Trade Organization.

The European Union's New International Investment Policy and the United Nation's Sustainable Development Goals

Integration as a Motor of Substantive Policy Change?

J. ROBERT BASEDOW

2.1 Introduction

The successful pursuit of the Sustainable Development Goals (SDGs) of the United Nations requires significant global financial efforts. Public development aid can only play a catalytic function and prepare the ground for private actors to invest in developing and least developed economies. Private capital in the form of foreign direct investment (FDI) is key to mobilising sufficient funds for the attainment of the SDGs. International investment agreements (IIAs) are one instrument states use to promote FDI flows into developing and least developed countries. IIAs seek to enhance the protection of foreign investors in host countries against discrimination and expropriation. They contain post-establishment treatment and protection standards as well as investor-to-state dispute settlement (ISDS) mechanisms and take the form of stand-alone bilateral investment treaties (BITs) or investment chapters of free trade agreements (FTAs). IIAs have, however, come under considerable criticism in recent years. While some observers suggest that IIAs hinder development in that they circumscribe the ability of states to regulate in the public interest (see Campact 2014; Corporate Europe Observatory 2014; Monbiot 2013; Poulsen and Aisbett 2013; Titi 2015), other commentators caution that only stringent IIAs provide the necessary protection to foreign investors to encourage investment activity (see Lavranos 2013, 2014).

Against the background of the debate about the developmental effects of IIAs, this chapter seeks to assess to what extent the European Union

(EU)'s emerging approach to IIAs supports the attainment of the SDGs. The EU is a fairly new actor in this policy domain and currently develops its approach to IIAs. In 2009, the Treaty of Lisbon transferred the exclusive competence to regulate FDI from the EU member states to the EU level and European institutions (Basedow 2017). The EU is now – by and large[1] – competent to conclude IIAs. In accordance with the views of many academics and policy-makers (Bonnitcha et al. 2017; European Commission 2016; European Parliament 2011; Kleinheisterkamp 2014; OECD 2004; Titi 2014, 2015), I assume here that EU IIAs have to strike a new balance between state and investor rights and interests so as to promote rather than to hinder development. Many older IIAs – notably of capital-exporting EU member states concluded prior to the Lisbon Treaty – arguably give too much consideration to investor interests and rights and unduly limit the ability of host states to regulate in the public interest and to advance development (Calamita 2012; Titi 2015). For EU IIAs to qualify as more development-friendly, they must thus give greater consideration to legitimate state interests and right to regulate.

The chapter builds on rational choice institutionalism (Hawkins et al. 2006; Majone 2001; Pollack 2003; Weingast 2002) to theorise why and how the competence transfer from the member state to the EU level may have translated into changes in policy substance and indeed more development-friendly IIAs. The core assumption of the aforementioned literature is that institutions shape state preferences and decision-making rules and thereby systematically influence policy outcomes. It follows that institutional changes – such as competence transfers – lead to changes in policy outcomes. The chapter develops three hypotheses on the basis of this institutionalist core assumption: First, the competence transfer legally embedded IIAs in the EU's external action, which is subject to primary law obligations to promote sustainable development. As few member states have similarly stringent legal commitments to the sustainable development, EU IIAs should be more development-friendly than member state IIAs. Second, the competence transfer entails that the much more diverse interests of EU member states have to be aggregated into one EU approach to IIAs. Whereas old and northern member states

---

[1] The Court of Justice of the European Union (2017) clarified in the recent Opinion 2/15 that certain core provisions of IIAs – such as rules applying to portfolio investments and investor-to-state dispute settlement – continue to come under shared competence. Standard IIAs thus require mixed ratification by the EU and individual member states. Policy debates and decision-making on IIAs nonetheless have clearly shifted from member state capitals to Brussels and the European Institutions.

tend to be capital exporters and their firms frequently use ISDS against host states (offensive interests), new and southern member states are capital importers and face ISDS claims from foreign investors (defensive interests). Hence, the EU's approach to IIAs should be more balanced in regard to state and investor rights than notably the IIAs of old and northern member states. Third, the competence transfer embedded IIA policy-making in the more politicised institutional and substantive context of the Common Commercial Policy. Primarily technocrats used to deal with IIAs at the member state level. At the EU level, IIAs are part of trade policy-making, which is by its nature more politicised as well as subject to stronger political oversight, namely by the European Parliament.

This chapter finds that the EU's IIA approach has become more development-friendly in comparison to the IIA approaches of EU member states. Institutional change in the form of a competence transfer has left an imprint on policy outcomes. The chapter finds that in particular the politicisation and aggregation of diverse member state preferences fuelled this shift in policy outcomes. Primary law obligations on the EU's IIA program played only a limited role. The chapter is structured as follows. It first discusses the link between the SDGs and IIAs. It then develops the three hypotheses in detail and measures policy shifts, comparing member state and EU IIA approaches. The chapter then assesses the explanatory power of the three hypotheses and concludes.

2.2   The Sustainable Development Goals and International Investment Policy

The SDGs comprise 17 development goals and goal-specific indicators to record progress (United Nations, 2018a). The following provides a brief summary:

1. **Poverty reduction:** Eradicate extreme poverty and half the number of people living under the international poverty line by 2030.
2. **Eradicate hunger:** Ensure access of all people to food all year round.
3. **Good health and wellbeing:** Reduce infant mortality, end major epidemic diseases, provide effective preventive care for major diseases and health problems, and establish universal health coverage for all.
4. **Access to education:** Ensure free access to quality primary and secondary education for all.

5. **Gender equality:** End discrimination against women and girls across the life cycle.
6. **Access to water and sanitation:** Provide universal, equitable, safe and affordable access to water and sanitation infrastructure for all.
7. **Access to energy:** Ensure universal access for all to affordable, reliable and sustainable energy sources including electricity and fuels.
8. **Sustain sustainable growth:** Ensure sustainable growth in gross domestic product (GDP) productivity and employment.
9. **Resilient infrastructure:** Develop quality, reliable, sustainable and resilient transport and communication infrastructure.
10. **Reduce inequalities:** Limit inequalities stemming from income, gender, age, sexual orientation, ethnicity and religion.
11. **Sustainable cities:** Ensure affordable and sustainable housing and resilient urbanism.
12. **Sustainable consumption:** Limit humanity's ecological footprint through more efficient use and recycling.
13. **Combat climate change:** Take action to protect people from climate hazards and natural disasters.
14. **Conserve the oceans:** Prevent and reduce marine pollution.
15. **Protect terrestrial ecosystems:** Promote the sustainable use of and restore forests and fight desertification.
16. **Peace and justice:** End all form of violence, abuse, trafficking, and exploitation and build a strong rule of law and inclusive political institutions.
17. **Strengthen implementation:** Mobilise more public and private resources dedicated to development, namely through the promotion of foreign direct investment, and ensure better cooperation and coordination of countries and international organisations.

The summary points to linkages between the realisation of the SDGs, FDI and IIAs (Alfaro et al. 2009; Demir 2016; Demir and Duan 2018). SDG number 17 even explicitly mentions FDI as a key instrument to promote sustainable development efforts. FDI can make a crucial direct contribution to achieving several SDGs. FDI, for instance, can directly enhance access to capital, technology, know-how, healthcare, water and sanitation, energy and infrastructure and promote GDP and employment growth (Alfaro et al. 2009; Demir 2016; Demir and Duan 2018). The potential effects of FDI, however, are not necessarily positive. FDI can be both a blessing and a curse for sustainable development, as a large literature reports. Irresponsible FDI and investors can also directly impinge on the successful pursuit of SDGs (Alfaro et al. 2009; Eskeland and Harrison 2002; Garsous and Kozluk 2017; Herzer 2012). FDI may contribute to pollution of the sea and land; deplete natural resources; amplify inequalities and social tensions; weaken host country institutions; and undermine access to infrastructure, water, energy and healthcare.

The development effects of FDI on home and host countries strongly depend on the governance of FDI. FDI governance is complex and crosscutting. It comprises inter alia IIAs, FDI screening mechanisms, as well as investment promotion programs (see Chapter 5). IIAs are only small – and in their effectiveness contested – building blocks of FDI governance (Bonnitcha et al. 2017, pp. 179–180; Busse et al. 2010; Egger and Merlo 2007; Neumayer and Spess 2005). Sectorial public policies – such as health, education, or transport policy – are often more important for foreign investment activities and their effects on sustainable development than IIAs. Sectorial public policies regulate in detail public and private activities in a given sector. They incentivise, prohibit or condition foreign investment. Some countries, for instance, prohibit foreign private investment in utilities and infrastructure. Other countries provide full market access to foreign private investors without any strings attached. Yet again other countries allow foreign private investments but impose price caps and require investors to provide universal access to grids and networks. Product market regulation, consumer and environmental protection, or trade policy, on the other hand, may determine whether countries attract vertical or horizontal FDI and whether FDI leads to positive know-how and technology spillovers (Dunning 2008; Navaretti and Venables 2004). It follows from this assessment that IIAs are best understood as creating an overarching policy framework laying down fundamental rules for the relationship between foreign investors and host and home states. The core purpose of IIAs is to ensure that foreign investors are effectively protected against discrimination and expropriation in host countries across sectors.

The insight that IIAs play a potentially important yet secondary role in ensuring that FDI contributes rather than hinders the pursuit of the SDGs is crucial for the purpose of this chapter. From a developmental perspective, the key challenge regarding IIAs is to ensure a socially beneficial balance between investor protection and states' public policy considerations, notably in the context of ISDS proceedings. IIAs need to ensure that investors are effectively protected against arbitrary and discriminatory expropriation without fair compensation while maintaining states' rights to regulate in the public interest. Adequate investor protection can increase beneficial FDI inflows into developing and least developed countries while insufficient investor protection can trigger a hold-up problem, slowing down sustainable development. Recent heated public debates on IIAs and ISDS in Europe demonstrate that it is contentious whether existing IIAs have struck a socially beneficial balance. A majority of policymakers, academics, non-governmental organisations (NGOs) and citizens demand that IIAs give greater weight to state interests and the right to regulate and cut back on investor rights and protection (Campact 2014; European Commission 2016; European Parliament 2011; Kleinheisterkamp 2014; Krajewski 2017; Monbiot 2013; Titi 2014, 2015). The underlying criticism is that investors exploit IIAs and ISDS to attack profit-reducing regulations and legitimate public policies, thereby imposing considerable financial costs on taxpayers and inhibiting social and economic development of host states (Pelc 2017). A widely discussed case was, for instance, *AWG v. Argentina* (ISDS Platform 2019). In 2001, a financial crisis hit Argentina, resulting in considerable hardship for millions of Argentinians. When a British-owned water company sought to increase water tariffs, the Argentinian government stepped in and revised the regulatory framework for the water sector so as to prevent water tariff increases and to ensure affordable access to water for Argentinians. AWG consequently sought compensation from Argentina through ISDS. Another example was the – ultimately unsuccessful – attempt of the French utility Veolia to seek compensation for Egypt's decision to increase the minimum wage (ISDS Platform 2018). Veolia claimed that the increase in the Egyptian minimum wage frustrated its business plan, eroded profits, and thus constituted an indirect expropriation of its Egyptian subsidiary. Both examples highlight how IIAs and ISDS can become serious obstacles to public policy.

2.3   Theorising the Impact of the Competence Transfer on EU Policy Substance

Does the competence transfer from the EU member states to the EU level lead to a recalibrating both of states' rights to regulate and investor rights under IIAs in line with the SDGs? In the following paragraphs, I develop three hypothetical arguments about *how* the competence transfer may have put the EU's IIA program onto a more development-friendly path than pre-existing member state policies. All three hypotheses build on rational choice institutionalism (Pollack 2003; Shepsle 2008; Weingast 2002). Rational choice institutionalism stipulates that institutions structure interactions between policy agents and therefore shape preferences, strategies, actions and ultimately outcomes. From a rational choice institutionalist perspective, the competence transfer and policy delegation to the EU has changed the rules structuring policy-making on IIAs, which is likely to structurally alter policy outcomes.

2.3.1   Primary Law Obligations

The competence transfer has a manifest legal implication for IIAs. Art. 3(5) of the Treaty on the European Union (TEU) – as amended by the Treaty of Lisbon – lays out fundamental objectives for the EU's external relations with third countries, which should according to rational choice institutionalism shape EU policy preferences and actions inter alia on IIAs:

> In its relations with the wider world, the Union shall uphold and promote its values and interests and contribute to the protection of its citizens. It shall contribute to peace, security, the *sustainable development of the Earth* [emphasis added], solidarity and mutual respect among peoples, free and fair trade, eradication of poverty and the protection of human rights, in particular the rights of the child, as well as to the strict observance and the development of international law, including respect for the principles of the United Nations Charter.

The EU is bound by primary law to promote through its external policies – including through its IIAs program – sustainable development as authoritatively defined by the United Nations. The promotion of the SDGs amounts to a quasi-constitutional obligation for the EU. Only few member state constitutions contain similarly strong legal commitments to the promotion of sustainable development, multilateralism and the United Nations. The competence transfer from the member states to the EU thus de jure amplified the weight of the SDGs with regard to European IIAs. Compatibility checks between EU measures and policies and the SDGs, for instance, now form part of EU impact assessments, stakeholder consultations and ex post evaluations (European Commission 2015a).

2.3.2   Aggregation Effects

The competence transfer is also likely to result in a more balanced approach to states' rights to regulate and to investment protection under IIAs owing to the necessity to aggregate diverse member state preferences into one European approach. This aggregation effect – while not tied to the sustainable development agenda – may nonetheless cause the EU's IIAs to become more development friendly than member state IIAs. The old and northern member states are predominantly net capital exporters and emitters of FDI (UNCTAD 2017). Their national firms invest abroad and frequently bring ISDS claims against host states in case of mistreatment. These member states thus typically hold offensive interests in ISDS proceedings. Hence, they historically sought to ensure highest levels of investment protection under their IIAs before delegating international investment policy-making to the EU under the Treaty of Lisbon. Belgium, France, Germany, Italy, Luxembourg, the Netherlands and the United Kingdom were very active and concluded more than 700 of the approximately 1,400 IIAs of EU member states (UNCTAD 2018). They shaped the so-called European 'gold standard' model IIA (Lavranos 2013; Titi 2015), which arguably provides for the highest level of investment protection in the international investment regime. This 'gold standard' contains broad and high substantive post-establishment treatment and protection standards and provides for easy access to ISDS for investors (see Sections 2.4.2 and 2.4.3). Most eastern and southern member states, on the other hand, are net capital importers and recipients of FDI (UNCTAD 2017). Foreign investors sink capital in these economies and frequently bring claims under IIAs, with ISDS provisions against these states in case of alleged mistreatment. Eastern and southern member states thus typically hold defensive interests in ISDS proceedings. The diverse preferences of old versus new and northern versus southern and eastern member states must now get aggregated into a European compromise approach to IIAs and ISDS. In comparison to the European 'gold standard' IIA of the old and northern member states, the European approach is likely to rebalance and to strengthen states' rights to regulate vis-à-vis investor interest. As assumed in rational choice institutionalism, a shift in policy-making institutions should translate into substantive policy changes.

2.3.3   Politicisation Effects

The competence transfer, moreover, embedded policy-making on IIAs into a more politicised context, which may result in a more balanced approach to IIAs and greater attention to states' rights to regulate. Technocratic policy-making allows narrow technocratic interests –

which are often closely aligned with special-interest groups – to shape policy outcomes. Politicised policy-making, on the other hand, entails broad social contestation and debate. Politicisation thereby is more likely to produce balanced policy outcomes, which reflect a broader set of social interests. In most member states, IIAs indeed used to be a highly technical domain with little involvement of politicians. Technocrats launched negotiations, developed national IIA approaches, and concluded IIAs with little political oversight. Germany – the country with the highest number of IIAs worldwide – illustrates the point. The German Ministry of Economics invented IIAs in the late 1950s as a highly technical component of German export policies. It negotiated IIAs with third countries to limit financial risks for German taxpayers under state-backed investment guarantee schemes (Basedow 2017). German IIAs were meant to enable German investors to seek compensation from host countries before requesting a pay-out of insurance coverage from investment guarantee schemes. The German Bundestag ratified IIAs for decades without in-depth deliberations (Interview with political appointee, German Ministry of Economics, June 13, 2013; Seidl-Hohenveldern 1977, pp. 54–59). Ratification of IIAs was seen as a constitutional formality rather than political deliberative process. The competence transfer has changed the dynamics of IIA negotiations. The competence transfer not only lifted policy-making from the national to the EU level, but also shifted it from a technocratic into a politicised environment. Art. 206 and 207 of the Treaty on the Functioning of the European Union empowers the EU to regulate FDI under the umbrella of the Common Commercial Policy. IIAs have thereby transformed into a sub-domain of the Common Commercial Policy. The embedding of IIAs into trade policy-making may trigger politicisation through two channels. First, trade policy is per se more politicised than international investment policy. IIAs are of regulatory nature. Unless they contain investment liberalisation provisions, they primarily deal with investment treatment and protection. IIAs do not redistribute or produce concentrated costs or benefits for specific societal interest groups. Trade policy and negotiations, in contrast, redistribute welfare within society and across economies, which entails political mobilisation and contestation (Hiscox 2002; Milner 1999; Rogowski 1989). As IIAs are increasingly negotiated as investment chapters of FTAs, the politicisation of trade policy may spill over into the realm of investment regulation.

Second, the European Parliament has emerged as a powerful co-legislator in the Common Commercial Policy under the Treaty of

Lisbon. The European Parliament used to play a limited role in trade policy and negotiations. The Treaty of Lisbon (2009), however, significantly extended the powers of the European Parliament, which now holds the power to ratify agreements coming under the Common Commercial Policy (Woolcock 2010). Since then, the European Parliament has emphasised its ambition to establish itself as a full-fledged co-legislator in trade policy next to the Council of Ministers. In accordance with its institutional self-understanding, the European Parliament positions itself vis-à-vis the Commission and the Council of Ministers as 'the advocate' of citizen interests and social and developmental concerns in European public policy in general and trade and investment policy in particular (Van den Putte et al. 2015). Efforts of the European Parliament to consolidate its role under the Common Commercial Policy should thus translate into greater politicisation and indeed consideration for non-economic issues such as the SDGs in policy-making.

2.4   Assessing the Developmental Focus of the EU's IIA Approach

I now turn to discussing preliminary empirical evidence to evaluate variation in my dependent variable – namely whether and how the EU's IIA approach may have become more development-friendly in comparison to member state policies and IIAs. It is important to note though that the EU's involvement in international investment policy and proper investment negotiations is recent. The EU currently negotiates IIAs and trade agreements with substantive investment chapters with thirteen countries. Only three agreements have entered the ratification stage yet and it is uncertain that the European Parliament will ratify these agreements. Hence, the empirical universe to assess the alignment between the EU's IIA approach and the sustainable development agenda is small and allows at best for tentative conclusions. To evaluate the effects of the competence transfer on IIAs, the section assesses (1) the choice of partner countries and (2) substantive and (3) procedural changes in EU IIA provisions in comparison to member state model IIAs.

2.4.1   Choice of Partner Countries

Inward FDI can make an important contribution to sustainable development in developing and least developed countries (Alfaro et al. 2009; Demir 2016). IIAs can facilitate FDI inflows through the creation of

a legal framework, which protects foreign investors but maintains the
ability of developing and least developed countries to regulate in the
public interest (Busse et al. 2010; Neumayer and Spess 2005). The EU's
choice of IIA partner countries suggests that the intent to channel FDI
into developing and least developed countries in line with the SDGs
cannot be the decisive motivation behind the EU's IIAs. The EU currently negotiates standalone IIAs or trade agreements with IIA-like
investment chapters with thirteen countries (Table 2.1). According to
the United Nations (2018b), only five qualify as lower middle or low-
income economies: China, India, Indonesia, Myanmar and Vietnam.
And apart from Myanmar, these countries can be seen as emerging
economies in lesser need of assistance than many other parts of the
world. The remaining eight partner countries of the EU qualify as high
or upper middle income economies, which shows that development
considerations do not play a role in these negotiations. A caveat applies
to this assessment though. The EU may see little urgency to negotiate

Table 2.1 *EU IIA Projects*

	Partner Country	Type of Agreement	Status Quo	Timing
1.	Canada	FTA	Provisionally applied	2009–2014
2.	Chile	FTA	In negotiation	2018–today
3.	China	BIT	In negotiation	2013–today
4.	India	FTA	In negotiation	2007–today
5.	Indonesia	FTA	In negotiation	2016–today
6.	Japan	FTA	Partly in force	2013–2017
7.	Malaysia	FTA	Paused	2010–2012
8.	Mexico	FTA	In negotiation	2018–today
9.	Myanmar	BIT	In negotiation	2013–today
10.	Singapore	FTA	Pending ratification	2010–2014
11.	Vietnam	FTA	Pending ratification	2012–2016
12.	USA	FTA	Paused	2013–today

BIT, Standalone Bilateral Investment Treaty; FTA, free trade and investment
agreement.
Source: European Commission (2018).

IIAs with developing and least developed countries, as the member states already have IIAs in place with many of them. France, Germany, the Netherlands and the United Kingdom, for instance, have hundreds of IIAs with mostly developing and least developed economies (UNCTAD 2018). Hence, a significant share of European outward FDI into many developing and least developed countries enjoys coverage and protection under existing member state IIAs. The EU's choice of partner countries may thus reflect gaps in member state IIA networks rather than an apparent disregard for developmental considerations.

2.4.2   Evolution of Substantive Treatment and Protection Standards

The substantive treatment and protection standards of IIAs matter for the development effects of FDI on states. In recent years, experts have lamented that many IIAs are overly business-friendly and impose high financial and political risks and costs on host states and called for a fundamental overhaul of IIAs (Bernasconi-Osterwalder 2013; Poulsen et al. 2015). The EU follows these calls, as becomes clear through a comparative analysis of the pivotal 'Fair and Equitable Treatment' (FET) clause in member state and EU IIAs. The FET clause commits parties to honour basic principles of 'due process' and the rule of law when dealing directly – or indirectly through regulation and legislation – with foreign investors. Unlike national or most favoured nation treatment, it is an absolute and contingent treatment standard in that it does not create relative obligations and is autonomous from other legal norms. According to the Organisation for Economic Co-operation and Development (OECD), the FET clause is the liability basis for the vast majority of investment arbitration proceedings against states and is also frequently cited as a potential threat to states' right to regulate (Gaukrodger 2017, p. 5). I focus on the FET clause as the key substantive treatment standard defining the balance between states' right to regulate and public policy considerations, on the one hand, and investor rights, on the other hand, in a given IIA.

A comparative assessment of the design of FET clauses in member state and European IIAs shows significant changes over time. The model IIAs of France (2006), Germany (2008), the Netherlands (2004), Italy (2003) and the United Kingdom (2006) contain concise FET clauses. FET is little defined. Vague FET clauses are seen to increase the level of investment protection and thereby to benefit investors (Jadeau and Gélinas 2016). Vague FET clauses allow arbitrators to broadly determine whether state treatment was unfair or inequitable in the spirit of the IIA and to order states to pay compensation. The EU adopted a fundamentally different approach to FET in the Comprehensive Economic and Trade Agreement (Canada) with Canada and in the EU-Singapore Free Trade Agreement (FTA). The agreements advance a detailed negative definition of FET through a list of treatment properties falling short of the FET standard (EU-Singapore FTA: 2.4.2; CETA: 8.10.2). The purpose of the Commission's efforts to provide a detailed definition of FET is to circumscribe the interpretative leeway and guide and constrain arbitrators so as to ring-fence states' right to regulate (Jadeau and Gélinas 2016). Furthermore, this intention is even more manifest with regard to a novel sub-clause empowering a joint committee formed by the respective parties to the agreements to regularly assess the application and interpretation and – if necessary – to amend the FET clause (EU-Singapore FTA: 2.4.4; CETA: 8.10.3). The subclause has the purpose of preventing unintentionally broad interpretations of FET and limiting financial risks for states. Critics have argued that the FET clause with its new substantive and procedural elaborations is effectively impossible to use for investors in arbitration proceedings. The threshold to proof a violation of FET is arguably so high that investors could not possibly invoke a violation of the FET standard to claim compensation (Lavranos 2014). While this criticism may be overstated, the EU's new approach to FET clearly seeks to strengthen states' rights to regulate and public policy space while maintaining investment protection against discriminatory treatment and expropriation.

2.4.3   Procedural Reforms of ISDS in EU IIAs

The balance between states' rights to regulate and investor rights under IIAs does not hinge exclusively on the substantive treatment and protection standards of IIAs. The procedural rules governing ISDS providing for the enforcement of substantive treatment and protection standards are another important determinant of the balance of state and investor rights and thus potentially of developmental effects of IIAs. The following section compares member state models and recent EU IIAs in two important regards: ease of access to ISDS and institutional setup of ISDS. The access to ISDS is of relevance here, because it determines the overall exposure of states to ISDS risks. The easier it is for foreign investors to use ISDS, the higher is the risk of states to face and lose ISDS proceedings.

Variation in the institutional setup of ISDS, as we shall see, affects the recruitment of arbitrators and their incentive structures, which may result in more or less attention given to states' rights to regulate, public policy considerations or investor rights.

A comparative assessment of the evolution of procedural rules governing access of investors to investment arbitration in member state and EU IIAs evidences a clear development trajectory over time. Access to arbitration is becoming more difficult in recent IIAs. French (2006), German (2008), Dutch (2004), Italian (2003) and the British (2006) models IIAs hardly condition access to investment arbitration. Recent EU IIAs, however, restrict access to investment arbitration. First, the EU-Singapore FTA and Comprehensive Economic and Trade Agreement (CETA) stipulate that only investors with 'substantial business activities' are covered and may bring claims against host countries (EU-Singapore FTA: 9.1.4; CETA: Art. 8.1). EU IIAs thereby exclude 'mailbox' or 'shell' companies from investment protection and arbitration proceedings. Taking into consideration the widespread practice of investment structuring and treaty shopping through shell companies, the new condition forecloses investment arbitration to a sizeable group of investors limiting ISDS risks for host states. Second, both EU agreements require investors to seek consultations to reach an amicable settlement during a compulsory six-month period (EU-Singapore FTA: Art. 9.17.b; CETA: Art. 8.22.b). Only after the end of this consultation period can an investment arbitration proceeding formally start. The model IIAs of member states also provide for an initial consultation period, which, however, is typically shorter and not necessarily compulsory. Third, both EU agreements require investors to withdraw from domestic legal proceedings and to waive their right to pursue a claim through other dispute resolution mechanisms (EU-Singapore FTA: Art: 9.17.1.f; CETA: Art. 8.22.1). Member state model IIAs do not contain equivalent clauses. This so-called 'fork in the road' clause may significantly complicate and even hinder investment arbitration proceedings. Large-scale investment projects are complex and touch upon many interrelated legal questions. Arbitration tribunals have found that investors could not pursue arbitration under an IIA, as the investor was still involved in a domestic lawsuit touching upon related legal questions.[2] The procedural requirement that arbitration proceedings and domestic lawsuits are fully independent may

---

[2] See *Pantechniki S.A. Contractors & Engineers (Greece) v. Republic of Albania* (ICSID No. ARB/07/21).

thus constitute a significant hurdle to using arbitration for investors. More importantly though, the prohibition of parallel proceedings may limit legal forum shopping and thereby prevent foreign investors from undermining the legitimacy of domestic legal systems in the eyes of citizens and national firms. To sum up, recent EU IIAs restrict access to investment arbitration in comparison to member state IIAs. The underlying policy rationale is to incentivise investors to use arbitration only in grave and major disputes and thereby to limit the exposure of states to ISDS.

The most significant changes to procedural rules of ISDS in IIAs concern the institutionalisation of investment arbitration. Most member state IIAs provide for conventional ad hoc arbitration as governed under the rules of the International Centre for Settlement of Investment Disputes (ICSID) or the United Nations Committee for International Trade Law (UNCITRAL). Investors file a claim, which entails the constitution of an ad hoc tribunal with private lawyers assuming the role of arbitrators. The ad hoc tribunal has the sole purpose to assess a given case. Once the case is decided, the tribunal ceases to exist. Arbitrators return to other functions. The ad hoc nature of investment arbitration creates a perverse incentive structure (Van Harten 2005, pp. 615–617). As only investors can bring arbitration claims, arbitrators theoretically face an incentive to rule in favour of investors to maintain the interest of potential claimants in investment arbitration in general and the services of individual arbitrators in particular. The incentive structure under ad hoc arbitration arguably weakens states' rights to regulate and public policy considerations including sustainable development objectives. What is more, the private sector and private law background of many arbitrators arguably limits the resonance of public law and public policy considerations in arbitration proceedings. While national administrative courts with permanent judges with a background in public and administrative law are seen to give state interests and public policy considerations – including sustainable development objectives – significant weight in their rulings, private arbitrators arguably attach less importance to such considerations because of their training and socialisation in commercial arbitration and private law. Finally, white male lawyers from OECD economies overwhelmingly serve as arbitrators in ISDS proceedings (Gaukrodger and Gordon 2012). The selection bias against women, other ethnicities and citizens from developing and least developed countries risks translating into a substantive bias in ISDS decision in that sustainable development concerns may receive less attention.

The EU advocates an institutionalisation of investor-to-state dispute resolution to address above discussed concerns. The EU has developed the so-called investment court system (ICS), which forms the basis for investor-to-state dispute resolution in CETA and the EU-Vietnam FTA. It needs to be mentioned that the EU-Singapore FTA still provides for conventional ad hoc arbitration but explicitly foresees the future integration of the agreement into the novel ICS. The ICS constitutes an inter se modification of the ICSID Convention (Reinisch 2016) and creates a standing arbitration tribunal (Art. 8.27). The tribunal will count fifteen judges vetted and appointed by the parties. The European Commission has declared that it aims to appoint diverse yet qualified judges with a background in international public and administrative law to the new tribunal. This legal-professional profile of future judges is meant to ensure that public policy and sustainable development considerations are given due consideration in the assessment of contested state action. The judges will hold a five-year tenure and will be randomly assigned to disputes. Their income will be decoupled from the number of disputes they arbitrate as well as any individual disputes. The institutionalisation of investment arbitration in the form of the investment court system thereby seeks to do away with the perverse incentive structure for arbitrators under the current system. The EU, furthermore, advocates the creation of a proper multilateral investment court under the umbrella of the United Nations in the long run (European Commission 2017). The success of this proposal, however, hinges on the yet uncertain support of other major economic powers.

2.5   Identifying the Drivers of Policy Reforms

The EU's IIA programs seem to strike a new, arguably more development-friendly balance between states' right to regulate and investor rights. How can one explain this policy change? Keeping in mind the foregoing theoretical discussion, does the policy shift reflect new primary law obligations, increased politicisation or aggregation effects resulting from the competence transfer? The following section produces evidence to empirically test these three theoretical hypotheses. It builds on process tracing, FDI and arbitration statistics and other policy documents.

2.5.1   The Importance of New Primary Law Obligations

The Treaty of Lisbon of 2009 transferred the competence to regulate FDI from the member states to the EU. If new primary law obligations played a significant role in making the EU rebalance states' rights to regulate and investor rights, it should have become particularly manifest from the outset in the months following the competence transfer. While policymakers typically need years to fully politically appropriate and penetrate new policy domains after competence transfers, new primary law obligations should become effective immediately. In other words, policymakers typically need some time to gain experience and become fully operational in new policy domains, yet legal requirements should constrain policymakers from the beginning. I therefore focus on the policy development and formulation phase to identify the causal significance of new primary law obligations for anchoring the sustainable development agenda in the EU's IIA programs.

The competence transfer was unintended and thus highly contentious (Basedow 2017). The member states criticised the European Commission for having surreptitiously usurped the competence despite their persistent and vocal opposition. Cooperation on IIAs between the European Commission and the Council of Ministers was tense in the months and years following the entry into force of the Treaty of Lisbon. It was clearly a phase of policy learning in terms of policy substance and reassigning of policy roles in the EU. In June 2010, the Commission published a first communication to develop its strategic vision for the EU's IIA program (European Commission 2010). Sustainable development concerns were mentioned only in passing in this document pointing to the limited weight of new primary law obligations on EU policy-making. First, the communication did not mention sustainable development as a key objective of a future EU IIA program (European Commission 2010, pp. 2–6) but clearly emphasised the economic interests of the European Union and European investors (Calamita 2012). Second, the communication insinuated that the Commission would seek to match the level of investment protection provided in 'gold standard' IIAs of the member states (European Commission 2010, p. 8). Third, the communication identified partner countries for future EU IIAs (European Commission 2010, p. 7). It suggested including IIA-like investment chapters in all ongoing FTA negotiations with countries such as Canada, Singapore, Mercosur and India. In the long run, the EU should aim to conclude IIAs with China and Russia. According to the United Nations (2018b), only one Mercosur member – namely Paraguay – qualifies as a lower middle income economy and can thus be considered as traditional developing country. All other potential partner countries are high income or upper middle income economies, which are not conventionally regarded as developing countries. The assessment shows that new primary law obligations regarding the promotion of the sustainable development agenda did not weigh in heavily in the formulation of the EU's new IIA program. Economic considerations were dominant.

This finding is remarkable in that the EU put markedly greater emphasis on sustainable development in its FTAs following the entry into force of the Treaty of Lisbon (see Chapter 1 by Adinolfi in this volume; Raess and Sari 2018). The EU-South Korea FTA of 2010 for instance contains an ambitious sustainable development chapter, which deals with labour rights and environmental protection. The apparent disregard for similar issues in the development of the EU's IIA approach might reflect the tense relationship between the Commission and member state investment officials after 2009. Member state investment officials typically had little experience with EU policy-making and trade policy prior to the entry into force of the Treaty of Lisbon. They had dealt with national IIA programs without interference from European Institutions. Many member state investment officials were thus highly circumspect of any deviation from their national IIA approaches and in particular the inclusion of non-economic issues such as developmental objectives. It seems likely that the Commission did not push for the inclusion non-economic issues into the EU's IIA approach so as not to further deteriorate the already tense working relationship with member state officials in this domain.

Finally, it needs to be mentioned though that the EU's trade and investment agreements are legally and automatically subject to impact assessments and sustainability impact assessments. In accordance with the Commission's 'Better Regulation' guidelines, the Commission must evaluate the economic, environmental, social and developmental effects of these treaties where appropriate (European Commission 2015a). Taking into consideration that the EU's IIA program deals primarily with high-income or newly industrialised economies for the time being, impact assessments and sustainability impact assessments can structurally make only a limited contribution to promoting sustainable development. The Commission nonetheless now negotiates on investment disciplines with five developing and least developed countries: China, India, Indonesia, Myanmar and Vietnam. The relevant assessments discuss potential developmental effects of the planned agreements (European Commission 2018), but it remains unclear to what extent this evaluation exercise does shape policy outcomes in the form of substantive agreement provisions.

2.5.2   The Importance of Aggregation Effects

Aggregation effects due to the pooling of diverse and evolving member state preferences on IIAs and ISDS played some role in making the EU's international investment policy more development-friendly over time. At the moment of the competence transfer in 2009, member states had different experiences with and exposures to the risks of IIAs and ISDS. The fifteen old member states had faced only five mostly unsuccessful ISDS cases (UNCTAD 2018). The twelve new member states, however, had already faced twenty-nine ISDS cases and lost several of them (UNCTAD 2018). Calculations based on OECD statistics (2018) statistics, moreover, suggest that at least 65 per cent of all inward FDI stocks of the new member states were covered by IIAs with ISDS provisions whereas at least 5 per cent of inward FDI stocks in old member states were covered in 2012–2013. Hence, the risk of new member states to face ISDS proceedings under IIAs was significantly higher than the risk of old member states. These structural differences meant that new member states and the Commission as guardian of the common European interest gave more consideration to defensive interests with regard to ISDS than old member states. The differences shaped to some limited extent debates between the Commission and the Council of Ministers on the substance of EU IIAs in the years following the competence transfer (Basedow 2017).

A significant shift in the aggregate preferences of the member states occurred after 2012–2013 and promoted development-friendly reforms. Since 2012–2013, investors have brought more than a hundred new ISDS claims against member states, mostly to limit the fallout of austerity programs and related regulatory reforms on business operations (see Figure 2.1). New member states faced seventy-two new cases, while old member states faced sixty-four new cases (UNCTAD 2018). Spain (forty-five) and Italy (eleven) were particularly hard hit over changes to renewable energy subsidy schemes. And even Germany had to face a high-profile claim from Vattenfall regarding its nuclear phase-out following the Fukushima incident (Bernasconi-Osterwalder and Hoffmann 2012). The preferences of new versus old, southern and eastern versus northern member states thus started converging toward a more defensive position and a rebalancing of states' right to regulate, public policy considerations and investor interests under IIAs. The convergence in preferences in the Council of Ministers – in conjunction with the heated debate over ISDS in the context of the negotiations on the Transatlantic Trade and Investment Partnership (TTIP) (see

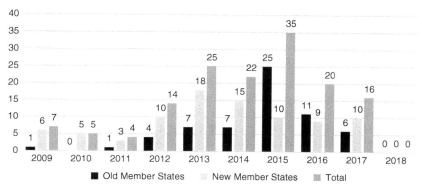

Figure 2.1   ISDS cases against member states of the European Union.
Source: Author's own calculation based on UNCTAD (2018).

later) – fuelled a significant shift in the EU approach to IIAs and ISDS. In consequence, the Commission in cooperation with the Council of Ministers and the European Parliament developed its investment court system and proposed the creation of a standing multilateral investment court under the umbrella of the United Nations (see Section 2.4.3). Both proposals seek to rebalance state and investor rights in view of better protecting states' rights to regulate. While these findings suggest that the shift in EU preferences and approach to IIAs and ISDS were driven primarily by the surge in ISDS cases, aggregation effects nonetheless played a role in the EU's shift toward a more development-friendly approach. This conclusion seems justified, as certain old member states faced no ISDS claims and would have in all likelihood continued to conclude old-fashioned 'gold standard' IIAs in the absence of a common EU IIA program. This counterfactual thus suggests that preference aggregation and policy delegation to the EU level indeed contributed to the policy shift.

2.5.3   *The Importance of Politicisation*

Empirical evidence suggests that the politicisation of international investment policy due to the competence transfer indeed plays a significant role in the promotion of the sustainable development agenda. First, the competence transfer entailed political oversight of the EU's IIA program through the European Parliament as part of the Common Commercial Policy. Following the entry into force of the Treaty of Lisbon in 2009, the European Parliament showed eager to assume and use its new role as co-legislator with the Council of Ministers under the Common Commercial Policy. In 2011, it formulated a critical response to the above-mentioned communication of the Commission (2010) and the Council of Ministers. Unlike the Commission and member state governments, the European Parliament insisted that future EU IIAs must protect developing countries' rights to regulate and make a contribution to the sustainable development agenda (European Parliament 2011). The European Parliament made clear that it would not ratify future IIAs that ignore non-economic objectives. Second, the embedding of international investment policy and negotiations into trade policy and negotiations led to unseen levels of politicisation and heated public debates on the effects of ISDS and IIAs on states' rights to regulate, democracy and sustainable development. In 2013, the launch of the negotiations on the so-called Transatlantic Trade and Investment Partnership (TTIP) between the EU and the USA triggered a forceful public campaign of non-governmental organisations, trade unions, parties and media. The campaign at first focused and criticised traditional trade provisions (Bauer 2016). Within a couple of months, the planned investment chapter and ISDS provisions of TTIP became the core topic of the campaign and public debate. A 'traditional' anti-trade campaign spilled over and turned into an anti-ISDS campaign. Millions of European citizens demonstrated against TTIP and ISDS (Spiegel Online 2015). The European Parliament was again a key focal point and played a catalytic role in the public campaign as a new co-legislator that was willing to oppose the Commission and the Council of Ministers on TTIP. TTIP was initially meant to contain rather old-fashioned – yet no 'gold standard' – investment protection and ISDS provisions. The Commission with the backing of the Council of Ministers sought to ease public opposition and resistance from the European Parliament by organising a public consultation on investment protection and ISDS (European Commission 2015b) and developing its new 'investment court system' and proposal for a multilateral investment court to replace ISDS (European Commission 2016). These proposals (see Sections 2.4.2 and 2.4.3) constitute an important policy shift toward an arguably more development-friendly approach to IIAs.

2.6 Conclusion

The international community is committed to attain the SDGs by 2030. The necessary efforts require huge public assistance and aid as well as private initiative and investment. International investment policy and IIAs can play a role in mobilising the necessary private capital and initiative to realise the SDGs. Critics stress, however, that conventional IIAs circumscribe states' rights to regulate in the public interest and thereby harm rather than support sustainable development. Developing and least developed countries require IIAs, which strike a better balance between investment protection, state interests and public policy considerations.

The chapter sought to assess whether the EU's recent empowerment to regulate FDI and to conclude IIAs is a stepping stone or stumbling block for efforts to make the international investment regime more development friendly. It finds that the EU's new international investment policy and IIA program indeed seem more development-friendly than preexisting member state policies in that they rebalance states' rights to regulate and investor interests. The chapter further finds that this effect of the competence transfer primarily results from the greater politicisation of IIA policy-making and aggregate effects. New primary law obligations under European law seem to have had little effect on policy changes. Finally, it is worthwhile emphasising that the arguably more development-friendly approach of the EU to international investment policy and IIAs is not so much the result of the EU's political commitment to the SDGs but reflects self-serving considerations about a surge in ISDS claims against Europe and thus growing public opposition against IIAs.

References

Alfaro, L., Kalemli-Ozcan, S. and Sayek, S. (2009). 'FDI, Productivity and Financial Development'. *The World Economy* 32: 111–135. Available at https://doi.org/10.1111/j.1467-9701.2009.01159.x.

Basedow, R. (2017). *The EU in the Global Investment Regime: Commission Entrepreneurship, Incremental Institutional Change and Business Lethargy.* UACES Contemporary European Studies. Routledge.

Bauer, M. (2016). 'Manufacturing Discontent: The Rise to Power of Anti-TTIP Groups'. ECIPE Occasional Papers. Brussels: ECIPE.

Bernasconi-Osterwalder, N. (2013). *A Response to the European Commission's December 2013 Document 'Investment Provisions in the EU-Canada Free Trade Agreement (CETA)'.* Geneva, Switzerland: IISD.

Bernasconi-Osterwalder, N. and Hoffmann, R. T. (2012). 'The German Nuclear Phase-Out Put to the Test in International Investment Arbitration? Background to the New Dispute Vattenfall v. Germany (II)'. Briefing Note. Geneva, Switzerland: IISD.

Bonnitcha, J., Poulsen, L. and Waibel, M. (2017). *The Political Economy of the Investment Treaty Regime*. Oxford University Press.

Busse, M., Königer, J. and Nunnenkamp, P. (2010). 'FDI Promotion through Bilateral Investment Treaties: More than a Bit?' *Review of World Economics* 146: 147–177. Available at https://doi.org/10.1007/s10290-009-0046-x.

Calamita, J. (2012). 'The Making of Europe's International Investment Policy: Uncertain First Steps'. *Legal Issues of Economic Integration* 39: 301–330.

Campact. (2014). A Corporate System of Injustice. Available at www.youtube.com /watch?v=dSuIGKSm7z0.

Corporate Europe Observatory. (2014). *TTIP: Debunking the Business Propaganda over Investor Rights.*, Brussels: Corporate Europe Observatory.

Demir, F. (2016). 'Effects of FDI Flows on Institutional Development: Does It Matter Where the Investors Are From?' *World Development* 78: 341–359. Available at https://doi.org/10.1016/j.worlddev.2015.10.001.

Demir, F. and Duan, Y. (2018). 'Bilateral FDI Flows, Productivity Growth, and Convergence: The North vs. The South'. *World Development* 101: 235–249. Available at https://doi.org/10.1016/j.worlddev.2017.08.006" https://doi.org/10 .1016/j.worlddev.2017.08.006.

Dunning, J. (2008). *Multinational Enterprises and the Global Economy*, 2nd ed. Edward Elgar.

Egger, P. and Merlo, V. (2007). 'The Impact of Bilateral Investment Treaties on FDI Dynamics'. *The World Economy* 30: 1536–1549.

Eskeland, G. A. and Harrison, A. E. (2002). 'Moving to Greener Pastures? Multinationals and the Pollution Haven Hypothesis'. Working Paper No. 8888. National Bureau of Economic Research. Available at https://doi.org/10 .3386/w8888.

European Commission. (2010). Towards a Comprehensive European International Investment Policy (COM(2010)343). Brussels.

European Commission. (2015a). Better Regulation Guidelines. Brussels. Available at https://ec.europa.eu/info/sites/info/files/better-regulation-guidelines.pdf.

European Commission. (2015b). Online Public Consultation on Investment Protection and Investor to-State Dispute Settlement (ISDS) in the Transatlantic Trade and Investment Partnership Agreement (TTIP). Brussels. Available at http://trade.ec.europa.eu/consultations/index.cfm?consul_id=179.

European Commission. (2016). The Multilateral Investment Court project. Brussels. Available at http://trade.ec.europa.eu/doclib/press/index.cfm?id=1608.

European Commission. (2017). Investment Provisions in the EU-Canada Free Trade Agreement (CETA). Available at http://trade.ec.europa.eu/doclib/docs/ 2013/november/tradoc_151918.pdf.

European Commission. (2018). Sustainability Impact Assessments. Available at http://ec.europa.eu/trade/policy/policy-making/analysis/policy-evaluation/sus tainability-impact-assessments/index_en.htm.

European Court of Justice. (2017). Opinion 2/15. EU:C:2017:376 (May 16, 2017).

European Parliament. (2011). Resolution of 6 April 2011 on the Future European International Investment Policy (No. (201072203(INI))). Brussels.

Garsous, G. and Kozluk, T. (2017). 'Foreign Direct Investment and the Pollution Haven Hypothesis – Evidence from Listed Firms'. OECD Working Paper.

Gaukrodger, D. (2017). 'Addressing the Balance of Interests in Investment Treaties – The Limitations of Fair and Equitable Treatment Provisions to the Minimum Standard of Treatment under Customary International Law'. OECD Working Papers on International Investment 2017/03.

Gaukrodger, D. and Gordon, K. (2012). 'Investor-State Dispute Settlement: A Scoping Paper for the Investment Policy Community'. OECD Working Papers on International Investment 2012/2013.

Hawkins, D., Nielson, D., Tierney, M. and Lake, D., eds. (2006). *Delegation and Agency in International Organizations*. Cambridge University Press.

Herzer, D. (2012). 'How Does Foreign Direct Investment Really Affect Developing Countries' Growth?' *Review of International Economics* 20: 396–414. Available at https://doi.org/10.1111/j.1467-9396.2012.01029.x.

Hiscox, M. (2002). *International Trade and Political Conflict: Commerce, Coalitions, and Mobility*. Princeton University Press.

ISDS Platform. (2018). 'Veolia Loses ISDS Case Against Egypt – After Six Years and Millions in Costs'. Available at https://isds.bilaterals.org/?veolia-loses-isds-case-against.

ISDS Platform. (2019). Arbitration. Challenge to *Republic of Argentina v. AWG Group* Ltd. Arbitration Award. Available at http://isds.bilaterals.org/?arbitration-challenge-to-republic.

Jadeau, F. and Gélinas, F. (2016). 'CETA's Definition of the Fair and Equitable Treatment Standard: Toward a Guided and Constrained Interpretation'. *Transnational Dispute Management* 13: 1–15.

Kleinheisterkamp, J. (2014). 'Who Is Afraid of Investor-State Arbitration? Or Comparative Law?' SSRN Scholarly Paper No. ID 2483775. Rochester, NY: Social Science Research Network.

Krajewski, M. (2017). *The European Commission's Proposal for Investment Protection in TTIP*. Friedrich Ebert Stiftung.

Lavranos, N. (2013). 'In Defence of Member States' BITs Gold Standard: The Regulation 1219/2012 Establishing a Transitional Regime for Existing Extra-EU BITs – A Member State's Perspective'. *Transnational Dispute Management* 10: 1–14.

Lavranos, N. (2014). 'The Lack of an FET-Standard in CETA'. Montreal. Available at www.mcgill.ca/fortier-chair/files/fortier-chair/2014_ceta_lavranos_nikos.pdf.

Majone, G. (2001). 'Two Logics of Delegation: Agency and Fiduciary Relations in EU Governance, Agency and Fiduciary Relations in EU Governance'. *European Union Politics* 2: 103–122. Available at https://doi.org/10.1177/1465116501002001005.

Milner, H. (1999). 'The Political Economy of International Trade'. *Annual Review of Political Science* 2: 91–114.

Monbiot, G. (2013). 'This Transatlantic Trade Deal Is a Full-Front Assault on Democracy'. *The Guardian*, 4 November 2013.

Navaretti, G. B. and Venables, A. (2004). *Multinational Firms in the World Economy*. Princeton University Press.

Neumayer, E. and Spess, L. (2005). 'Do Bilateral Investment Treaties Increase Foreign Direct Investment to Developing Countries?' *World Development* 33: 1567–1585.

OECD (Organisation for Economic Co-operation and Development). (2004). Indirect Expropriation and the Right to Regulate in International Investment Law. Working Papers on International Investment 2004/4.

OECD (Organisation for Economic Co-operation and Development). (2018). FDI Positions by Country. Available at https://stats.oecd.org/Index.aspx?DatasetCode=FDI_FLOW_INDUSTRY#.

Pelc, K. J. (2017). 'What Explains the Low Success Rate of Investor-State Disputes?' *International Organization* 71: 559–583.

Pollack, M. A. (2003). *The Engines of European Integration: Delegation, Agency, and Agenda Setting in the EU*. Oxford University Press.

Poulsen, L., Bonnitcha, J. and Yackee, J. W. (2015). 'Transatlantic Investment Treaty Protection', CEPS Special Report. CEPS, Brussels.

Poulsen, L. N. S. and Aisbett, E., (2013). 'When the Claim Hits: Bilateral Investment Treaties and Bounded Rational Learning'. *World Politics* 65: 273–313. Available at https://doi.org/10.1017/S0043887113000063.

Raess, D. and Sari, D. (2018). 'Labor Provisions in Trade Agreements (LABPTA): Introducing a New Dataset', *Global Policy* 9: 451–466. Available at https://doi.org/10.1111/1758-5899.12577.

Reinisch, A. (2016). 'Will the EU's Proposal Concerning an Investment Court System for CETA and TTIP Lead to Enforceable Awards? The Limits of Modifying the ICSID Convention and the Nature of Investment Arbitration', *Journal of International Economic Law* 19: 761–786. Available at https://doi.org/10.1093/jiel/jgw072.

Rogowski, R. (1989). *Commerce and Coalitions: How Trade Affects Domestic Political Alignments*. Princeton University Press.

Seidl-Hohenveldern, I. (1977). *Verischerung nichtkommerzieller Risiken und die Europäische Gemeinschaft, Kölner Studien zur Rechtsvereinheitlichung, Band 1*. Carl Heymanns Verlag KG.

Shepsle, K. (2008). 'Rational Choice Institutionalism'. In R. A. W. Rhodes, S. Binder and B. Rockman, (eds.), *The Oxford Handbook of Political Institutions*. Oxford University Press, pp. 23–38.

Spiegel Online. (2015). 'Massendemo gegen TTIP – So viele kamen noch nie'. Available at www.spiegel.de/wirtschaft/unternehmen/ttip-demonstration-in-berlin-stellt-teilnehmerrekord-auf-a-1057187.html.

Titi, C. (2014). *The Right to Regulate in International Investment Law*. Bloomsbury Publishing.

Titi, C. (2015). 'International Investment Law and the European Union: Towards a New Generation of International Investment Agreements', *European Journal of International Law* 26: 639–661. Available at https://doi.org/10.1093/ejil/chv040.

UNCTAD (United Nations Conference on Trade and Development). (2018). 'Investment Policy Hub'. Available at http://investmentpolicyhub.unctad.org/IIA.

UNCTAD (United Nations Conference on Trade and Development). (2017). *World Investment Report 2017 – Investment and the Digital Economy*. Geneva, Switzerland: UNCTAD.

United Nations. (2018a). 'Sustainable Development Goals'. Available at https://sustainabledevelopment.un.org/?menu=1300.

United Nations. (2018b). *World Economic Situation and Prospect 2018*. New York: United Nations.

Van den Putte, L., De VIlle, F. and Orbie,J. (2015). 'The European Parliament as an International Actor in Trade'. In S. Stavrids and D. Irrera (eds.), *The European Parliament and Its International Relations*. Routledge, pp. 52–69.

Van Harten, G. (2005). 'Private Authority and Transnational Governance: The Contours of the International System of Investor Protection'. *Review of International Political Economy* 12: 600–623.

Weingast, B. (2002). 'Rational-Choice Institutionalism'. In I. Katznelson and H. Milner, (eds.), *Political Science: State of the Discipline*. W.W. Norton & Company, pp. 660–692.

Woolcock, S. (2010). 'The Treaty of Lisbon and the European Union as an Actor in international Trade'. ECIPE Working Paper 1/2010.

Natural Resources Management in the Sustainable Development Goals Era

Insights from World Trade Organization Case Law

ILARIA ESPA

3.1 Introduction

Since its inception in the 1987 Brundtland Report (WCED 1987), the concept of sustainable development has gone a long way in international law with regards to both its conceptual development and its practical implementation (Schrijver 2008). While its exact contours remain difficult to define today (Bacchus 2018, p. 15), and most likely because of it, the objective of sustainable development has virtually informed all fields of international law because of its economic, social and environmental connotations (United Nations 2002; ILA 2018). Accordingly, what it is now commonly referred to as the *corpus* of international law on sustainable development has rapidly evolved in the latest decades (Cordonier Segger et al. 2004; Schrijver et al. 2004; Gehring et al. 2005; Cordonier Segger et al. 2010), with an increasingly important role played by international courts and tribunals in the furtherance of key international law principles relating to sustainable development (Cordonier Segger et al. 2017).

Among such principles, the principle of sustainable use of natural resources has gained prominence in latest years as a result of a number of factors (ILA 2002), from increased competition for access to natural resources brought about by the 2000's commodity 'super-cycle' to the growing awareness of the social costs and environmental impacts linked to natural resources exploitation, from increased levels of price commodity volatility to the resurgence of disputes concerning natural resource protection in a wide range of different international arenas including law of the sea, human rights, trade law, investment law (Espa 2015, pp. 8–31; 2017, pp. 86–88). Global policy agendas have aligned to reflect the growing attention towards sustainable natural resource management concerns, as epitomized by the outcomes of the 2012 United Nations (UN) Conference on Sustainable Development (Rio+20), namely the Agenda 2030 and the global Sustainable Development Goals (SDGs) (United Nations 2012, 2015). The SDGs, in particular, cover a broad spectrum of natural resources, from water to forests, from energy to landscapes and biodiversity, in addition to specifically addressing the issue of resource efficiency more comprehensively by means of SDG 12: 'Ensure sustainable consumption and production patterns', which explicitly mentions 'sustainable management and efficient use of natural resources' among its core, cross-cutting targets (United Nations 2013).

As much as the SDGs' regulatory agenda is clearly cognisant of the prominence of sustainable natural resources management concerns nowadays, the principle of sustainable use for natural resources for development is, however, not (yet) fully reflected in international legal instruments. As of now, only few international treaties contain explicit provisions on natural resources management (one notable example is the 2015 Paris Agreement), whereas the majority touch upon sustainable management of different natural resources somewhat incidentally in the context of the pursuit of other regulatory purposes (ILA 2018, pp. 9–11). The World Trade Organization (WTO) Agreement is no exception to this trend despite the potential of trade policy to contribute to the sustainable use of natural resources (WTO 2010, pp. 160–199; Sell 2012; WTO 2018c). The progressive consolidation and furtherance of the principle of sustainable use of natural resources has instead essentially occurred through case law developments (Cordonier Segger et al. 2017, pp. 13–14). Here again, the multilateral trading system is no exception to the more general 'growing salience' of 'sustainable development jurisprudence' (ILA 2018, p. 5). The WTO is in fact the typical example of a regime in which judicial developments have far outpaced developments on the normative side (Van den Bossche 2017, pp. 91–101).

Against this backdrop, this chapter aims to explore how the principle of sustainable use of natural resources has been reflected in the SDGs, on the one hand, and on the law and practice of the WTO, on the other hand. The bottom line is that, as will be shown in the text that follows, sustainable natural resources management concerns have figured prominently in the SDGs but at the same time, and regretfully, trade was not systemically integrated into the SDGs' goals and targets concerned with sustainable natural resources management. More generally, trade has played a much smaller than optimal role in the SDGs' conceptual and implementation frameworks (Messerlin 2017, pp. 9–31). To the extent that SDGs accommodate the principle of sustainable use of natural resources, however, assessing WTO's responsiveness to such principle can inform on whether the multilateral trading regime is de facto sufficiently aligning on its own with the SDGs' regulatory agenda on sustainable natural resource management.

The remainder of this chapter is thus articulated as follows. Section 3.2 gives an account of the normative content of the principle of sustainable use in natural resources, followed by an assessment of how this principle is reflected in the SDGs and the role of trade in such relevant SDGs (Section 3.3). Section 3.4 illustrates how and to which extent sustainable natural resources management concerns are addressed in the WTO rulebook. Section 3.5 then focuses on how relevant WTO rules and exceptions have been interpreted in recent WTO case law, paying due regard to the relationship between such rules and the principle of sustainable development enshrined in the Preamble of the WTO Agreement. Based on this analysis, Section 3.6 discusses whether the WTO regime has proven sufficiently responsive to natural resource management challenges as enshrined in the SDGs, that is, whether WTO adjudicatory bodies have interpreted existing rules in a way that preserves sufficient flexibility for members to pursue sustainable natural resource management goals through trade-related policy instruments in accordance with the international law principle of sustainable use of natural resources as reflected into the SDGs. Finally, Section 3.7 concludes.

3.2 On the Principle of Sustainable Use of Natural Resources

After more than thirty years since its first formulation, the international community has yet to agree on an exact, thorough definition of sustainable development. Over the decades, the notion has invariably been stretched and squeezed on either side of the environment-development spectrum (Dupuy et al. 2015, pp. 20–24), and the malleability of the concept is perhaps one of the main reasons of its success (Birnie et al. 2009). Yet, in the words of James Bacchus, the Brundtland Report definition of sustainable development 'is open to endless further defining' (Bacchus 2018, p. 15).

Within such context, the work of the International Law Commission has, in particular, proved crucial to understanding how international law has contributed to defining the normative content of sustainable development. The Commission has identified seven key principles of international law whose consolidation and furtherance would be, in its own words, 'instrumental in pursuing the objective of sustainable development'. Such principles were first formulated in the 2002 *New Delhi Declaration of Principles of International Law Relating to Sustainable Development* and then reaffirmed and elaborated in 2012 in light of subsequent judicial developments (ILA 2012). As inherently interrelated principles, each of them disentangles a fundamental component of the evolving international law of sustainable development, while at the same time cumulatively contributing to refining sustainable development as a principle of international law: (1) the duty of States to ensure sustainable use of natural resources; (2) the principle of equity and the eradication of poverty; (3) the principle of common but differentiated responsibilities; (4) the principle of the precautionary approach to human health, natural resources and ecosystems; (5) the principle of public participation and access to information and justice; (6) the principle of good governance (ILA 2002, pp. 3–4). Among these principles, the principle of sustainable use of natural resources has been gaining centre stage for several reasons: first, the centrality of good resource management in the very notion of sustainable development, which involves, according to the *New Delhi Declaration*, 'a comprehensive and integrated approach to economic, social and political processes, which aims at the sustainable use of natural resources of the Earth and the protection of the environment on which nature and human life, as well as social and economic development depend' (ILA 2002, pp. 3–4); second, the *momentum* built by pressing sustainable natural resources management challenges (ILA 2002, rec. 13); and third, the parallel prominence acquired by disputes concerning natural resources before international courts and tribunals (ILA 2018, pp. 50–55).

According to the *New Delhi Declaration*, the principle of sustainable use of natural resources embodies both the (sovereign) right and the duty of all states to manage their own natural resources 'in a rational, sustainable and safe way' (ILA 2002, paras. 1.1–1.2). This means that, on the one hand, states can pursue their own environmental and developmental policies but, on the other hand, they also have the responsibility to ensure that such policies attain the conservation and sustainable use of natural resources for both present and future generations and do not cause harm to the environment of others or in areas beyond the limits of national jurisdiction. This is because 'the protection, preservation and enhancement of the natural environment, particularly the proper management of the climate system, biological diversity and fauna and flora of the Earth are the common concern of humankind' (ILA 2002, para. 1.3; Dupuy et al. 2015, p. 98). Ultimately, the principle of sustainable use of natural resources descends and at the same time expands on the principle of sovereignty over natural resources, the no harm principle, the prevention principle, and the principle of intra- and inter-generation equity having due regard to both their environmental and developmental connotations (Schrijver 2008).

The normative content of the principle of sustainable use of natural resources places it at the very heart of sustainable development, reflecting the fact that, in the words of the International Law Commission, '[f]or sustainable development, effective governance of resources is crucial' (ILA 2018, p. 2). And yet, the status of the principle of sustainable use of natural resources is yet to be definitively determined. Back in 2012, the International Law Commission had expressed the view that 'as a matter of common concern, the sustainable use of all natural resources represents an emerging rule of general customary international law' (ILA 2012, No. 3). The matter is however still far from settled and requires a reality check in light of the latest developments in the international legal framework.

3.3 Sustainable Use of Natural Resources in the SDGs' Regulatory Agenda and the Role of Trade

This section aims at a better understanding of how and to which extent the SDGs' regulatory agenda reflects the centrality of natural resources governance for the furtherance of sustainable development. Although the SDGs are not legally binding for states, they are revelatory of a broad international consensus on how governments should act to incorporate sustainable development concerns into national and international regulations in all fields and sectors. In this perspective, assessing whether SDGs fully accommodate for the *New Delhi* principle of sustainable use of natural resources may contribute not only to ascertaining the legal status of the principle; it may also contribute to shedding light on whether and, if so, to which extent the multilateral trading system aligns to the SDGs' regulatory agenda for the purposes of attaining sustainable natural resource governance by means of implementing the principle of sustainable use of natural resources. As will be shown in the text that follows, this is particularly important because SDGs do not pay sufficient consideration to the importance of harnessing trade as an instrument for attaining sustainable development more generally and sustainable natural resources governance more specifically.

3.3.1   Resource-Related SDGs and the Principle of Sustainable Use in Natural Resources

Sustainable natural resource management concerns feature prominently in the structure of the SDG goals and core targets. The SDGs cover virtually all main categories of natural resources, as identified by the Glossary of Statistical Terms elaborated by the Organisation for Economic Co-operation and Development (OECD) (OECD 2008, p. 352), from extractive (mineral and energy) resources to soil resources, from water resources to biological resources, either directly or indirectly, and with a more or less explicit focus on the environmental dimension of resource management alongside its economic and social implications (OECD 2008, p. 352). Among the SDGs focused directly on particular natural resources are SDG 6: 'Ensure availability and sustainable management of water and sanitation for all'; SDG 14: 'Conserve and sustainably use the oceans, seas and marine resources for sustainable development'; and SDG 15: 'Protect, restore and promote sustainable use of territorial ecosystems, sustainably manage forests, combat desertification, and halt and reverse land degradation and halt biodiversity loss.' There is no SDG goal which explicitly tackles the sustainable use and management of extractive resources. However, as shall be seen in the text that follows, SDG 12: 'Ensure sustainable consumption and production patterns', indirectly touches upon the issue through (1) Target 12.2, which mentions 'the sustainable management and efficient use of natural resources' more generally and (2) Target 12.c, which calls on, inter alia, the elimination of 'inefficient fossil-fuel subsidies' based on considerations related to 'their environmental impact' (United Nations 2017, p. 17). Furthermore, the very fact that SDG 7 aims to 'Ensure access to affordable, reliable, sustainable and modern energy for all', hence providing for adequate mechanisms aimed at facilitating the shift to renewables, also has a bearing, although indirectly, on the pace of extraction of energy resources (United Nations

2017, p. 11). While each of the natural resource–specific SDGs encompasses several core targets (eight, ten and twelve targets, respectively), which overall take into account environmental as well as developmental (economic and social) considerations, the environmentally centred targets can be clustered into two main categories: (1) one related to the protection/restoration and sustainable use of the specific resource, hence touching upon issues of environmental protection more at large (i.e. pollution reduction, ecosystems protection), and (2) one related to the rational management of the specific resource, hence touching upon conservation and resource efficiency issues. While the line between the two may sometimes be relatively thin, examples of the former kind of core targets include Target 6.6: 'By 2020, protect and restore water-related ecosystems, including mountains, forests, wetlands, rivers, aquifers and lakes'; Target 14.1: 'By 2025, prevent and significantly reduce marine pollution of all kinds, in particular from land-based activities, including marine debris and nutrient pollution'; and Target 15.1: 'By 2020, ensure the conservation, restoration and sustainable use of terrestrial and inland freshwater ecosystems and their services, in particular forests, wetlands, mountains and drylands, in line with obligations under international agreements.' By contrast, examples of the latter type of core target include Target 6.5: 'By 2030, implement integrated water resources management at all levels, including through transboundary cooperation as appropriate'; Target 14.4: 'By 2020, effectively regulate harvesting and end overfishing, illegal, unreported and unregulated fishing practices, and implement science-based management plans, in order to restore fish stocks in the shortest time feasible . . . '; and Target 15.2: 'By 2020, promote the implementation of sustainable management of all types of forests, halt deforestation, restore degraded forests and substantially increase afforestation and reforestation globally' (United Nations 2017, pp. 11 and 18–19). Clear interlinkages among them reflect the complex multidimensional nature of each of the specific goals and the spillovers inherent to sustainable use and management of different natural resources. Let's think, for instance of the implications of oceans, seas and marine resources protection for biodiversity as reflected in the interactions between Target 6.6 and Target 15.1, or of the effects of water-related ecosystems protection on land and forests, as apparent in the interlinkages between Target 14.2 and Target 15.5 (United Nations 2017, pp. 11 and 18–19).

Under the same logic, a number of other SDGs have furthermore an indirect link with sustainable resource management: for instance, SDG 11: 'Make cities and human settlements inclusive, safe, resilient and sustainable' is clearly centred on the economic and social dimensions of urban planning and does not tackle issues related to resource management specifically; yet, it includes targets such as Target 11.6, which reads: 'By 2030, reduce the adverse *per capita environmental impact of cities*, including by paying special attention to air quality and municipal and other waste management', and Target 11.b, which states: 'By 2020, substantially increase the number of cities and human settlements adopting and implementing integrated policies and plans towards inclusion, *resource efficiency, mitigation and adaptation to climate change, resilience to disasters, . . . "* (emphasis added). This clearly impacts on the quality of soil, water and biological resources, in addition to exhibiting evident links to goals such as SDG 13: 'Take urgent action to combat climate change and its impacts', making thus cities more resilient and prone to adapting to climate change (which, in turn, enhances sustainability of resource usage). See, for instance, Target 13. 1, which prescribes to '[s]trengthen resilience and adaptive capacity to climate-related hazards and natural disasters in all countries' (United Nations 2017, p. 17). Other examples include SDG 2: 'End hunger, achieve food security and improved nutrition and promote sustainable agriculture', which includes targets such as Target 2.4: 'By 2030, ensure sustainable food production systems and implement resilient agricultural practices that increase productivity and production, *that help maintain ecosystems, that strengthen capacity for adaptation to climate change*, extreme weather, drought, flooding and other disasters *and that progressively improve land and soil quality'* (emphasis added).

Finally, what is not captured, either directly or indirectly, under each of the specific resource-related SDGs falls anyways within the purview of SDG 12: 'Sustainable consumption and production patterns', which has a broad cross-cutting coverage when it comes to natural resources through its core Target 12.2: 'By 2030, achieve the sustainable management and efficient use of natural resources.' Further synergies with the aforementioned SDGs are incorporated through Target 12.4: 'By 2020, achieve the environmentally sound management of chemicals and all wastes throughout their life cycle, in accordance with agreed international frameworks, and significantly reduce their release to air, water and soil in order to minimize their adverse impacts on human health and the environment' (United Nations 2017, p. 16). SDG 12 incorporates, in essence, the issue of resource efficiency and, quite significantly, it is considered 'at the hard and soul of the 2030 Agenda' (Paul 2018).

When looking at the SDGs' overall framework, it seems fertile ground for accommodating and advancing the implementation of sound natural resource management practices in accordance with the principle of sustainable use of natural resources identified in the ILA *New Delhi Declaration*. It covers the full-fledged spectrum of natural resources, it pays due regard to both environmental and developmental consider-ations linked to the use of natural resources and related environmental spillovers and goes all the way from ensuring natural resources protec-tion to attaining conservation objectives.

3.3.2   The Marginal Role of Trade in Resource-Related SDGs

While sustainable natural resources concerns have figured prominently in the SDGs, trade was not systemically integrated into the SDG goals and targets concerned with natural resources use and management. This reflects, on the one hand, a more general 'lack of interest' in trade policy and trade-related measures during the SDGs production process and in its resulting working framework (Messerlin 2017, pp. 12 and 26). On the other hand, and more directly relevant for our purposes, it results from the fact that the SDGs' regulatory agenda is geared towards the economic dimension of trade and fails to innovatively account for its environmental dimension. In the words of C. Bellmann and A. V. Tipping: 'The trade-related targets included in the 2030 Development Agenda are not fundamentally new and many, particularly those in the SDGs, tend to repeat earlier commitments included in the WTO negotiations' (Bellmann et al. 2015).

What is more, many scholars have noticed that the vision encapsulated into the economically targeted SDGs is quite conservative:

> 'The focus in the SDGs is on improving market access for developing countries, including through WTO negotiations and [duty-free and quota-free (DFQF)] treatment for exporters in [least developed coun-tries (LDCs)], and ensuring that developing countries have "policy space" – matters that have long been on the international agenda. ... The language on trade and trade policy in the various SDGs consti-tutes "business as usual" – the underlying approach that has been pursued in the UN and the General Agreement on Tariffs and Trade (GATT)/WTO context for decades. The only specific target, that is, to double the global share of LDC exports by 2020, is already included in the Istanbul Programme of Action (United Nations 2012). There is a mercantilist flavour to how trade is included in the SDGs: the focus is on exports as opposed to trade (imports and exports) and improv-ing governance and the business environment confronting firms in developing countries is underemphasized.' (Hoekman, 2017, pp. 42–43)

Accordingly, the core of the targets that relate to trade and the WTO are included in SDG 17: 'Strengthen the means of implementation and revitalize the Global Partnership for Sustainable Development', which, however, reflects a relatively old-fashioned vision of trade as a means of implementation for sustainable development basically centred on development assistance, policy space and preferential market access. This is evident when reading the three specific targets related to trade as a means of implementation for the 2030 Agenda for Development, that is, (1) Target 17.10: 'Promote a universal, rules-based, open, non-discriminatory and equitable multilateral trading system under the World Trade Organization, including through the conclusion of nego-tiations under its Doha Development Agenda'; (2) Target 17.11: 'Significantly increase the exports of developing countries, in particular with a view to doubling the least developed countries' share of global exports by 2020'; and (3) Target 17.12: 'Realize timely implementation of duty-free and quota-free market access on a lasting basis for all least developed countries, consistent with World Trade Organization deci-sions, including by ensuring that preferential rules of origin applicable to imports from least developed countries are transparent and simple, and contribute to facilitating market access.' Other trade-related targets are included under the sub-heading 'Systemic Issues: Policy and Institutional Coherence'. They are (1) Target 17.13: 'Enhance global macroeconomic stability, including through policy coordination and policy coherence'; (2) Target 17.14: 'Enhance policy coherence for sustainable development'; and (3) Target 17.15: 'Respect each country's policy space and leadership to establish and implement policies for poverty eradication and sustainable development' (United Nations 2017, p. 20).

In a similar fashion, the bulk of the remaining trade-related targets are listed in a few economically targeted SDGs such as (1) SDG2: 'End hunger, achieve food security and improved nutrition and promote sustainable agriculture', and Target 2.b therein: 'Correct and prevent trade restrictions and distortions in world agricultural markets, including through the parallel elimination of all forms of agricultural export subsidies and all export measures with equivalent effect, in accordance with the mandate of the Doha Development Round' (United Nations 2017, p. 3); (2) SDG 8: 'Promote sustained, inclusive and sustainable economic growth, full and productive employment and decent work', and Target 8.a therein: 'Increase Aid for Trade support for developing countries, in particular least developed countries, including through the Enhanced Integrated

Framework for Trade-related Technical Assistance to Least Developed Countries' (United Nations 2017, p. 9); and (3) SDG 10: 'Reduce inequality within and among countries', and Target 10.a therein: 'Implement the principle of special and differential treatment for developing countries, in particular least developed countries, in accordance with World Trade Organization agreements' (United Nations 2017, p. 11).

Only residually and incidentally are trade-related commitments incorporated into environmentally targeted SDGs devoted to natural resources use and management. This is the case of a handful of goal-related targets focusing on removing trade distortions, that is, phasing out global commons-depleting subsidies on both fisheries and fossil fuels. See for instance, in relation to fisheries, Target 14.6:

> By 2020, prohibit certain forms of fisheries subsidies which contribute to overcapacity and overfishing, eliminate subsidies that contribute to illegal, unreported and unregulated fishing and refrain from introducing new such subsidies, recognizing that appropriate and effective special and differential treatment for developing and least developed countries should be an integral part of the World Trade Organization fisheries subsidies negotiation.

and, in relation to fossil fuels, Target 12.c:

> Rationalize inefficient fossil-fuel subsidies that encourage wasteful consumption by removing market distortions, in accordance with national circumstances, including by restructuring taxation and phasing out those harmful subsidies, where they exist, to reflect their environmental impacts, taking fully into account the specific needs and conditions of developing countries and minimizing the possible adverse impacts on their development in a manner that protects the poor and the affected communities.

3.4   Sustainable Use of Natural Resources in the WTO Rulebook

Although trade was not systemically integrated into the SDGs' goals and targets concerned with sustainable natural resources management, the multilateral trading system may still de facto play an important role in attaining the SDGs' regulatory agenda to the extent that the WTO system practically implements the principle of sustainable use of natural resources. This section sets the premises for such analysis by looking into the WTO rules relevant to natural resources management for sustainable development.

3.4.1   WTO Rules Relevant to Natural Resource Management

The WTO Agreement does not contain sectoral rules dealing specifically with trade in natural resources. Internationally traded natural resources are treated just like any other goods in WTO law once they are extracted and exchanged (Yanovich 2011, p. 3). Because of that, they primarily fall within the scope of the General Agreement on Tariffs and Trade (GATT), which essentially contains rules on the gradual elimination of tariffs, the absolute prohibition of quantitative restrictions and the non-discriminatory application of non-tariff barriers (Van den Bossche et al. 2017, pp. 305–324, 341–398, and 415–516). Depending on the exact type of trade instruments used by governments, a number of specialized WTO agreements may also come into play. To the extent that governments resort to national regulatory instruments (e.g. labelling requirements), the WTO Agreement on Technical Barriers to Trade (TBT Agreement) is relevant, as it requires that technical regulations and standards do not create unnecessary obstacles to trade (Van den Bossche et al. 2017, pp. 883–931). The same holds true in the case of the WTO Agreement on Sanitary and Phytosanitary Measures (SPS Agreement), which deals with a subcategory of technical regulations, namely sanitary and phytosanitary measures aimed at protecting human, animal or plant life or health from risks arising from pests or diseases of plants or animals or from food safety risks. The WTO agreements regulating unfair trade and trade remedies (the WTO Agreement on Subsidies and Countervailing Measures [ASCM], the WTO Anti-dumping Agreement [ADA] and the WTO Agreement on Safeguards) may also be applicable to trade in natural resources inasmuch as members impose countervailing duties, anti-dumping duties or safeguards on raw materials (let's think, for instance, of anti-dumping duties imposed on softwood lumber).

When looked through the lens of the principle of sustainable use of natural resources, however, not all such agreements are directly relevant for dealing with sustainable natural resource management concerns. The SPS Agreement focuses on the relationship between health and trade liberalisation of primary and processed agricultural products rather than the sustainable management of land and soil resources as targeted by the principle of sustainable use of natural resources as defined by the International Law Commission (ILA 2018). The ASCM, the ADA and the WTO Agreement on Safeguards, on the other hand, are technical agreements which do not address sustainability issues but rather discipline trade in natural resources merely from the side of its economic profitability. Here again, the focus of trade remedies is not on natural resources in the way intended by the ILA principle of sustainable use of natural resources, but rather on internationally traded raw materials (Espa 2015, pp. 41–44).

The GATT and the TBT Agreement, on the other hand, do allow for a certain margin of manoeuvre to members to fulfil legitimate non-economic objectives, some of which bear a more proximate relevance when it comes to sustainable natural resource management for development. As to GATT disciplines, Article XX GATT lists a number of legitimate public policy goals under paragraphs (a) to (j), which may be invoked to justify otherwise GATT-inconsistent measures. Under paragraph (b), in particular, members may seek justification for measures 'necessary to protect human, animal or plant life or health', whereas paragraph (g) allows members to deviate from standard GATT disciplines when they introduce measures 'related to the conservation of exhaustible natural resources if such measures are made effective in conjunction with restrictions on domestic production or consumption'. As per the chapeau of Article XX, moreover, a measure that falls within the range of policies enumerated under the letters (a) to (j) can seek justification only if it is not 'applied in a manner which would constitute a means of arbitrary or unjustifiable discrimination between countries where the same conditions prevail, or a disguised restriction on international trade'.

Somewhat similarly, the TBT Agreement contains a few provisions which may open the door to sustainable natural resources management concerns. After recognizing that 'no country should be prevented from taking measures necessary . . . for the protection of human animal or plant life or health, of the environment, . . . at the level it considers appropriate', de facto incorporating Article XX-chapeau-like language in the sixth recital of its Preamble,[1] Article 2.1 TBT and Article 2.2 TBT prescribe, respectively, that technical regulations shall be applied non-discriminatorily, and that they shall not be more trade-restrictive than necessary to fulfil a legitimate objective . . . *inter alia*: . . . 'protection of human health or safety, animal or plant life or health, or the environment'. Such flexibilities are all the more important if one considers that the TBT Agreement applies to requirements regarding processes and production methods (PPMs), both product-related

---

[1] The sixth recital indeed adds, in the relevant part: 'subject to the requirement that they are not applied in a manner which would constitute a means of arbitrary or unjustifiable discrimination between countries where the same conditions prevail, or a disguised restriction on international trade'.

and, at the very least in certain instances covered under Annex 1.1, second sentence and Annex 1.2, second sentence, non-product related PPMs (*US – Tuna II (Mexico)(2012)*, discussed in Section 3.5.2; Van den Bossche et al. 2017, pp. 885–895).

3.4.2   *Sustainable Development in the WTO Agreement*

Although neither the GATT nor the TBT Agreement mention the principle of sustainable development explicitly, express reference to sustainable development can be found in the preamble of the Agreement Establishing the World Trade Organization.[2] According to the first recital of the preamble, trade in and of itself is not the ultimate goal of the global trading system. Rather, WTO members recognize that 'their relations in the field of trade and economic endeavour should be conducted with a view to raising standards of living; ensuring full employment and a large and steadily growing volume of real income and effective demand; and expanding the production of and trade in goods and services, *while allowing for the optimal use of the world's resources in accordance with the objective of sustainable development, seeking both to protect and preserve the environment* and to enhance the means for doing so in a manner consistent with their respective needs and concerns at different levels of economic development' (emphasis added).

The preamble of the Marrakesh Agreement is particularly important when it comes to assessing how responsive is the WTO system to issues pertaining to sustainable natural resource management. Based on a consistent WTO jurisprudence, the preamble informs all the covered agreements. In *US – Shrimp*, in particular, the Appellate Body noted:

> this language demonstrates a recognition by WTO negotiators that optimal use of the world's resources should be made in accordance with the objective of sustainable development. As this preambular language reflects the intentions of negotiators of the WTO Agreement, we believe it must add colour, texture and shading to our interpretation of the agreements annexed to the WTO Agreement, in this case, the GATT 1994. (para. 153)

---

[2] Agreement Establishing the World Trade Organization (15 April 1994) 1867 UNTS 154, (1994) 33 ILM 1144, entered into force 1 January 1995 [hereinafter 'Marrakesh Agreement'].

This reasoning is all the more relevant as the measure at issue in the *US – Shrimp* dispute was an import ban implemented by the United States for resource conservation purposes, namely the protection of sea turtles from certain harmful shrimp fishing techniques. The Appellate Body affirmed in that occasion that the preamble of the Marrakesh Agreement imparts meaning to Article XX(g) GATT (*US – Shrimp*, Appellate Body Report, paras. 129–131). The objective of sustainable development can thus have a bearing in the interpretation of WTO rules relevant for natural resource management.

3.5 Sustainable Use of Natural Resources in WTO Jurisprudence

Building on Section 3.4, this section looks into whether WTO dispute settlement bodies have practically interpreted existing WTO rules and exceptions related to sustainable management of natural resources in accordance with the principle of sustainable use of natural resources. It hence contributes further qualifying the status of the principle since the *New Delhi Declaration*, while at the same time informing on whether the WTO de facto aligns with the SDGs' regulatory agenda on natural resource governance.

At a first glance, and reflecting the variety of WTO agreements governing, at various levels, trade in natural resources, a large number of WTO disputes are at least somewhat related to natural resources management (ILA 2018, pp. 58–68). On a general level, these disputes have dealt with a wide range of issues at the intersection of trade and environment intended broadly to incorporate a wide range of issues, from food safety through animal and plant protection issues to renewable energy promotion. Similar to what was noted earlier, however, not all such disputes bear a direct relevance for the purposes of discussing to which extent the WTO system has accommodated sustainable natural resource management concerns in line with the ILA principle of sustainable use of natural resources. More specifically, only in a handful of cases have the WTO adjudicatory bodies elaborated on the interplay between WTO rules, the principle of sustainable development and/or other international law principles relevant to sustainable natural resources management. The *trait d'union* among such disputes is that they revert around the notion of conservation, on the one hand, and on the notion of sovereignty of states, and the limits imposed to sovereign states by WTO rules, on the other hand – namely, two defining aspects of the principle of sustainable use of natural resources. In a few instances, WTO dispute settlement bodies have engaged in such discussions directly within the scope of Article XX(g) GATT: this is the case of the two disputes concerning China's export restrictions on mineral raw materials, that is, measures that were purportedly meant to manage the extraction and the exploitation of classical exhaustible natural resources, albeit at the expenses of access opportunities (*China – Raw Materials* and *China – Rare Earths*). A third, similar dispute (*China – Raw Materials II*) is still pending (WTO 2019). In a few other cases, the issue of conservation lay at the heart of classical non-product related PPM measures aimed at preserving living natural resources under Article XX(g) GATT and Article 2.2 TBT (sea turtles in *US – Shrimp* and dolphins in *US – Tuna II*). Here, the interplay between WTO rules and sovereignty of states is not apparently dealt with, but it indirectly comes into play because of the issue of extraterritoriality of PPM measures.

3.5.1   Access to Natural Resources in WTO Disputes

In *China – Raw Materials* and *China – Rare Earths*, the WTO dispute settlement bodies clarified the contours of the GATT conservation exception in cases in which members explicitly evoked their inalienable right to pursue sustainable national resources management goals. At issue in casu was the use by China of export restrictions (mainly export taxes and quotas) compromising fair and predicable access to a number of mineral raw materials. According to the Chinese government, such measures purported to achieve a more sustainable pace of extraction domestically, within the context of a more comprehensive conservation policy inspired by 'sustainable economic development' needs; net-importing countries, however, firmly contested them as industrial policy measures de facto subsidising Chinese domestic producers to the detriment of foreign competitors (Espa 2017, pp. 86–91).

Ultimately, China's measures did not pass the test under Article XX(g) GATT (Espa 2015, pp. 193–226). Prima facie, one may think that this outcome reflects the mantra of trade liberalization at any cost. Quite the contrary, the WTO adjudicatory bodies deeply delved into the question of policy space left to members to pursue sustainable natural resources management goals within the purview of the conservation exception. For our purposes, a few points should be retained here. First, they made clear that the term 'conservation' is to be interpreted in light of the objective of sustainable development as recognized in the preamble of the Marrakesh Agreement (Panel Reports, *China – Rare Earths*, para. 7.261 and Panel

Reports, *China – Raw Materials*, para. 7.373) and the international law principle of sovereignty over natural resources (Panel Reports, *China – Raw Materials*, paras. 7.377–7.381; Panel Reports, *China – Rare Earths*, para. 7.262) as a 'relevant rule of international law applicable in the relations between the parties' in accordance with Article 31(3) of the Vienna Convention on the Law of Treaties. Second, and following from the previous point, they acknowledged that WTO members have the right to design their own conservation programmes on the basis of a full range of policy considerations and goals, including their own economic and sustainable development needs (Panel Reports, *China – Raw Materials*, paras. 7.375 and 7.381; Panel Reports, *China–Rare Earths*, paras. 7.257–7.267), also by means of comprehensive policies consisting of 'a series of interconnected measures and programmes … which are designed to manage the extraction and supply of [the challenged] resources' (Panel Reports, *China – Rare Earths*, para. 7.375). The important thing here is that there exists a real, rational connection between the measure at issue and the conservation goal (Appellate Body Reports, *China – Raw Materials*, para. 355; Appellate Body Reports, *China – Rare Earths*, para. 5.90). This leads to the third point, namely that the conservation exception cannot be transformed into an exception protecting measures designed to pursue 'sustainable economic development' goals in and of themselves:

> As we have already explained, that panel did not say that "sustainable economic development" was, in itself, a goal that could be pursued under the rubric of "conservation". As we have further explained, the need for "sustainable development" may impact a Member's decision whether or not and how to implement a conservation policy. It may also affect the final form of any conservation policy eventually adopted, as well as the form or manner of any conservation actions taken. But measures adopted for the purpose of economic development are not automatically measures "relating to the conservation of exhaustible natural resources". Indeed, the Panel considers that measures the objective of which is to promote economic development are not "measures relating to conservation" but measures relating to industrial policy. (para. 7.461)

It is precisely in such a context that China's export restrictions were condemned by WTO adjudicatory bodies. More specifically, the use of measures restricting exports, and thus burdening foreign consumers only, was not considered to have a rational connection to the goal of reducing consumption (and thus achieving conservation) domestically in *China – Rare Earths* (Panel Reports, *China – Rare Earths*, paras. 7.436–7.439). This conclusion was reached after noticing the so-called perverse signalling function associated with export quotas, according to which 'whereas export quotas may reduce foreign demand for [the restricted goods], they will also *stimulate* domestic consumption by effectively reserving a supply of low-price raw materials for use by domestic downstream industries (Appellate Body Reports, *China – Rare Earths*, para. 5.156, citing Panel Reports, *China – Rare Earths,* para. 7.444).

The *China – Raw Materials* and *China – Rare Earths* reports remain nevertheless crucial for the definition of the relationship between conservation, sustainable development and permanent sovereignty over natural resources under Article XX(g) GATT. This is because, in essence, the WTO adjudicatory bodies did recognize that WTO members are free to design conservation policies aimed at managing extraction for sustainability purposes; what they cannot do is to defend measures centred on 'sustainable economic development' objectives such as supply management as conservation-related measures, especially when they simply discriminate between domestic and foreign consumers (Panel Reports, *China – Rare Earths*, para. 7.460). The bottom line here is that the relationship between 'conservation', sustainable development and permanent sovereignty over natural resources cannot be intended as to allow a WTO member to allocate the available stock of a natural resource between foreign and domestic consumers under the purview of Article XX(g) GATT because, once extracted and in commerce, natural resources are subject to WTO law (Panel Reports, *China – Rare Earths*, para. 7.462). Importantly, this conclusion lies in the premise that the permanent sovereignty over natural resources has to be exercised within the limits imposed by the requirements of Article XX(g) GATT:

> As noted by the panel in *China – Raw Materials*, a State's sovereignty is also expressed in its decision to ratify an international treaty and accept the benefits and obligations that such ratification entails. In becoming WTO Member[s], [States] ha[ve] of course not forfeited permanent sovereignty over [their] natural resources, which [they] enjoy as a natural corollary of [their] statehood. Nor [have they] 'given up' [their] right to adopt export quotas or any other measure in pursuit of conservation. [They have], however, agreed to exercise [their] rights in conformity with WTO rules, and to respect WTO provisions when developing and implementing policies to conserve exhaustible natural resources. (Panel Reports, *China – Rare Earths*, para. 7.270)

Accordingly, export regimes as such are unlikely to pass the test of Article XX(g) GATT; yet, they can reinforce or complement alternative instruments which countries may still legitimately resort to for the

purposes of conservation, including resource taxes, extraction and production quotas and volume restrictions on consumptions.

Such alternatives were explicitly indicated by WTO dispute settlement bodies as examples of domestic restrictions which ensure that the
burden of conservation is evenly distributed between foreign producers
and domestic producers or consumers, as required under the second
prong of Article XX(g) GATT, that is, the even-handedness requirement (Panel Reports, *China – Rare Earths*, paras. 7.521–7.550).
Importantly, the WTO adjudicatory bodies clarified that, for international trade restrictions to fulfil the even-handedness requirement,
factors to be weighted in include the existence of any coordination in
the level and timing of the announcements of domestic and international trade restrictions, correspondence in the product coverage of
such measures and the absence of a temporal disconnect between
domestic and international trade restrictions (Panel Reports, *China –
Rare Earths*, paras. 7.572–7.599).

3.5.2 PPMs in WTO Disputes

Questions pertaining to sustainable natural resources management have
also been addressed in a few WTO disputes concerning the conservation
of living natural resources: *US – Shrimp* and *US – Tuna II*. The former
targeted a US import ban on shrimps and shrimp products harvested
from countries where commercial fishing technologies might adversely
affect endangered sea turtles (Ahn 1997). The latter concerned a series of
US measures setting out the parameters for using the 'dolphin-safe' label
on tuna and tuna products (Howse et al. 2013, pp. 353–357). Ultimately,
both measures were aimed at the conservation of living natural resources
(namely, biological resources), albeit assessed under different WTO
agreements – i.e. the GATT and the TBT Agreement, respectively.

While the reports of the WTO adjudicatory bodies exhibit a high level
of technicality in discussing whether such measures are legitimate under
WTO law or not, both disputes bear relevance for the purposes of further
assessing the responsiveness of the WTO system to the emerging principle of sustainable use of natural resources. The complexity of the matter
before the dispute settlement bodies is also exemplified by the fact that
both disputes were subject to compliance proceedings and, in the case of
US – Tuna II, to the following recourse to Article 22.6 arbitration and
a second recourse to Article 21.5 proceedings, finalized only very recently
(the Appellate Body report was adopted on 14 December 2018, after ten

years since the first original dispute arose between Mexico (complainant) and the United States (respondent) (WTO 2018).

The importance of *US – Shrimp* in this perspective is many-fold. First, the Appellate Body interpreted the notion of 'exhaustible natural resources' under Article XX(g) GATT as encompassing both non-living (i.e. classically finite or non-renewable resources such as extractive resources) and living resources 'susceptible of depletion, exhaustion and extinction', thus expanding the scope for justification of otherwise GATT-inconsistent measures under the rubric of conservation (Appellate Body Report, *US – Shrimp*, paras. 128–132). Second, and importantly, the Appellate Body urged for such an evolutionary interpretation by means of explicitly recalling the preamble of the WTO Agreement and acknowledging the objective of sustainable development incorporated therein.[3] More specifically, it hinged upon the language of the preamble to interpret the notion of exhaustible natural resources in accordance with the latest pertinent sources (hard and soft) of international environmental law:

> From the perspective embodied in the preamble of the WTO Agreement, we note that the generic term "natural resources" in Article XX(g) is not "static" in its content or reference but is rather "by definition, evolutionary". It is, therefore, pertinent to note that modern international conventions and declarations make frequent references to natural resources as embracing both living and non-living resources. (Appellate Body Report, *US – Shrimp*, para. 130)

It was thus after perusing a number of such sources, including the 1982 United Nations Convention on the Law of the Sea, the 1992 Agenda 21 and the 1992 Convention on Biological Diversity that the Appellate Body concluded that

> Given the recent acknowledgement by the international community of the importance of concerted bilateral or multilateral action to protect living natural resources, and recalling the explicit recognition by WTO Members of the objective of sustainable development in the preamble of the WTO Agreement, we believe it is too late in the day to suppose that Article XX(g) of the GATT 1994 may be read as referring only to the conservation of exhaustible mineral or other non-living natural resources. Moreover, two adopted GATT 1947 panel reports previously found fish to be an "exhaustible natural resource" within the meaning of Article XX(g). We hold that, in line with the principle of effectiveness in treaty interpret-

---

[3] See Section 3.4.2.

ation, measures to conserve exhaustible natural resources, whether living
or non-living, may fall within Article XX(g). (Appellate Body Report, *US –
Shrimp*, para. 131)

Third, the Appellate Body cautiously approached the issue of extraterritoriality, thus indirectly touching upon the issue of how far can sovereign
states go in the pursuance of legitimate but unilateral conservation
policies. Here, the Appellate Body apparently refrained from inquiring
into the specific question of 'whether there is an implied jurisdictional
limitation in Article XX(g) and, if so, the nature or extent of that limitation', but declared it sufficient to note that 'there is a sufficient nexus
between the migratory and endangered marine populations involved and
the United States for the purposes of Article XX(g)' (*US – Shrimp*,
Appellate Body Report, para. 133; Howse et al. 2000, p. 249; Gehring
et al. 2017, pp. 362–363). As a matter of principle, however, it considered
it admissible for WTO members seeking a certain unilaterally determined level of conservation protection to adopt regulations having
extraterritorial effects within the purview of Article XX GATT:

> It appears to us, however, that conditioning access to a Member's domestic
> market on whether exporting Members comply with, or adopt, a policy or
> policies unilaterally prescribed by the importing Member may, to some
> degree, be a common aspect of measures falling within the scope of one or
> another of the exceptions (a) to (j) of Article XX. Paragraphs (a) to (j)
> comprise measures that are recognized as exceptions to substantive obliga-
> tions established in the GATT 1994, because the domestic policies
> embodied in such measures have been recognized as important and legit-
> imate in character. It is not necessary to assume that requiring from
> exporting countries compliance with, or adoption of, certain policies
> (although covered in principle by one or another of the exceptions) pre-
> scribed by the importing country, renders a measure a priori incapable of
> justification under Article XX. Such an interpretation renders most, if not
> all, of the specific exceptions of Article XX inutile, a result abhorrent to the
> principles of interpretation we are bound to apply. (para. 121)

Overall, the Appellate Body's approach to Article XX(g) broadened the
reach of the conservation exception and, arguably, the policy space
available to WTO members to resort to natural resources management
policies more generally. In casu, the US shrimp ban was considered to be
provisionally justified under Article XX(g) by the Appellate Body (*US –
Shrimp*, Appellate Body Report, para. 145).

Finally, a fundamentally similar approach to the issue of extraterritoriality inspired the Appellate Body's Article XX chapeau analysis. The issue

was first addressed in the original proceedings: here, the US shrimp ban was considered to fail the test because of its inflexibility (namely, the fact that it was formulated in a way that intentionally and effectively coerced foreign governments into adopting a 'regulatory programme that is not merely comparable, but rather essentially the same' [*US – Shrimp*, Appellate Body Report, para. 124] as the US programme to protect sea turtles while harvesting shrimp) and the lack of serious negotiations on the part of the United States prior to the imposition of the ban. In the compliance proceedings, the Appellate Body further elaborated on the matter and clarified that (1) the chapeau does not require on members to conclude a formal international agreement before imposing unilateral trade restrictions as long as serious and good faith negotiating efforts have been undertaken (*US – Shrimp (Article 21.5)*, Appellate Body Report, para. 124); (2) unilateral measures which condition market access on the adoption of a programme 'comparable in effectiveness' can pass the chapeau test (*US – Shrimp (Article 21.5)*, Appellate Body Report, paras. 141–144). Such developments on the issue of extraterritoriality allowed the Appellate Body to consider, for the first time in the history of WTO jurisprudence, the measure at issue in compliance with the requirements of the chapeau of Article XX. Importantly, the objective of sustainable development as enshrined in the preamble of the WTO Agreement was explicitly evoked by the Appellate Body as informing its interpretation of the chapeau requirements (Gehring et al. 2017, p. 365).

In *US – Tuna II*, the issue of conservation of living natural resources (in casu, dolphins) was addressed under the TBT agreement inasmuch as the US dolphin-safe labelling requirements at issue were found, albeit quite controversially, to constitute a technical regulation within the meaning of Annex 1.1 TBT, second sentence (Howse et al. 2013, pp. 353–357). In the original proceedings, the US measure was ultimately considered by the Appellate Body inconsistent with the non-discrimination obligation under Article 2.1 TBT for reasons pertaining to the preservation of the balance of competitive opportunities for imports of Mexican tuna products as compared to like US tuna products and tuna products of other countries (*Tuna II*, Appellate Body Report, para. 240). The Appellate Body reached this conclusion (and reverted the panel) on the basis of a relatively recent approach (see, in particular, the Appellate Body report in *US – Clove Cigarettes*) revolving around (1) whether a measure has a 'detrimental impact' on imported products of a member compared to the like products of the importing member or imported products of any other members and, in the affirmative, (2) whether such detrimental impact 'stems exclusively from a legitimate regulatory distinction rather than reflecting discrimination against the group of imported products' (*US – Tuna II*, Appellate Body Report, paras. 215 and 234–235).

Yet, a few points raised in *US – Tuna II* in the context of the Article 2.2 TBT analysis still contribute refining our understanding of the interplay between WTO rules and the principle of sustainable use of natural resources. The first point is that both the panel and the Appellate Body maintained an essentially open approach to the issue of extraterritoriality in the context of the TBT Agreement in accordance with the approach espoused in *US – Shrimp* with regards to GATT (*US – Tuna II*, Panel Report, para. 7.370). In particular, they accepted that WTO members can be legitimately concerned about the protection of dolphins *outside* of their own territory and acknowledged that a unilateral measure aimed at altering the environmental practices of another sovereign country (in casu, its tuna fishing techniques) may still be legitimate within the meaning of Article 2.2 TBT. Such an approach is not only consistent with *US – Shrimp* (para. 121) but also goes even further in two important respects: (1) the Appellate Body did not engage in discussing whether there was a 'sufficient nexus' between dolphins and the US – otherwise said, the very fact that the US measure might concern the protection of dolphins that never crossed the US territory did not make it per se violate Article 2.2 TBT. The bottom line here is that it remained a measure targeting the sale of tuna products on the US domestic market (Pauwelyn 2012); (2) admitting that classical extraterritorial legislation can be legitimate amounts to, in the words of Robert Howse, 'consigning the product/process distinction to irrelevance' (Howse et al. 2013, p. 358).

This leads to the second point, namely that *US – Tuna II* clarified the admissibility of non-product-related (npr) PPMs within the scope of the TBT Agreement, at least for what concerns labeling requirements covered under Annex 1.1, second sentence. Interestingly, however, this was done by explicitly eluding any actual debate on PPMs as such and simply focusing on the fact that US labelling requirements 'applied' to a *product*, namely tuna products' (*US – Tuna II*, Panel Report, para. 7.78). In other words, the panel considered it sufficient that the labelling provisions 'applied' to tuna as a 'product' irrespective of the fact that they regulated how the tuna was produced (i.e. caught) outside the US territory (as opposed to regulating something physically in the product) (Pauwelyn 2012). Were the essence of the *US – Tuna II* approach retained in future WTO disputes, what was aptly defined by Joost Pauwelyn as the 'end of the PPM distinction' may carry important consequences for the policy space left to members to adopt 'extraterritorial' natural resources protection regulations. This is particularly important in light of the progressive deterioration of global trade relations and the more general crisis of multilateralism which, at the present juncture, makes international cooperation increasingly difficult not only in trade but also in other areas, which are dependent on collective action. As the latest Insight Report of the World Economic Forum showcases, today's world is indeed characterized by 'countries moving into a new phase of strongly state-centred policies', making collective progress on global risks such as climate change and other environment-related risks of a global nature (e.g. biodiversity loss) more challenging (World Economic Forum 2019, pp. 14–15).

Accordingly, the contemporary political economy context is expected to increasingly prioritize unilateral/bilateral solutions over multilateral solutions. In the global trading system, countries have rapidly switched towards the conclusion of so-called preferential trade agreements (either bilateral, regional or, most recently, mega-regionals) as an 'antidote' to the stalemate of the Doha negotiations (Dür et al. 2015). In the environment arena, the use of trade policy instruments is on the rise but remains controversial precisely because of the jurisdictional 'stretch' such instruments imply when they are based on npr-PPMs (let's think, for instance, of the alarm caused by recent discussions on the introduction of border carbon adjustments).

Against this background, the issue becomes whether the most recent developments in WTO jurisprudence can accommodate for the use of trade policy instruments as a means to achieve not only natural resource conservation goals but also, more generally, other legitimate regulatory purposes recognized within the purview of relevant WTO disciplines. In this respect, it is worth noting that WTO dispute settlement bodies have not confined the admissibility of extraterritorial regulations to measures aimed at natural resources conservation only. On the contrary, the Appellate Body in *US – Shrimp* made a general statement on the jurisdictional boundaries within Article XX GATT, hence encompassing all the sub-paragraphs rather just Article XX(g) GATT (see Appellate Body report, para. 121). This includes, inter alia, Article XX(b) GATT, which arguably may cover, inter alia, climate change measures. Mutatis mutandis, the same holds true for matters governed under the TBT Agreement to the extent that Article 2.2 lists explicitly 'protection of human health or safety, animal or plant life or health, or the environment' among the objectives considered legitimate.

While *US – Tuna II* arguably points to an increasing receptivity for the usage of 'extraterritorial' measures, the responsiveness of the WTO dispute settlement bodies should, however, be assessed against the implications of the so-called 'detrimental impact' approach developed under the non-discrimination rules in latest TBT (and GATT) cases for npr-PPM measures. In this respect, it should be noted that the conclusion of the second compliance proceedings, albeit resolved in favour of the United States, was marked by a fierce critique of the Appellate Body's 'detrimental impact' approach to Article 2.1 of the TBT (and Article I:1 and Article III:4 GATT) by the US delegation:

> For the past ten years, the United States has been trying to establish that the dolphin safe labelling measure is not discriminatory but is a legitimate environmental measures concerned with the protection of dolphins and, as such, is consistent with the U.S. WTO obligations. . . . In the course of the dispute, the Appellate Body developed increasingly demanding legal standards under Article 2.1 of the TBT Agreement and Articles I:1 and III:4 of the GATT 1994. These legal standards were not based on the text of the relevant provisions, and the United States was forced to expend considerable resources over nearly a decade trying to defend successfully what was always an environmental measure with no element of protectionism. It is unclear how many other Members would have been able to invest such resources. . . . ' (United States 2019, pp. 3–4)

Such discussions are even more relevant if one considers that, just as Articles I:1, III:4 and XX of the GATT 1994, 'Articles 2.1 and 2.2 of the TBT Agreement are intended to strike a balance between trade liberalization and regulatory autonomy' (European Communities 2013, para. 124).

Finally, *US – Tuna II* importantly made clear that animal welfare is a legitimate objective under Article 2.2 TBT Agreement even when the conservation of an endangered species is not at stake:

> Similarly, the protection of dolphins may be understood as intended to protect animal life or health or the environment. In this respect a measure that aims at the protection of animal life or health need not, in our view, be directed exclusively to endangered or depleted species or populations, to be legitimate. Article 2.2 refers to "animal life or health" in general terms, and does not require that such protection be tied to a broad conservation objective. We therefore read these terms as allowing Members to pursue policies that aim at also protecting individual animals or species whose sustainability as a group is not threatened. (para. 7.437)

This significant development paved the way for a further broadening of the reach of Article XX(g) GATT after *US – Shrimp*. The GATT conservation exception was as a matter of fact evoked by the United States in the context of the compliance proceedings with the aim to seek justification for its amended tuna labelling provisions challenged by Mexico (*US – Tuna II (Article 21.5 – Mexico)*; WTO 2015). Here, it is worth noting that the panel (not reverted by the Appellate Body) agreed with both parties that dolphins are exhaustible resources within the meaning of Article XX(g) GATT (*US – Tuna II (Article 21.5 – Mexico)*, para. 7.521). What is more, the panel (also not reverted by the Appellate Body) found that the amended measure 'related to' conservation of dolphins:

> We believe that measures designed to reduce the harm done to dolphins in commercial fishing practices concern the protection of dolphins, and as such can properly be said to relate to the conservation of dolphins. Accordingly, to the extent that the goal of the amended tuna measure is to contribute to the protection of dolphins, even on an individual scale, that measure can be said to relate to the conservation of dolphins.

Ultimately, the revised US measure failed the Article XX chapeau test inasmuch as it relied on a system of different certification requirements that were not applied consistently in all circumstances of comparably high risk, thus amounting to arbitrary or unjustifiable discrimination (*US – Tuna II (Article 21.5 (Second Recourse by Mexico)*, Appellate Body Report, para. 7.605). Eventually, and following proceedings under Article 22.6 DSU, the US further revised its tuna regulations in 2016. The new US Tuna Measure was subsequently subject to new Article 21.5 proceedings and, at the Appellate Body stage, it was finally found consistent with both Article 2.1 of the TBT Agreement, as a measure whose 'detrimental impact stems exclusively from a legitimate regulatory distinction', as well as with Article XX(g) GATT and the requirements of the chapeau (WTO 2017). At the second compliance proceedings, however, the issue of extraterritoriality was not discussed, not even incidentally, inasmuch as the main point of contention revolved around Article 2.1 of the TBT Agreement. The Appellate Body, in particular, extensively relied on the calibration analysis developed under such Article to conclude that the 2016 Tuna Measure was in compliance with the chapeau of Article XX GATT (*US – Tuna II (Article 21.5 (Second Recourse by Mexico)*, Appellate Body Report, paras. 7.12–7.14).

3.6 Conclusions

This chapter focused on the latest developments in WTO jurisprudence
with a view to assessing whether sustainable natural resources management concerns have been accommodated in the multilateral trading
regime in line with the emerging principle of sustainable use of natural
resources as reflected in the SDGs' regulatory agenda. It found that, since
its inception, the WTO dealt with a number of disputes bearing direct
relevance to discussing the policy space left to members to pursue
sustainable natural resources management goals. These disputes have
mainly reverted around the notion of conservation under Article XX(g)
GATT and, to a limited extent, Article 2.2 TBT. Although such measures
were either found definitively inconsistent with WTO rules or at last
considered WTO-compatible after the conclusion of (at times multiple)
compliance proceedings, our analysis has shown that WTO adjudicatory
bodies have proved much inclined to engage in the debate over sustainability in the management and use of natural resources, both living and
non-living. This is already worth noting in and of itself inasmuch as the
conventional wisdom on WTO law is that, as it stands now, it does not
sufficiently accommodate for twenty-first-century sustainable development issues compared to other international trade law instruments
(WTO 2018b), namely the new generation of 'deep' preferential trade
agreements (PTAs) concluded by leading actors in the sustainable development narrative such as the EU. And yet, as it is convincingly argued by
a number of scholars, including one of the authors of this edited volume,
the sustainable development chapters included in the latest PTAs do to
a certain extent contribute to advance the legal framing on treatment of
sustainable development concerns (Adinolfi, Chapter 1 in this volume),
but remain relatively toothless to the extent that their provisions are
mainly hortatory in language and that they lack an effective enforcement
mechanism most of the times (this is the case, for instance, of EU PTAs);
furthermore, even when the provisions of such chapters are subject to
dispute settlement procedures, they have largely remained underused
because of excessive lengthiness and inefficiencies (Adinolfi, Chapter 1 in
this volume).

By contrast, and interestingly enough from a sustainable natural
resources management standpoint, WTO dispute settlement bodies
have consistently broadened the reach of the GATT conservation
exception by means of referring explicitly to the importance of the
objective of sustainable development, as enshrined in the preamble of

the WTO Agreement and thus informing all covered agreements; the principle of sovereignty over natural resources as a relevant rule of international law applicable in the relations between the members; and, a wide range of soft and hard law instruments of international environmental law. The main outcomes of such evolutionary interpretation seem in harmony with the principle of sustainable use of natural resources, namely that (1) the conservation exception incorporates the notion of exercising rights over natural resources in the interests of a member's economic and sustainable development so that members retain the right to design their conservation programmes based on 'their own assessment of various, sometimes competing, policy considerations and in a way that responds to their own concerns and priorities' (Panel Reports, *China – Rare Earths*, para. 7.459); (2) members can legitimately pursue conservation policies for the sake of protecting both non-living and living natural resources, even when the resources are not endangered or threatened by extinction; (3) natural resources conservation policies, as so broadly intended, can have extraterritorial effects irrespective of whether they are product- or non-product-related (as shown supra, mutatis mutandis, points (2) and (3) apply to Article 2.2 TBT too). On the other hand, when looking at the reasons why targeted measures were found incompatible with WTO rules, they have mainly concerned the failure to establish a rational connection with the conservation goal, either at the level of the relatedness requirement under Article XX(g) or at the level of the arbitrary/ unjustifiable discrimination requirement under the chapeau. In other words, WTO adjudicatory bodies were keen to make clear that the conservation exception can and must attend to issues of sustainable natural resources management, even when this entails restricting international trade, but can neither be transformed into an economic development exception nor can it be stretched into protecting measures that are not applied even-handedly.

As much geared towards trade preservation as this may sound prima facie, at a closer look the approach of the Appellate Body to Article XX GATT does essentially preserve the 'environmental' connotation of the conservation exception. This is important not only to the extent that, as noted earlier, WTO case law is practically the only body of jurisprudence explicitly touching upon sustainability issues in the international trade law regime due to the enforceability limits of trade and sustainable development chapters included in PTAs (Adinolfi, Chapter 1 in this volume). It also critically reveals no contradiction with a sound implementation of the principle of sustainable use of natural resources, inasmuch as it indeed revolves extensively around the environmental (i.e. conservation-related) dimension of sustainable natural resource management.

References

Ahn, D. (1997). 'Environmental Disputes in the GATT/WTO: Before and After US–Shrimp case'. *Michigan Journal of International Law* 20: 819–870.

Bacchus, J. (2018). *The Willing World: Shaping and Sharing a Sustainable Global Prosperity*. Cambridge University Press.

Bellmann, C. and Tipping, A. (2015). 'The Role of Trade and Trade Policy in Advancing the 2030 Development Agenda'. *International Development Policy* 6. Available at http://journals.openedition.org/poldev/2149.

Birnie, P., Boyle, A. and Redgwell C., eds. (2009). *International Law and the Environment*. Oxford University Press.

Centre for Climate and Energy Solutions. (2018). 'Outcomes of the UN Climate Change Conference in Katowice'. Available at www.c2es.org/site/assets/uploads/2018/12/cop-24-katowice-summary.pdf.

Cordonier Segger, M.-C., Gehring, M. and Newcombe, A., eds. (2010). *Sustainable Development in World Investment Law*. Kluwer Law International.

Cordonier Segger, M.-C. and Khalfan A. (2004). *Sustainable Development Law: Principles, Practices and Prospects*. Oxford University Press.

Cordonier Segger, M.-C. and Weeramantry C. G., eds. (2017). *Sustainable Development Principles in the Decisions of International Courts and Tribunals*. Routledge.

Crowley, M. A. and Howse, R. (2014). 'Tuna – Dolphin II: A Legal and Economic Analysis of the Appellate Body Report'. *World Trade Review* 13: 321–356.

Dupuy, P.-M. and Viñuales, J. E., eds. (2015). *International Environmental Law*. Cambridge University Press.

Dür, A. and Elsig, M., eds. (2015). *Trade Cooperation: The Purpose, Design and Effects of Preferential Trade Agreements*. Cambridge University Press.

Espa, I. (2015). *Export Restrictions on Critical Minerals and Metals: Testing the Adequacy of WTO Disciplines*. Cambridge University Press.

Espa, I. (2016). 'New Raw Materials Dispute Revives Trade Tensions Between China and the US/EU'. *International Economic Law and Policy Blog*. Available at http://worldtradelaw.typepad.com/ielpblog/2016/09/guest-post-new-raw-materials-dispute-revives-trade-tensions-between-china-and-the-useu.html.

Espa, I. (2017). 'Natural Resource Management and Sustainable Development in the WTO Legal System: Implications for the Investment Regime'. In

A. Shawkat, B. J. Hossain and J. Razzaque (eds.), *International Natural Resources Law, Investment and Sustainability*. Routledge, pp. 86–107.

Espa, I. and Marín Durán, G., eds. (2018). 'Renewable Energy Subsidies and WTO Law: Time to Rethink the Case for Reform Beyond Canada – Renewable Energy/FIT Program'. *Journal of International Economic Law* 21: 621–653.

European Communities. (2013). Measures Prohibiting the Importation and Marketing of Seal Products (DS400, DS401: European Union's Responses to the First Set of Questions from the Panel, Geneva, Switzerland, 13 March 2013). Available at http://trade.ec.europa.eu/doclib/docs/2013/july/tradoc_151660.pdf.

Gehring, M. and Cordonier Segger, M.-C., eds. (2005). *Sustainable Development in World Trade Law*. Kluwer Law International.

Gehring, M. and Genest, A. (2017). 'Disputes on Sustainable Development in the WTO Regime: 1992–2012'. In Marie-Claire Cordonier Segger and H. E. Judge C. G. Weeramantry (eds.), *Sustainable Development Principles*. Oxford University Press, pp. 357–383.

Hoekman, B. (2017). 'Trade and the Post-2015 Development Agenda'. In Helble Matthias and Shepherd, Ben (eds.), *Win-Win: How International Trade Can Help Meet the Sustainable Development Goals*. Asian Development Bank Institute, pp. 32–60.

Howse, R. and Levy, Ph. I. (2013). 'The TBT Panels: US – Cloves, US – Tuna and US – Cool'. *World Trade Review* 12: 327–376.

Howse, R. and Regan, D. (2000). 'The Product/Process Distinction – An Illusory Basis for Disciplining "Unilateralism" in Trade Policy'. *Journal of International Economic Law* 11: 249–290.

ILA (International Law Association). (2002). 'New Delhi Declaration of Principles of International Law Relating to Sustainable Development', 2 April 2002. Available at http://cisdl.org/tribunals/pdf/NewDelhiDeclaration.pdf.

ILA (International Law Association). (2012). 'Sofia Guiding Statements on the Judicial Elaboration of the 2002 New Delhi Declaration of Principles of International Law Relating to Sustainable Development'. ILA Resolution No. 7/2012.

ILA (International Law Association). (2018). 'Second Report of the Committee on the Role of International Law in Sustainable Natural Resource Management for Development (2016–2018)'. Final Draft, Sidney Conference. Available at www.ila-hq.org/images/ILA/DraftReports/DraftReport_SustainableNaturalResources.pdf.

Kein, D., Carazo, M. P., Doelle, M., Bulmer, J. and Higham, A., eds. (2017). *The Paris Agreement on Climate Change*. Oxford University Press.

Messerlin, P. (2017). 'From MDGs to SDGs: The Role of Trade'. In Helble Matthias and Shepherd, Ben (eds.), *Win-Win: How International Trade Can Help Meet the Sustainable Development Goals*. Asian Development Bank Institute, pp. 9–31.

OECD (Organisation for Economic Co-operation and Development). (2008). Glossary of Statistical Terms. Available at www.oecd-ilibrary.org/docserver/download/3008121e.pdf.

Paul, D. (2018). 'SDG12 Review at HLPF Calls for Circular Economies, Sustainable Lifestyles', 13 July 2018. Available at http://sdg.iisd.org/news/sdg-12-review-at-hlpf-calls-for-circular-economies-sustainable-lifestyles/.

Pauwelyn, J. (2012). 'Tuna: The End of the PPM Distinction? The Rise of International Standards?' Guest Post, International Economic Law and Policy Blog. Available at http://worldtradelaw.typepad.com/ielpblog/2012/05/tuna-the-end-of-the-ppm-distinction-the-rise-of-international-standards.html.

Pauwelyn, J. and Alschner, W. (2015). 'Forget About the WTO: The Network of Relations between Preferential Trade Agreements (PTAs) and Double PTAs'. In Andreas Dür and Elsig, Manfred (eds.), *Trade Cooperation: The Purpose, Design and Effects of Preferential Trade Agreements*. Cambridge University Press, pp. 497–532.

Schrijver, N. (2008). *The Evolution of Sustainable Development in International Law: Inception, Meaning and Status*. Brill Nijhoff.

Schrijver, Nico (2008). *Sovereignty Over Natural Resources: Balancing Rights and Duties*. Cambridge University Press.

Schrijver, N. and Weiss, F., eds. (2004). *International Law and Sustainable Development: Principles and Practice*. Martinus Nijhoff.

Sell, M. (2012). 'Cutting to the Core: Using Trade Tools for Sustainable Natural Resources Management'. *Biores* 6. Available at www.ictsd.org/bridges-news/biores/news/cutting-to-the-core-using-trade-tools-for-sustainable-natural-resources.

United Nations. (2002). Johannesburg Declaration on Sustainable Development. UN Doc. A/CONF.199/20, 4 September 2002.

United Nations. (2012). Report of the United Nations Conference on Sustainable Development, Rio de Janeiro, Brazil, 20–22 June 2012. UN Doc. A/CONF.216/16.

United Nations. (2013), UN Environment, 'The 10-Year Framework of Programmes on Sustainable Consumption and Production'. Available at https://sustainabledevelopment.un.org/content/documents/944brochure10yfp.pdf.

United Nations. (2015). Transforming Our World: The 2030 Agenda for Sustainable Development, 25 September 2015, UN Doc. A/RES/70/1.

United Nations. (2017). General Assembly (GA) Resolution, A/RES/71/313, Annex 'Global Indicator Framework for the Sustainable Development Goals and Targets of the 2030 Agenda for Sustainable Development', 10 July 2017. Available at http://ggim.un.org/documents/A_RES_71_313 .pdf, p. 17.

United States (2019). Meeting of the WTO Dispute Settlement Body, Geneva, Switzerland, 11 January 2019. Available at https://worldtradelaw.typepad.com /files/usa.pdf.

Van den Bossche, P. and W. Zdouc (2017). *The Law and Policy of the World Trade Organization*. Cambridge University Press.

WCED (World Commission on Environment and Development). (1987). *Our Common Future.* Oxford University Press.

WTO (World Trade Organization). (2010). *World Trade Report 2010: Trade in Natural Resources.*

WTO (World Trade Organization). (2017). Doc. WT/DS381/45, 6 December 2017.

WTO (World Trade Organization). (2018a). Docs. WT/DS381/AB/RW/USA, WT/DS381/AB/RW2, 14 December 2018.

WTO (World Trade Organization). (2018b). Doc. WT/CTE/25, Report (2018) of the Committee on Trade and Environment, 10 December 2018.

WTO (World Trade Organization). (2018c). 'Mainstreaming Trade to Attain the Sustainable Development Goals'. Available at www.wto.org/english/res_e/pub lications_e/sdg_e.htm.

World Economic Forum. (2019). *The Global Risks Report 2019,* 14th ed.

Yanovich, Alan (2011). 'WTO Rules and the Energy Sector'. In Yulia Selivanova (ed.), *Regulation of Energy in International Trade Law.* Kluwer Law International, pp. 1–47.

PART II

Top-Down: Public Approaches to Achieving the
Sustainable Development Goals

The Trade Effects of Environmental Provisions in Preferential Trade Agreements

AXEL BERGER, CLARA BRANDI, JEAN-FREDERIC MORIN,
AND JAKOB SCHWAB

4.1 Introduction

The international community has acknowledged that international trade can be an effective means of helping to achieve the 2030 Agenda for Sustainable Development and the 17 Sustainable Development Goals (SDGs) (UN 2015). The 2030 Agenda covers a broad range of indicators comprising three interrelated goals of sustainability. It aims to simultaneously improve economic, social and environmental conditions worldwide. Given the all-encompassing nature of the 2030 Agenda, contradictions and trade-offs between the different goals seem inevitable (Nilsson et al. 2016). This is exacerbated by the fact that implementing the 2030 Agenda depends on improving the coordination of different international policy regimes addressing issues relating to trade, climate, deforestation and biodiversity, to name just a few.

One of the potential core trade-offs that needs to be carefully managed is between trade liberalization and environmental protection. The relationship between trade and the environment is often described as one of divergence rather than synergy (Esty 1994). One key concern is that more international trade implies more production and consumption, which in turn means higher resource use and greater environmental pollution and degradation. A further concern is that environmental regulations may be used as a disguised form of protectionism. For instance, subsidizing technologies for generating renewable energy can protect domestic producers from competitive imports from abroad.

Traditionally, rules on trade and the environment were negotiated in different regimes. Now, we are witnessing increasing overlaps and interactions between the various regimes (e.g. Zelli et al. 2013; Johnson 2015). In this respect, one of the most striking developments is the integration of environmental provisions in preferential trade agreements (PTAs) that are negotiated on the bilateral or regional level (Lechner 2016; Milewicz et al. 2018; Morin et al. 2018).[1] While trade agreements traditionally set out to eliminate tariffs, they now tend to be more comprehensive and also include non-economic policy areas, such as the environment. Environmental provisions have become a regular feature of preferential trade agreements. Already roughly 85 percent of all PTAs that have been signed until 2016 include environmental provisions alongside trade-related issues (Morin et al. 2018).

In principle, environmental provisions in PTAs can affect both the environmental and the economic dimension of sustainability. The current literature focuses largely on the environmental effects of PTAs (Baghdadi et al. 2013; Bastiaens and Postnikov 2017; Brandi et al. 2019; Morin et al. 2019). Recent PTAs include prescriptions on numerous environmental issues that are directly linked to many SDGs, including provisions to encouraging trade of energy efficient goods and renewable energy (SDG 7), reduction of greenhouse gas emissions and the ratification of the Paris Climate Agreement (SDG 13), the prevention of maritime pollution (SDG 14) and the protection and sustainable management of forests (SDG 15). Therefore, it is reasonable to expect that environmental provisions in PTAs have the potential to promote several SDGs, as well as the environmental dimension of the 2030 Agenda for Sustainable Development more generally.[2]

In contrast, little is known about how environmental provisions in PTAs affect the economic dimension of sustainable development. Despite the ubiquity of environmental provisions in PTAs and their potential importance for sustainable development, how they affect economic variables such as trade flows is uncertain. Frequently, international trade is presented as being a key driver of economic development. Indeed, it is argued that many important synergies exist between trade and the SDGs. While trade liberalization always generates winners and losers and can increase inequalities, it does have positive effects on a broad range of economic variables (e.g. Baier and Bergstrand 2007; Baccini 2019). Manifold studies show that trade liberalization

---

[1] For an overview of the uptake of environmental provisions, see www.trendanalytics.info.
[2] For a legal analysis of the environmental provisions in European Union PTAs in relation to the 2030 Agenda on Sustainable Development, see Chapter 1 by Adinolfi in this volume.

enhances productivity, generates higher income, increases growth and helps alleviate poverty (Winters and Martuscelli 2014). Thus, PTAs can be an effective means to help developing countries achieve a number of SDGs, including those relating to poverty (SDG 1), growth (SDG 8) and industry (SDG 9).

How does the inclusion of environmental provisions in PTAs affect this overall positive contribution to the economic dimensions of the SDGs? Can the PTA signatories pursue economic and environmental goals simultaneously or do they face a trade-off, which amounts to protecting the environment at the expense of the economy? Little is known about how environmental provisions in PTAs affect trade flows and whether they restrict trade, thereby potentially undermining the economic aspects of sustainable development. To address these questions in this chapter, we investigate the impact of PTA environmental provisions on contracting parties' exports.

This question is particularly relevant to developing countries. Developing countries are often concerned that high-income countries misuse environmental provisions in PTAs, which is tantamount to green protectionism. Political leaders of poorer countries tend to reject demands for environmental provisions in PTAs, sometimes pointing to "green imperialism" and to lower environmental standards simply being part of developing countries' comparative advantage (Bernauer and Nguyen 2015). Subsequently, environmental provisions in PTAs may not only undermine the purpose of the agreements (which is to increase trade), but also the overall objective of the 2030 Agenda for Sustainable Development designed to promote the environment and the economy simultaneously. In this chapter, we seek to shed more light on the interplay between trade and the environment by empirically investigating the economic effects of environmental provisions in PTAs.

We use a novel data set that tracks environmental provisions across a broad range of PTAs. We estimate the effects of environmental provisions in PTAs using a gravity-type panel regression. We hypothesize that the number of environmental provisions in PTAs has a negative effect on trade flows, particularly for developing countries. In line with our expectations, we find that higher number of environmental provisions in PTAs is associated with less trade between the partner countries. This negative effect is particularly apparent in South–North trade flows as the inclusion of more environmental provisions restrict developing countries' export opportunities in terms of market access in developed countries.

This chapter contributes to the literature on the design features of PTAs and their economic impact. Furthermore, it sheds light on the interplay between trade and sustainable development. We provide new evidence on the effects of including environmental provisions in PTAs, which improves our understanding of the role of trade measures when it comes to achieving the 2030 Agenda for Sustainable Development.

The chapter is organized as follows. Section 4.2 shows that environmental provisions are now a standard feature of many PTAs and describes the main design features of these provisions. Section 4.3 reviews the literature and presents the hypotheses. Section 4.4 sets out our data and our empirical approach. Section 4.5 presents and discusses the empirical findings. Section 4.6 summarizes the results and discusses ways forward for both policymakers and researchers.

4.2   Environmental Provisions in PTAs

In the past two decades, scholars have studied the drivers and effects of a number of key innovations in PTA design (e.g. Horn et al. 2010; Büthe and Milner 2014; Dür et al. 2014; Kohl et al. 2016). Traditionally, PTAs focused primarily on eliminating at-the-border measures, such as tariffs and quotas. Since the 1990s, negotiating parties increasingly include behind-the-border measures in their PTAs. For example, these measures concern investment, services, intellectual property or regulatory cooperation. Recent PTAs cover a broad range of behind-the-border issues and are designed to have a deep impact on domestic policymaking (Dür et al. 2014).

Following this rise of behind-the-border measures in PTAs, environmental provisions have also become increasingly common in PTAs. Figure 4.1 shows that the average number of environmental provisions per PTA has skyrocketed in the 2000s. In 2016, each new PTA contained on average around 100 different environmental provisions (Morin et al. 2018). The prevalence of environmental provisions is particularly high in agreements negotiated by developed countries.

These environmental provisions are increasingly heterogeneous and far-reaching (Lechner 2016; Milewicz et al. 2018; Morin et al. 2018). Initially, they were limited to exceptions to trade commitments that can be used to protect human, animal or plant life or health or to conserve exhaustible natural resources. However, environmental provisions now tackle an increasingly broad range of environmental issues, such as hazardous waste, deforestation, the protection of fish stocks and

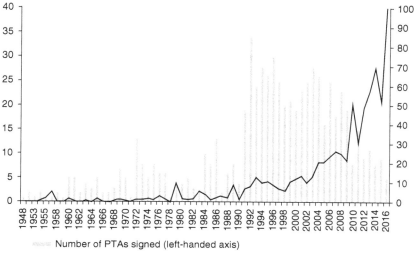

Figure 4.1   Average number of environmental provisions per PTA.
Source: Own compilation based on the Trade and Environment Database (TREND), Morin et al. (2018).

the mitigation of CO_2 emissions. Other environmental provisions in PTAs facilitate the harmonization of environmental policies, strengthen multilateral environmental agreements (MEAs) or require the transfer of green technologies to developing countries.

While the proliferation of deep PTAs is often explained by the spread of regional and global value chains, where companies' international activities combine trade with foreign investments and the transfer of technology abroad, the reasons for including environmental provisions in PTAs are more puzzling. Three main explanations can be identified. First, some argue that the "greening of PTAs" is a strategic move to win the support of societal groups, which would otherwise be opposed to economic liberalization (Hufbauer et al. 2000; Gallagher 2004). Empirical works supports this explanation and finds that a majority of citizens in different countries are in favour of the inclusion of environmental provisions in PTAs (Esty 2001; Bernauer and Nguyen 2015). More recent empirical work supports these findings for citizens in developed countries but finds that citizens in developing countries view the inclusion of environmental provisions in PTAs as a form of protectionism (Bastiaens and Postnikov 2019). Furthermore, democratic countries include on average more environmental provisions in their PTAs than autocratic countries (Morin et al. 2018).

A second explanation is that countries use PTAs to promote higher environmental standards globally (Johnson 2015; Jinnah and Lindsay 2016). In contrast to environmental treaties, trade agreements are often perceived to offer more effective enforcement mechanisms and are therefore better suited to promote environmental concerns.[3] Furthermore, PTAs covering a number of different issue areas from trade and investment liberalization, the protection of intellectual property rights to labor rights and environmental protection open the possibility of trade-offs across issue areas, they might therefore be seen as more effective instruments for environmental diplomacy than traditional multilateral negotiations focusing solely on environmental protection.

A third explanation is that the inclusion of environmental provisions in PTAs serves economic motivations (Bhagwati and Hudec 1996; Krugman 1997; Bechtel et al. 2012). Countries with higher environmental standards might want to level the playing field with foreign competitors by correcting global differences in regulatory environment (George 2014). From the perspective of countries with lower environmental standards, environmental provisions can be used to restrict their exports and are often regarded as a green cover for protectionist interests in high-income countries. A number of studies provide evidence of the link between protectionist interests and the inclusion of environmental provisions in PTAs (Runge 1990; Subramanian 1992; Ederington and Minier 2003; Lechner 2016). While the research is being conducted on the motivations for including environmental provision in PTAs, their actual effects remain unclear.

4.3   Literature and Hypotheses

Multiple economic studies assess the economic effects of PTAs. In theory, PTAs can lead to the creation and diversion of trade. However, existing empirical research commonly shows that PTAs tend to increase trade between their members (Baier and Bergstrand 2007, 2009; Egger et al. 2008, 2011; Magee 2008; Freund and Ornelas 2010; Fugazza and Nicita 2013). More recent research has focused on the differential trade effects that PTAs have across various sectors (Baccini et al. 2017; Spilker et al.

---

[3] Hafner-Burton et al. (2019) make a similar argument in the case of worker rights protection in the US General System of Preferences.

2018; Brandi et al. 2020). In light of new data on PTA design, recent studies have also investigated whether design determines the impact of PTAs. Existing research suggests that deep PTAs tend to generate more trade than more basic agreements (Baier et al. 2014; Dür et al. 2014; Mattoo et al. 2017).

Increased trade has uncertain implications for the environment because of scale, composition and technique effects (Grossman and Krueger 1993; Copeland and Tyler 2004). Therefore, it may not be possible to achieve environment-related SDGs that cover issues, such as water (SDG 6), climate (SDG 13), oceans (SDG 14) and land (SDG 15). First, the scale effect concerns the negative environmental consequences of increased output or greater economic activity as a result of the opening up of trade. Second, the composition effect indicates how trade opening leads to the reallocation of a country's productive resources towards the products for which it has a comparative advantage. It is difficult a priori to determine whether the composition effect will increase or decrease the negative environmental impact, since the overall impact depends on the specific sectors in which a given country enjoys a comparative advantage. Third, the technique effect of trade liberalization can improve environmental protection because trade opening reduces the cost of environmentally friendly goods, services and technologies, making them more accessible. In addition, the increased income generated by trade can lead society to demand better environmental quality.[4] The effects of scale and technique tend to work in opposite directions, while the composition effect depends on the countries' comparative advantage. Therefore, it is difficult to predict how trade will affect the environment overall.

Just a handful of studies look at the consequences of PTAs' environmental provisions. Most of them focus on their environmental impact. Baghdadi et al. (2013) distinguish PTAs with and without environmental provisions and find that the former lead to lower levels of absolute CO_2 emissions and find a convergence of emissions among the partner countries. Two papers, by Martínez-Zarzoso and Oueslati (2016) and Zhou et al. (2017), find similar results for air quality measures. In a more recent paper Brandi et al. (2019) focus on the direct link of PTAs with environmental provisions on domestic environmental legislation. They find a positive relationship between the number of environmental provisions

---

[4] On the link between individual-level environmental concerns associated with foreign direct investment and a country's level of economic development, see Kim and Lee's chapter in this volume.

included in PTAs and the adoption of domestic environmental laws, in particular in developing countries. Furthermore, the authors analyse the effects of particular issue-specific environmental provisions and find strong effects in the case of water (SDG 6), air (SDG 11) and soil (SDG 15). Fewer studies investigate environmental provisions' economic consequences. One rare exception is an article by Lisa Lechner (2018) that examines how PTAs environmental provisions affect the behavior of US investors. In her study, Lechner finds that environmental provisions in PTAs reduces foreign direct investment (FDI) in polluting industries while they have a promoting effect in environmentally clean industries. Yet, little is known about how environmental provisions in PTAs affect trade flows across a large number of countries.

This chapter argues that environmental provisions in PTAs can restrict trade flows in two different ways. First, countries with high environmental standards can use environmental provisions to "level the playing field" with countries that have lax environmental regulations (e.g. Bhagwati 1995). A number of environmental provisions are "offensive" in nature and demand partner countries, for example, to protect the ozone layer, enforce domestic environmental legislation, and ratify international environmental agreements. Such "offensive" environmental provisions can be used to reduce the competitive advantage of countries with formerly lower environmental standards (Blümer et al. 2019).

Second, the "defensive" nature of some environmental provisions may reduce trade flows directly. One important example is that of environmental exceptions, which allow countries to restrict trade to protect biodiversity or conserve natural resources (Blümer et al. 2019). These exceptions were included in the 1947 General Agreement on Tariffs and Trade (GATT) and were later incorporated into hundreds of PTAs. In addition to general exceptions, PTAs now include more and more issue-specific exceptions that concern investment, services and public procurement, among others. As PTAs become deeper, businesses and environmental groups are calling for more exceptions to help cushion the impact of economic liberalization.

In light of these arguments, we expect environmental provisions to reduce the additional trade induced by the PTA.

Hypothesis 1: The higher the number of environmental provisions in PTAs, the greater the negative effect on trade flows between the partner countries.

Furthermore, the effects of environmental provisions in PTAs may vary across different country groups. Developing countries are often concerned that high-income countries use environmental provisions in PTAs to restrict market access and level the playing field in foreign countries. Therefore, we expect that environmental provisions will specifically impede market access for developing countries.

Hypothesis 2: The higher the number of environmental provisions in PTAs, the greater the negative effect on exports from developing to high-income countries.

4.4   Data and Empirical Approach

To test the aforementioned hypotheses, we construct a panel on bilateral trade flows and combine it with data on the environmental provisions in PTAs ratified between the trading partners.

We use bilateral country-pair goods exports, drawn from the UN Comtrade database, as our main, as our main dependent variable. The data cover the period 1984 to 2016 and provide the total volume of exports in manufacturing, mining and agricultural products from one country to another (in current thousand US$ for the available years). As common in the literature, we use the natural log of total exports as dependent variable (*EXPORTS*). The resulting panel is unbalanced, with a total of roughly 780,000 trade flow observations, involving approximately 50,000 exporter–importer pairs. Therefore, on average, there are fifteen trade flow observations for each country pair in a given direction.

For our independent variables, namely different environmental provisions in PTAs, we use information from the Trade and Environment Database (TREND) to capture the contractual arrangement for each exporter-importer dyad. TREND, introduced by Morin et al. (2018), is the most comprehensive and fine-grained dataset of environmental provisions in PTAs. It identifies 286 environmental provisions in 598 PTAs that have entered into force. This list of PTAs is based on the Design of Trade Agreements (DESTA) dataset, which is by far the most comprehensive collection of PTAs (Dür et al. 2014). Thus, the data also cover PTAs that do not include any environmental provisions. On average, all PTAs ever signed until 2016 include 14.5 environmental provisions. However, this number varies widely, with a maximum of 120 provisions (the 2014 agreement between the European Union and Moldova) and a median number of 5 provisions. In general, more recent PTAs have more environmental provisions. Given that WTO agreements concern almost every country in the trade flow sample, we do not include them in our analysis. We consider that external EC/EU treaties involve all members and the respective partner country.

Our main explanatory variable is the maximum number of environmental provisions in a PTA between a pair of countries (*ENVPROVS*). Thus, we assume that if the same provision is included in more than one PTA between two countries, it does not add any content to the contractual relationship.

In order to analyze separately the effect of the content from the plain existence of PTAs in place, in our estimation, we control for whether a PTA is in force between the trading partners. We thus construct a binary variable, whether between any exporter-importer dyad, one or more PTA(s) was (were) in place in a given year (*PTA*). Often, more than one PTA has been signed between two countries. However, the value attributed for the *PTA* is still 1 for this country pair in a given year.

To control for the varying depth of PTAs commitments related to trade liberalization, we use the DESTA depth index in our empirical analysis (Dür et al. 2014).[5] The index in the sample ranges from -1.4 to 2.3, which we normalize to range from zero to 3.7. Again, we use the maximum depth of *any* PTA between a country pair to measure the depth of PTAs between a country pair (*DEPTH*). We include this as a control variable, since deeper agreements are also likely to have more environmental provisions (the correlation coefficient between the two variables in all PTAs is 0.68), and we specifically want to examine the effect of environmental provisions.

We use the World Bank classification of (non-) high-income countries as of 2000 to classify exporters and importers as developed or developing countries. The use of the classification in the year 2000 is not decisive for the results, but using only one classification facilitates the interpretation of our findings by keeping the country group samples constant over time. The year 2000 is the available classification closest to the middle of the time span covered by the sample and thus a good proxy for how a country was classified over the majority of years analyzed.

The aim of the identification strategy is to compare the change in exports between two countries that enter into a PTA with more environmental provisions to the change in exports between two countries that enter into a PTA with fewer environmental provisions. Given this strategy, those countries that never enter into any PTA throughout the period

---

[5] The DESTA Depth index does not include information about environmental provisions in PTAs.

covered by our sample do not contribute to identification. We therefore simply drop them from the sample. This choice does not significantly affect our results. Thus, our sample includes only country pairs that signed a PTA at some point during the period studied. This corresponds to roughly 36 percent of all trade flow partners. To be able to relate the effect of including environmental provisions in PTAs to the situation of no PTA whatsoever, we include the exports between trading partners in our sample also for the time period before they signed the PTA. Furthermore, we only include countries as exporters or importers for which data are available on the country group classification in order to keep the different samples of the estimations depending on the country group classification comparable to that of the estimation on the entire sample. This reduces the overall sample of trade flow observations to 250,014.

Table 4.3 in the Appendix to this chapter lists all the countries included in the sample as either exporters or importers and their classification (high-income and developing countries). The summary statistics of all variables on the PTA level are listed in Table 4.4 in the Appendix. Note that 13 percent of the PTAs in the sample are between high-income countries only, 32 percent between high income and non-high-income countries and 54 percent between non-high-income countries only. Table 4.5 lists the summary statistics for all variables at the country-pair level. Of all dyadic trade flows taken as observations, 76 percent are under a PTA (only 24 percent before signing any PTA). On average, each dyadic trade flow is under 1.6 PTAs.

Our main interest is how environmental provisions affect trade flows between partner countries. We exploit the data's panel structure using country-pair fixed effects in order to control for unobserved heterogeneity and the time-invariant characteristics of a trading relationship, such as distance and common border fixed effects. By using country-pair fixed effects, we can also partially control for selection effects into signing PTAs and the inclusion of environmental provisions. This strategy allows us to capture time-invariant selection effects on a country-pair level, such as distance or the average level of trade. It cannot control for bilateral trends in or expectation of future trade levels, which could also drive selection into signing a PTA or including environmental provisions. We furthermore include exporter- and importer-year fixed effects in order to capture multilateral resistance and country-specific time-variant developments. Although this generally gives a slight downward bias to our results, it allows us to control for all time-variant country-specific variables, such as gross domestic product (GDP), or a general opening up to

international trade by individual countries. Thus, our baseline regression
equation is as follows:

$$EXPORTS_{eit} = \beta * ENVPROVS_{eit} + \gamma * PTA_{eit} + \delta * DEPTH_{eit} + \alpha_{ei}$$
$$+ \alpha_{et} + \alpha_{it} + \varepsilon_{eit} \qquad (4.1)$$

where e is the index for the exporter, i for the importer and t for the
respective year. α_{ei}, α_{et} and α_{it} are the country-pair and exporter- and
importer-year fixed effects, respectively, and ε_{eit} is an error term. Since
EXPORTS is measured in logs, the estimated results for the coefficients
give the percentage change in exports per change in the independent
variables (i.e. particularly for one additional environmental provision in
a PTA). To account for common shocks on the country-pair level, we
cluster standard errors on that level.

In 4,239 cases of an exporter–importer relationship, the number of
environmental provisions in force between two countries increased when
they were already in an existing PTA. In almost all cases this occurred
when a new PTA (usually involving third countries) entered into force.
To ascertain that the changes in exports are driven by the number of
environmental provisions in place rather than by the additional PTA, we
add the number (#) of PTAs in force at a given time between the trading
partners as a control variable. Further robustness tests include the non-
linear estimation via panel pseudo-maximum likelihood (PPML), and
excluding all major oil exporting countries from the sample. We refer to
the results of these while discussing the results of the main estimation.

4.5   Findings

First, we estimate Equation (4.1) for the entire panel. The results are
shown in column 1, Table 4.1. In line with Hypothesis 1, we find that
environmental provisions in PTAs, in general, decrease trade between
partner countries.[6] When an additional environmental provision is

---

[6] However, this finding is not very robust. In some other specifications, the statistical
significance of the coefficient vanishes, such as when including all trade flow observations
including between countries that never signed a PTA, or when adding up sectoral trade
flows to compute aggregate trade flows, which implies a loss of observations. The point
estimates are similar to the ones reported here in all these estimations, however. The
finding of a negative overall effect is also statistically robust to replacing the fixed effects by
constant bi- and time-variant unilateral variables, which is often pursued in the literature
when no panel data is available (see Baier and Bergstrand 2007). The results on the country
groupings reported in the text that follows are not affected in any of these cases.

Table 4.1 *Effect of Environmental Provisions in PTAs on Trade*

	(1)	(2)
	EXPORTS	EXPORTS
ENVPROVS	−0.002***	−0.003***
	(0.001)	(0.001)
PTA	0.127***	0.162***
	(0.034)	(0.034)
# of PTAs		0.126***
		(0.015)
DEPTH	0.016	−0.026
	(0.019)	(0.019)
Country-pair FE	Yes	Yes
Exporter- and importer-year FE	Yes	Yes
Observations	250,014	250,014
Share of flows under PTA	0.76	0.76
Average no. of PTAs if trade flow under any PTA	2.14	2.14
Average no. of ENVPROVS per trade flow under PTA	27.36	27.36
R^2	0.890	0.890

This table shows the results from running a panel regression of the log of bilateral exports (*EXPORTS*) between 1984 and 2016 on whether a PTA was signed and the environmental provisions (*ENVPROVS*) included in the PTA. Robust standard errors clustered at the exporter-importer level are reported in parentheses. ***$p < 0.01$; **$p < 0.05$; *$p < 0.1$.

included in a PTA, it decreases trade between two countries by an average of 0.2 percent, compared to countries with a PTA of equivalent depth and initial export volumes. This result is economically significant, given that on average, trade flows under a PTAs are subject to 27.36 environmental provisions.[7] Therefore, trade between countries that are party to a PTA with an average number of environmental provisions is 5 percent less on

---

[7] The number differs from the average number of environmental provisions in PTAs on the PTA level, as a PTA with a given number of provisions can affect several trade flow observations. The fact that the average number of environmental provisions per trade flow is higher than the PTA average shows that those PTAs with more environmental provisions on average affect more bilateral trade relationships.

average in the years following the PTA's entry into force than between countries that sign a PTA with no environmental norms.

For our control variables, our results show that when a PTA is in place, it increases trade between two countries by about 13 percent, which is roughly in line with previous studies (see e.g. Baier and Bergstrand 2007). Our findings reveal that the depth of a PTA has no significant effect on overall trade flows, which runs counter to previous findings (for example, see Dür et al. 2014).[8] We also control for the fact that when countries have signed various PTAs, there are usually more environmental provisions in place between them by including the absolute number of PTAs in place between them (see results in column 2). While the number of PTAs, given their maximum depth, does matter, the result on the effect of ENVPROVS remains constant or even increases. For a given number of PTAs, the more environmental provisions they include, the less (of an increase in) trade there is between countries.

Next, we analyze the effects of environmental provisions separately for whether the exporter and the importer are developed or developing economies. Table 4.2 shows the results of estimating Equation (4.1) for the samples of trade flows between the different country categories: from developed to developed economies (column 1), from developing to developed economies (column 2), from developed to developing countries (column 3) and from developing to developing economies (column 4), respectively.

In line with Hypothesis 2, our findings show that the negative effect of environmental provisions on aggregate trade flows occurs only for trade relationships involving exports from a developing country to a developed economy (column 2). There does not seem to be any significant effect on trade between developed economies (column 1), exports from developed to developing economies (column 3) or exports between developing economies (column 4). We see that trade flows in the framework of a PTA between countries with different levels of development are on average subject to more environmental provisions than those between countries with a similar level of development. However, this has a significant negative effect only on developing countries' exports to developed countries. For the subsamples, we repeat the estimation, while controlling for the absolute number of PTAs in place between the countries. The result is shown in Table 4.6 in the Appendix. The variation

---

[8] However, this result is not driven by the correlation with environmental provisions, but can be explained by the extension of our sample to 2016, compared to previous studies using samples up to 2009. Thus, it appears that the positive effect of depth is worn away in recent years. We cannot identify this type of change over time for the effect of environmental provisions.

Table 4.2 *Effect of Environmental Provisions in PTAs in Relation to the Level of Development of Trading Partners*

	(1)	(2)	(3)	(4)
	North–North	South–North	North–South	South–South
	EXPORTS	EXPORTS	EXPORTS	EXPORTS
ENVPROVS	−0.003	−0.005**	−0.003	−0.001
	(0.003)	(0.002)	(0.002)	(0.001)
PTA	−0.086	0.437***	0.198**	−0.080*
	(0.105)	(0.102)	(0.077)	(0.048)
DEPTH	0.119**	−0.090	0.007	0.054*
	(0.060)	(0.057)	(0.040)	(0.032)
Share of flows under PTA	0.790	0.696	0.709	0.808
Average no. of ENVPROVS per trade flow under PTA	26.6	44.2	45.59	13.67
Country-pair FE	Yes	Yes	Yes	Yes
Exporter- and importer-year FE	Yes	Yes	Yes	Yes
Observations	20,071	53,690	55,576	120,315
R^2	0.965	0.896	0.927	0.848

This table shows the results from running a panel regression of the log of bilateral exports (*EXPORTS*) between 1984 and 2016 on whether a PTA was signed and the environmental provisions (*ENVPROVS*) included in the PTA. The four columns report the results for the split sample by level of development of the exporter and importer, according to the World Bank definition of High Income (North) and non-High Income (South) countries. Robust standard errors clustered at the exporter–importer level are reported in parentheses. ***$p < 0.01$; **$p < 0.05$; *$p < 0.1$.

in the numbers of PTAs in force does not appear to drive the results, although the number of environmental provisions increases as the number of PTAs increases.

Our findings are in line with the literature, which suggests that the concern expressed by developing countries about the effect of environmental provisions may be justified. For example, some "offensive" provisions require developing countries to implement international environmental agreements and enforce domestic environmental laws because, typically, they have less stringent environmental regulations. This reduces developing countries' comparative advantage, which partially stems from the exploitation of regulatory differences. Developing countries' exports to developed countries may decline as a direct consequence. In this context, developed countries may use environmental provisions as an instrument to achieve their "offensive" trade and environmental interests.

An alternative explanation for the negative trade effect of environmental provisions relates to countries' "defensive" interests. Trade agreements are getting deeper and more comprehensive as a result of, inter alia, the inclusion of provisions designed to facilitate trade flows, services and FDI, as well as to protect intellectual property rights and open up public procurement markets. Including deep provisions requires domestic policy reforms that may weaken domestic environmental regulations. Including environmental exceptions in PTAs may be interpreted as a cushioning system to mitigate the unintended regulatory effects of deep PTAs.

We also apply a pseudo maximum likelihood (PPML) estimation to the data (Santos Silva and Tenreyro 2010).[9] The dependent variable is the sum of exports (non-logarithmized). The results are presented in Table 4.7 in the Appendix. They suggest that the effects of environmental provisions are not statistically significant across the entire sample (column 1) or for exports between any of the different country groups (columns 2–5). Still, the sign is again only negative for exports from developing to developed countries.[10]

Furthermore, it is likely that for countries that export many particularly environmentally harmful goods, such as oil and petroleum products, the effects of environmental provisions in trade agreements on trade

[9] PPML estimations are often used as robustness tests in the literature on the trade effects of PTAs, and sometimes even as main gravity model specification. However, not only do they constitute a black box, but also their efficiency, particularly in fixed effects models, has come under some discussions recently; see Pfaffermayr (2019). So far, PPML estimations appear to be slightly more efficient for indicator explanatory variables, such as the effect of an existing PTA. Further research is required to examine this discrepancy.

[10] We use the log-linear estimation in this chapter to facilitate interpretation and because the results of the log-linear approach on the PTA variable is in line with previous findings. The handling of zeros is one advantage of the PPML estimation, but our trade flow data does not contain any zeros. Therefore, we treat missing trade values as zeros for the PPML estimation in Table 4.7 in order to exploit the strength of PPML estimation. At the same time, not including them does not change the results of the PPML estimation substantially.

flows are somewhat different, as might be their motivation to include these provisions in a PTA in the first place. To exclude that this is what drives our results, we also estimate the general equation excluding all trade flows that involve the main oil exporting countries. Table 4.8 in the Appendix reports the results. Column 1 shows the results on the whole sample when all major oil exporting countries are excluded from the sample, column 2 the results excluding only Organization of the Petroleum Exporting Countries (OPEC) member countries. The main result that the inclusion of environmental provisions reduces the trade creation effect of PTAs also holds in the sample without oil exporters. Columns 3–6 report the breakdown by country income group of exporter and importer for the sample excluding the top oil exporters. We see that also in this sample, it is particularly export flows from developing to developed countries that are affected by the inclusion of environmental provisions. However, although on average subject to much fewer environmental provisions, trade flows *between* developing countries are also negatively affected by the inclusion of environmental provisions in this reduced sample without major oil exporting countries (column 6).

4.6   Conclusion

Our main finding shows that including environmental provisions in PTAs has a restrictive effect on trade flows, albeit only slightly. We hypothesize that trade flows between two countries will be negatively affected and that this effect is stronger, the higher the number of environmental provisions included in a PTA signed by the two parties. We furthermore hypothesized that the trade-restricting effect of environmental provisions will affect developing countries more strongly than other countries. Our findings confirm both hypotheses. To be clear, PTAs in general do increase trade flows. However, the inclusion of environmental provisions in PTAs moderates this trade-increasing effect. In line with our expectations, we find empirical evidence to justify the fear expressed by developing countries, namely, that environmental provisions in PTAs have a trade restrictive effect on their economies. When PTAs include environmental provisions, there is a negative effect on developing country exports in terms of trade flows to developed countries. This suggests that there is a trade-off between the economic and environmental aims of the SDGs. Environmental provisions in PTAs can help promote environmental sustainability (e.g. SDG 13 and 15) and trade is a key engine for economic development (e.g. SDG 8). Our results suggest that developing country governments that want to sign comprehensive PTAs with developed countries are faced with this trade-off.

However, some types of environmental provisions are more likely to promote trade flows than others. Some actually facilitate trade by calling for the liberalization of trade in environmental goods and the reduction of environmentally harmful subsidies. Unfortunately, PTAs rarely include environmental provisions of this type. Therefore, trade negotiators keen to achieve the SDGs should focus specifically on environmental provisions that do not generate trade-offs between the environmental and economic goals of the 2030 Agenda for Sustainable Development. Alternatively, trade negotiators could consider offering additional trade concessions to developing countries to offset the negative effects of some environmental provisions. Further research is needed to improve our understanding of the trade effects of different types of environmental provisions.

References

Baccini, L. (2019). "The Economics and Politics of Preferential Trade Agreements." *Annual Review of Political Science* 22: 75–92.

Baccini, L., Pinto, P. and Weymouth, S. (2017). "The Distributional Consequences of Preferential Trade Liberalization: A Firm-Level Analysis." *International Organization* 71: 373–395.

Baghdadi, L., Martinez-Zarzoso, I. and Zitouna, H. (2013). "Are RTA Agreements with Environmental Provisions Reducing Emissions?" *Journal of International Economics* 90: 378–390.

Baier, S. L. and Bergstrand, J. H. (2007). "Do Free Trade Agreements Actually Increase Members" International Trade?" *Journal of International Economics* 71: 72–95.

Baier, S. L. and Bergstrand, J. H. (2009). "Estimating the Effects of Free Trade Agreements on International Trade Flows Using Matching Econometrics." *Journal of International Economics* 77: 63–76.

Baier, S. L., Bergstrand, J. H. and Feng, M. (2014). "Economic Integration Agreements and the Margins of International Trade." *Journal of International Economics* 93: 339–350.

Bastiaens, I. and Postnikov, E. (2017). "Greening Up: The Effects of Environmental Standards in EU and US Trade Agreements." *Environmental Politics* 26: 1–23.

Bastiaens, I. and Postnikov, E. (2019). "Social Standards in Trade Agreements and Free Trade Preferences: An Empirical Investigation", *Review of International Organizations*. Available at https://doi.org/10.1007/s11558-019-09356-y.

Bättig, M. and Bernauer, T. (2009). "National Institutions and Global Public Goods: Are Democracies More Cooperative in Climate Change Policy?" *International Organization* 63: 281–308.

Bechtel, M. M., Bernauer, T. and Meyer, R. (2012). "The Green Side of Protectionism: Environmental Concerns and Three Facets of Trade." *Review of International Political Economy* 19: 837–866.

Bernauer, T. and Nguyen, O. (2015). "Free Trade and/or Environmental Protection?" *Global Environmental Politics* 15: 105–129.

Bhagwati, J. N. (1995). "Trade Liberalisation and Fair Trade Demands: Addressing the Environmental and Labour Standards Issues." *The World Economy* 18: 745–759.

Bhagwati, J. N. and Hudec, R. E., eds. (1996). *Fair Trade and Harmonization: Prerequisites for Free Trade?" Economic Analysis.* MIT Press.

Blümer, D., Morin, J.-F., Brandi, C. and Berger, A. (2019). "Environmental Provisions in Trade Agreements: Defending Regulatory Space or Pursuing Offensive Interests?" *Environmental Politics* 29: 866–889.

Brandi, C., Blümer, D. and Morin, J.-F. (2019). "When Do International Treaties Matter for Domestic Environmental Legislation?" *Global Environmental Politics* 19: 14–44.

Brandi, C., Schwab, J., Morin, J.-F. and Berger, A. (2020). "Do Environmental Provisions in Trade Agreements Make Exports from Developing Countries Greener?" *World Development* 129: May, 104899. Available at https://doi.org /10.1016/j.worlddev.2020.104899.

Business Europe (2014). Trade-Roadmap for the European Commission. Available at www.businesseurope.eu/sites/buseur/files/media/imported/2014–01000-E.pdf.

Büthe, T. and Milner, H. (2014). "Foreign Direct Investment and Institutional Diversity in Trade Agreements: Credibility, Commitment, and Economic Flows in the Developing World, 1971–2007." *World Politics* 66: 88–122.

Copeland, B. R. and Taylor, M. S. (2004). "Trade, Growth and the Environment." *Journal of Economic Literature* 46: 7–71.

Dür, A., Baccini, L. and Elsig, M. (2014). "The Design of International Trade Agreements: Introducing a New Dataset." *Review of International Organizations* 9: 353–375.

Ederington, J. and Minier, J. (2003). "Is Environmental Policy a Secondary Trade Barrier? An Empirical Analysis." *Canadian Journal of Economics* 36: 137–154.

Egger, H., Egger, P. and Greenaway, D. (2008). "The Trade Structure Effects of Endogenous Regional Trade Agreements." *Journal of International Economics* 74: 278–298.

Egger, P., Larch, M., Staub, K. E. and Winkelmann, R. (2011). "The Trade Effects of Endogenous Preferential Trade Agreements." *American Economic Journal: Economic Policy* 3: 113–143.

Esty, D. C. (1994). *Greening the GATT: Trade, Environment, and the Future.* Columbia University Press.

Esty, D. C. (2001). "Bridging the Trade-Environment Divide." *The Journal of Economic Perspectives* 15: 113–130.

Freund, C., and Ornelas, E. (2010). "Regional Trade Agreements." *Annual Review of Economics* 2: 139–166.

Fugazza, M. and Nicita, A. (2013). "The Direct and Relative Effects of Preferential Market Access." *Journal of International Economics* 89: 357–368.

Gallagher, K. (2004). *Free Trade and the Environment: Mexico, NAFTA, and Beyond.* Stanford University Press.

George, C. (2014). Environment and Regional Trade Agreements: Emerging Trends and Policy Drivers. OECD Trade and Environment Working Papers. Paris: OECD.

Grossman, G. M. and Krueger, A. B. (1993). "Environment Impacts of a North American Free Trade Agreement." In P. M. Garber (ed.), *The Mexican-US Free Trade Agreement.* MIT Press, pp. 1–10.

Hafner-Burton, E. M., Mosley, L. and Galantucci, R. (2019). "Protecting Workers Abroad and Industries at Home: Rights-Based Conditionality in Trade Preference Programs." *Journal of Conflict Resolution* 63: 1253–1282.

Horn, H., Mavroidis, P. C., and Sapir, A. (2010). "Beyond the WTO? An Anatomy of EU and US Preferential Trade Agreements." *World Economy* 33: 1565–1588.

Hufbauer, G. C., Esty, D. C., Orejas, D., Rubio, L. and Schott, J. J. (2000). *NAFTA and the Environment: Seven Years Later.* Peterson Institute for International Economics.

Jinnah, S. and Lindsay, A. (2016). "Diffusion through Issue Linkage: Environmental Norms in US Trade Agreements." *Global Environmental Politic* 16: 41–61.

Johnson, T. (2015). "Information Revelation and Structural Supremacy: The World Trade Organization's Incorporation of Environmental Policy." *The Review of International Organizations* 10: 207–229.

Kohl, T., Brakman, S. and Garretsen, H. (2016). "Do Trade Agreements Stimulate International Trade Differently? Evidence from 296 Trade Agreements." *World Economy* 39: 97–131.

Krugman, P. (1997). "What Should Trade Negotiators Negotiate About?" *Journal of Economic Literature* 35: 113–120.

Lechner, L. (2016). "The Domestic Battle over the Design of Non-trade Issues in Preferential Trade Agreements." *Review of International Political Economy* 23: 840–871.

Lechner, L. (2018). "Good for Some, Bad for Others: US Investors and Non-trade Issues in Preferential Trade Agreements." *The Review of International Organizations* 13: 163–187.

Magee, C. S. (2008). "New Measures of Trade Creation and Trade Diversion." *Journal of International Economics* 75: 349–362.

Martínez-Zarzoso, I. and Oueslati, W. (2016). "Are Deep and Comprehensive Regional Trade Agreements Helping to Reduce Air Pollution?" CEGE Discussion Papers.

Mattoo, A., Mulabdic, A. and Ruta, M. (2017). "Trade Creation and Trade Diversion in Deep Agreements. World Bank Policy Research Working Paper No. 8206.

Mayer, T. and Zignago, S. (2011). "Notes on CEPII's Distances Measures: The GeoDist database." CEPII Working Paper 2011–25.

Milewicz, K., Hollway, J., Peacock, C. and Snidal, D. (2018). "Beyond Trade: The Expanding Scope of the Nontrade Agenda in Trade Agreements." *Journal of Conflict Resolution*, 62: 743–773.

Morin, J.-F., Bluemer, D., Brandi, C. and Berger, A. (2019). "Kick-Starting Diffusion: Explaining the Varying Frequency of PTAs" Clauses by Their Initial Conditions." *The World Economy* 42: 2602–2628.

Morin, J.-F., Dür, A. and Lechner, L. (2018). "Mapping the Trade and Environment Nexus: Insights from a New Dataset." *Global Environmental Politics* 18: 122–139.

Nilsson, M., Griggs, D. and Visbeck, M. (2016). "Policy: Map the Interactions between Sustainable Development Goals." *Nature News* 534: 320–322.

Pfaffermayr, M. (2019). "Gravity Models, PPML Estimation and the Bias of the Robust Standard Errors." *Applied Economics Letters* 26: 1–5.

Runge, C. F. (1990). "Trade Protectionism and Environmental Regulations: The New Nontariff Barriers." *Northwestern Journal of International Law & Business* 11: 47–61.

Santos Silva, J. M. C. and Tenreyro S. (2010). "On the Existence of the Maximum Likelihood Estimates in Poisson Regression." *Economics Letters* 107: 310–312.

Spilker, G., Bernauer, T., Kim, I. S., Milner, H., Osgood, I. and Tingley, D. (2018). "Trade at the Margin: Estimating the Economic Implications of Preferential Trade Agreements." *The Review of International Organizations* 13: 189–242.

Subramanian, A. (1992). "Trade Measures for Environment: A Nearly Empty Box?" *World Economy* 15: 135–152.

United Nations (UN) (2015). Transforming Our World: The 2030 Agenda for Sustainable Development. Resolution adopted by the General Assembly A/RES/70/1, pp. 1–35.

Winters, L. A. and Martuscelli, A. (2014). "Trade Liberalization and Poverty: What Have We Learned in a Decade?" *Annual Review of Resource Economics* 6: 493–512.

Zelli, F., Gupta, A. and van Asselt, H. (2013). "Institutional Interactions at the Crossroads of Trade and Environment: The Dominance of Liberal Environmentalism?" *Global Governance* 19: 105–118.

Zhou, L., Xi Tian, X. and Zhou, Z. (2017). "The Effects of Environmental Provisions in RTAs on PM2.5 Air Pollution." *Applied Economics* 49: 2630–2641.

APPENDIX

Table 4.3 *List of Countries by World Bank Country Group Classification (as of 2000)*

High-Income Countries

Andorra	French Polynesia	Monaco
Argentina	Germany	Netherlands
Aruba	Greece	New Caledonia
Australia	Greenland	New Zealand
Austria	Guam	Norway
Bahamas	Hong Kong	Portugal
Barbados	Iceland	Qatar
Bermuda	Ireland	San Marino
Brunei	Israel	Singapore
Canada	Italy	Slovenia
Cayman Islands	Japan	Spain
Cyprus	Kuwait	Sweden
Denmark	Liechtenstein	Switzerland
Faroe Islands	Luxembourg	Taiwan
Finland	Macao	United Arab Emirates
France	Malta	United Kingdom
		USA

Low-Income, Middle-Income, Upper Middle-Income Countries

Afghanistan	Gambia	Panama
Albania	Georgia	Paraguay
Algeria	Ghana	Peru
American Samoa	Grenada	Philippines
Angola	Guatemala	Poland
Antigua and Barbuda	Guinea	Republic of Congo
Armenia	Guinea-Bissau	Republic of Moldova
Azerbaijan	Guyana	Romania
Bahrain	Haiti	Russian Federation
Bangladesh	Honduras	Rwanda
Belarus	Hungary	Saint Kitts and Nevis
Belgium	India	Saint Lucia
Belize	Indonesia	Saint Vincent and the Grenadines

Table 4.3 (*cont.*)

Benin	Iran	Samoa
Bhutan	Iraq	São Tomé and Príncipe
Bolivia	Jamaica	Saudi Arabia
Bosnia Herzegovina	Jordan	Senegal
Botswana	Kazakhstan	Serbia
Brazil	Kenya	Serbia and Montenegro
Bulgaria	Kyrgyzstan	Seychelles
Burkina Faso	Latvia	Sierra Leone
Burundi	Lebanon	Slovakia
Cabo Verde	Lesotho	Solomon Islands
Cambodia	Liberia	Somalia
Cameroon	Libya	South Africa
Central African Republic	Lithuania	South Korea
Chad	Madagascar	Sri Lanka
Chile	Malawi	Sudan
China	Malaysia	Suriname
Colombia	Maldives	Swaziland
Comoros	Mali	Syria
Costa Rica	Marshall Islands	Tajikistan
Côte d'Ivoire	Mauritania	Tanzania
Croatia	Mauritius	Thailand
Cuba	Mayotte	Togo
Czech Republic	Mexico	Tonga
Democratic Republic of the Congo	Mongolia	Trinidad and Tobago
Djibouti	Morocco	Tunisia
Dominica	Mozambique	Turkey
Dominican Republic	Myanmar	Turkmenistan
Ecuador	Namibia	Uganda
Egypt	Nepal	Ukraine
El Salvador	Nicaragua	Uruguay
Equatorial Guinea	Niger	Uzbekistan
Eritrea	Nigeria	Vanuatu
Estonia	North Korea	Venezuela
Ethiopia	North Macedonia	Viet Nam
Fiji	Oman	Yemen
Gabon	Pakistan	Zambia
	Palau	Zimbabwe

Table 4.4 *Summary Statistics PTAs*

Variable	Observations	Mean	Std. Dev.	Min	Max
ENVPROVS	598	14.50502	21.79951	0	120
DEPTH	568	1.582993	1.019131	0	3.687593
Only North–North Agreement (Dummy)	588	0.1309524	0.3376355	0	1
North–South Agreement (Dummy)	588	0.3282313	0.4699693	0	1
Only South–South Agreement (Dummy)	588	0.5408163	0.4987555	0	1

Table 4.5 *Summary Statistics Trade Data*

Variable	Observations	Mean	Std. Dev.	Min	Max
EXPORTS	250,014	8.501814	3.861231	−6.907755	19.76745
ENVPROVS	250,014	20.79433	26.84317	0	120
PTA	250,014	0.7600054	0.4270807	0	1
No. of PTAs	250,014	1.628669	1.641328	0	9
DEPTH	250,014	0.9088943	1.080169	0	3.687593
High-Income Importer	250,014	0.2957114	0.4563628	0	1
High-Income Exporter	250,014	0.303279	0.4596756	0	1

Table 4.6 *Effect of Environmental Provisions in PTAs by Level of Development of Trading Partners, Controlling for the Number of PTAs*

	(1)	(2)	(3)	(4)
	North–North	South–North	North–South	South–South
	EXPORTS	EXPORTS	EXPORTS	EXPORTS
ENVPROVS	−0.003	−0.006***	−0.002	−0.001
	(0.003)	(0.002)	(0.002)	(0.001)
PTA	−0.077	0.460***	0.163**	−0.012
	(0.106)	(0.103)	(0.076)	(0.048)
No. of PTAs	0.017	0.088*	−0.140***	0.175***
	(0.032)	(0.047)	(0.042)	(0.030)
DEPTH	0.113*	−0.112*	0.046	−0.035
	(0.059)	(0.058)	(0.043)	(0.035)
Share of flows under PTA	0.790	0.696	0.709	0.808
Average no. of PTAs if any PTA in place	2.51	2.64	2.64	1.69
Average no. of ENVPROVS per trade flow under PTA	26.6	44.2	45.59	13.67
Country-pair FE	Yes	Yes	Yes	Yes
Exporter- and importer-year FE	Yes	Yes	Yes	Yes
Observations	20,071	53,690	55,576	120,315
R^2	0.965	0.896	0.927	0.848

This table shows the results from running a panel regression of the log of bilateral exports (*EXPORTS*) between 1984 and 2016 on whether a PTA was signed and the environmental provisions (*ENVPROVS*) included in the PTA. The four columns report the results for the split sample by level of development of the exporter and importer, according to the World Bank definition of High Income (North) and non-High Income (South) countries. Robust standard errors clustered at the exporter–importer level are reported in parentheses. ***$p < 0.01$; **$p < 0.05$; *$p < 0.1$.

Table 4.7 *Effect of Environmental Provisions in PTAs by Level of Development of Trading Partners, Controlling for the Number of PTAs – PPML Regressions*

	(1) Full Sample	(2) North–North	(3) South–North	(4) North–South	(5) South–South
	EXPORTSSUM	EXPORTSSUM	EXPORTSSUM	EXPORTSSUM	EXPORTSSUM
ENVPROVS	0.001	0.000	–0.000	0.001	0.001
	(0.001)	(0.002)	(0.002)	(0.001)	(0.001)
PTA	0.080**	–0.029	0.209**	0.083	0.056
	(0.035)	(0.065)	(0.098)	(0.065)	(0.052)
No. of PTAs	0.017	–0.026*	0.126***	–0.069	0.018
	(0.012)	(0.015)	(0.038)	(0.055)	(0.027)
DEPTH	–0.021	–0.027	–0.073	0.019	–0.024
	(0.017)	(0.037)	(0.049)	(0.028)	(0.027)
Share of flows under PTA	0.737	0.782	0.687	0.697	0.808
Average no. of PTAs if any PTA in place	2.02	2.50	2.61	2.61	1.60
Average no. of ENVPROVS per trade flow under PTA	25.9	26.5	44.5	45.3	14.4

Country-pair FE	Yes	Yes	Yes	Yes	Yes
Exporter- and importer-year FE	Yes	Yes	Yes	Yes	Yes
Observations	315,276	20,511	59,099	58,854	176,114
R^2	0.996	0.997	0.999	0.998	0.990

This table shows the results from running a panel pseudo maximum likelihood (PPML) regression of the total amount of bilateral exports (*EXPORTSSUM*) between 1984 and 2016 on whether a PTA was signed and the environmental provisions (*ENVPROVS*) included in the PTA. Column 1 reports the results for the entire sample, Columns 2–5 report the results for the split sample by level of development of the exporter and importer, according to the World Bank definition of High Income (North) and non-High Income (South) countries. Robust standard errors clustered at the exporter–importer level are reported in parentheses. $***p < 0.01$; $**p < 0.05$; $p < 0.1$.

Table 4.8 *Effect of Environmental Provisions in PTAs on Trade, Sample Without Oil Exporters*

	(1) Non-oil-exporting countries	(2) Non-OPEC countries	(3) Non-oil-exporting North–North	(4) Non-oil-exporting South–North	(5) Non-oil-exporting North–South	(6) Non-oil-exporting South–South
	EXPORTS	EXPORTS	EXPORTS	EXPORTS	EXPORTS	EXPORTS
ENVPROVS	−0.004***	−0.003***	−0.002	−0.006**	−0.001	−0.003*
	(0.001)	(0.001)	(0.003)	(0.003)	(0.002)	(0.002)
PTA	0.118***	0.169***	−0.129	0.553***	0.098	−0.034
	(0.039)	(0.035)	(0.111)	(0.115)	(0.085)	(0.056)
No. of PTAs	0.136***	0.137***	0.095**	0.184***	−0.090*	0.173***
	(0.018)	(0.016)	(0.042)	(0.054)	(0.046)	(0.038)
DEPTH	−0.001	−0.036*	0.090	−0.177***	0.024	−0.019
	(0.022)	(0.019)	(0.070)	(0.066)	(0.046)	(0.042)
Country-pair FE	Yes	Yes	Yes	Yes	Yes	Yes
Exporter- and importer-year FE	Yes	Yes	Yes	Yes	Yes	Yes
Observations	178,280	224,941	15,108	43,726	45,737	73,193
Share of flows under PTA	0.74	0.75	0.78	0.71	0.72	0.79

Average no. of PTAs if trade flow under any PTA	2.26	2.13	2.49	2.73	2.72	1.72
Average no. of ENVPROVS per trade flow under PTA	32.54	28.59	28.82	47.90	48.77	15.89
R^2	0.899	0.895	0.962	0.895	0.930	0.868

This table shows the results from running a panel regression of the log of bilateral exports (*EXPORTS*) between 1984 and 2016 on whether a PTA was signed and the environmental provisions (*ENVPROVS*) included in the PTA. The sample excludes in columns 1, 3, 4, 5, and 6 all top oil exporters (Angola, United Arab Emirates, Azerbaijan, Bahrain, Canada, Democratic Republic of the Congo, Colombia, Algeria, Ecuador, Egypt, Gabon, Equatorial Guinea, Indonesia, Iran, Iraq, Kazakhstan, Kuwait, Libya, Malaysia, Nigeria, Norway, Qatar, Russian Federation, Saudi Arabia, Sudan, Venezuela, Viet Nam, Yemen) and in column 2 all OPEC member countries (Angola, United Arab Emirates, Republic Congo, Algeria, Ecuador, Gabon, Equatorial Guinea, Iran, Iraq, Kuwait, Libya, Lithuania, Nigeria, Qatar, Saudi Arabia, Venezuela). Robust standard errors clustered at the exporter-importer level are reported in parentheses.
***$p < 0.01$; **$p < 0.05$; *$p < 0.1$.

Facilitating Sustainable Investment

The Role and Limits of Investment Promotion Agencies

SARAH BAUERLE DANZMAN AND GEOFFREY GERTZ

5.1 Introduction

The Sustainable Development Goals (SDGs), agreed to in 2015 by the members of the United Nations (UN), set out an ambitious agenda for global development over the subsequent fifteen years. Given the scope and scale of these global goals, achieving the SDGs will require significant financial investments, including private investment. The UN has estimated an additional US$2.5 trillion in annual public and private finance will be needed to meet the SDG targets.

The need to catalyze private investment to developing countries has generated considerable interest in new international financing mechanisms, including various blended finance projects that bring together public and private funds (World Economic Forum 2015; Kharas and McArther 2016). In this chapter, we examine the potential contributions of one mechanism which has been relatively unstudied in both the policy and academic literature: developing countries' own investment promotion agencies (IPAs), which almost every country has and which are tasked with promoting and facilitating greater inward foreign direct investment (FDI).

In principle, IPAs are an appealing mechanism for catalyzing FDI, one that is aligned with the aid effectiveness principles of the Paris Declaration (Paris Declaration on Aid Effectiveness, March 2, 2005). These principles stress that development cooperation should privilege country ownership, reflecting the fact that host country governments,

The authors would like to thank the World Bank Group for making data available for analyses included in this chapter; the views presented here are those of the authors alone and should not be attributed to the World Bank Group.

rather than donor agencies or other outside actors, should be in the driver's seat of their own development strategies. If the international development community wants to help catalyze FDI to achieve the SDGs, then partnering with developing country IPAs will allow them to do so in a way that is country-led, works through domestic institutions, and is aligned and integrated into the government's own development strategy.[1]

To date, however, relatively little is known about the potential development contributions of IPAs, and specifically how the political economy of IPA governance influences their activities. In this chapter, we assess what role IPAs could play in advancing the sustainable development agenda. We argue that IPAs' potential contribution is shaped by how they manage a fundamental tension in their work. IPAs have a dual nature, functioning both as the face of government to foreign investors and as an advocate for foreign firms within the bureaucracy. Both these roles are important for achieving IPAs' underlying goal of promoting economic development by attracting foreign investment. By having a foot in the private sector, IPAs can better understand the needs and constraints facing would-be investors, gaining crucial (and often implicit) knowledge that government bureaucracies frequently lack. And by having a foot in the public sector, IPAs can also see the bigger picture of how foreign investment can contribute to broader development strategies. Yet this dual nature also creates tensions, as the interests of governments and foreign investors are not always aligned, and IPAs thus must make choices on whether to privilege the concerns of investors (such as advocating for a more business-friendly investment climate) or those of the government (such as regulating foreign investment to serve broader policy agendas).

---

[1] In emphasizing IPAs, we do not diminish the role that other geographic, regulatory, and governance factors play in structuring investment flows. IPAs cannot entirely compensate for weak local institutions or trade rules that discourage MNEs from developing local linkages. Nor can they impose regulatory requirements on firms to influence the social and environmental sustainability of investor activities. However, IPAs can and do target particular industries and firms, use an array of techniques to entice firms they view to be particularly 'attractive,' and are generally the arm of the government most actively engaged in trying to influence the type of investment a country receives. To the extent that countries view IPAs as tools to discriminate between and differentially support some kinds of FDI over others, the strategies and activities these agencies undertake can have important implications for the sectoral and business activity composition of investment inflows as well as the achievement of the SDGs.

We develop a theory that explains how variation in IPAs' governance structures shapes how they manage these tensions, and in turn how these choices influence their strategies and activities and ultimately their contributions to the sustainable development agenda. We argue that when an IPA's governance structure is designed to be highly autonomous from the rest of the government bureaucracy, it is more likely to align itself with the interests of foreign investors. Autonomous IPAs are likely to be highly professionalized, staffed with more private expertise, and interact more fluently with potential investors; yet are less likely to internalize a government's developmental agenda. Conversely, when an IPA's governance structure is more integrated into the government bureaucracy, it is more likely to align itself with the interests of the government. Integrated IPAs are thus more likely to actively build linkages between foreign investors and domestic firms, and to consider the social and environmental impact of potential investments; yet they may be less effective at attracting potential foreign investors in the first place.

This is the trade-off at the heart of contemporary investment promotion. It follows that there is no single 'best practice' approach to investment promotion, but rather a number of varying approaches that privilege different sets of interests and consequently have different effects. If IPAs are to play a more substantial role in discussions on financing the sustainable development agenda – as we argue they should – these policy debates should focus on grappling with these trade-offs, rather than advocating for a single 'best practice' model.

The remainder of this chapter is structured as follows. First, we briefly survey the small existing literature around IPAs and investment attraction. We emphasize the tendency in this literature to place analytic focus on the 'best' institutional form of IPAs. In contrast, we argue a political economy perspective allows us to develop insights into how and why IPA structure and behavior differs in various domestic institutional and policy contexts. Second, we develop a framework clarifying the tensions between investors' and governments' interests in IPAs and argue that the extent to which an IPA is integrated or autonomous from the government will shape how it navigates these tensions. Third, we present suggestive quantitative and qualitative evidence that IPA governance structure helps explain variation in IPA behavior. Finally, we conclude by discussing the policy implications of our framework, particularly with respect to strategies to achieve the SDGs, and by considering avenues for future research.

5.2 The Rise of Investment Promotion Agencies

While today almost every country has an IPA, these agencies were not always so prevalent. The diffusion of IPAs followed from the rise of neo-liberalism and the aftermath of the Cold War. Countries which had previously been skeptical of foreign investment embraced a view of attracting new capital to ensure their countries remained 'competitive' in a rapidly globalizing economy (Linsi 2016). The creation of IPAs was one among a suite of policy interventions to attract new FDI, along with liberalizing domestic regulations, privatizing state-owned companies, and signing onto trade and investment agreements (Bauerle Danzman 2019).

IPAs carry out a range of activities to attract FDI. At a minimum, agencies provide marketing and advertising functions that assist in the attraction phase of the investment life cycle. Traditionally, IPAs have invested the core of their budgets and person-power to such activities. They market their country as an attractive destination to investors, for instance through advertising in foreign media and participating in trade shows around the world. They also act as business generation agents, actively seeking out foreign firms that are potential investors and recruiting them to the country.

As IPAs became a standard component of governments' investment attraction strategies, their remit also widened as practitioners realized aggressive marketing had limited potential to attract high quality investment. Many IPAs began helping investors navigate bureaucratic and regulatory red tape, often through a 'one stop shop' for licensing. Today, many IPAs also have responsibilities over promoting, negotiating, approving, and managing investment incentives, such as tax holidays. Additionally, contemporary IPAs often provide ancillary aftercare services such as matchmaking foreign firms with domestic suppliers and partners, serving as an ombudsman to address investor complaints and disputes, and providing other 'aftercare' activities to assist already established foreign investors.

IPAs' activities interact with a number of SDG-related policy priorities. The most immediate links are to SDGs 8 (Decent Work and Economic Growth) and 9 (Industry, Innovation and Infrastructure). IPAs influence employment both directly, in terms of jobs created by new foreign investors, and indirectly, in jobs created by domestic companies that are suppliers and customers to the new foreign investors. More generally, the decisions IPAs make in terms of what sectors to target and how successful they are in encouraging linkages between foreign and domestic firms influence both the quantity and quality of jobs created per dollar of FDI attracted. Similarly, IPAs' ability to attract investors in infrastructure and other strategic industries, and their success in promoting spillovers from FDI to the domestic economy, shapes their contributions to industrialization and technological innovation. Finally, at a more general level, new foreign investments can either improve or worsen a country's progress towards the gender (SDG 5), energy (SDG 7), inequality (SDG 10) and environmental (SDGs 13, 14, and 15) goals. Thus, variation in IPAs activities impact many SDGs by facilitating foreign investment projects that either contribute to SDG-compatible development or worsen environmental, socioeconomic, and gender equity concerns.

Despite the near ubiquity of IPAs, there is only limited literature on their operations and effectiveness. In one of the earliest studies of IPAs, Wells and Wint (2000) focused on marketing and image-building to promote inward FDI. They found that investment promotion can successfully attract export-oriented FDI, and that the most effective IPAs tend to have quasi-government organizational structures, combining elements of public and private governance. Morriset and Andrews-Johnson (2004) also found some suggestive evidence that countries that spend more on investment promotion do in fact receive more inward-FDI, though that this relationship only holds in countries with strong investment climates. Harding and Javorcik (2011) showed that when IPAs target a particular sector of the economy, FDI subsequently increases in that sector (relative to others within the same economy). While these studies provide some evidence that IPAs can have an important effect in helping countries attract more FDI, research on the use of investment incentives points in the opposite direction: a number of recent analyses on incentives suggest they rarely play a catalytic role in generating new investment (Tavares-Lehmann et al. 2016; Jensen 2017; Jensen and Malesky 2018). Furthermore, since investment incentives narrow the tax base, there are real concerns that attracting investment in this way can undermine broader sustainable development goals. For example, governments tend to offset the revenue losses associated with investment incentives through reducing education and other social welfare spending and through increasing regressive sales taxes (James 2010; Tavares-Lehmann et al. 2016; Jensen and Malesky 2018). The budgetary squeeze that incentives produce, then, can directly counteract SDGs associated with human development and income equality. This further underlines the need for more information on what specifically IPAs are doing, and disaggregating any investment effects among these various activities.

Another line of research grows out of a World Bank effort to benchmark best practices for IPAs. Scholarship in this vein tends to be applied rather than theoretical and emphasizes the importance of political independence to IPA effectiveness. In a series of studies (2006, 2009, 2012), the World Bank developed a framework to measure IPA performance on basic promotional activities, such as having a user-friendly website and responding to investor requests for information in a timely fashion. This research has generally found that IPA performance varies significantly, and though levels of economic development are correlated with IPA performance there is still substantial variation across countries of similar income levels. Using the same benchmarking data, Whyte, Ortega, and Griffin (2011) found that IPAs whose mandates include tasks related to investment regulation, rather than a narrower focus on promotion, tend to perform worse on the promotion benchmarking metrics. Meanwhile, Harding and Javorcik (2013) demonstrated that IPAs that perform better on basic benchmarking tasks – such as prompt, professional, and accurate handling of project inquiries – tend to attract more FDI. Nelson (2005, 2009) uses comparative case studies of Brazil, Chile, and Costa Rica to argue that operational independence is crucial for IPA effectiveness. He emphasizes that effective investment promotion rests on the ability of the government to shield IPAs from special interests, the extent to which technocrats have operational autonomy necessary to implement 'best practices' rather than respond to the particularistic interests of politicians or specific firms, and the extent to which the IPA can engage in transnational learning to better anticipate the needs of new and high-growth transnational firms.

While the scholarship outlined in the foregoing conceptualizes IPA performance as contingent on insulating IPA officials from political pressures, another strand of research emphasizes the importance of integrating investment promotion activities into broader governmental strategies on targeting high-value investments that complement existing and growing domestic comparative advantages. Scholars embracing this perspective tend to emphasize the role of FDI in technological upgrading and the importance of well-considered industrial policy integrated and coordinated across multiple government ministries. For example, Egan (2018) found that when IPAs pursue more active policies, including strategically discriminating between sectors and directly incentivizing linkages with domestic firms, foreign investors are more likely to invest in innovation and produce valuable spillovers for the local economy. Moran et al. (2018) are more skeptical of the effectiveness of state-led development strategies, but do advocate for a 'light touch' industrial policy in investment promotion, including targeting specific strategic sectors and explicitly strengthening spillovers and linkages with the domestic economy, such as through trainings and matchmaking services connecting suppliers to client firms.

Overall, the current literature on IPA activities and performance is under-theorized and fragmented. One strand, which is focused mostly on assessing the cost–benefit of investment incentives, tends to view IPAs as functional equivalents cross-sectionally. That is, research that explores whether the presence of IPAs and incentives increase FDI flows implicitly assume that IPA activities are similar enough to generate analytic insights from measuring IPA efforts without regard to their differences in strategies or tactics. However, IPA targeting may have heterogeneous effects on potential investors depending on whether the IPA chooses appropriate sectors to target and how it goes about targeting those sectors. Another strand, which emphasizes the importance of insulating IPA officials from special interests, provides evidence for how IPAs can become captured by particularistic interests, but does little to explain why IPA officials may have more public-interest oriented preferences to begin with, or how IPA officials generate beliefs over what is the 'correct' technocratic solution. A third literature emphasizes the importance of integrating IPA activities to broader development goals of the state, but with little treatment of when the state is able to focus on broad versus particular interests.

We argue more can and should be done to integrate the insights from these literatures in order to build a richer, more theoretically grounded understanding of the roles and limits of investment promotion. In particular, while many policy-oriented treatments of IPAs focus on identifying best practices and a totalizing 'correct' IPA structure and strategy, recent developments in global political economy suggest a more ecumenical vantage point has several advantages. First, a theory that explains why governments approach investment promotion in different ways embeds our understanding of IPA structure and behavior within the broader political economy in which these agencies operate. Second, as economic nationalism and the returning legitimacy of industrial policy become more central to political realities in the global economy, it is useful to more fully develop a theory to explain differences in investment promotion among governments that embrace different beliefs over whether it is better to manage capitalism or defer to markets. Third, a theory of IPA structure and behavior that is rooted in political economy frames allows researchers to better explore the distributive implications – at both the national and international levels – of investment promotion. Finally, our approach shifts analysis from 'effectiveness' to behavior. This reorientation is important because 'effectiveness' is in itself a contested concept. Different countries may have varying goals for their IPAs. For example, low-wage countries such as Bangladesh may prioritize investments in low-skill, labor-intensive industries. Middle-income and emerging markets, however, may wish to avoid such investments all together and instead use FDI projects to facilitate technical upgrading. Conceptualizing and measuring effectiveness in a cross-national context is even more problematic when we consider how countries may decide to forego some kinds of foreign investments – in mining and resource extraction as an example – in service to their broader SDG commitments. By centering our analytic gaze on behavior, we avoid these pitfalls.

5.3 The Dual Nature of Investment Promotion Agencies

Our understanding of IPAs begins with the insight that they act as agents serving two different principals. On the one hand, IPAs are agents of their host government, tasked with carrying out the government's preferences in its economic development strategy. These preferences include attracting and retaining foreign investors, but also (potentially) imposing obligations on investors to encourage technology transfer, high labor standards, environmental protection, and other policy objectives. On the other hand, IPAs are agents of existing and would-be foreign investors, tasked with communicating the views and concerns of investors to the government and advocating for pro-investment policies.

On some issues, the preferences of the government and the foreign investor community will be relatively similar, and thus IPAs can reasonably act as agents of both these principals. Yet on many important questions, these preferences might diverge. This is most obvious on explicit distributive issues between the two parties, i.e. the government will want to minimize the amount of an investment incentive (conditional on the investment being made), while an investor will want to maximize it. But it is also true for many broader policy questions. Consider, for instance, the widespread adoption of 'one stop shop' offices, where new investors are able to quickly and seamlessly achieve all of the licensing requirements that are needed to operate. Such policy reforms are frequently billed as creating efficiencies and reducing red tape, which is unambiguously positive for the investor. For the government, however, eliminating steps of regulatory review may ultimately make it more difficult to implement strong and effective social and environmental regulatory regimes. Thus, the drive to streamline regulatory processes may benefit investors at the expense of government control.

On issues where the preferences of foreign investors and governments diverge, IPAs will need to choose which principal's interest they seek to advance. These are both explicit and implicit decisions; IPAs choose what to focus on and, as importantly, what not to focus on. These decisions drive how IPAs interpret their mandates, and in turn the activities they pursue and ultimately the extent and manner in which they may contribute to their country's development.

We argue that IPAs' governance structures play a crucial role in shaping these decisions. The key dimension is the extent to which IPAs are autonomous or integrated into the government bureaucracy. Highly autonomous IPAs may either be non-governmental agencies, or standalone, professionalized government agencies. They are typically overseen by a board of directors and/or advisory board featuring private sector representatives, and mimic private sector companies. They tend to recruit staff from the private sector and have performance-based promotion and compensation policies, and are funded outside of the government's typical budgeting process, either through fee-for-service charges assessed on private sector beneficiaries or through foreign aid.

IPAs with an integrated governance structure, conversely, look much more like any other government agency. Rather than existing as autonomous agencies, they are typically integrated into existing ministerial hierarchies, for instance operating as an office within the Ministry of Economy or Ministry of Planning. Their staff recruitment and compensation policies are similar to those found in other government agencies, and their budgets are set as part of the normal government budgeting process. Staff are evaluated based on policies and procedures applied throughout the bureaucracy and are usually not subjected to market-driven key performance indicators during annual review for promotion and compensation. While integrated IPAs may have some channels to receive information from the private sector, private actors have no formal role in setting the agency's agenda or strategy.

IPAs' governance structures can influence three levels of their operations: their mandates, strategies, and activities. An IPA's mandate provides its overall mission statement and sets the general parameters for its work. It can be either narrow (for instance, focused explicitly on foreign investment) or broad (for instance, including domestic investment and export promotion in addition to foreign investment). IPA mandates are defined externally, typically in the domestic legislation creating the agency. An IPA's strategy is the broad vision of how it interprets its mandate, and typically includes for instance what industries the IPA wants to target. IPA strategies are set by the agency's leadership, though often with oversight from and in response to demands from an external authority, such as the agency's board of directors or a government minister. Finally, an IPA's activities are its day-to-day operations and policies, including questions such as how to allocate staff time and resources among priorities, how to define and measure agency effectiveness, and recruitment and promotion policies. An IPA's choice of activities reflects its decision on how to execute the agreed-on strategy.

Choices over the governance structure of IPAs entail trade-offs, and policymakers as well as international development organizations hold differing opinions over the relative benefits and costs of each structure. On one side, some groups such as the World Bank's Investment Policy and Promotion team often suggest IPAs should be as autonomous from the government as possible (Ortega and Griffin 2009). Such agencies have the benefit of developing their own investment promotion priorities and strategies, and their distance from their governments confers upon them legitimacy in the eyes of potential investors, who view autonomous agencies as allies in negotiations with government officials. Yet, autonomy also entails costs. Because these IPAs are less integrated into government, they may find themselves without a strong voice within policy making circles of the government; this limits their ability to coordinate investment promotion strategy and activities among multiple agencies and ministries such as those responsible for export promotion, trade, finance, and labor. Because of these costs, other groups view integration as vital for IPA performance. For example, United Nations Conference on Trade and Development (UNCTAD) officials tend to advise governments to integrate their IPAs closely into their governments and to make the head of these agencies a cabinet-level official (interview with UNCTAD official July 18, 2016; interviews with multiple IPA officials October 14, 2016).

We contend that the trade-offs associated with IPAs' governance structures are also evident in their strategies and activities. Autonomous IPAs are likely to focus on improving the climate for inward investment and marketing their country as an attractive destination to potential new investors. They work within the government policymaking process to represent the views and interests of foreign investors, encouraging the government to ease general constraints to doing business. Their close connections to foreign investors provide them with accurate insights into the most important obstacles to increasing investment, and they can work with government bureaucracies to prioritize and address these issues. They tend to view foreign investors as clients, and the services they provide will be driven by 'consumer' demand. Crucially, autonomous IPAs develop any targeting strategy they employ in-house, and have the authority to make their own assessments about how to best attract 'high-quality' FDI without much government involvement. Accordingly, they may be better insulated from political considerations when pursuing investment, but that also means they are less likely to target specific firms based on a broader government mandate or to coordinate investment promotion efforts with other developmental strategies.

Integrated IPAs, on the other hand, take their direction from the government rather than treating foreign investors as clients. They tend to play a more active direct role in managing inward FDI flows, targeting specific firms and partnering closely with them in pursuit of developmental goals. Integrated IPAs place more specific demands on new investors, such as commitments to create new jobs and supply linkages with domestic firms, particularly small and medium-sized firms. They often receive strategies for targeting specific industries and firms from above. That is, cabinet-level ministers generate beliefs over what investment attraction strategies are most beneficial to achieving state development objectives and then direct IPA officials and staff to align their activities with these state-led objectives. While integration may make coordinating investment targeting easier, it also leaves such agencies susceptible to bureaucratic inefficiencies and interest group lobbying that often characterize top-down planning.

In brief, variation in IPAs' governance structures lead to distinct configurations of power and interests within IPAs, which in turn leads to different assessments of which priorities should be privileged. As we demonstrate in the next section, the distinction between autonomous and integrated agencies helps us understand what roles different IPAs can and should play in attracting sustainable FDI, and how these agencies manage the tension between investors' and state's interests. The goal of this exercise is not to make a judgement claim as to the superiority of integrated or autonomous agencies; indeed, the optimal IPA institutional framework will likely vary by context and may be best characterized as an exercise in balancing two competing priorities. Understanding IPA behavior in this way allows policymakers to assess whether the governance architecture surrounding their IPAs facilitates or hinders agencies' ability to fulfill the development objectives that political leaders have tasked them with. While this chapter largely leaves questions of 'effectiveness' to the side in favor of instead explaining variations in IPA behavior, it is worth noting that how to measure agency effectiveness should ultimately depend on governance structure because autonomous and integrated agencies are incentivized to prioritize different sets of development goals.

5.4 Explaining Variation in IPA Strategies and Activities

In this section, we leverage World Bank surveys of IPAs in 2009 and 2017 to examine how agency structure influences their behavior. We find IPA activities vary systematically with the degree of autonomy afforded to the agency. Even as IPAs have converged over time on several 'best practices' such as hiring staff with professional backgrounds and prioritizing advocacy for foreign investors, autonomous and integrated IPAs retain distinctive patterns of activities. In contrast to autonomous IPAs, integrated agencies spend more time on activities designed to enhance positive spillovers from FDI into the local economy and are also more likely to consider broader social objectives when targeting potential investors. These findings complicate a previous policy consensus that IPAs become increasingly effective the more autonomous they are from government. Instead, governments must find a balance between providing their IPAs with sufficient autonomy to respond to the needs and desires of potential investors and integrating the agency enough so that investment promotion officials are incentivized and given the tools necessary to align investment promotion strategies and activities to broader development goals.

5.4.1 Leveraging Survey Data of IPA Activities

Since 2002, the World Bank's Facility for Investment Climate Advisory Service (previously called the Foreign Investment Advisory Service) has conducted occasional cross-national surveys of IPAs. These surveys ask respondents a series of questions concerning their governance structures and operations as well as their strategies and investment promotion activities. Unfortunately for our purposes, these surveys are neither panel nor trend data; the population of IPAs included in the surveys changes across survey waves as do the questions asked of them.[2] Therefore, direct comparisons across surveys are challenging. Nevertheless, we conduct analysis on the two most recent survey waves (2009, 2017), first assessing the waves independently and then by matching IPAs that are included in both rounds of surveys. Our approach allows us to provide descriptive data of IPA operations and activities and changes in these attributes over time.

We begin by providing basic descriptive statistics of the governance and operational structure of IPAs in 2009. This survey round asked respondents to identify the legal status of their agency as a subunit of a ministry (which we identify as a marker of bureaucratic integration) or as an autonomous public agency or a non-governmental entity (both of which we identify as autonomous agencies). Table 5.1 reports average responses for agencies subset by governance structure. The column 'Integrated Agency Premia' reports coefficient estimates for ordinary least squares regressions in which the dependent variable is the characteristic described in the respective row, the main explanatory variable is an indicator variable equal to '1' if the IPA is integrated and '0' if it is autonomous, and control variables include indicator variables for country income group as defined by the World Bank in 2009 with lower middle income being the excluded, referent group. These results illustrate that, as expected, many operational characteristics of IPAs were statistically significantly different across governance structures. Autonomous agencies were more likely to have a board, have a greater share of employees with university degrees and private sector experience, and to pay salaries on par with the private sector. In contrast, integrated IPAs tended to have more employees relative to the size of their budgets and pay scales at par with the public sector.

To what extent did these differences in operational structure influence agency activities? We find some evidence that autonomous IPAs were more effective in 'client-facing' aspects of their job, as measured by the World Bank's Global Investment Promotion Best Practices (GIPB)

---

[2] These surveys were designed for purposes other than cross-national, time series analysis, which explains their structure.

Table 5.1 *Operational attributes and activities of IPAs by governance structure, 2009*

	Integrated Agency	Autonomo-us Agency	All Agencies	Integrated Agency Premia
Has a board?	71%	87%	82%	−0.21*
With public sector representation	60%	57%	58%	0.17
With private sector representation	42%	43%	43%	0.00
Budget	4,422,268	14,560,572	11,382,895	−1.11*
Number of employees	174	114	133	−0.35
Operational employees	52	79	71	−0.53
Employee intensity (staff per US$1 mil budget)	79	31	46	0.89**
Share of staff with private sector experience	28%	52%	45%	−0.23*
Share of staff with university degree	77%	90%	86%	−0.11
Share of staff with >5 years' experience	32%	26%	28%	0.05
Pay at par with private sector	4%	23%	17%	−0.17+
Pay between public and private sector	17%	46%	37%	−0.31*
Pay at par with public sector	78%	31%	45%	0.48***
Age as of 2009 (years)	16	11	13	0.34
GIPB score	0.439	0.532	0.504	−0.10*
GIPB website score	0.633	0.693	0.675	−6.27
GIPB inquiry handling score	0.246	0.382	0.34	−14.07**
N	24	53	77	77

Average values reported in each cell. $+p < 0.1$; $*p < 0.05$; $**p < 0.01$; $***p < 0.001$, two-tailed tests. Regressions include World Bank country-income group fixed effects with lower middle income as the referent group. GIPB, Global Investment Promotion Best Practices. Source: Authors' calculations based on data provided by the World Bank.

system (see Table 5.1). GIPB assesses IPAs on the quality of their website and their timeliness in responding to potential investors' requests for information. A similar World Bank analysis of these data concluded that IPAs' with a 'private sector-minded culture' that prioritized hiring from the private sector, paying higher salaries, and rewarding a client-centered approach to investment facilitation and promotion tended to score better on the GIPB (Ortega and Griffin 2009, p. 2).

Moreover, we also find compelling evidence that IPAs' governance structure influenced how they interpreted their mandates. The 2009 survey wave asked respondents to identify the top three activities they were mandated to perform. Figure 5.1 shows that, among IPAs most integrated into the government bureaucracy, 42 percent prioritized regulatory aspects of managing FDI, such as issuing licenses and permits. In contrast, autonomous IPAs were less likely to prioritize regulatory aspects: only 21 percent of these agencies listed this as a core activity. Meanwhile, we see that IPAs less integrated into the government bureaucracy were more likely to emphasize policy advocacy: 25 percent of autonomous agency IPAs prioritized policy advocacy, while only 8 percent of those integrated into government bureaucracies did.

Finally, it is also notable that in the entire survey, only one IPA mentioned linkages and other elements of industrial policy as one of its core activities. Consistent with our theory, this IPA is an integrated agency.

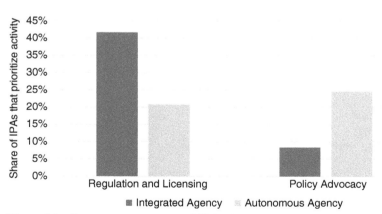

Figure 5.1   Governance structure and IPA priority activities.
Source: Authors' calculations based on data provided by the World Bank.

5.4.2   IPA Convergence and Continued Differences in Recent Years

The data from the 2009 IPA survey suggest that agencies' governance structures can exert a powerful influence on both operational characteristics and interpretation of investment promotion mandates. Indeed, at least partially motivated by the results of the 2009 survey, the World Bank subsequently advised IPAs to undertake a variety of reforms, in particular to adopt a more private-sector minded approach (Ortega and Griffin 2009). In line with this emerging consensus and international advice, IPAs began to adopt several characteristics associated with autonomous agencies, as results from the 2017 survey suggest.

Unfortunately, differences across the two survey waves make it difficult to compare across time: questions change across survey waves as do respondents. Notably, the 2017 survey did not ask respondents to identify their legal status as either integrated or autonomous, our key explanatory variable of interest.[3] For this reason, we limit our analysis to the thirty-six IPAs that are included in both survey waves – an unfortunate but unavoidable decrease in sample size – and assume that the legal status of agencies has not changed in the intervening years.[4] We focus on comparing questions across the two waves that are either identical (such as the presence of a board and its make-up as well as the percentage of staff with private sector experience) or conceptually similar (for instance, the 2017 survey asked IPAs to place their agencies' budgets into discrete categories while the 2009 survey asked for exact budgetary appropriation).

Table 5.2 reports the average values of operational attributes in 2017, grouping IPAs by their governance structure.[5] Overall, we see that IPAs

---

[3] Instead, the 2017 survey asks respondents to which ministry or government agency the IPA reports, which is an imperfect measure of IPA governance because it does not specify how autonomous the agency is from the rest of government.

[4] It is of course possible that some IPAs have changed their governance structure since 2009. Given the development community's growing belief in the importance of autonomy, we would expect more IPAs to have become autonomous over the time period than for IPAs that were previously autonomous to become more integrated into government, which would likely bias our analysis against finding any significant differences between governance structures. Second, a long lag in measurement of IPA governance allows us to ascertain the effect of institutional histories – even if governance structures undergo de jure changes, an IPA that was previously integrated into the government bureaucracy will have developed institutional cultures and memories that persist over time.

[5] We are able to perform OLS regression analyses for 2009 survey data because we have a larger sample ($n = 77$). Table 5.2 reports results from analysis of means because our sample for the 2017 survey is substantially smaller ($n = 36$), which reduces the usefulness of regression analysis.

Table 5.2 *Operational attributes of IPAs by governance structure, 2017*

	Governance Structure			
	Integrated Agency	Autonomous Agency	All Agencies	Integrated – Autonomous Difference
Has a board?	55%	76%	67%	−21%
Public sector representation on board	44%	46%	46%	−2%
Private sector representation on board	55%	51%	52%	4%
Budget	1–2 Million	2–5 Million	1–2 Million	
Share of staff with private sector experience	58%	59%	59%	−1%
Share of staff with public sector experience	43%	59%	54%	−16%
Share of staff with technical background	43%	41%	41%	2%
Share of staff with foreign language	79%	79%	79%	0%
N	11	25	36	

Average values are reported in each cell. Source: Authors' calculations based on data provided by the World Bank.

have become more alike in their operations and staffing decisions. In contrast to Table 5.1, no characteristics display statistically significant differences across groups in the 2017 data.[6] While autonomous agencies are more likely to have a board and a larger operating budget, these differences are not statistically significant. Most telling, both types of

[6] While this is partially due to the smaller sample size, results presented in Tables 5.2 and 5.3 show that statistically significant differences are perceptible even given the limited sample.

agencies seem to have substantially increased the share of staff with private sector experience; from 28 to 58 percent for integrated agencies and from 45 to 59 percent for autonomous ones.

Despite the convergence in operational characteristics across IPA governance structures, however, further inspection illustrates that the integrated-autonomy dichotomy remains relevant for explaining variations in IPA activities. Unlike in 2009, the 2017 IPA survey asked respondents to identify whether they had engaged in a list of investment promotion and facilitation activities over the previous six months rather than to identify their top three mandated activities. Table 5.3 reports the average number of activities related to attraction, entry, operations, and linkages in which IPAs engaged, accounting for agency governance structure. In general, integrated IPAs report carrying out a greater variety of activities than autonomous agencies, and these differences are statistically significant in one-tailed tests even accounting for a small sample. Both integrated and autonomous agencies report far less linkage activities than other types of investment promotion, and in the aggregate the difference between the two is not statistically significant. However, more fine-grained analysis shows that a larger percentage of integrated IPAs engage in a variety of domestic firm, educational, and technological linkage activities than do autonomous agencies and that this difference is statistically significant for programs designed to link domestic suppliers to foreign firms. Additionally, the difference between integrated and autonomous IPAs with respect to educational linkage activities slips just under traditional levels of statistical significance with a p-value of 0.11.

Finally, we look beyond IPA activities to examine the association between governance structures and agencies' budgetary choices, mandates, and evaluations of investment projects. Table 5.4 presents descriptive statistics and difference in means tests for these behaviors; a few findings stand out.

To begin with, there appears to have been considerable convergence among IPAs with respect to their regulatory and advocacy mandates.[7]

---

[7] Note that the 2009 survey asked respondents to identify their top three mandated activities, while the 2017 survey asked respondents to check all boxes that applied with respect to their mandate; thus, comparisons between the two waves of surveys should be interpreted very cautiously. In supplemental analysis, available upon request, we analyze whether governance structures are statistically significantly associated with differences in agency mandates. We find no evidence to support this, which further supports our

Table 5.3 *Activities of IPAs by governance structure, 2017*

	Integrated Agency	Autonomous Agency	All Agencies	Integrated – Autonomous Difference
No. of attraction activities	11.5	9.8	10.3	1.7+
No. of entry activities	12.3	8.7	9.8	3.6**
No. of operations activities	10.5	7.8	8.6	2.7*
No. of linkage activities	5.5	3.8	4.3	1.7
% with domestic linkage	82%	52%	61%	0.3*
% with educational linkage	91%	72%	78%	0.19
% with tech linkage	55%	52%	53%	0.03
N	11	25	36	

Average values are reported in each cell. $+p < 0.1$; $*p < 0.05$; $**p < 0.01$; $***p < 0.001$, one-tailed tests. Source: Authors' calculations based on data provided by the World Bank.

Table 5.4 provides a descriptive analysis of IPA mandates and behaviors, using 2017 survey data. In contrast to the 2009 survey, which found integrated IPAs were more likely to prioritize regulatory functions while autonomous IPAs were more likely to emphasize advocacy, the 2017 survey indicates that integrated and autonomous agencies hold regulatory mandates at similar rates (55 versus 52 percent). While autonomous agencies are more likely to be tasked with advocacy responsibilities than their integrated counterparts (92 versus 82 percent), this difference is not statistically significant.

interpretation that IPA governance continues to influence agency *activities* even as agency *mandates* and *operational characteristics* converge.

Yet, despite this seeming convergence in mandates, important differences in behavior continue to persist. Autonomous agencies are statistically significantly more likely to devote more resources to wooing large foreign firms than are integrated IPAs. The average autonomous agency in our sample spends about 34 percent of its resources on attracting and maintaining investments from large foreign firms, while the average integrated agency spends just 22 percent of resources on these sorts of projects. In contrast, integrated IPAs spend more resources on cultivating joint ventures between foreign and domestic firms than do autonomous agencies; this difference is again statistically significant. Finally, we also find some suggestive evidence that integrated IPAs are more disposed to evaluating investment proposals for their impact on society-wide economic, socio-environmental, and gender objectives than are autonomous IPAs. While these differences are not statistically significant, the difference between governance structures approaches significance for gender-based evaluation criteria ($p = 0.1287$).

Taken together, what can we conclude from these survey results? We find that as of 2009 autonomous IPAs were more likely to adopt a client-focused approach to investment promotion – such as prioritizing policy advocacy – than integrated IPAs. More recently, however, this gap appears to have narrowed considerably, consistent with the definition of a best practice for investment promotion that mimics private-sector agencies.

Yet we also find that some differences have persisted between integrated and autonomous agencies – differences that may have important implications for policy advice encouraging countries to adopt more autonomous IPAs. Indeed, the differences between integrated and autonomous IPAs described in Tables 5.3 and 5.4 are particularly important when viewed through the lens of the growing literature on the links between FDI and local economic growth. This research has generally found that the positive effect of FDI on domestic growth is not automatic but instead depends on the absorptive capacity of the local economy as well as the extent to which foreign firms develop backward and forward linkages with domestic firms (Alfaro et al. 2004; Havranek and Irsova 2011; Irsova and Havranek 2013). There is a growing understanding that to foster more inclusive growth through FDI, governments often need to provide capacity building among local firms, facilitate mutually beneficial joint ventures, and fill informational gaps to assist foreign firms searching for local suppliers (Javorcik and Spatareanu 2005, 2008; Alfaro and Chen 2018). These realities, combined with a growing understanding that

Table 5.4 *Other behaviors of IPAs by governance structure, 2017*

	Governance Structure			
	Integrated Agency	Autonomo- us Agency	All Agencies	Integrated – Autonomous Difference
% Resources devoted to:				
Large foreign firms	22%	34%	31%	−12%*
SME foreign firms	20%	22%	22%	−2%
Joint ventures	18%	10%	12%	8%*
SME domestic firms	18%	22%	21%	−4%
Large domestic firms	12%	11%	11%	1%
Regulatory mandate	55%	52%	53%	3%
Advocacy mandate	82%	92%	89%	−10%
Investment Projects evaluated on:				
Economic impact	91%	80%	83%	11%
Environmental/ social impact	73%	56%	69%	17%
Gender impact	27%	12%	17%	15%
N	11	25	36	

Average values reported in each cell. $+p < 0.1$; $*p < 0.05$; $**p < 0.01$; $***p < 0.001$, one-tailed tests. Source: Authors' calculations based on data provided by the World Bank.

ensuring FDI is SDG-compatible means evaluating potential projects through their impacts on gender (SDG 5), the environment (SDG 6, 7, 11, 12, and 13), inequality (SDG 10), and labor (SDG 8), suggest that integrated IPAs have important advantages over autonomous agencies that are less likely to prioritize these goals through their activities. Moreover, these differences persist despite the convergence of IPAs across operational characteristics and mandates. These results suggest that IPA autonomy entails trade-offs, and governments interested in restructuring their IPAs should carefully weigh how increased autonomy may influence the degree to which investment agencies can help fulfill sustainable development objectives.

5.5 Case Study Evidence: Investment Promotion in Costa Rica

In this section, we examine qualitative evidence on how IPAs' organizational structures influence how they define their missions and in turn the activities they carry out. We use a single case study of Costa Rica's national IPA, Coalicion Costarricense de Iniciativas de Desarrollo, known by its acronym CINDE. We choose CINDE as our case because it is one of the most prominent and well-known IPAs, and is frequently cited within the investment promotion literature for embodying best practices (Spar 1998; Nelson 2009; OECD 2013, p. 104). By focusing on temporal, within-case variation, we can better identify how changes in the agency's organizational structure are associated with shifts in its approach to facilitating sustainable development, while holding other country-level factors constant.

We examine variation in CINDE's activities across three periods: from its inception in 1982 to 1993, from 1993 until 2010, and from 2010 through 2018. As discussed in further detail in the text that follows, this periodization corresponds to changes in CINDE's funding and organizational structure, changes which saw CINDE move from being completely autonomous to the Costa Rican government to becoming moderately more integrated. This within-case variation is more modest than the across-case variation that exists in comparing different IPAs: while CINDE is more integrated into the government today than it was a few decades earlier, it is still far more autonomous than most other IPAs. By showing that even relatively small steps from autonomy toward integration are associated with different policy priorities, this research suggests that the larger cross-country variation will have even more prominent effects.

5.5.1 The USAID Era: 1982–1993

CINDE was created directly out of an alliance between the US Agency for International Development (USAID) and a small group of executives from Costa Rica's private sector. The country had experienced a sharp recession in the early 1980s, leading to the ouster of the previous government and a new administration taking power in 1982. The same year, a new director of the USAID office, Daniel Chaij, arrived in Costa Rica and began holding twice a week breakfast meetings with local business executives, to discuss the roots of the crisis and possible economic recovery strategies (Clark 1997, pp. 80–81). It was at one of these meetings that Chaij proposed a new initiative to promote non-traditional exports, the agency that would become CINDE. Chaij and the Costa Rican executives hand-picked the members of CINDE's board, a group of "nationally respected independent businessmen and intellectuals" (Clark 1997, p. 82).

From its inception, then, there was significant distance between CINDE and the Costa Rican government. CINDE was created by a foreign aid agency partnering with local business executives, neither at the direction of, nor reporting to, the government. Moreover, USAID provided 100 percent of CINDE's budget, and as a result, USAID exerted significantly more control over the agency than any local Costa Rican constituencies. Indeed, it was USAID officials that pushed CINDE to make attracting foreign investors its primary focus, in 1985; this was considered the best way to achieve the agency's original goal of promoting non-traditional (i.e. non-primary product) exports (Clark 1997, p. 85).[8] This autonomy allowed CINDE (and its funders at USAID) to define its own mandate and set its own agenda.

During these early years, CINDE's activities focused overwhelmingly on changing Costa Rican government policy, in line with how our theory suggests autonomous agencies will act. The agency effectively served as a conduit for USAID suggestions to the Costa Rican government on how to liberalize the economy and operated far more as the voice of the business community toward the government than vice versa. Clark (1997) describes CINDE's hands-on approach in ushering through government reforms: "Consultants contracted by CINDE drew up these sections of the legislation [providing incentives for investors and simplifying regulations for exporting], and CINDE board members led the way in lobbying them through the Legislative Assembly by meeting with government functionaries, congressional representatives, ministers, and the president himself, usually on an informal and individual basis" (pp. 86–87). Crucially, while CINDE was autonomous from the

---

[8] This decision was taken after hiring experts from the Ireland Development Authority, Ireland's very successful IPA, as consultants.

government, its leaders were still respected and well-connected to high-level officials; these high-level connections contributed to CINDE's success in shifting government policy.

In addition to lobbying for policy changes, from the late 1980s into the early 1990s CINDE also began to target particular sectors for increased FDI. The agency initially focused on attracting US textile and apparel firms to Costa Rica (Clark 1995, p. 183), and later also began to target the electronics industry (Spar 1998, p. 14). During this era Costa Rica was successful in diversifying its export base to non-traditional products; between 1985 and 1995, the share of primary products in Costa Rica's exports fell from 65 to 38 percent (UNCTAD 2002, p. 167). While this was part of a broader shift in the economy, many observers at least partially credit CINDE with this shift (Clark 1995, 1997; UNCTAD 2002). CINDE itself claimed responsibility for attracting 146 individual FDI projects to Costa Rica between 1886 and 1990, accounting for 18,000 jobs – just over half of which were in the textile industry (quoted in Clark 1995, p. 183).

5.5.2   Becoming a Self-Sufficient Agency: 1993–2010

By the early 1990s, USAID was beginning to withdraw some of its financial support to Costa Rica, and in 1994 the agency announced it would soon be leaving Costa Rica altogether. USAID's withdrawal forced a deep restructuring of CINDE. With USAID funding, the agency had expanded to include 8 overseas offices and some 300 employees; at the lowest point following the restructuring, CINDE closed all its overseas offices and had only around 10 employees (interview with former CINDE official, October 29, 2018). The agency managed to string together enough funds to cover a bare bones budget, drawing on a number of sources (Clark 1995; Lanza 1995; CINDE 2011; OECD 2013, p. 104; interview with former CINDE official, October 29, 2018). These included an endowment, which the agency had built up from USAID's initial contributions and which was further buoyed by selling the company's main office building. Another important source of funding were fees assessed to Costa Rican industrial parks; these parks were seeking foreign investors as tenants, and collectively benefited from a centralized marketing strategy to attract new companies. Yet CINDE's scaled back operations made it difficult to generate the quantity of new leads the industrial parks demanded, and thus in turn they were inconsistent in their funding (interview with former CINDE official, October 29, 2018). A final source of funding was support from the Costa Rica United States Foundation for Cooperation (CRUSA), a Costa Rican non-profit agency created as part of USAID's exit strategy.

While USAID's withdrawal forced CINDE to shift strategies, it did not lead the agency to become more integrated with the Costa Rican government. Throughout this period, CINDE did not receive any substantial financing directly from the Costa Rican government. CINDE also continued to hire private sector workers and reported to a board made up primarily of business executives. This institutional set-up ensured CINDE continued to enjoy considerable autonomy. During the 1990s the agency developed a strategy to target high-technology firms, with a particular focus on electronic component manufacturing. A former CINDE official confirms that this strategy was set "entirely independently" of the government, and that the government was "reactive" to CINDE's initiatives, rather than CINDE following the government's lead (interview with former CINDE official, October 29, 2018).

CINDE helped bring a number of smaller electronics firms to Costa Rica in the mid-1990s, and then in late 1996 landed the deal that would establish the agency as a world-class IPA: Intel's major Latin American expansion. CINDE beat out a number of larger, more established markets in this competition, including Brazil, Mexico, and Chile. Several case studies examine why Intel chose Costa Rica, and what role CINDE played in the decision (see, for example, Spar 1998; Nelson 2000; Hilb and Roitstein 2005). These analyses suggest that CINDE's business-like approach to wooing Intel's executives, combined with the direct personal involvement of Costa Rica's president, convinced the company that the country provided a business-friendly environment for its Latin American plant. CINDE took a proactive approach, making the initial contact with Intel, organizing and coordinating site visits for company executives, and eventually lobbying the Ministries of Transportation and Education to make policy changes that would alleviate some of Intel's concerns about infrastructure and workforce skills (Spar 1998, pp. 18–20). Throughout the process CINDE treated Intel as a potential client and worked with the company to ensure its needs were met. The agency's private sector experience and culture allowed it to successfully execute this strategy, while an IPA more tightly integrated into the government bureaucracy would likely have struggled to partner so seamlessly with a multinational firm. At the same time, the strong support from Costa Rica's president gave CINDE's appeals to Intel more credibility, highlighting the importance of political backing for autonomous IPAs. Indeed, a former official noted that without the president's personal commitment to the project, CINDE would have struggled to engage other government bureaucrats, as CINDE had "no clout" with any other ministries-another drawback of autonomous IPAs (interview with former CINDE official, October 29, 2018).

The successful Intel recruitment gave CINDE a new lifeline, with CRUSA agreeing to increase funding and the Costa Rican government for the first time providing some public financial support to the agency, US$300,000 to open an office in Silicon Valley (interview with former CINDE official, October 29, 2018). In the years after CINDE successfully recruited Intel, a number of other technology and medical services companies also invested in Costa Rica, establishing a small cluster of high-technology firms. Yet, while CINDE's success in attracting these firms demonstrates some of the advantages of autonomous IPAs, Costa Rica's broader experience with FDI during this period also reveals the downsides of such an approach. There were only limited spillovers and linkages between many of the foreign investors CINDE helped bring in and the domestic economy, limiting the positive impact FDI had on the country's broader development. For instance, even a generally very positive World Bank assessment of Intel's impact on the country notes that locally acquired direct materials make up only 2 percent of the total value that Intel exports from its Costa Rican factories (MIGA 2006, p. 16). An analysis from the Economist Intelligence Unit concluded that Costa Rica's "focus on high-tech effectively created a dual economy since the spillovers to the rest of the domestic economy were never particularly strong. On one hand was a vibrant, highly productive, export-oriented sector working at the cutting edge of technology. On the other hand was a mass of unproductive, mostly service-related firms with little or no export prospects. These ultimately accounted for the bulk of employment" (Aguilera 2014). Similarly, another study found that even where some backward linkages did exist between foreign investors and local suppliers, these relationships did not result in any significant knowledge transfer; instead, knowledge transfers occurred primarily horizontally, within the community of foreign investors (Giuliani 2008).

This outcome at least partially reflects CINDE's limited interest in proactively building linkages and spillovers between foreign and local firms. Ciravegna (2012) notes that in the ICT sector in Costa Rica, "MNCs interact mainly with CINDE ... which also assists them after their initial investment. CINDE, however, has no contact with local producers, as this falls outside its mission" (pp. 577–578). CINDE is responsive to foreign investors, and understands their needs and ways of doing business, but is not similarly knowledgeable of domestic firms. There is in fact a separate matchmaking service in the country, Costa Rica Provee, part of the export promotion agency PROCOMER (discussed further in the text that follows). Ciravegna (2012) notes that Costa Rica Provee has a small budget insufficient to hire experienced professionals, and thus "its capacity to interact with MNCs was lower than that of CINDE" (p. 571). Another analysis of Costa Rica's FDI strategy finds that "the proaction aimed at FDI attraction has not been matched by analogous consistent policies to promote indigenous linkage capabilities" (Paus and Gallagher 2008, p. 76). While it is difficult to say what if any effect a more active linkages strategy might have had on Costa Rica's development, it is clear that facing a hard budget constraint CINDE chose to focus on attracting new investors rather than on promoting linkages between foreign and domestic enterprises. Again, this follows our expectations of how autonomous IPAs will interpret their mandates and choose to privilege certain interests over others.

5.5.3 Small Steps Toward Greater Integration with the Government: 2010–2018

More recently, CINDE has taken some steps to establish closer ties with the Costa Rican government and has become marginally more integrated into the bureaucracy. In 2010, CINDE signed a formal partnership agreement with two sister agencies: COMEX, the Ministry for External Trade, and PROCOMER, the export promotion agency (OECD 2013, p. 104). The agreement has become an important source of funding for CINDE and has also increased cooperation between the three agencies. Moreover, CINDE's current head, Jorge Sequeira, previously served as the head of PROCOMER – thus he brings greater awareness and experience of the needs and concerns of domestic Costa Rican firms seeking to enter global value chains. To be sure, the agency is still quite autonomous relative to most other IPAs – it remains a non-profit private organization and receives only a small share of its financing from its agreement with the government. But it is less autonomous than it used to be.

There are some signs that, as CINDE has become more integrated in the government, it is adapting its operations to put more emphasis on implementing the state's development strategy, rather than focusing on serving foreign investors as clients. For instance, CINDE has adopted an explicit goal to attract investors to less developed rural areas of the country, places that have traditionally received less investment. A former CINDE official described this as a "compromise" the agency had accepted as part of a funding agreement with the government, and noted that it could in principle create a conflict for CINDE if the agency was encouraging firms to locate in rural areas even if those locations weren't necessarily in the investors' best interest (interview with former CINDE official, October 29, 2018). CINDE is also placing greater emphasis on linkages between foreign investors and the domestic economy, including through closer collaboration with PROCOMER. CINDE's three-year strategic plan adopted in 2015 identifies promoting productive linkages as one of seven core objectives for the agency (CINDE 2015). And at a July 2018 forum organized by CINDE that brought together high-level government officials and representatives from multinational companies, Costa Rican President Carlos Alvarado remarked that "our challenge is to promote linkages with the rest of the economy to generate more and better employment opportunities in all the country, specially, in the most vulnerable regions" (CINDE 2018).

Finally, it should be noted that CINDE is also in the midst of revising its strategy and evaluation metrics to better incorporate the SDGs. A current CINDE official confirmed that the agency is currently discussing how to measure its contributions to the SDGs, and how to revise its key performance indicators along these lines (phone interview with current CINDE official, Costa Rica, November 26, 2018). Sustainability already features prominently in the country's "Essential Costa Rica" branding, which is managed by CINDE. Companies hoping to use the brand must be certified by the agency, which requires adhering to a particular set of environmental and corporate social responsibility standards. As CINDE further develops its SDG strategy, it continues to balance its autonomy and its relationship with the central government. Though CINDE does not directly take direction from the central government, a CINDE official noted that the agency does seek to align its activities and contributions to the broader Costa Rican SDG strategy developed by the central government.

These developments all suggest that CINDE has somewhat rebalanced its activities in light of its evolving positionality relative to the government. Though overall the agency still has a client-first approach to investment promotion, as its links to the government have strengthened, so too has its interest in promoting linkages and ensuring incoming FDI serves a broader development strategy organized around the SDGs.

5.6   Conclusions and Policy Implications

In this chapter, we explain why research on IPAs' contributions to sustainable development must consider how the structure of such agencies influences the activities in which they engage. We develop a new framework for exploring variation in how IPAs manage these tensions as intermediaries between investors and governments. We argue that agencies' governance structures lead them to privilege certain ideas and interests over others, which in turn incentivize IPAs to approach their mandates of investment attraction in different ways. We differentiate between two ideal types of IPAs: integrated IPAs, that sit within the government bureaucracy and function like any other public sector office, and autonomous agencies, that have more independence from the government. While autonomous agencies are likely to better understand investors' needs and more effectively work alongside private sector actors, their strategic distance from the government's economic development policy team makes it less likely that they will closely align their activities with other government priorities. Consequently, the degree to which an IPA is integrated or autonomous from the bureaucracy influences the extent and manner in which it contributes to its country's sustainable development agenda.

We interrogate these claims in two ways. First, we use data from World Bank surveys of IPAs to demonstrate that variation in IPAs' governance structures help explain variations in their activities and investment promotion strategies. Autonomous IPAs spend more time courting large foreign projects and prioritize activities that are designed to increase overall inflows of foreign investment. In contrast, integrated IPAs are more likely to structure their activities in ways that privilege their countries' industrial policy priorities, such as by emphasizing joint ventures, by devoting more resources to developing local linkages, and by considering broader social goals when evaluating the desirability of investment proposals. Second, we use the Costa Rican experience with investment promotion from the 1980s until 2018 to explore how changes to the country's IPA governance structure influenced its activities and the development outcomes associated with investments it helped attract.

Ultimately, we argue that these variations in promotional strategies and tactics condition IPAs' potential and limits in contributing to sustainable, inclusive development. Over the past decade, the development community has pushed IPAs to become more autonomous from government in order to achieve the operational authority and private-sector mindset thought necessary to best serve the needs of potential investors. Indeed, more autonomous agencies fare better on metrics of IPA performance, which are largely conceptualized as how responsive agency officials are to the requests of investing firms. The Costa Rica case also demonstrates how bureaucratic autonomy can provide IPAs insulation from politicized investment promotion activities so that they can more effectively implement highly targeted, long-term facilitation strategies. Preventing IPAs from becoming a political tool of governing parties is necessary to ensure that investment promotion adds value to the local economy rather than is used to pander to politically important constituents (Jensen and Malesky 2018).

However, our analysis demonstrates there are important trade-offs associated with autonomy. More autonomous IPAs are less likely than their bureaucratically integrated peers to allocate time and resources to activities designed to enhance the positive spillovers that FDI can, under certain circumstances, generate for local economies. Additionally, integrated IPAs demonstrate a greater commitment to social and environmental justice-oriented criteria when evaluating and prioritizing specific investment projects. In the context of the SDGs, integrated IPAs are better poised to balance the exigencies of economic growth with larger social goals of equality, environmental protection, and stronger rights for labor and marginalized groups. As governments increasingly turn to targeted investment promotion in the service of their industrial policy goals (UNCTAD 2018, chapter 4), they will find that institutional form conditions the ability of IPAs to effectively assume a central role in the achievement of sustainable development goals. The policy implication here is not that integrated IPAs are necessarily superior to autonomous ones, but that individual countries will need to calibrate their IPAs' institutional framework to balance the competing priorities of fostering business acumen and translating broad sustainable development objectives into agencies' strategies and everyday activities.

While this chapter speaks to the link between governance structures and IPAs' strategies and activities, we have only touched on one part of a broader process. For now, we have treated the choice between governance structures as exogenous and have bracketed the processes through which these institutional configurations emerge. However, a fuller understanding of the political economy of IPAs should interrogate this further. Where do governance structures come from and why do some countries set up particular types of IPAs? How does governance relate to how IPAs conceptualize, measure, and perform with respect to effectiveness? And how can we move beyond a dichotomous conceptualization of IPA governance to instead explore how agencies might carefully balance operational autonomy with strategic integration into broader governmental objectives? While these issues are beyond the scope of the current study, they are important questions for future research.

The analysis we present in this chapter also suggests a rich policy research agenda related to ensuring investment promotion activities contribute to a country's sustainable development.

First, through what processes can IPAs undergo meaningful governance reform? The Costa Rican case indicates that the degree of autonomy afforded to IPAs can shift over time. What political calculations affect these structural transformations? How do evolutions of IPA governance relate to broader changes in political and policy orientations toward global markets? Under what conditions can states best balance the trade-offs associated between autonomy and integration?

Second, how does policy learning and mimicry function across IPA governance models? Many IPA officials strive to replicate the success of a few particularly efficacious agencies such as Ireland's and Singapore's. But the institutional forms of aspirational IPAs may not lend themselves well to replicating the particular functions of these well-known cases. How does the institutional form of IPAs, then, condition the adoption and implementation of best practices around investment promotion? Rather than coalescing around one exemplary model, is it the case that multiple successful models of investment promotion can coexist?

Finally, while policymakers often consider how weak rule of law and corruption can stymie investment promotion activities, it is worthwhile to consider the reverse causal pathway. Under what conditions, if at all, can the structure and activities of IPAs create new opportunities for corruption and cronyism? As IPAs become increasingly autonomous organizations for connecting foreign and domestic firms with resources of the state, what organizational and political structures guard against capture? We look forward to exploring these questions further in future work.

References

Aguilera, R. (2014). "Costa Rica: Life After Intel." *The Huffington Post*, May 1, 2014.
Alfaro, L., Areedam C., Sebnem K.—O., and Selin Sayek. (2004). "FDI and Economic Growth: The Role of Local Financial Markets." *Journal of International Economics* 64: 89–112.

Alfaro, L and Maggie X. Ch. (2018). "Selection and Market Reallocation: Productivity Gains from Multinational Production." *American Economic Journal: Economic Policy*, 10: 1–38.

Bauerle Danzman, S. (2019). *Merging Interests: When Domestic Firms Shape FDI Policy*. Cambridge University Press. DOI:10.1017/9781108657143.

CINDE (Costa Rican Investment Promotion Agency). (2011). "Annual Report 2011." Available at www.cinde.org/en/resources.

CINDE (Costa Rican Investment Promotion Agency). (2015). "Strategic Plan CINDE 2015–2018." Available at www.cinde.org/en/resources.

CINDE (Costa Rican Investment Promotion Agency). (2018). "Press Release: Government Reaffirms Its Support to Foreign Direct Investment in a High-Level Dialogue with More Than 250 Representatives of Multinational Companies." July 27, 2018. Available at www.cinde.org/en/news.

Ciravegna, L. (2012). "Linkages in the New ICT Clusters of Latin America." *Journal of Latin American Studies* 44: 553–580.

Clark, M. (1995). "Nontraditional Export Promotion in Costa Rica: Sustaining Export-Led Growth." *Journal of Interamerican Studies and World Affairs* 37: 181–223.

Clark, M. (1997). "Transnational Alliances and Development Policy in Latin America: Nontraditional Export Promotion in Costa Rica." *Latin American Research Review* 32: 71–97.

Egan, P. J.W. (2018). *Globalizing Innovation: State Institutions and Foreign Direct Investment in Emerging Economies*. MIT Press.

Giuliani, E. (2008). "Multinational Corporations and Patterns of Local Knowledge Transfer in Costa Rican High-Tech Industries." *Development and Change* 39: 385–407.

Harding, T. and Beata J. (2011). "Roll Out the Red Carpet and They Will Come: Investment Promotion and FDI Inflows." *Economic Journal* 121: 1445–1476.

Harding, T. and Beata J. (2013). "Investment Promotion and FDI Inflows: Quality Matters." *CESifo Economic Studies* 59: 337–359.

Havranek, T. and Irsova Z. (2011). "Estimating Vertical Spillovers from FDI: Why Results Vary and What the True Effect Is." *Journal of International Economics* 85: 234–244.

Hilb, M. and Florencia R. (2005). "Intel in Costa Rica: A Success Story?" INSEAD Case 205–092–1.

Irsova, Z. and Havranek T. (2013). "Determinants of Horizontal Spillovers from FDI: Evidence from a Large Meta-Analysis." *World Development* 42: 1–15.

James, S. (2010). "Providing Incentives for Investment: Advice for Policy Makers in Developing Countries." Investment Climate in Practice Note 54017, World Bank Group.

Javorcik, B. S. and Spatareanu M. (2005). "Disentangling FDI Spillover Effects: What Do Firm Perceptions Tell Us?" In T. Moran, E. M. Graham, and M. Bloström (eds.), *Does Foreign Direct Investment Promote Development?* Institute for International Economics, pp. 45–72.

Javorcik, B. S. and Spatareanu M. (2008). "To Share or Not to Share: Does Local Participation Matter for Spillovers from Foreign Direct Investment?' *Journal of Development Economics* 85: 194–217.

Jensen, N. (2017). "Job Creation and Firm-Specific Location Incentives." *Journal of Public Policy* 37: 85–112.

Jensen, N. and Malesky E. (2018). *Incentives to Pander: How Politicians Use Corporate Welfare for Political Gain*. Cambridge University Press.

Kharas, H. and McArthur J. (2016). "Links in the Chain of Sustainable Finance: Accelerating Private Investments for the SDGs, Including Climate Action." *Brookings Global* Views, No. 5, September 2016.

Lanza, K. (1995). "Institutionalizing Export and Investment Promotion Organizations: The Case of Costa Rica's CINDE." CIDR Working Paper Series, November 1995.

Linsi, L. (2016). *How the Beast Became a Beauty: The Social Construction of the Economic Meaning of Foreign Direct Investment Inflows in Advanced Economies, 1960–2007*. PhD thesis, The London School of Economics and Political Science (LSE).

MIGA (Multilateral Investment Guarantee Agency). (2006). *The Impact of Intel in Costa Rica: Nine Years After the Decision to Invest*. The World Bank.

Moran, Th., Görg H., Serič A., and Krieger-Boden C. (2018). "Attracting FDI in Middle-Skilled Supply Chains." Economics E-Journal Discussion Paper, No. 2018-2.

Morisset, J. and Andrews-Johnson K. (2004). "The Effectiveness of Promotion Agencies at Attracting Foreign Direct Investment." FIAS Occasional Paper No. 16, The World Bank Group.

Nelson, R. (2000). "Case Study: Intel's Site Selection Decision in Latin America." *Thunderbird International Business Review* 42: 227–249.

Nelson, R. (2005). "Competing for Foreign Direct investment: Efforts to Promote Nontraditional FDI in Costa Rica, Brazil, and Chile." *Studies in Comparative International Development* 40: 3–28.

Nelson, R. (2009). *Harnessing Globalization: The Promotion of Nontraditional Foreign Direct Investment in Latin America*. The Pennsylvania State University Press.

OECD (Organisation for Economic Cooperation and Development). (2013). Costa Rica: OECD Investment Policy Reviews.

Ortega, C. and Griffin C. (2009). "Investment Promotion Essentials: What Sets the World's Best Investment Facilitators Apart from the Rest?" World Bank Investment Climate in Practice Policy Brief No. 6, Summer 2009.

Paus, E. and Gallagher K. (2008). "Missing Links: Foreign Investment and Industrial Development in Costa Rica and Mexico." *Studies in Comparative International Development* 43: 53–80.

Spar, D. (1998). "Attracting High Technology Investment: Intel's Costa Rican Plant." Foreign Investment Advisory Service Occasional Paper No. 11. The World Bank.

Tavares-Lehmann, A. T., Toledano P., Johnson L., and Sachs L., eds. (2016). *Rethinking Investment Incentives: Trends and Policy Options.* Columbia University Press.

UNCTAD (United Nations Conference on Trade and Development). (2002). World Investment Report 2002: Transnational Corporations and Export Competitiveness. United Nations Publications.

UNCTAD (United Nations Conference on Trade and Development). (2018). World Investment Report 2018: Investment and New Industrial Policies. United Nations Publications.

Wells, L. and Wint A. (2000). "Marketing a Country: Promotion as a Tool for Attracting Foreign Investment (Revised Edition)." FIAS Occasional Paper No. 13. The World Bank Group.

Whyte, R., Ortega C. and Griffin C. (2011). "Investment Regulation and Promotion: Can They Coexist in One Body?" World Bank Investment Climate in Practice Research Note No. 16, March 2011.

World Bank. (2006, 2009, 2012). *Global Investment Promotion Benchmarking Report.* The World Bank Group.

World Economic Forum. (2015). Blended Finance, Vol. 1: A Primer for Development Finance and Philanthropic Funders. Available at http://www3.weforum.org/docs/ WEF_Blended_Finance_A_Primer_Development_Finance_Philanthropic_Funde rs.pdf.

PART III

Bottom-Up: Private Sector and Civil Society
Initiatives on the Sustainable Development Goals

6

Voluntary Standards, Trade, and Sustainable Development

MATTEO FIORINI, HINNERK GNUTZMANN, AREVIK
GNUTZMANN-MKRTCHYAN AND BERNARD HOEKMAN

6.1 Introduction

High-income countries import goods from other countries that may be
produced by very poorly paid workers under unsafe conditions and with
severe environmental consequences. This is both an important social
justice issue associated with international trade that is of concern to many
consumers of imported products, and one that has salience in light of
international commitments made by countries to protect the environment and defend human rights. In recent decades, a number of policy
initiatives have been implemented to improve labour and environmental
standards through trade. Some governments of developed countries have
sought to incentivize adoption and implementation of International
Labour Organization (ILO) Core Labor Standards through tariff preferences under the Generalized System of Preferences (an example is the
GSP+ regime of the EU, under which developing countries that comply
with ILO norms are granted deeper preferential access than developing
countries that do not do so) and increasingly include provisions on
labour standards and environmental protection in their trade agreements. Multinational companies have implemented codes of conduct
aimed at improving labour conditions in their international supply
chains (Locke 2013). Development aid projects and programs have
been conceived to help improve infrastructure, institutions and administrative capacity needed to enforce social and environmental regulation in
exporting countries.

Perhaps the fastest growing set of initiatives in this area are voluntary
sustainability standards (VSS), under which firms in exporting countries
and distributors in importing countries (wholesalers and retailers)

voluntarily commit to maintaining certain social and environmental standards. Private sector operators – both producers and distributors – document compliance with VSS through a label, permitting consumers to identify products that comply with certain standards that differentiate them from similar (competing) products when they make purchasing decisions. A label potentially secures a price premium for producers and distributors that in principle can cover the costs of defining, implementing and certifying compliance with a given VSS.

The norms and criteria established by VSS are determined by private sector actors – companies, business and industry associations or non-commercial non-governmental organizations (NGOs). They differ from technical product regulations set by public bodies through legislation and/or regulation that generally aim to safeguard public, animal or plant health and safety or to protect the natural environment.[1] First, they are voluntary, not mandatory (legally binding). Second, they are private, created by NGOs or (associations of) companies. Third, they go beyond the domain of mandatory product regulation by establishing standards for the process of production (e.g. requiring use of 'organic' inputs) and other criteria (such as gender equality) the attainment of which cannot be determined through physical inspection of the products – i.e., they constitute credence goods.

The VSS landscape is complex. Some voluntary standards systems compete with each other; others may complement each other. Some become de facto mandatory for certain exports in the sense that not complying with them excludes producers from major distribution channels in import markets. Empirical research on the effects of VSS has found that the multiplicity of VSS may lead producers to invest in multiple certifications for the same product, potentially increasing costs of VSS on smallholder farmers significantly. For instance, 50 per cent of Fairtrade-certified and 15 per cent of Rainforest Alliance–certified farmers were also certified as Organic in 2008 (Rainecke et al. 2012). Some 80 per cent of Fairtrade-certified producers had at least one other certification label in 2011 (Dragusanu et al. 2014). Second, voluntary standards can become a de facto requirement for exporters in some industries and destinations. A well-studied example is GlobalGAP, a farm assurance program that translates consumer requirements into Good Agricultural

---

[1] See WTO (2005) Section II.B for theoretical discussion of the differences between mandatory (public) and voluntary (private) standards. A comprehensive economic analysis and literature review on public standards can be found in Swinnen et al. (2015).

Practices. A survey of 102 fresh produce firms in 10 sub-Saharan countries in 2007 that exported to the European Union (EU) revealed that 79 per cent reported being required by buyers to be certified as meeting GlobalGAP horticultural standards, with 58 per cent of exporters having concluded the GlobalGAP certification process (Henson et al. 2011).

The rapid proliferation of VSS in the marketplace suggests they may be a tool for economic development and attainment of the Sustainable Development Goals (SDGs). Using a difference-in-differences methodology, Distelhorst and Locke (2018) found that producers that become compliant with VSS labour standard-related requirements see a 4 per cent increase in annual purchases, with a particularly strong effect in the apparel industry, a sector in which social movements are strong. Many field studies have shown encouraging results of VSS on both incomes of producers and the realization of social and environmental objectives. Fiorini et al. (2018) argue there is a considerable overlap in aims between VSS and the SDGs. What is less clear is the effectiveness and scale at which VSS can address SDGs, and through which mechanisms such impacts could occur (Thorstensen et al. 2015).

This chapter develops a conceptual framework to analyse the market access (trade) effects of VSS created by actors in developed countries that target producers and supply chains in developing countries. We focus on four questions: (1) whether and how VSS improve smallholder access to developed-country markets, (2) how rents created by VSS are distributed through the value chain; (3) how the impacts of VSS are mediated through the design of the certification process; and (4) whether and how VSS can contribute to the attainment of SDGs. Existing research on these questions has largely focused on mandatory (public) standards and come to ambiguous answers, in part reflecting model parameters (Swinnen et al. 2015; Swinnen 2016).

To address these questions, in line with Ruben and Zuniga (2011), we categorize VSS into two groups: 'Fair Trade' standards (FT-VSS) and 'Corporate-Backed Voluntary Sustainability Standards' (CB-VSS). Fair Trade standards tend to be rooted in NGO sponsorship, going back to a faith-based inspiration of increasing the income gains from trade for marginalized farmers in developing countries (Dragusanu et al. 2014). CB-VSS differ from FT-VSS by having strong corporate backing, although in practice some CB-VSS may be certified by NGOs with focus on sustainability. We show that these two kinds of VSS systematically differ in key provisions that affect market access – ranging from price policy, through supply chain factors to investment and capacity-building support given to producers.

While VSS undoubtedly have been successful in the marketplace, the extant empirical evidence on their effectiveness is mixed. Meta-studies by Blackman and Rivera (2010) and Oya et al. (2017) identify a large set of potential outcome variables that may be affected by the presence of VSS. Most studies find generally limited impacts. Moreover, results are not necessarily statistically significant. Indeed, in some cases, VSS are associated with outcomes that are worse than those of a comparison (control) group of firms that is not certified. One issue, highlighted by Oya et al. (2017), is that VSS operate in complex environments, and outcomes may be specific to a particular institutional or economic setting. This limits the external validity of studies undertaken in any particular developing country setting. Furthermore, VSS may also have positive spillover effects to uncertified producers. This insight emerges from the theoretical literature – for example, if a particular VSS creates competition in the supply chain, this will tend to reduce mark-ups charged by uncertified supply actors (Podhorsky 2015). Thus, like a rising tide, VSS may lift all boats. This presents a challenge for even the most rigorous empirical studies, which often rely on exploiting difference-in-difference variation between certified and uncertified producers, biasing these studies towards finding a weak or no effect.

In terms of traded quantities, the coverage of CB-VSS far exceeds that occurring under FT-VSS. However, Fair Trade is an important benchmark for our analysis. Partly this reflects the strong sustainability and (implicit) SDG focus of Fair Trade-VSS and partly it reflects the dominance of FT certification as a focal point for extant research.[2] For example, in a critical assessment of the literature by Blackman and Rivera (2010), seventeen of thirty-seven reviewed empirical studies on VSS certification systems concern Fairtrade. Moreover, one should not underestimate the influence that Fairtrade has had on other VSS certification schemes: UTZ, Starbucks and Nespresso (all CB-VSS) report the average price premium paid to producers to highlight the economic benefits of certification for farmers (Reinecke et al. 2012).

This chapter proceeds as follows. In Section 6.1 we provide some context by briefly characterizing the state of play as regards the prevalence of VSS across types, countries and products. Section 6.2 discusses

---

[2] In a review of VSS literature, Loconto and Dankers (2014) found that Organic and Fairtrade are by far the most studied standards, followed by GlobalGAP.

different channels through which VSS may impact on producers and summarizes the extant empirical evidence on each of them. Section 6.3 turns to the relationship between VSS and the SDGs, providing a 'mapping' between the various channels identified in Section 6.2 and the different SDGs. Section 6.4 concludes.

6.2   VSS Landscape

This section presents some stylized facts on the most prominent VSS systems, focusing on their market size, price effects and design characteristics. Systems differ in their main area of emphasis, but each VSS covers a multitude of issues. This is demonstrated in Table 6.1, which draws on the survey by Loconto and Dankers (2014).

The VSS set by NGOs tend to focus on social and environmental requirements, and incorporate a broad set of stakeholders, usually incorporating producers and public sector bodies. This group includes Fairtrade certification through the Fairtrade Labelling Organizations International (FLO), an NGO created in 1997 (a scheme we discuss in more detail in the text that follows), which has a strong focus on social equity and producer welfare and Organic and Rainforest Alliance standards, which are production management systems that focus on environmental issues, such as biodiversity, water and soil preservation and ecosystem conservation.

Table 6.1 *Focus Areas and Standard-Setting of Key VSS Systems*

Standard	Year of Inception	Main Focus	Standard-Setting Body			
			NGO	Producers	Public	Private
Fairtrade	1997	Social equity	✓	✓		
Organic	1972	Environment	✓		✓	
Rainforest Alliance	1987		✓			
UTZ Certified	2002	Food safety	✓			✓
GlobalGAP	1999	and quality				✓
C.A.F.E. Practices	2004	Quality				✓

C.A.F.E., Coffee And Farmer Equity (Starbucks).
Source: Authors' elaboration based on Loconto and Dankers (2014).

Standards originating in the private sector tend to have a strong focus on product safety and quality. GlobalGAP certification, for example, is set and managed by private sector actors and offers better access to large buyers in export markets, who are likely to require GlobalGAP certification. Importantly, GlobalGAP targets business-to-business transactions –it does not come with a label that makes compliance with this VSS visible to consumers. UTZ Certified is similar to GlobalGAP in its requirements but has a stronger focus on supply chain transparency and sustainability criteria. Another example is Coffee And Farmer Equity (C.A.F.E.) Practices, a certification system with a focus on quality set by Starbucks. Starbucks now sources practically all its coffee from farmers with this certification, but farmers may also have other certificates, such as Fairtrade (Craves 2015). What makes Starbucks C.A.F.E. Practices special is that it appears to be the only company-specific VSS, which also makes up almost 100 per cent of purchases, at least among large coffee roasters. In comparison, Nestlé and JAB Holding Co have much higher share in global coffee purchases than Starbucks but they source only a small share from VSS-certified producers: 9 per cent and 20 per cent, respectively (Craves 2018).[3]

These standards have an important presence in agricultural markets. Table 6.2 presents information on sales value, price premia and farmland covered by VSS systems. The information is collected from annual reports of the standard setting organizations. Due to the heterogeneity in reported metrics and level of detail, figures should be treated as indicative rather than definitive.[4] Moreover, annual reports appear to have become less informative in recent years.

Organic farming has by far the largest retail market value and farmland of all VSS systems. However, only a 24 per cent of Organic farmland is in developing countries (Willer and Lernoud 2019),[5] which limits its potential impact on the SDGs and in particular smallholder welfare in developing countries. Organic is also by far the largest VSS in terms of retail sales, but only a small share of total VSS retail sales are imports from developing countries. For example, for the US organic retail market, which accounts for half of the global total, only 5 per cent of the retail

---

[3] Nestlé has an internal company Nespresso AAA quality program, which is based on Rainforest Alliance principles, but is not in fact a certification system, the inclusion criteria appear to be less stringent than those of certification systems and statistics are not well-reported. On top of that, total purchases of Nespresso make up less than 8 per cent of Nestlé's coffee purchases (Craves, 2016).

[4] Fairtrade International Organization has the most comprehensive reports.

[5] About half of the Organic-certified farmland is in Australia.

Table 6.2 *Market presence by VSS*

Standard	Value, billion EUR, 2017	Total Premiums, million EUR	Farmland, million ha, 2016	Farmland, %, 2016
Fairtrade	8.49 retail sales	178 (2017)	2.48 (2015)	0.05
Organic	86 retail sales	—	57.8[a]	1.20
Rainforest Alliance	2.90 (in UK, 2016)	—	1.93	0.04
UTZ certified	—	48.4[b] (2013)	2.73	0.06
GlobalGAP	—	—	3.29	0.07
C.A.F.E. Practices	0.57 (Coffee purchases, 2014)	—	—	—

C.A.F.E., Coffee and Farmer Equity (Starbucks).
[a]Including planned certification area.
[b]Coffee and Cocoa, in 2013.
Sources: UTZ (2014), Ethical Consumer (2017), Fairtrade International (2018), Lernoud et al. (2018), and Willer and Lernoud (2019).

value are due to imports.[6] Certified farmland for other VSS systems reported in Table 6.2 are more concentrated in developing countries, as implied by their objectives, although specific shares are not available.

Some VSS incorporate a 'price premium' relative to non-certified produce, which is paid to producers to support their sustainability objectives. This instrument was pioneered by Fairtrade, who enforce a mandatory price premium. In 2017, Fairtrade paid a total of 178 million EUR in premia, as shown in Table 6.2. Other standards leave the determination of price premia purely to market forces or direct negotiation, e.g., Organic and UTZ. For Organic, we were not able to find data on total premia paid. UTZ reports that in 2013 it paid premia totaling 48.4 million EUR to cocoa and coffee farmers. Values for other products are not available but likely to be much smaller in magnitude. Rainforest Aliance,[7] GlobalGAP and C.A. F.E. Practices do not incorporate price premia.

[6] Data from https://statistics.fibl.org.
[7] In January 2018, UTZ officially merged with the Rainforest Alliance.

6.3 Channels of VSS Impact

Following the early Fair Trade labeling initiatives launched in the late 1980s, voluntary sustainability standards have proliferated. Hundreds of VSS are now active in the global marketplace, and their number and scope are continuing to grow. Initially focused only on agricultural products, VSS now cover a broad range of manufactured products as well (Fiorini et al. 2018). There is considerable diversity in VSS requirements, certification criteria, and assistances offered to producer to satisfy norms. To better understand this complexity, it is useful to distinguish between Fair Trade standards, which follow the tradition of the earliest initiatives, and corporate-backed private standards that are of more recent vintage.

Fair Trade (FT) labeling initially spread through faith-based initiatives launched in the Netherlands. The label was initially designed to reward coffee importers who incorporated specific, producer-friendly policies into their sourcing agreements, with the goal that smallholders should be guaranteed a 'living wage'. The key features of FT labels have remained constant: they offer a guaranteed minimum price to protect producers from drastic price decreases, a guaranteed price premium over the non-certified commodity price and some element of advance payment to ease liquidity constraints on producers. The FT model generally also encourages importers (retailers) to develop direct relations with producer co-operatives in exporting countries, with the aim of reducing the share of rents (price premia) that may be captured by intermediaries in the global value chain. In return for these benefits, the FT model places requirements on producers, such as limiting the use of certain inputs like pesticides or water.

Corporate-backed VSS (CB-VSS) are developed and/or used by corporations. What distinguishes CB-VSS from the FT model is that business-related objectives and practices are the primary focus of certificate design. Fairtrade also collaborates with large retailers such as Starbucks, Sainsbury's and LIDL, but CB-VSS tend to follow a more market-based approach, as opposed to an explicit focus on increasing price premia for producers. The goal instead is to improve production – increasing productivity (e.g., raising yields), boosting product quality, and/or the process of production, including use of more environmentally sustainable practices. While criteria or requirements may overlap to some extent with FT-VSS, a basic difference is in the approach to pricing. In the case of CB-VSS any price premium arising from certification over conventional price is negotiated between producer and buyer, not mandated by the standard. Another difference is that in contrast to FT, CB-VSS do not seek to reduce the role of intermediaries in the supply chain.

As already noted, CB-VSS need not be developed by businesses. Some of the most widely adopted certification schemes, such as Rainforest Alliance (RA), have strong backing from multinational enterprises (MNEs), were established by NGOs. Some private sector-established CB-VSS standards, such as UTZ, GlobalGAP, and Starbucks C.A.F.E., are regarded as belonging in the same group and have similar requirements. Sometimes single-actor systems are developed in collaboration with private standard setters, e.g. the 'Nespresso AAA Sustainable Quality Program' was developed in partnership with RA. In other cases, adoption of a VSS by large buyers is crucial – for example, Forest Stewardship Council (FSC) certification has obtained the backing of large retailers such as Ikea and The Home Depot (Bartley 2018).

Not all VSS are private. Some are issued by government actors (Public VSS). These mostly concern organic produce. Such organic standards centre on the use of production inputs and methods and do not have the supply chain/GVC focus of private VSS. The three types of VSS are not mutually exclusive; many producers may hold two or more certifications simultaneously. This increases overall VSS compliance (certification) costs but permits producers to optimize their use of alternative sales channels depending on market conditions prevailing for each VSS segment.

Figure 6.1 shows two major stages of a typical agricultural supply chain for products such as coffee, tea, or cocoa where producers are smallholders. Farmers may sell directly to an intermediary (which may be a

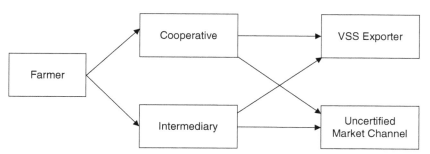

Figure 6.1 Agricultural supply chain: certified versus uncertified.
Source: Authors' elaboration.

processor) or organize themselves into cooperatives. FT-VSS generally focus on the latter situation, certifying the output of cooperatives that is exported. VSS may also apply to situations where certified farm output is sold to intermediaries that operate within a GVC or that have contractual relationship with large foreign buyers. In practice, output channeled through cooperatives or intermediaries may be sold on markets with certification. The issue of interest is to determine the effect of certification on the various agents in the supply chain. As we discuss in the text that follows, VSS potentially impacts each stage of the value chain. This starts with the inputs, financing terms and production technology available to the producer. To satisfy documentation and reporting requirements, VSS tend to strengthen the market presence of farmer cooperatives which may increase competitive pressure on intermediaries and increase incentives for farmers to obtain certification.

The theoretical and empirical literature that assesses the potential impacts of VSS identifies five potential channels through which VSS may impact on trade (Table 6.3): (1) increasing the price of the export good, (2) affecting the competitiveness of the supply chain, (3) through the design of certification process, (4) influencing production techniques and finally (5) indirectly, through a 'public good' channel. The last channel operates through the effects of VSS may have on the environment, health and social standards in the exporting community or region which in turn is valued by consumers in export markets.

Table 6.3. *Fair trade versus corporate-backed VSS*

| Channel | Type of Private VSS System | |
	Fair Trade	Corporate-Backed VSS
Pricing	Explicit price support, quantity constrained	Market-based
Supply chain competitiveness	Own supply chain	Own supply chain, may displace traditional supply chain
Certification design	Co-op	Importer
Production process	Upgrade to higher level of processing	Financing/investment for better inputs
Indirect: public goods	Yes	No

Source: Authors' elaboration.

1. **Pricing Channel**: VSS certification can increase benefits from exporting if certification helps to achieve higher sales prices.[8] The price effect can be directly embodied into the VSS design or through signaling to the consumers who value sustainable production processes. Thus, the effects on the export price depend on the type of VSS adopted. Under FT, producers have a guaranteed floor price as well as a guaranteed 'social premium' over the market price that can reach up to 15 per cent. Thus, conditional on selling their produce as FT, the producer gets more revenue. However, it is not guaranteed that producers are able to sell their output as FT – this depends on whether demand is sufficient. In practice, a large share of FT-certified produce is not sold through FT; i.e. producers end up using the non-certified channel. For most commodities (with the exception of bananas), a majority of FT produce is not sold as FT. Small FT producer organizations rely on the FT channel more than farms that employ wage workers (large farms; plantations): in 2013–2014, the share of producers in both groups that sold more than half of their production on FT terms was 43% and 29%, respectively (Fairtrade International, 2015, figures 5.4 and 5.5). In contrast, CB-VSS are more market-oriented, leaving it to direct negotiation between producer and importer whether a premium is paid. In this case, prices adjust to clear the market, so farmers can expect to sell all their certified produce. This leaves open the possibility that price premia could be low or non-existent.

The evidence points to a significant price premium for FT compared to non-certified produce. Results for UTZ and organic are more ambiguous. Chiputwa et al. (2015) found that FT price is higher partly because of the price premium of FT certification, and partly due to higher levels of processing. However, the positive effect of higher prices is reduced as a result of demand-side constraints: the market for FT-certified output is limited. Dragusanu and Nunn (2018) studied a panel of coffee mills in Costa Rica and found that FT-certified mills do receive higher prices but their total sales do not increase – they are similar to those of non-certified mills. The evidence further suggests that price advantages of certified products reduce over time. Van Rijsbergen et al. (2016) analysed certification of Kenyan cooperatives. Their findings support higher coffee prices received by the certified farms (both Fairtrade and UTZ) but initial

---

[8] Note that for there to be a benefit from VSS participation through the pricing channel, certification and compliance costs must be less than the price premium of certified product.

advantages tend to reduce over time and there is no significant impact on value chains as measured by the value added received by the producers.

Systematic review of studies on certification schemes by Oya et al. (2017) and Nelson and Martin (2013) concluded the empirical importance of the pricing channel is small. The literature surveyed reports significantly higher supply than demand of certified output for many products, particularly in the case of FT certification, resulting in goods meeting the certification requirements being sold without a label. A key motivation for certification is argued to be the effect on export market access, not gains through the pricing channel. Small farmers are unlikely to overcome high barriers of accessing export markets without certification, and VSS provide new reliable export channel. The inability of studies to find a significant price premium for certified producers may also reflect certification 'raising all boats'. If certification creates new export market access opportunities for farmers, this translates into higher aggregate demand and higher equilibrium price for all farmers and makes it difficult to measure the true differential impact of certification on price.

Theoretical analyses predict (eventual) exhaustion of fair trade rents (premia) (Janvry et al. 2015). The reasoning is that, with a large number of potential FT smallholders, premia will induce entry, over time eliminating the net income gains of FT participation. In principle, a larger number of participants does not lead to a fall in prices in FT schemes, since the premium is fixed, but entry will lower the share of output that participants can sell into certified markets given that these are limited in size. Janvry et al. (2015) showed that in the long run producer benefits of FT are equal to participation costs. They confirm that this theoretical prediction holds for data from an association of coffee cooperatives in Central America. Thus, the benefits and sustainability of price premia are determined by the number of participating producers and the overall demand for certified produce.

2. **Supply Chain Competitiveness**: VSS can provide access to alternative supply channels to participating farmer organizations and make the overall value chain more competitive. FT-VSS can improve market access for certified product by providing an alternative sale channel even if there are no gains from the pricing channel. Imperfect competition among intermediaries may reduce prices obtained by individual farmers or cooperatives when selling to processors or wholesalers.[9] CB-VSS systems

---

[9] A commonly used term for intermediaries by Mexican farmers is 'coyotes'. See Milford (2012).

may operate through intermediaries, co-ops, large agricultural enterprises (plantations or estates) or large buyers. Thus, their impact on smallholder cooperatives is more ambivalent than in the case of FT-VSS.

In contrast, one of the key features of FT is to work with farmer cooperatives rather than commercial intermediaries, reflecting a goal to cut out the middleman. By strengthening the role of co-ops, FT-VSS certification seeks to reduce the effect of monopsony power of intermediaries by providing an alternative sales channel to farmers. This pro-competitive role of FT-VSS is less of a feature of CB-VSS. However, CB-VSS may also give producers access to new distribution channels that are linked to large buyers that use the VSS system and may be owned and controlled by them. The associated volume (demand) effect may be important. It is well documented that only a small proportion of the total output is distributed through the FT channel.

The pro-competitive benefits of FT model have been analysed theoretically by Podhorsky (2015). The paper compares welfare impact of FT model with a much simpler direct transfer to farmers. The FT is found to be better than direct transfer if and only if the intermediary market is insufficiently competitive and the price is not too high above the efficient wage. This result highlights that main benefits to the FT model lie in improvement of competition in the intermediaries' market.

Empirical studies confirm the theory. In a study on Chiapas, Mexico, Milford (2012) found that cooperatives have a pro-competitive effect, offsetting the price-suppressing effects of limited competition between intermediaries and reducing cheating by intermediaries. At the same time the study finds that the farmers might choose selling through an intermediary due to immediate payment and loan offers. Ronchi (2006) found similar positive impacts, with FT support for cooperatives improving their market power and increasing prices received in the coffee sector in Costa Rica. Dragusanu and Nunn (2018), similarly, found in a panel setting that FT certification increases the incomes of skilled coffee farmers and hurts the intermediaries. Although incomes of unskilled farm workers, who comprise 60 per cent of coffee industry workers, are unaffected, the overall effect of FT certification can be seen as positive and reducing inequality due to the transfer of income from intermediaries to high-skill farmers. Nelson and Martin (2013), an impact assessment of Fairtrade and Rainforest Alliance/Organic certification of cocoa in Ecuador comes to similar findings: certified farmers sell higher share of their produce through producer organizations and rely less on intermediaries. Certification creates pressure on intermediaries to raise purchase prices.

3. **Certification Design**: The design and associated costs of the certification system determines whether producers can comply with a VSS and the net gains from certification. High costs of certification and implementation may turn the VSS into a market access barrier rather than an additional sales channel and opportunity. Thus, it is important to know who bears the certification and implementation costs.

Certificate design, specifically the nature of certificate ownership, is an important distinction between FT and CB-VSS. Under FT, the co-op pays for certification and owns the certificate. Under CB-VSS, the intermediary/exporter organization often subsidizes or pays for certification but also owns the certificate (intermediary mode). This exporter company subsidizes – partially or fully – the certification cost for farmers, and has the explicit objective of trade facilitation for producers (Nelson and Martin 2013; Chiputwa et al. 2015). This comes at the cost that farmers don't own the certification documents – certified sales are 'locked' to a specific sales channel. Thus, the co-op has to deal with a specific exporter for their certified channel, rather than shop around for the best deal as under FT.

Identification of the value chain participant bearing the certification costs can be a challenge. For instance, smallholder farmers can organize into groups to be jointly certified to meet GlobalGAP standards. This first appears to be similar to the FT design. It is, however, very different in practice. Any trader or agricultural producer that represents the farmers can become the certificate owner. Thus, although it might appear that farmers/farmer organizations in traditional sense pay for the certificate, in practice, independent intermediaries/exporters often cover the costs of certification and auditing, own the certificate and contract the individual farmers. The arrangement is then that of an intermediate-pays model rather than that of producer-pays mode of FT where the co-operative is more than a legal entity that owns and pays for the certificate.

Which scheme is preferable from the producers' perspective? Under producer-pays, an initial investment must be financed by the producers, but afterwards the cooperative can sell to the highest bidder (if one exists). In contrast, with intermediary-pays mode, the risk to producers is lower – no initial investment is required, and access is obtained to a stable sales channel – but the potential upside is smaller because the producers face a monopsonist (the intermediary they have an obligation to sell their produce to). In either case, the outside option is to sell uncertified.[10] Empirical studies of UTZ and Organic-certified coffee farmers in Uganda (Chiputwa et al. 2015) and RA-certified tea farmers in India (Nelson and Martin, 2013) found that farmers face one buyer and thus are dependent on this buyer, the bargaining power for price limited by the risk of losing the contract. Bolwig et al. (2009) describe a contract farming scheme in Uganda. Here, an operating company makes a contract with multiple smallholder farmers. The operator manages and finances certification on behalf of the farmers. Certification may be with multiple label operators. Farmers are then obliged to sell all their certified produce to the contract operator, who decides through which sales channel (label) to sell it on. The intermediary guarantees to purchase all output from the cooperative – and bears the risk that it may not be able to sell all output as certified.

Certificate design can have far-reaching impact on supply chain. Colen et al. (2012) examined the contribution of GlobalGAP to the horticultural landscape in Senegal between 2000 and 2010. The data cover firms that become certified under GlobalGAP Option 1 – certification of individual producers. Such design creates significant increasing returns to scale of certification costs and can cause dramatic shifts in the supply chain. The study reports shift of exporters sourcing from smallholders to own production or large estates: from about 100 per cent in the beginning of the sample to 50 per cent in 2010. Later, group certification has been introduced where producer groups or exporter/trading company can be certified and represent a group of farmers (Option 2). Asfaw et al. (2009) analysed the costs and benefits of GlobalGAP certification under Option 2 for smallholders in Kenya. In these analysed cases the exporter firms cover the certification and auditing costs while individual farmers bear the costs of infrastructure investment. The paper found that the certified smallholder farmers benefited substantially from adopting private standards.

4. **Production Process**: Certification standards can influence the producers' production quantity, processing level and production technology. VSS systems vary along these dimensions. Some VSS can motivate producers to upgrade in the value chain. When applicable, such as for instance in the case of coffee, FT encourages its members to sell more processed produce, rather than just raw commodities. Value chain

[10] That is, the output that is produced satisfies the VSS criteria, but is not sold as VSS.

upgrading partly explain why FT prices are higher (i.e., a higher level of processing). Such upgrading is often the focus of capacity-building assistance provided by the VSS system. A constraint, however, in moving up the value chain is that FT producers often are not able to sell all their output on the FT terms. In contrast, CB-VSS systems are generally not designed to incentivize producers to move along the extensive margin by doing more processing.

VSS certification often has an impact on production technologies used and productivity. For example, FT cooperatives are often also organic certified, as this allows them to sell through the organic channel some of their output that cannot be not sold through the FT channel. This may limit the use of productivity-enhancing fertilizers, reduce output and increase the labour intensity of production. Both FT and CB-VSS provide training and product-specific assistance that can increase productivity and offset the effect of changing the input mix to satisfy the VSS requirements. Empirical studies assess which certification approach is associated with higher productivity. CB-VSS may provide financing, or inputs directly, to support production, for example, financing of fertilizer, etc. similar to contract farming. CB-VSS is more focused on productivity.

In their impact assessment of Fairtrade and Rainforest Alliance (RA) certification focusing on five case studies of cocoa producers in Ghana and Ecuador and tea producers in Kenya and India Nelson and Martin (2013) found that VSS certification has a positive impact on productivity and yields, due to training and technical assistance leading to improved management practices and fertilizer use. In addition, the possibility to use Fairtrade premiums on fertilizer purchase, reforestation and soil conservation which can help productivity allowed FT-certified farmers in Ecuador to achieve higher yields than Organic certified producers.

Nelson and Martin (2013) found that certification leads to higher quality of production but also higher production costs. Higher quality is attributed to the disciplining effect of VSS rules regarding management, hygiene and use of chemicals. Importantly, the cooperative managers consider that consumers value and pay the premium for certified products more because of higher quality of the products than because of label. Increased production and certification costs of certified farmers are a barrier for poor farmers; however, this also means that marginalized producers, with more available labour, are more likely to benefit from the certified cooperatives (Milford 2014).

There is some evidence that a producer's current level of capacity interacts with the effectiveness of a particular VSS. As Ruben and

Zuniga (2011) found in a study of Nicaraguan smallholder coffee produ-cers, FT certification can be an important first step for smallholder farmers to improve market access and update their production methods. However, once this level of capacity has been reached, there is limited evidence in their setting that FT can take producers further. Instead, CB-VSS standards perform better in subsequent stages of upgrading. An important insight emerging from these findings is that different VSS systems may usefully be seen as complements, targeting producers at different stages, rather than substitutes. The literature review of Loconto and Dankers (2014) presents a more detailed discussion of quality and productivity impacts of VSS for some of the most important standards based on twenty-nine empirically rigorous studies.

5. **Public Goods Channel**: VSS tend to have some form of support for public goods such as improvement in water use, water quality, or provi-sion of common infrastructure. These can improve competitiveness and thereby market access, e.g., by increasing productivity via plant disease reduction or lowering transportation costs via better infrastructure. This channel is particularly important for FT certification, as FT requires setting aside part of the premium for social projects that benefit the entire community. Community-improving premia can be present also in cor-porate-backed VSS but have a smaller role. All forms of VSS certification can benefit producers in developing countries through promotion of environmental and other sustainability goals (Podhorsky, 2009).

Empirical studies have most extensively covered the public goods impact of Fairtrade certification. Dragusanu and Nunn (2018) find in a panel setting that FT premiums have positive educational impact. Nelson and Martin (2013) report using FT premium in a cocoa-producing FT organization in Ghana on boreholes, schools, toilets, corn mills and developing the organization's website. Dragusanu et al. (2014) review of Fairtrade concludes that FT-certified farmers are more likely to engage in environmentally friendly farming practices. Chiputwa and Qaim (2016) report positive impact of certification (Fairtrade, UTZ and Organic) on gender equity as women have more control over the pro-duction and sales revenues in certified households.

6.4   VSS and the SDGs

The impact VSS can have on sustainable development has attracted considerable attention across several research fields in social sciences, fueling a lively debate with contrasting theoretical arguments and empirical evidence (see UNFSS, 2018 for a recent discussion). Sustainable development is a multidimensional outcome variable as it encompasses a wide range of areas, from poverty reduction to gender equality to environmental sustainability. Matters are complicated further, as potential tensions may arise between different dimensions of sustainable development insofar as these are affected by VSS. Thus, Brandi (2016) shows that in the palm oil sector in Indonesia the positive effect of VSS on environmental sustainability is often accompanied by a negative impact on market participation of smallholder producers, reducing incomes. Similarly, Tayleur et al. (2018) uses geo-localized data on certified farms to demonstrate that VSS tend to be concentrated in geographic areas that are important for biodiversity conservation but that are not the most important in terms of poverty alleviation.

In a recent contribution, UNFSS (2018) provided an empirical assessment of the potential impact of a broad population of 122 VSS on 10 of the 17 SDGs. The report maps SDG targets to more than 800 detailed VSS requirements and criteria as reported in the Standards Map Database of the Geneva-based International Trade Centre. Through a goal-to-goal comparison, the report identifies three areas where VSS appear best positioned to contribute to the SDGs: goal 8 (promote decent work and economic growth), goal 12 (ensure sustainable consumption and production patterns) and goal 15 (promote environmental sustainability and protect life on land). That study provided an empirical assessment of the direct effect of VSS on SDGs, i.e. an assessment based on the specific certification requirements of the standards.

In what follows we complement the exercise conducted in UNFSS (2018) by investigating the implications for sustainable development (as defined in the SDGs) of the five channels noted previously linking VSS and trade: pricing, supply chain competitiveness, certificate design, production, and public good spillover effects. Our focus is on the sustainability impacts of VSS that arise indirectly through their effect on trade. Questions of interest are whether the five trade-VSS channels discussed in the preceding text can support sustainable development; whether some dimensions of sustainable development are more affected than others across different channels; and if specific channels give rise to trade-offs between different SDGs. To answer these questions, we use the SDGs as indicators of the different dimensions of sustainable development. Table 6.4 summarizes the implications of VSS for sustainable development by channel.

Table 6.4 *SDG impacts of VSS by channel*

Channel	Qualifying SDGs
Pricing	1, 2
Supply chain competitiveness	1, 2
Certificate design	1, 2, 16
Production channel	1, 2, 5, 8, 12, 13, 14, 15
Public goods channel	3, 4, 6, 7, 9, 11, 16

Source: Authors' elaboration.

To the extent that a VSS-related increase in output prices allows producers to register higher revenues from their sales, and under the condition that the costs associated with obtaining VSS certification labels are such that greater revenues generate higher profits, the VSS pricing channel raises the income of producers. This income effect has direct implication for the reduction of poverty (SDG 1) and hunger and malnutrition (SDG 2). Similarly, the supply chain competitiveness channel, by reducing market power of intermediaries, may increase real incomes of producers and therefore contribute to SDGs 1 and 2.

Analogous implications derive from the certificate design channel. Which economic agent(s) bear the costs of certification and/or implementation is an important parameter for the effect of VSS on the income of producers in developing countries. Moreover, certificate design can help trigger a positive effect of VSS for SDG16, by promoting fairer and/ or stronger institutions for the governance of sustainable production.

Some SDGs may be affected by VSS through effects on production. VSS may trigger a potential income effect insofar as the standards trigger an increase in productivity that results in higher profits for producers. VSS might also lead to changes in the production technology used so as to positively affect gender equality (SDG 5) – e.g., by providing services (e.g., transport; childcare) that permit women to better combine household with paid work, the quality of work (SDG 8), the efficiency of the use of natural resources such as water and land or better waste management through requirements specifying efficiency enhancing practices in resource management (SDG 12), climate phenomena (SDG 13), marine resources (SDG 14) and terrestrial ecosystems (SDG 15). However, VSS-induced changes in production technology can also generate tensions between different dimensions of sustainability. For instance, technology requirements designed to protect biodiversity might come with high implementation costs, excluding the poorest producers from the use of the associated VSS and potentially increasing income inequality (SDG 1, SDG 5). More than others, the production channel can be associated with trade-offs in terms of the impact of VSS on different dimensions of sustainable development.

Finally, there is a potential public good dimension of VSS that can have effects on a variety of SDGs without implying associated trade-offs. VSS can support investments in or increase the effectiveness of infrastructure that is valuable for broad groups in society, including health services (SDG 3), education (SDG 4), water-related infrastructures (SDG 6), energy-related infrastructures (SDG 7), transport infrastructures (SDG 9), urban infrastructures (SDG 11), and accountable and inclusive institutions (SDG 16).

6.5   Concluding Remarks

Voluntary sustainability standards have become mainstream in many sectors, particularly agriculture and related processing activities. Their rapid spread in the marketplace strongly suggests that consumers have a desire to take social and environmental factors into account in their purchasing decisions. Notwithstanding the large number of high-quality studies investigating different dimensions of VSS, the empirical evidence on their effectiveness is mixed. In this chapter, we focused on two types of standards – FT-VSS and CB-VSS – and isolated five potential channels of impact. Importantly, the two types of VSS implement these channels differently, raising the question of which approach works better in specific development settings.

FT-VSS emphasize capacity-building, making them especially suitable for producers with a low initial level of capacity. This focus on capacity-building is apparent throughout the different channels. In terms of the pricing mechanism, producer prices are one crucial concern. Here, FT standards have historically focused on low commodity prices as a part of the problem, with standards designed to offer a 'price premium' for FT-certified producers. The evidence points to an economically significant price premium for FT producers, although the sustainability of this effect depends on the size of both supply and demand. In contrast, CB-VSS leave the determination of a premium to direct negotiation between producer and exporter; in practice, premia for CB-VSS are likely lower than under FT. The key caveat of the FT price premium is that it leads to quantity constraints: producers can generally only sell a small share of their qualifying produce under FT terms. For smallholder farmers working without hired labour, even a price premium for a small share of the harvest may be very valuable in terms of poverty reduction. In contrast, for larger enterprises with accordingly much larger production volumes, the insecurity and low scalability of the FT channel may be a serious limitation.

In FT, the mechanisms underlying the supply chain channel are also designed with inclusion in mind. FT explicitly promotes the development of farmers' cooperatives, since these co-ops manage access to the FT sales channel. Fostering co-ops may be especially helpful for development to the extent that co-ops also provide other services, such as agricultural training and access to inputs. In contrast, under CB-VSS, the main gain for producers is access to large markets in developed countries. This benefit is more valuable the larger a producer already is.

The literature finds a stronger focus on modernization of production practices in CB-VSS standards. However, FT producers also experience productivity increases, especially when starting from a low base. Once more these findings suggest that FT can be a 'stepping stone' for producers: building an initial level of capacity, which enables farmers to take advantage of CB-VSS in a subsequent stage. Finally, the relatively stronger focus of FT systems on the public good channel makes them a better solution for producers operating in environments characterized by weak infrastructures and poor provision of basic services such as health and education. A separate question is how rents are divided along the supply chain. Both FT and CB-VSS introduce new intermediary actors into the supply chain, which generates greater local competition for farmers' produce. The evidence suggests that both types of VSS have a beneficial effect on participating farmers. However, non-participating farmers will also benefit from any increase in competition. Thus, VSS may have positive externalities on non-participants, which could bias empirical studies towards finding weaker effects.

Disentangling the sustainability impact of VSS is complex. The five channels proposed here help to unpack the role that VSS may play in attaining the SDGs through their impact on trade. Depending on how different channels manifest in FT and CB-VSS, one type of system can be more effective than the other in contributing to a specific sustainability dimension. Analysis of the various channels can help to identify the most appropriate design of VSS given the priorities of supply chain actors with regards to sustainable development.

References

Asfaw, S., Mithöfer, D. and Waibel, H. (2009). 'Investment in Compliance with GlobalGAP Standards: Does It Pay Off for Small-Scale Producers in Kenya?' *Quarterly Journal of International Agriculture* 48: 337–362.

Bartley, T. (2018). *Rules Without Rights: Land, Labor, and Private Authority in the Global Economy*. Oxford University Press.

Blackman, A. and Rivera, J. E. (2010). 'The Evidence Base for Environmental and Socioeconomic Impacts of "Sustainable" Certification'. Available at https://media.rff.org/documents/RFF-DP-10-17.pdf.

Bolwig, S., Gibbon P. and Jones S. (2009), 'The Economics of Smallholder Organic Contract Farming in Tropical Africa'. *World Development* 37: 1094–1104.

Brandi, C. A. (2016). 'Sustainability Standards and Sustainable Development: Synergies and Trade-Offs of Transnational Governance'. *Sustainable Development* 25: 25–34.

Chiputwa, B. and Qaim, M. (2016). 'Sustainability Standards, Gender, and Nutrition Among Smallholder Farmers in Uganda'. *The Journal of Development Studies* 52: 1241–1257.

Chiputwa, B., Spielman, D. J. and Qaim, M. (2015). 'Food Standards, Certification, and Poverty Among Coffee Farmers in Uganda'. *World Development* 66: 400–412.

Colen, L., Maertens, M. and Swinnen, J. (2012). 'Private Standards, Trade and Poverty: GlobalGAP and Horticultural Employment in Senegal'. *The World Economy* 35 1073–1088.

Craves, J. (2015). 'Starbucks Claims 99% "Ethically Sourced" Coffee, But What Does That Even Mean?' Daily Coffee News. Available at https://dailycoffeenews.com/2015/05/15/starbucks-claims-99-ethically-sourced-coffee-but-what-does-that-even-mean/.

Craves, J. (2016). 'Nespresso AAA Quality Program Guidelines. Coffee and Conservation'. Available at www.coffeehabitat.com/2015/06/nespresso-aaa-guidelines/.

Craves, J. (2018). 'How Much Eco-certified Coffee Is Purchased by the Big Coffee Companies? Coffee and Conservation. Available at www.coffeehabitat.com/2012/01/market-share-update–2012/.

De Janvry, A., McIntosh C. and Sadoulet E. (2015). 'Fair Trade and Free Entry: Can a Disequilibrium Market Serve as a Development Tool?' *Review of Economics and Statistics* 97: 567–573.

Distelhorst, G. and Locke, R. M. (2018). 'Does Compliance Pay? Social Standards and Firm-Level Trade'. *American Journal of Political Science* 62: 695–711.

Dragusanu, R., Giovannucci, D. and Nunn, N. (2014). 'The Economics of Fair Trade'. *Journal of Economic Perspectives* 28: 217–236.

Dragusanu, R. and Nunn, N. (2018). 'The Effects of Fair Trade Certification: Evidence from Coffee Producers in Costa Rica'. NBER Working Paper No. 24260. Available at www.nber.org\\papers\\w24260"www.nber.org/papers/w24260.

Ethical Consumer. (2017). Markets Report. Available at www.ethicalconsumer .org/sites/default/files/inline-files/ec%20markets%20report%202017.pdf.

Fairtrade International. (2015). *Scope and Benefits of Fairtrade: Seventh Edition 2015*. Available at http://fairtrade.org.nz/~/media/Fairtrade%20Australasia/ Files/Resources%20for%20pages%20-%20Reports%20Standards%20and% 20Policies/2015-Fairtrade-Monitoring-Scope-Benefits_web.pdf.

Fairtrade International. (2018). 'Working Together for Fair and Sustainable Trade: Annual Report 2017–2018'. Available at www.fairtrade.net/fileadmin/user_up load/content/2009/about_us/annual_reports/2017–18_FI_AnnualReport.pdf.

Henson, S., Masakure, O. and Cranfield, J. (2011). 'Do Fresh Produce Exporters in Sub-Saharan Africa Benefit from GlobalGAP Certification?' *World Development* 39: 375–386.

Kersting, S. and Wollni, M. (2011). *Public-Private Partnerships and GLOBALGAP Standard Adoption: Evidence from Small-Scale Fruit and Vegetable Farmers in Thailand. In EAAE 2011 Congress: Change and Uncertainty, Challenges for Agriculture, Food and Natural Resources*. ETH Zurich.

Milford, A. B. (2012). 'The Pro-Competitive Effect of Coffee Cooperatives in Chiapas, Mexico'. *Journal of Agricultural & Food Industrial Organization*, 10: 1–29.

Milford, A. B. (2014). 'Co-Operative or Coyote? Producers' Choice Between Intermediary Purchasers and Fairtrade and Organic Co-operatives in Chiapas. *Agriculture and Human Values*, 31: 577–591.

Fiorini, M., Hoekman, B., Jansen, M., Schleifer, P., Solleder, O., Taimasova, R. and Wozniak, J. (2018). 'Institutional Design of Voluntary Sustainability Standards Systems: Evidence from a New Database'. *Development Policy Review*, 37: O193–O212.

Lernoud, J., Potts, J., Sampson, G., Schlatter, B., Huppe, G., Voora, V., et al. (2018). *The State of Sustainable Markets 2018: Statistics and Emerging Trends*. Geneva, Switzerland: International Trade Centre.

Locke, R. M. (2013). *The Promise and Limits of Private Power: Promoting Labor Standards in a Global Economy*. Cambridge University Press.

Loconto, A. M. and Dankers, C. (2014). 'Impact of International Voluntary Standards on Smallholders' Market Participation in Developing Countries: A Review of the Literature'. Food and Agriculture Organization of the United Nations.

Nelson, V. and Martin, A. (2013). 'Assessing the Poverty Impact of Sustainability Standards. Department for International Development UK. Available at https:// assets.publishing.service.gov.uk/media/57a08a55e5274a27b2000543/ AssessingThePovertyImpactOfSustainabilityStandards.pdf.

Oya, C., Schaefer, F., Skaligou, D., McCosker, C. and Langer, L. (2017), 'Effects of Certification Schemes for Agricultural Production on Socio-economic

Outcomes in Low- and Middle-Income Countries: A Systematic Review'. *Campbell Systematic Reviews* 2017:3.

Podhorsky, A. (2009). 'Environmental Labeling'. Working Paper 2009/3, York University. Available at https://econpapers.repec.org/paper/ycawpaper/2009_5f3.htm.

Podhorsky, A. (2015). 'A Positive Analysis of Fairtrade Certification'. *Journal of Development Economics* 116: 169–185.

Reinecke, J., Manning, S. and Von Hagen, O. (2012). 'The Emergence of a Standards Market: Multiplicity of Sustainability Standards in the Global Coffee Industry'. *Organization Studies* 33: 791–814.

Ronchi, L. (2006). *Fairtrade and Market Failures in Agricultural Commodity Markets*. Washington, DC: The World Bank.

Ruben, R. and Zuniga, G. (2011). 'How Standards Compete: Comparative Impact of Coffee Certification Schemes in Northern Nicaragua'. *Supply Chain Management* 16: 98–109.

Swinnen, J. (2016). 'Economics and Politics of Food Standards, Trade, and Development'. *Agricultural Economics* 47: 7–19.

Swinnen, J., Deconinck, K., Vandemoortele, T. and Vandeplas, A. (2015). *Quality Standards, Value Chains, and International Development: Economic and Political Theory*. Cambridge University Press.

Tayleur, C., Balmford, A., Buchanan, G. M., Butchart, S. H. M., Corlet Walker, C., Ducharme, H. and Phalan, B. (2018). 'Where Are Commodity Crops Certified, and What Does It Mean for Conservation and Poverty Alleviation?' *Biological Conservation*, 217: 36–46.

Thorstensen, V., Weissinger, R. and Sun, X. (2015). 'Private Standards: Implications for Trade Development, and Governance, E15Initiative. International Centre for Trade and Sustainable Development (ICTSD) and World Economic Forum.

UNFSS. (2018). 'Voluntary Sustainability Standards, Trade and Sustainable Development'. 3rd Flagship Report of the United Nations Forum on Sustainability Standards. Available at https://unfss.org/wp-content/uploads/2018/09/UNFSS-3rd-Flagship-Report-FINAL-for-upload.pdf.

UTZ. (2014). 'Bringing Good Practice to Scale'. Available at https://utz.org/wp-content/uploads/2016/01/Annual-report-2013-UTZ.pdf.

Van Rijsbergen, B., Elbers, W., Ruben, R. and Njuguna, S. N. (2016). 'The Ambivalent Impact of Coffee Certification on Farmers' Welfare: A Matched Panel Approach for Cooperatives in Central Kenya'. *World Development* 77: 277–292.

Willer, H. and Lernoud, J. (2019). *The World of Organic Agriculture. Statistics and Emerging Trends 2019* (pp. 1–336). Research Institute of Organic Agriculture FiBL and IFOAM Organics International. Available at https://shop.fibl.org/CHen/mwdownloads/download/link/id/1202/?ref=1.

WTO (World Trade Organization). (2005). *World Trade Report 2005. Trade, standards and the WTO*. World Trade Organization.

The Role of Voluntary Sustainability Standards in Sustainable Livelihoods for Cocoa Farmers in Côte d'Ivoire

LEE ANN JACKSON AND KOSSIVI BALEMA

7.1 Introduction

Fluctuations in cocoa prices have generated increased attention over the past few decades to the economic and social conditions of cocoa farmers. The issue is especially critical in countries where cocoa represents a large share of the national economy, such as Côte d'Ivoire. Despite investment in sustainability initiatives, cocoa farmers in West Africa continue to experience low productivity due to aging trees, declining soil fertility, and pest and diseases. Few young farmers are prepared to tackle these challenges, leading to a situation in which projected cocoa production is stagnating, while global demand is expected to increase.

The system of incentives for farmers involved in the cocoa sector is complex. While private standards have garnered a great deal of media attention, the landscape of the cocoa sector is shaped by a complex system of government regulations and market interventions, in addition to private sector standards.

Government intervention to support prices can alter farmers' incentives to invest in improved production practices. Western Africa governments have intervened in cocoa markets by providing guaranteed minimum prices to farmers. Côte d'Ivoire has implemented various approaches to address the challenge of supporting cocoa farmers, including direct market interventions and liberalization of the sector. In 2018, the Côte d'Ivoire government adopted a strategic partnership agreement with Ghana to pursue a common strategy for the improvement of prices for cocoa producers (Government of Ghana 2018).

At the same time some large private sector companies have developed a joint action plan, bringing together the world's largest cocoa and chocolate companies and the governments, to define and address priority issues in cocoa sustainability (World Cocoa Foundation 2016). This voluntary industry-wide strategy, Cocoa Action, seeks to achieve alignment in corporate sustainability initiatives in the areas of productivity, community development, and environmental sustainability to catalyse public–private action to accelerate cocoa sustainability.

Some companies have explicitly framed their strategies in terms of the Sustainable Development Goals (SDGs), since many of these are relevant to addressing the challenges specific to the cocoa sector (see, for example Cargill 2019) such as food insecurity, lack of access to education, and gender inequality in the sector. Companies can identify how to target actions to contribute to outcomes for specific SDGs such as no poverty (SDG 1), zero hunger (SDG 2), quality education (SDG 4), and gender equality (SDG 5). In the area of environmental outcomes, companies highlight SDGs such as climate action (SDG 13) and life on land (SDG 15). Private firms increasingly focus attention on specific SDGs through their sustainability standards, communicating to customers how their actions may contribute to global sustainability outcomes.

This chapter seeks to evaluate the ways in which public and private sector actions affect the choices of smallholder farmers in the cocoa sector in Côte d'Ivoire and to identify key factors that determine farmer adoption of voluntary sustainability standards (VSS) and resulting socioeconomic outcomes. Analysis of a comprehensive household dataset highlights the different economic and environmental outcomes for certified and uncertified farmers. Section 7.2 summarizes key literature related to the adoption and impacts of VSS. Section 7.3 describes the specific context of cocoa in Côte d'Ivoire. Section 7.4 provides some details on the landscape of sustainability standards, focusing on those standards that play a role in the case of cocoa. In Section 7.5 we describe the dataset and methodology used to develop quantitative insights into the role of VSS in cocoa in Côte d'Ivoire. In Section 7.6 we examine the household determinants of adoption and the impacts of certification. Results highlight the importance of access to credit, size of land in cocoa cultivation, and participation in training to enhance sustainable practices in determining farmers' adoption of VSS.

7.2   Literature on Adoption and Impacts of VSS

Private sector initiatives have developed with a view to strengthen the links between smallholder cocoa producers and global consumers. With growing consumer attention to the socio-economic conditions in the cocoa sector, an increasing number of firms adopted labelling schemes to highlight products that were produced in ways to support smallholders. According to Bacon (2010) VSS provide a useful tool to enhance the livelihoods of cocoa farmers through prices and improve environmental outcomes. However, Giovannucci and Ponte (2005) considered that implementing VSS along the value chain, and providing opportunities for certification, would not be sufficient to ensure that farmers would invest adequately in their production systems for economic and environmental sustainability. After several decades of experience with these systems, the results with respect to farmers' livelihoods and environmental impact are mixed (Chiputwa et al. 2015; Ibanez and Blackman 2016; Fiorini et al., Chapter 6, this volume).

The literature on the impacts of VSS at the local level has focused primarily on the economic benefits farmers perceive from participating in the standards adoption (Blackman and Rivera 2010; Beuchelt and Zeller 2011). These benefits, however, are often subject to price variability (Rueda and Lambin 2013), which offers only a partial explanation of why farmers adopt these certifications. Several factors including the socio-economic aspects and environmental benefits may also act as drivers that motivate farmers to join and adopt these VSS. Indeed, the adoption of VSS by cocoa farmers can potentially improve farmers' income and food and nutrition security of farmers' household through product quality and eco-environment strategies, yields improvement, sustainable agricultural technologies use, and access to market (Perez-Aleman 2012). Certification can also generate spillover effects on the adjacent farms and communities through technological diffusion and improved transparency and traceability in the market. Markelova and Mwangi (2010) indicated that the involvement of smallholders in the markets can contribute to higher productivity and income growth, which can in turn enhance food security, poverty reduction efforts, and overall economic growth.

VSS cover diverse objectives, including fair trade, organic production, environmental sustainability, and product certification (Minten et al. 2015). The means of achieving these objectives varies among VSS. The main objective of Fairtrade labelling is to ensure that producers will realize sufficient incomes by assuring minimum price and price premiums (Minten et al. 2015). Chiputwa et al. (2015) found that Fairtrade certification increased smallholder living standards by 30 per cent and reduced the prevalence and depth of poverty in Uganda. The adoption of VSS can also imply additional costs for producers and these trade-offs mean that the result of adoption of VSS on farmers' net income and welfare is uncertain. For example, the results of Chiputwa et al. (2015) also reveal that organic and UTZ certifications have no statistically significant impacts on household welfare indicators. Giovannucci and Ponte (2005) mentioned that the impact of VSS on farmers' income depends on the balance between the additional cost of matching the VSS and the extra income generated from VSS price premium and changing farming practices impact on yield and product quality.

The question of the impact of VSS adoption on smallholder households' livelihoods is particularly important in the context in developing countries where farmers have high production costs and are less competitive. Less attention has been given to agricultural commodities such as cocoa in Cote d'Ivoire with regards to the adoption of VSS and its impacts on smallholder farmers' livelihood. As certification expands geographically and to diverse agricultural commodities, understanding the determinants of its adoption and potential to improve livelihoods and landscapes becomes more urgent.

7.3   Cocoa Production in Côte d'Ivoire

Côte d'Ivoire is the largest cocoa producing country, with almost 2.7 million hectares dedicated to cocoa production (FAOSTAT 2017). In 2017, Côte d'Ivoire accounted for 40 per cent of the world production of cocoa. Small farmers account for more than 70 per cent of the production, with farm sizes typically between 2 and 4 hectares. About 900,000 farmers growing cocoa in Côte d'Ivoire and 3.5 million of the country's 22 million inhabitants depend on the crop for their livelihoods. While cocoa production accounts for about 10 per cent of the gross domestic product (GDP) – about one third of agriculture's contribution to national GDP (CIA 2012) – cocoa generated 30 per cent of the national export earnings in the period 1995–2014 (Gayi and Tsowou 2015).

Government involvement in the Côte d'Ivoire cocoa sector has shifted over time. Historically, the marketing of cocoa beans had been controlled through a national commodity board and then was fully liberalized in the early 2000s. In 2012, the government of Côte d'Ivoire created a new central body – the Conseil du Café-Cocoa (CCC) – which is responsible for the management regulation, development, and price stabilization of cocoa (Gayi and Tsowou 2015).

Within the Côte d'Ivoire cocoa sector, a handful of large companies dominate the cocoa trade and processing: Barry Callebaut, Cargill, Cemoi, ECOM-Zamacom, Olam, and Transmar. In 2014, these firms adopted a voluntary industry-wide strategy, called CocoaAction. Through this strategy, the cocoa and chocolate industry work with government and other stakeholders to facilitate harmonized interventions to accelerate sustainability in the cocoa sector (World Cocoa Foundation 2016). Interventions focus on addressing a variety of challenges, including low productivity, pest and disease, environmental concerns, and market challenges.

In most cocoa producing countries, fluctuations in the world market price have an immediate influence on the price the farmer receives for his or her cocoa. However, the situation in Côte d'Ivoire is different. The country has a national cocoa marketing board that pre-sells part of the farmers' harvest in the year before the harvest season starts. The marketing board then determines a fixed price around 1 October each year, the beginning of the annual main-crop season based on the prices established in futures market (Fountain and Hutz-Adams 2018). The government intervention in prices therefore reduces, without eliminating, instability in farmer incomes. For example, in 2017 future prices for cocoa dropped from US$ 2.90/kilo to US$ 1.80/kilo due to increased international production. Since the CCC's guaranteed price is benchmarked off the futures prices, farm gate prices for cocoa producers are not insulated from these types of declines (Confectionary News 2017). Farmers in the country have not been successful in achieving levels of income that would allow them to improve their socio-economic situation. A Fairtrade International report estimated that a living income for cocoa farmers in Côte d'Ivoire would be $2.51 per day, whereas farmers' actual incomes are less than one dollar per day (Rusman et al. 2018). This daily income is well below the World Bank's benchmark for extreme poverty, which is currently defined as $1.90 per day.

Côte d'Ivoire experienced a dramatic increase in cocoa production from 900,000 tons in 1995 to 1,500,000 tons in 2011, largely driven by a significant increase in the farm gate price due to government policies to stimulate cocoa growing as an export crop (Wessel and Quist-Wessel 2015). The increase in production was accompanied by a growing number of cooperatives involved in the certification process for their export cocoa under different schemes. In 2011, an estimate of 55,387 farmers were certified under UTZ and Fairtrade schemes. This number has increased since then by almost four times to reach 225,938 farmers in 2015 (see Table 7.6 in the Appendix to this chapter). The share of certified production of cocoa to the total national production of Cote d'Ivoire has increased from 23 per cent to 69.5 per cent between 2008 and 2016 (see Figure 7.1 in the Appendix to this chapter). The important surge in exports of certified cocoa in Cote d'Ivoire was to a large extent enabled by the increase of certified area of production and the rise in the global demand for certified cocoa by chocolates companies mainly in Europe.

The early adoption of VSS certification did not lead to improved environmental outcomes in the cocoa sector. Cocoa farmers would traditionally plant their cocoa as part of an agroforestry system, where thinned forest cover would provide shade for the cocoa trees. The traditional agroforestry production methods require few inputs, relying instead on natural forest soil fertility and shade from other trees. As cocoa production shifted towards more intensive production systems, more inputs such as fertilizer were required to address depleted soil fertility. In addition, intensification led to widespread occurrence of pest and disease because less diverse crop-ping systems are more prone to disease and pest outbreaks. For example, in Côte d'Ivoire the Cocoa Swollen Shoot Virus Disease, which was thought to have been eradicated in the 1950s, resurfaced in 2014. In addition, increased production was accompanied by deforestation and land degradation, as farmers expanded their pro-duction area and intensified production on existing land without investing in land management improvements.

The adoption of different varieties of cocoa trees may also contribute to unsustainable management practices. When certain cocoa hybrids were introduced, such as the Upper Amazon hybrid cocoa, farmers were able to begin growing their cocoa without shade. This change in light conditions meant that farmers needed to weed more frequently and apply fertilizer more regularly to sustain production. Still, many farmers were unable to adopt these cultivation practices either due to lack of financial resources or lack of adequate training (Wessel and Quist-Wessel 2015). These conditions create a feedback loop. Poor cocoa farmers who use a low amount of inputs and inadequate pest and disease controls experience low yields and are stuck in a system that limits their ability to increase their income and lift themselves out of poverty.

7.4   Private Sector Sustainability Standards

As high-income consumers have become increasingly aware of environ-mental challenges in the agrifood system, the private sector has developed strategies to take advantage of consumers' willingness to pay for sustainable outcomes. Products that are certified to be consistent with the sustainability standards should, in principle, be able to be sold at a higher price, since the standards identify product characteristics that are desirable to consumers. Therefore, the adoption of these standards by importing firms influences how consumers perceive products. They bridge consumers' concerns for the way goods are produced with globalized commodity chains that depend on standardized quality attributes to reach international markets (Ponte and Gibbon 2005). While research has shown the existence of consumer demand for Fairtrade products (see for example Hiscox et al. 2015), in practice, there is limited evidence of consumer willingness to pay for chocolate that is certified as sustainably produced. Furthermore, the outcomes on productivity and farmer livelihoods have been mixed.

Different VSS regimes include different provisions that will affect market access and trade. Fiorini et al. (Chapter 6, this volume) distinguish between VSS regimes developed by nongovernmental organizations (Fairtrade VSS and those developed by private firms (corporate backed VSS) and identifying possible channels through which these two types of VSS will impact trade and sustainable development. The authors highlight the importance of understanding the impact of VSS on pricing, supply chain competitiveness, certificate design, and production and provision of public goods, such as education. They conclude that the effectiveness of each regime with respect to achieving particular sustainability outcomes will depend on how these channels are affected.

Standards include diverse requirements that cocoa farmers need to meet to be certified and gain access to high-value markets. The two dominant VSS standards for cocoa in Côte d'Ivoire, Fairtrade and UTZ/Rainforest alliance, reflect different views on the type of intervention that will lead to sustainable production outcomes. According to the classification developed in Chapter 6 by Fiorini et al. in this volume, the UTZ/RA systems can be considered 'corporate backed' standards, while Fairtrade standards fall into the category of 'fair trade' labelling initiatives.

The UTZ Certified and Rainforest Alliance (RA) systems place a strong emphasis on encouraging farmers to adopt good production practices, which is expected to increase productivity and improve working conditions for farmers and labourers. The UTZ/RA sustainable agriculture standard includes four main principles: effective management, biodiversity conservation, natural resource conservation, and improved livelihoods. The UTZ/RA standard also incorporates a set of pesticide management policies that seek to reduce the use of hazardous pesticides and to promote, as an alternative, integrated pest management. The standard is developing two lists of pesticides – the first identifying pesticides that are prohibited on UTZ/RA certified farms and the second identifying pesticides that can be used only under certain conditions and that will be phased out. The UTZ/RA standard does not intervene directly in pricing based on the underlying philosophy that long-term sustainability is possible only if the underlying market conditions support the decisions to satisfy the standards requirements.

VSS regimes are also evolving so that technology and satellite images may play a larger role assisting farmers to determine what targeted interventions will improve their productivity. For example, Rainforest Alliance has launched the Ag-Tech Developer Challenge, a competition to create a remote sensing data product to support the mobile-enabled farm development plans (FDPs) on cocoa farms (Rainforest Alliance 2019). In addition to the FDPs, the remote sensing can allow tracking of land use and deforestation and the adoption of good agricultural practices by cocoa farms, enabling the assessment of how individual farms are performing in relation to standards.

Fairtrade, on the other hand, focuses on providing economic stability to producers by ensuring minimum prices and providing price premiums (Minten et al. 2015). The approach intervenes directly on prices and farmers' economic incentives, ensuring more income predictability, rather than following the UTZ/RA approach, which allows markets to determine prices for cocoa beans. When the market price is higher than the Fairtrade minimum price, producers should receive the current market price or the price negotiated at contract signing. The impact of the Fairtrade minimum price on farmer income is also related to the price stabilization efforts of the governments. In a low-price environment the Fairtrade minimum price may not take effect. For example, in 2018 the world price of cocoa fell making the price premium established by Fairtrade unworkable because it was less than the price guaranteed by the government of Côte d'Ivoire (Fairtrade 2018). In 2018, Fairtrade increased both the minimum price for cocoa as well as the premium provided to farmers organizations to be used on projects of their choice (Fairtrade 2018). Fairtrade requires farmers to organize into democratic organizations and create a development plan to address challenges such as health care, education, and clean water. These projects are financed through the Fairtrade premiums that the organizations receive from selling their products to exporters.

The difference in the structure of standards and certification has implications for the incentives that farmers face to adopt and maintain specific sustainable agricultural practices, and thus deserves closer scrutiny. However, because of limited data availability the following analysis was not able to identify differences in outcomes economic and environmental outcomes between these two approaches.

7.5   Data and Methodology

7.5.1   Data

The analysis presented in this chapter relies on publicly available data collected by the KIT Royal Tropical Institute based in the Netherlands in the context of a research project entitled "Demystifying the Cocoa Sector in Ghana and Côte d'Ivoire" (Bymolt et al, 2018)[1]. That study serves as descriptive desk research that provides household data and analyses the major aspects of cocoa production and marketing. Fieldwork was carried out in the cocoa growing regions of Ghana and Côte d'Ivoire in late 2016 and early 2017. This study focuses on Côte d'Ivoire because of the gaps in the data collected in Ghana. A random sample of approximately 1,500 household surveys was collected in each country. This was complemented by thirty-seven focus group discussions in each country. The data are structured around households rather than individual producers and highlight the various roles played by different household members in the production of cocoa. Unfortunately, the dataset did not provide adequate variation in the adoption of the two main standards to allow for a deeper analysis of why farmers choose one type of standard over another. Among the certified producers interviewed in 2017, only 11 per cent certified with Fairtrade, while 89 per cent with UTZ/RA and 15 per cent with both Fairtrade and UTZ/RA. Therefore, the empirical analysis that follows treats Fairtrade and UTZ/RA standards together and does not differentiate between the determinants of adoption for these two different standards.

The survey included a set of variables to check a posteriori whether the sample selection method had effectively controlled for possible selection bias (Blackman and Rivera 2010). Those variables include household socio-economic characteristics (age and sex of the household head; size of the household, i.e. number of people in household [HH]; level of

---

[1] Data available for download at www.kit.nl/project/demystifying-cocoa-sector.

education of head of HH); farm-specific features such as land size, number of trees, use of soil management techniques, and ecosystem conservation; and other socio-economic factors such as access to credit and training and engagement in local networks (ability of farmers to network and get agricultural related information aspects including prices). Other variables include the importance of cocoa for the household economy, off-farm opportunities, and land tenure.[2]

The survey identified current agronomic and environmental practices relating to land use, following the 2010 version of the SAN standard (Sustainable Agriculture Network 2010): ecosystem conservation, water use, pests, and soil. Since the survey asked certified farmers about their practices before joining certification, the data can highlight whether farmers changed their practices after joining certification schemes.

7.5.2 Methodology

The household survey data provide reliable information to better understand the determinants of VSS adoption. In addition, household data allow the examination of how VSS adoption would lead to changes in production and management practices at the household level and subsequently to different environmental and economic outcomes.

The data were analysed using a pair-matched case control method. This method is frequently employed in epidemiological (Jewell 2003) and ecological studies (Benayas et al. 2009) to compare pairs of like individuals whose only observable difference was whether or not they participated in a particular treatment. In this study the treatment is whether they had chosen to become certified for particular standards. Outcomes for the paired samples were compared using the Wilcoxon signed rank test, which tests whether there are systematic differences within pairs, and the McNemar chi-square test for marginal homogeneity, which tests differences between paired proportions for discrete variables. This method's approach ensures that, based on the information at hand a priori, pairs of farms share similar biophysical and accessibility attributes. A total of 94 farms were matched (47 pairs) during the months of January to February of 2017, ranging in size from 0.4 to 11 hectares. Pairs were obtained from adjacent neighbours. For large farms, identifying a suitable pair sometimes required selecting farms from neighbouring municipalities. In the absence of the baseline survey, information obtained

---

[2] See Appendix Table 7.7 for the list of variables used in the study.

was only that for the period after the adoption of certification. To understand farmers' previous state before certification, the survey used recall questions to those who adopt certification. As for those who did not adopt the certification, the survey investigated on their use of agricultural practices including land intensification and soil, water, and ecosystem conservation over the years.

Other available methods used for the adoption and impact of cocoa certification include econometric modelling, such as logit models (Bryk and Raudenbush 1992; Arrègle 2003). The Logit model is used to derive the probability of an event in function of a set of characteristics observed on farmers in the sample. In fact, the explanatory variable Yi takes the value 1 if the farmer (1) adopts the VSS, and 0 otherwise. In general, the adoption of VSS may be attributed to a combination of determinants, both from farmers and certification schemes. However, the data in the chapter relate only to household level because of limited data available on specific schemes.

7.6   Household Determinants and Impacts of Certification

7.6.1   Analysis of the Determinants of Cocoa Certification

To understand the determinants associated with the type of farmers who participate in selling certified cocoa, we estimated a logit of certified versus non-certified farmers (Table 7.1) and looked at the probability that a farmer adopts the VSS (Fairtrade or UTZ). We include on the right-hand side of the regression socio-demographic characteristics of households (age and sex of the household head, size of the household, i.e. number of people in household [HH], level of education of head of HH); farm-specific features (land size) and other socio-economic factors such as access to credit and technical assistance. Hence, the certification status of a farmer is regressed upon those socio-demographic characteristics of households- and farm-specific features that can potentially affect the decision to adopt the certification.

The results show that the heads of VSS-certified households are older and more likely to have been involved in cocoa training school. Older farmers are seen as more experienced to household heads. The variable measuring farm size for cocoa production is significant indicating that certified farmers devoted most of their production land to cocoa cultivation. In addition, farmers have access to credit for their cocoa production, which allows them to adopt VSS.

The analysis presented in this chapter also examines farmer motivation to join certification. According to the survey data, farmers' motivation to join

Table 7.1 *Determinants of Participation in Certification Schemes at Farmer Level* (n = 47)

Variables	Unit	Coef.	p-Value
Socio-demographic Characteristics			
Gender of head of household	Male = 1	0.06	0.957
		(0.277)	
Age]65, + [	Years	1.018*	0.09
		(0.678)	
Head of household completed primary school	Yes = 1	1.100	0.551
		(1.167)	
Head of household other education (informal)[3]	Yes = 1	0.209*	0.066
		(1.398)	
Household size [11, + [	Number	0.031	0.198
		(0.324)	
Dependency ratio	Share	0.420***	0.000
		(0.082)	
Farm-Specific Features			
Cocoa land size cultivated	Ha	0.058*	0.099
		(0.029)	
Non-cocoa land size owned	Ha	−0.049(0.043)	0.259
Other socio-economic factors Training on cocoa	Yes = 1	1.142*** (0.308)	0.000
Credit received for cocoa (finance)	Yes = 1	1.050*** (0.276)	0.000
Cocoa most important crop	Yes = 1	− 0.562(0.368)	0.127
Constant		−2.692**(1.310)	0.04
R^2		0.30	

***Significant at 1%; **significant at 5%; *significant at 10%. Figures in parentheses are estimated standard deviations. Nb Obs. = 47. Dependent Variable: Adoption of VSS (yes/no) using the Logit model.
Source: Authors' calculations based on Dataverse survey 2017.

certification schemes relate to a combination of economic and social factors. The results highlight the importance of services provided by the certification schemes, such as training on sustainable cocoa production and the provision

---

[3] Farmers in our sample had access to informal education such as trainings and workshops either in their local language or in French.

of crucial market and financial information. The fact that farmers participated in trainings and workshops on cocoa sustainability even though their
level of formal education is low as well as experience gained over time created
awareness of the importance of certification and its benefits. Other factors
included the accessibility to credit and the size of land devoted to cocoa
cultivation, which provides scope for planting and expanding cocoa production. Most certified households reported that cocoa was their main crop,
whereas noncertified households had other priority crops.

In sum, many factors can influence cocoa farmers to join and adopt the
voluntary sustainability standards. The analysis of the farmers under
study captured socio-economic, environmental, and other factors
which included the accessibility to credit, capacity building through
technical assistance and training on cocoa's sustainability in production,
the size of land devoted to cocoa cultivation which provides scope for
planting, and expanding cocoa production.

7.6.2   Impact of Cocoa Certification on Farmers

7.6.2.1   Difference in Practices Between Certified and Non-certified Farms

The study attempts to evaluate the effects of certification on a number of
variables related to VSS, including farmers' livelihood, economic benefits
of certification, land expansion, and environment aspects.

The majority of land tenures among cocoa farmers under study were
owned by farmers themselves (95 per cent of certified against 79 per cent of
non-certified). These two groups were not significantly different (Table 7.3).
Farmers from both certified and non-certified cocoa farms reported that
other members in the households contribute to the household income,
indicating no significant difference between the two groups, as shown in
Table 7.3. However, there exists a significant difference in the role that cocoa
plays in household economy. As noted earlier, the majority of certified
households reported that cocoa was their main crop as opposed to non-
certified households and that they devoted a larger proportion of their farm
to cocoa (Tables 7.2 and 7.3: land devoted to cocoa in hectares and number
of farmers for whom cocoa is the main activity).

Certification will likely have an impact on the production choices of
farmers, including land expansion and input use. Certification schemes
influence the producers' decisions related to quantity of production, crop
selection, and level of processing and production technology (Fiorini

et al., Chapter 6, this volume). Tables 7.2 and 7.5 show that certified cocoa farmers have increased the land cultivation devoted to cocoa after certification with significant difference at the 5 per cent level. For example, Table 7.2 shows that the median number of cocoa producing hectares for certified farmers increased by 2 hectares after certification. This implies that voluntary sustainability schemes create incentives for farmers to adopt more sustainable production practices. However, non-certified farmers have also increased the total area from 135.4 hectares to 195 hectares. The land devoted to cocoa increased from 204.6 hectares to 331.9 hectares, an increase of 62 per cent during from 2012 to 2017. This situation has made the supply chain more competitive with certified and non-certified producers seeking to gain access to global markets. In view of the difference in competitiveness observed in the supply of cocoa products between certified and non-certified farmers, adopting a VSS scheme can provide access to alternative supply channels for participating farmer organizations and improve market access for certified products (Fiorini et al., Chapter 6, this volume).

Most VSS recognize the importance of securing the long-term supply of cocoa products. This trend is visible in cocoa production in Cote d'Ivoire, where climate change and land use pressures threaten to reduce future supply. Certified farmers who belong to farmers' organizations agreed that adopting VSS helped them in several ways. First, addressing environmental problems that limit production, vulnerability to climate change and farmer incomes, will make the production more viable into the future and help ensure continued supply. Second, VSS create linkages between cocoa producers and buyers, which can help ensure that farmers can sell their certified product and firms can access the supply they need. Finally, VSS linkages help to drive change at the production level because the predictable relationship can reassure farmers that their investments will be repaid at a later stage. Table 7.3 shows that certified farmers were more likely than uncertified farmers to choose environmentally friendly practices, such as ecosystem conservation, water use, and water management. Certified farms showed significant differences in renovation of cocoa plantation by stumping over the previous five years with a view to increase and enhance land productivity: 64 per cent of certified farmers as compared to 51 per cent of non-certified farmers. Both certified and non-certified farmers applied synthetic and organic fertilizers and used soil analysis methods and biological control. However, the use of synthetic and organic fertilizer is not significant for certified or non-certified farmers. In contrast, there was a significant difference in the use of soil

Table 7.2 *Difference in Practices Between Certified and Non-certified*
Farms: Continuous Variables (n = 94)

Variables	Non-certified Median Values	Certified	Wilcoxon Test	p-Value	% Difference
Land Expansion					
Land size devoted to cocoa (ha)	3.492	3.990	595	0.004*	14.26
No. of ha expanded since certification/ previous 5 years	1.03	2	670	0.100	94.17
Ecosystem Conservation					
No. of trees per hectare	1	3	493	0.042*	200
No. of trees aged 5 years per hectare	1	2	489.5	0.752	100
Socio-demographic Characteristics					
Age of household's head	55	56	559	0.801	1.81
No. of people in the household	5	5	596.50	0.368	0
Education level of the head of household	2	2	232.5	0.106	0
Highest educational level of HH members	7	10	368.5	0.031*	42.85

*Significant at the 0.05 level.
Source: Authors' calculations based on Dataverse survey 2017.

analysis for proper application of fertilizer: 9.57 per cent certified farmers used it as compared to 3.19 per cent for non-certified farmers. Waste management activities were significantly different between certified and non-certified farmers: 89 per cent of certified farmers collected their trash from the field while only 11 per cent of non-certified farmers did so; 25 per cent of non-certified farmers recycled their trash while 70 per cent of them burned or buried their trash (Table 7.4).

Table 7.3 *Difference in Practices Between Certified and Non-certified Farms: Dichotomous Variables (n = 94)*

Variables	Non-certified	Certified	McNemar's Chi-square Test	p-Value	% Difference
	Median Values				
Land Intensification					
No. of farmers who renovated the cocoa plantation by new planting since certification/ previous 5 years	24	30	2.049	0.123	+25
No. of farmers who renovated the cocoa plantation by stumping since certification/ previous 5 years	17	23	3.051	0.024*	+35.29
Soil Management and Conservation					
No. of farmers who use organic fertilizer	32	41	3.694	0.1363	+28.12
No. of farmers who use synthetic fertilizer	37	32	2.421	0.132	−13.51
No. of farmers who use soil analysis	3	9	5.214	0.021*	+200
Integrated Crop Management and Waste Management					
No. of farmers who use biological control	3	9	1.265	0.04	+200
No. of households that collect trash from the field	10	42	23.954	0.001*	+320
No. of households that recycle	12	42	25.014	0.000*	+250
No. of households that burn or bury trash	33	3	20.325	0.000*	−90
Water Conservation					
No. of farmers who use water-saving technologies	13	27	9.259	0.002*	+107.7

Table 7.3 (*cont.*)

Variables	Non-certified	Certified	McNemar's Chi-square Test	p-Value	% Difference
	Median Values				
No. of farmers who throw waste water to the field	12	1	5.001	0.012*	−91.67
Ecosystem Conservation					
No. of farmers who planted trees outside the cocoa plots	17	35	5.895	0.012*	+105
Socio-demographic Characteristics					
No. of farmers for whom cocoa is the main activity	31	42	8.591	0.010*	+44
No. of households that have other members contributing to HH income	25	27	0.17	0.56	+8
No. of farmers with land title	38	43	5.879	0.052*	+13.15
No. of households that have off-farm income	25	28	0.365	0.458	+12
Other Socio-economic Factors					
No. of households that have access to information on prices	39	41	0.002	0.978	+5.13
No. of households who sell to the cooperative	17	43	16.326	0.000*	+170.59
No. of households who had access to credit	16	40	6.235	0.002*	+150
No. of farmers who belongs to organizations	12	39	19.324	0.000*	+2.25

*Significant at the 0.05 level.
Source: Authors' calculations based on Dataverse survey 2017.

7.6.2.2   Difference in Practices for Certified Farms Before and After Joining Certification

The data indicate that the use of these good practices increased in the years after farmers join the certification schemes. Certified farmers increased the use of integrated waste management strategies after the adoption of VSS (Table 7.4). In terms of the management of soil and its conservation, both certified and non-certified farmers used organic and synthetic fertilizers; however, certification leads to an increased practice of analysing the soil which can lead to better targeted use of fertilizers (Tables 7.3 and 7.4). Before certification, cocoa farmers preferred not to use soil analysis methods. However, the number significantly increased after they joined the schemes. Before certification, the majority of certified farmers were not involved in any of the required practices. They used to burn or bury plastics (87 per cent) and very few used to recycle those plastics (only 5 per cent). Overall, the adoption of practices such as water conservation, soil management, integrated waste management, and eco-system conservation significantly increased after farmers joined the certification program (Table 7.4).

In terms of socio-economic benefits for families, income from cocoa constituted on average 62 per cent of the total income of the farmers interviewed. Data on the cocoa prices obtained from farmers indicate that certification can lead to higher prices (Table 7.5). The certified farmer's average price was 9 per cent higher than non-certified farmers' price – US$ 1.75/kg as compared to US$ 1.63/kg. Results on VSS adoption and revenue generated indicate a statistically significant difference in the income of cocoa farmers. The average income earned from cocoa production was US$ 683.54 per hectare and US$ 520 per hectare for certified and non-certified farmers respectively (Table 7.5). Certified producers obtained an increase of 31.44 per cent in income generated for certified cocoa sales. Income results are determined by the interaction between improved yields and higher prices. Certified farmers obtained higher yields (414.14 kg/ha higher than that of non-certified farmers 328.57 kg/ha). The increased yield for certified farms compared to non-certified ones can be partly attributed to the improved efficiency generated by changing production methods and technical knowledge from training programmes associated with certification system. In terms of profits generated, the results indicated a statistically significant difference with an increase of 7.4 per cent higher for certified farmers than for non-certified farmers (US$ 653.33/ha compared to US$ 608.47/ha).

Table 7.4 *Difference in Practices for Certified Farms Before and After Joining Certification* (n = 94)

Variables	Before Certification	Current	Wilcoxon/ McNemar Test	*p*-Value	% Difference
	Median Values				
Water Conservation					
No. of farmers who use water-saving technologies	14	27	9.015	0.001*	+92.86
No. of farmers who throw waste water to the field	25	1	19.875	0.000*	−0.96
Soil Management and Conservation					
No. of farmers who use soil analysis	0	9	6.521	0.000*	−
Integrated Waste Management					
No. of farmers who collect trash from the field	3	42	35.251	0.000*	+1,300
No. of farmers who recycle	4	42	32.781	0.000*	+2,000
No. of farmers who burn or bury trash	41	3	34.325	0.000*	+92.68
Ecosystem Conservation					
No. of trees per hectare	1	3	215.6	0.004*	+200
No. of farmers who planted trees outside the cocoa plots	12	35	21.365	0.000*	+191.66

*Significant at the 0.05 level.

Source: Authors' calculations based on Dataverse survey 2017.

This analysis highlighted that the adoption of VSS increases both costs and revenues along the value chain. However, producers tend to be better off financially when participating in VSS. As the adoption of VSS leads to an increase of additional costs, for example due to investment requirements to environmental practices, farmers reported the need to be cautious when choosing the certification schemes. In either case, these variables reinforce each other to produce important socioeconomic and environmental benefits (on household livelihoods and welfare) at the local and country level. The study found that socio-economic characteristics (age and sex of the household head, size of household, level of education of the head) and farm-specific factors such as size of land devoted to cocoa cultivation determine farmers' adoption of certification programs in Côte d'Ivoire.

Fiorini et al. (Chapter 6, this volume) argued that in the certification membership, certificate design, and the nature of certificate ownership, were important elements to be considered. Premiums for certified cocoa provide incentives to invest in improved cocoa products and social standards. As noted earlier, among the certified producers interviewed in 2017, only 11 per cent certified with Fairtrade, while 89 per cent certified with UTZ/RA and 15 per cent with both Fairtrade and UTZ/RA. Most of the farmers interviewed reported that over the previous five

Table 7.5 *Adoption of VSS and Influence of Some Characteristics*

Indicators	Certified	Non-certified	p-Value
Average cocoa income (US$/ha)	683.54	520.05	0.000*
Average cocoa price (US$/kg)	1.75	1.63	0.000*
Average productivity (kg/ha)	414.14	328.57	0.001*
Average cocoa profit (US$/ha)	653.33	608.47	0.004*
Average cocoa land cultivated(ha)	3.990	3.492	0.004*

* Significant at the 0.05 level using Wilcoxon's rank sum test.
Source: Authors' calculations based on Dataverse survey 2017.

years the premium has been lower than expected. Even though Fairtrade does have a fixed premium price, as well as a minimum price under which Fairtrade-certified cocoa cannot be sold, this minimum price has been well below the current world market price and the price guaranteed by the government. In a high-price environment, the Fairtrade minimum price does not take effect. Double certified farmers reported that although Fairtrade failed to meet the expectation of premiums payment, there are other benefits of working with certification, such as training and capacity building which can lead to higher yields and better quality of cocoa products. In addition, with Fairtrade, farmers organize themselves into democratic organizations and create a Development Plan to address challenges such as health care, education, and clean water. These public goods are financed through the Fairtrade premiums that the organizations receive from selling their products to exporters.

7.7   Conclusion

The literature examining the participation of cocoa farmers in certification schemes has primarily emphasized the economic gains farmers perceive from joining these schemes and has offered less insight into the other determinants. Despite the increasing global demand for VSS and the growing number of cocoa producers that supply their products under these schemes, less attention has been given to the adoption of cocoa certification and its impact on smallholder farmers livelihood in Cote d'Ivoire. From our analysis, we conclude that economic gain is only one factor influencing adoption of certification schemes.

The study found that socio-economic characteristics of cocoa households and farm-specific factors determine farmers' adoption of certification programs in Côte d'Ivoire. Older farmers are likely to adopt certification, and the probability is even higher when they have access to training and credit devoted to cocoa cultivation. Through certification, cocoa farmers received training and have gained new skills and capacities that helped them mobilize assets to invest in more sustainable production practices. In addition, farmers gained access to information and new technology to increase yield. This result raises questions regarding the need to incorporate young producers in public and private interventions targeting future sustainable production.

In terms of impact of certification, the analysis suggested that the adoption of private VSS by cocoa farmers has had positive impacts on household livelihoods and welfare through the increase of land devoted to cocoa cultivation and sustainability practices by farmers. Voluntary sustainability standards provide a useful tool to enhance the livelihoods of cocoa farmers through prices and improve environmental outcomes. The adoption of practices such as water conservation, soil management, integrated waste management, and ecosystem conservation has significantly increased after farmers joined the certification program. Incomes from cocoa sales have increased for certified farmers owing to the increased yield through the improved efficiency generated by changes in production methods and improved technical knowledge from training programmes associated with the certification system.

Cocoa certification in Côte d'Ivoire demonstrated that VSS can create connections between local social-ecological systems and market forces and have the potential to generate incentives for improved management which can lead to positive environmental outcomes and improved farmers' incomes and welfare. Efforts from the public and private sector's actors to connect farmers to global supply chains in the institutional arrangement governing agricultural trade have the potential to improve final sustainability outcomes as well as the costs of achieving these outcomes.

References

Arrègle, J.-L., (2003). Les modèles linéaires hiérarchiques: principes et illustration, *Management* 6: 1–28.

Bacon, C. (2010). 'A Spot of Coffee in Crisis: Nicaraguan Smallholder Cooperatives, Fair Trade Networks, and Gendered Empowerment'. *Latin American Perspectives* 37: 50–71.

Benayas, J. M. R., Newton, A. C., Diaz, A. and Bullock, J. M. (2009). 'Enhancement of Biodiversity and Ecosystem Services by Ecological Restoration: A Meta-analysis'. *Science* 325: 1121–1124.

Beuchelt, T. and Zeller, M. (2011). 'Profits and Poverty: Certification's Troubled Link for Nicaragua's Organic and Fairtrade Coffee Producers'. *Ecological Economics* 70: 1316–1324.

Blackman, A and Rivera, J. E. (2010). 'The Evidence Base for Environmental and Socioeconomic Impacts of "Sustainable" Certification'. RFF Discussion Paper 10–10. Washington, DC: Resources for the Future.

Bryk, A. S. and Raudenbush, S. W. (1992). *Hierarchical Linear Models: Applications and Data Analysis Methods.* Sage Publications.

Bymolt, R., Laven, A. and Tyszler, M. (2018). *Demystifying the Cocoa Sector in Ghana and Côte d'Ivoire.* The Royal Tropical Institute (KIT).

Cargill. (2019) 'Re-defining Our Goals. How We Are Evolving the Cargill Cocoa Promise. Available at www.cargill.com/sustainability/cocoa/re-defining-our-goals.

Central Intelligence Agency. (2012). *World Factbook*. Washington, DC: CIA.

Chiputwa B., Spielman D. and Qaim M. (2015). 'Food Standards, Certification, and Poverty among Coffee Farmers in Uganda'. *World Development* 66: 400–412.

Confectionary News. (2017). 'Cocoa Price for Ivorian Farmers May Drop 30% amid Widespread Poverty'. Available at www.confectionerynews.com/Article/2017/03/24/Cocoa-price-for-Ivorian-farmers-may-drop30?utm_source=copyright&utm_medium=OnSite&utm_campaign=copyright.

Confectionary Production. (2019). 'Rainforest Alliance Calls on Developers to Help Cocoa Farms'. 8 February 2019. Available at www.confectioneryproduction.com/news/25345/rainforest-alliance-calls-on-developers-to-help-cocoa-farms/.

Fairtrade International. (2018). 'Cocoa Farmers to Earn More through a Higher Fairtrade Minimum Price'. Available at www.fairtrade.net/new/latest-news/single-view/article/cocoa-farmers-to-earn-more-through-a-higher-fairtrade-minimum-price.html.

FAOSTAT. (2017). *FAO On-lineStatistical Database on Crop Production*. Food and Agriculture Organization. Available at www.fao.org/faostat/en/#data/QC.

Fountain, A. and Huetz-Adams, F. (2018). 'Cocoa Barameter 2018'. Voice Network. Available at www.voicenetwork.eu/wp-content/uploads/2019/08/Cocoaborometer2018_web4.pdf.

Gayi, S. and Tsowou, K. (2015). *Cocoa Industry: Integrating Small Farmers into the Global Value Chain*. United Nations Conference on Trade and Development.

Giovannucci, D. and Ponte, S. (2005). 'Standards as a New Form of Social Contract? Sustainability Initiatives in the Coffee Industry'. *Food Policy* 30: 284–301.

Government of Ghana. (2018). Available at www.ghana.gov.gh/index.php/news/4512-ghana-cote-d-ivoire-sign-agreement-on-cocoa.

Hiscox, M. J., Hainmueller, J. and Sequeira, S. (2015). 'Consumer Demand for the Fair Trade Label: Evidence from a Multi-Store Field Experiment'. *Review of Economics and Statistics* 97: 242–256.

Ibanez, M. and Blackman, A. (2016). 'Is Eco-Certification a Win–Win for Developing Country Agriculture? Organic Coffee Certification in Colombia'. *World Development* 82: 14–27.

Jewell, N. (2003). *Statistics for Epidemiology*. Chapman & Hall/CRC.

Markelova, H. and Mwangi, E. (2010). 'Collective Action for Smallholder Market Access: Evidence and Implications for Africa'. *Review of Policy Research* 27: 621–640.

Minten, B., Tamru, S., Engida, E., and Kuma, T. (2015). 'Transforming Staple Food Value Chains in Africa: The Case of Teff in Ethiopia'. *The Journal of Development Studies* 52: 627–645.

Perez-Aleman, P. (2012). 'Global Standards and Local Knowledge Building: Upgrading Small Producers in Developing Countries. *Proceedings of the National Academy of Sciences of the USA* 109: 12344–12349.

Ponte, S. and Gibbon, P. (2006). 'Quality Standards, Conventions and the Governance of Global Value Chains'. *Journal of Economic and Society* 34: 1–31.

Rainforest Alliance. (2019). 'How Can Digital Technology Improve Supply Chain Sustainability?' https://utz.org/better-business-hub/sourcing-sustainable-products/how-can-digital-technology-improve-supply-chain-sustainability/.

Rueda, X. and Lambin, E. (2013). 'Linking Globalization to Local Land Uses: How Eco-consumers and Gourmands Are Changing the Colombian coffee landscapes'. *World Development* 41: 286–301.

Rusman, A., de Adelhart Toorop, R., de Boer, J., de Groot Ruiz, A. (2018). 'Cocoa Farmer Income. The Household Income of Cocoa Farmers in Côte d'Ivôire and Strategies for Improvement. True Price/Fairtrade, April 2018. Available at www .fairtrade.net/fileadmin/user_upload/content/2009/resources/2018–04_Report_Fairtrade_Cocoa_Farmer_Income.pdf.

Sustainable Agricultural Network. (2010). 'Sustainable Agriculture Standard 2010'. Available at https://sustainableagriculturenetwork.squarespace.com/.

Wessel, M., and Quist-Wessel, P. M. (2015). 'Cocoa Production in West Africa: A Review and Analysis of Recent Developments'. *NJAS – Wageningen Journal of Life Sciences* 74–75: 1–7.

World Cocoa Foundation. (2016). 'Learning as We Grow'. *Putting CocoaAction into Practice*. Abidjan: World Cocoa Foundation. Available at www .worldcocoafoundation.org/wp-content/uploads/2016-CocoaActionReport-English_WEB_10-30.pdf.

Appendix

Table 7.6 *Number of Producers/Operators of Certified Cocoa by Standard*

Label	2011	2012	2013	2014	2015	2016	2017
Fairtrade	20,518	33,668	32,723	31,436	32,494		
UTZ	34,869	81,986.5	129,104	170,435	193,444	265,000	329,978
Total	55,387	115,654.5	161,827	201,871	225,938	265,000	329,978
Relative growth	108.81%	39.92%	24.74%	11.92%	17.29%	24.52%	—

Source: Compiled using data in Potts et al. (2014) and data supplied by Rainforest Alliance.

Table 7.7 *List of Variables Used in the Study*

Variables	Metrics/Modalities
Socio-demographic Characteristics	
Age of the household head	Number
Gender of the household head	1 = Male, 2 = Female
Household size	Number
People in household	Number
Education level of head of HH	1 = Primary, 2 = Secondary, 3 = University, 4 = Informal, 5 = Formal
Farmers with off-farm income	Number
Farm-Specific Features	
Land size	Hectare
Number of trees per hectare	Number
Other Socio-economic Factors	
Access to credit	1 = Yes; 2 = No, Number
Training	1 = Yes; 2 = No, Number
Local networks/organizations	1 = Yes; 2 = No, Number
Land Intensification and Soil Management and Conservation Aspects	
Renovation	1 = Yes; 2 = No
Use of organic fertilizer	1 = Yes; 2 = No
Use of synthetic fertilizer	1 = Yes; 2 = No
Farmer who use soil analysis	Number
Farmer who use biological control	Number
HHs that collect trash from field	Number
HHs that recycle	Number
HHs that burn or bury trash	Number
Farmers who plant trees outside cocoa plots	Number
Water Conservation Aspects	
Farmers who use water-saving technologies	Number
Farmers who throw waste water to the field	Number
Economic Factors	
Cocoa income	USD
Cocoa price	USD
Productivity	Kg
Profit	USD

HH, household.
Source: Authors' compilations.

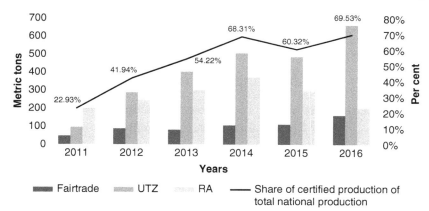

Figure 7.1 Trend in the three VSS adopted in the cocoa sector in Côte d'Ivoire over years. *Source*: Data from standard-setting organizations and FAO (2018).

8

Unblocking the Trade Pipes

Using Blockchain Technology to Facilitate Trade
for Sustainable Development

ALISA DICAPRIO, CHRISTINE MCDANIEL, BADRI G.
NARAYANAN, AND HANNA C. NORBERG

8.1 Introduction

There is an interesting paradox in modern international trade. According to theory and empirical evidence, the closer two countries are to one another, the more they trade, all else being equal (e.g., Head and Mayer 2013). What we witness, however, is that the countries that are situated geographically or economically distant from advanced economies tend to be those that stand to gain the most from more trade. For instance, states of the Pacific and Caribbean Islands are geographically distant from most high income and developed countries, and economically distant in terms of different institutions, cultures, and political and governance structures. Countries of Southeast Asia and Africa are not great distances from high growth areas, but there is a great deal of economic distance between them. Overcoming these distances to increase cross border exchange for these countries will require new ways to facilitate bilateral trust, transparency, and accountability.

Blockchain technology was first invented to facilitate transactions between parties that did not necessarily know or trust each other. One of its first applications – and what most people still commonly confuse it with – was cryptocurrencies, such as Bitcoin. Blockchain technology's most basic function, however, is to facilitate exchanges between

The authors are grateful for helpful comments by Cosimo Beverelli, Jürgen Kurtz, Damian Raess, Joseph Francois, Andrea O'Sullivan, Walter Valdivia, Jacqueline Yang, and the participants of the 2018 World Trade Forum at the World Trade Institute in Florence, Italy, for helpful comments. Any remaining errors are our own.

untrusting parties and provide a permanent record of the transactions. Trust, transparency, and accountability are the most important factors in trading across great distances; and so it is unsurprising that blockchain's characteristics make it particularly relevant to international commerce, where the use of several intermediaries including banks, customs brokers, and online exchanges serves as a proxy for trust.

Blockchain is best seen not as a stand-alone solution to trade frictions but rather part of the second wave of the information communications technology (ICT) revolution that can bring trade facilitation to the next level. The first wave of the ICT revolution made it easier for ideas to move across borders, and cross border separation of factories soon followed. Production was unbundled and carried out in the most cost-effective location, and digital data flows have kept factories, entities, and persons along the supply chain in constant communication regardless of distance (Baldwin 2016). This can work well within an entity as long as there is a central point of information, although once the exchange occurs between entities that are at arm's length, frictions tend to appear in the form of administrative costs and delays as each side takes necessary steps for transparency, accountability, and trust.

The novelty of blockchain is that it obviates the need for centralization and offers a decentralized way to exchange information and documents. This not only reduces frictions in the trade process, but also has direct implications for the attainment of several of the Sustainable Development Goals (SDGs).

In this chapter we discuss the potential effects that the emerging technology of blockchain stand to have on the SDGs, by mapping the impact of blockchain to global trade and the resulting effects on trade to the SDGs. To the extent that blockchain technology can facilitate trade, it contributes to the achievement of many of the defined goals by empowering international trade. The 2030 Agenda, as defined by the United Nations in 2015, specifically mentioned the completion of the World Trade Organization (WTO) Doha round as an important venue for realizing the goals. Completion of the round appears unlikely and the political climate for engaging in multilateral liberalization has diminished since the inception of that report. Yet the importance of increased trade for the realization of the goals remains, which only underscores the need for new avenues to trade facilitation.

New emerging technologies such as blockchain do not require multilateral negotiations. In practical terms, blockchain technology offers an avenue "operationalize" trade, thereby adding to the facilitation of SDG attainments (Hoekman 2017). By smoothing the trade process (reducing costs, removing frictions at the border) increased trade can empower small business to trade and grow, and consumers to attain more, and lower priced, goods and food. We dissect three particularly tangible parts of the trade process, which are generally regarded as bottlenecks and have the potential to be relieved by the use of blockchain technology, with disproportionately large benefits for smaller firms and firms in developing countries and least developed countries.

We pursue three WTO (2018b) recommendations for mainstreaming trade to accelerate progress in pursuing the SDGs, namely by lowering trade costs, increasing utilization rates, and supporting small and medium-sized enterprises (SMEs) to engage in international trade. More specifically the implementation of blockchain technology stands to directly impact the following SDGs; according to the 2030 agenda it is vital for SDGs 8 (Decent Work and Economic Growth) and 9 (Industry, Innovation and Infrastructure) that companies have access to national, regional, and global markets, which in turn is imperative for foreign investments, which can provide an important contribution to employment innovation, technology transfer, and productive capacity. The use of blockchain technology facilitates trade and lowers the threshold for firms to enter the global market in general. Furthermore, these innovations are shown to be particularly useful for empowering SMEs to participate in international trade, which corresponds well with SDG 10 (Reduced Inequalities), i.e., to empower the social, economic and political inclusion of all. As discussed in the text that follows, blockchain stands to lower the risks of making international transactions, streamline important paperwork, increase the speed with which goods move thru customs, and make it easier for smaller firms to both adhere to rules of origin and access crucial trade credit.

Furthermore, successful implementation of blockchain technology requires interoperability stemming from multistakeholder engagement, such as governments, the private sector, and civil society as a whole, thereby making SDG 17 (Partnerships) a key component as well.

We find that the potential economic effects of integrating blockchain technology across the trade landscape to increase the preference utilization rate, close part of the trade finance gap, and improve customs processes to be relatively large. Adopting blockchain in the customs space could narrow the preference utilization gap and improve customs processes, which could generate an estimated $1.7 trillion in additional trade and $916.5 billion in economic welfare.[1] In addition, we find blockchain technology could eliminate many of the inefficiencies in trade finance and has the potential to close the trade finance gap by $189 billion. But policymakers will have to figure out regulatory approaches that enable scalability and interoperability for these gains to be fully realized.

Our research strategy employs a mixed methods approach to account for the lack of transactional blockchain data, which remain proprietary and limited given the nascent stage of applications. Instead, we detail how blockchain technology is able to reduce information asymmetries and inefficiencies in trade finance, automate rules of origin and the confirmation process to increase the preference utilization rate, and eliminate the back-and-forth of the same document in the customs process.

Section 8.2 introduces a framework for understanding blockchain as a technology and how it impacts trade. Sections 8.3–8.5 detail each of the three disrupted areas in depth. Section 8.6 estimates the impact of blockchain on trade facilitation through preference utilization, and Section 8.7 concludes with policy implications.

8.2   Conceptual Framework for Blockchain's Impact on Trade

Digital technologies such as blockchain impact trade facilitation largely through the channel of paperless trade.[2] Because of the volume and variety of documentation that accompanies goods when they cross a border, successful trade facilitation increasingly depends on digital technology. Electronic trade documentation systems have clear advantages over paper-based manual customs and border clearance processes. This has spurred many countries to pursue ways to make cross border trade paperless.[3]

The Internet has been the default and primary information transport option for digital data (except for telephone lines) but it is only one type of "transport layer" for digital data. Blockchain can also use the Internet but will require a different approach to businesses and governments

---

[1] All dollar figures are in US dollars unless otherwise noted.

[2] Writ large, trade facilitation is defined as the simplification, modernization, and harmonization of export and import processes. Export and import processes are the 'activities, practices and formalities involved in collecting, presenting, communications and processing data required for the movement of goods in international trade' (WTO 2015).

[3] Implementation of paperless trade measures varies across regions. Developed economies have made the most progress overall, while Latin America and the Caribbean economies have progressed on electronic submission of air cargo manifests and electronic submission of customs declarations. See Trade Facilitation and Paperless Trade Implementation Report (United Nations 2017, p. 20) for a full comparison.

sharing data. There are two important limitations to real-world applications. First, blockchain technology is so fundamentally different from previous technologies that have disrupted trade that it presents a steep learning curve for the decision makers who will apply it. Second, the application of blockchain technology in many cases will require changing regulatory structures in ways that governments participate and do so seamlessly.

It is worth emphasizing that existing structures did not foresee digital distributed technology. Blockchain was not mentioned in 2006 when the United Nations Economic Commission for Europe came out with the paperless trade roadmap, and it was not yet well known or even mentioned in 2013 when the WTO completed negotiating the Trade Facilitation Agreement (UNECE 2006).

Table 8.1 describes the links between the major features of blockchain and articles of the WTO Trade Facilitation Agreement. Each of the four fundamental characteristics of blockchains can solve different problems in trade and trade facilitation.

Much of international trade theory focuses on the physical properties of cross border trade and the role of digital distributed technology is not obvious. Facilitating trust, transparency, and information is one possibility because, in principle, blockchain reduces trade frictions that arise from multiple parties and their corresponding intermediaries reconciling information. In practice, however, blockchain technology can eliminate the need for the intermediary and reconcile information that has been traditionally seen, confirmed, and sometimes even transformed by those intermediaries, including multiple and arm's length (distrusting) parties.[4]

In the text that follows, we provide a brief tour of blockchain technology for a trade audience. Next, we use the framework in Table 8.1 to shine a spotlight on the specific parts of the trade process where blockchain can facilitate trust, transparency, and information, and thereby facilitate trade itself.

8.2.1   A Brief Tour of Blockchain for a Trade Audience

The needs for trust, transparency, and accountability are among the most salient drivers of cross border trade frictions. It is then unsurprising that

---

[4] The bill of lading, as an example, needs to be verified by the buyer, the buyer's bank, the supplier, the supplier's bank, the carrier, as well as others. Confirming that there are no errors and the information in the document is as expected is costly and time consuming.

Table 8.1 *Mapping Blockchain Features to the WTO Trade Facilitation Agreement (TFA)*

Blockchain Characteristic	Features that Blockchain Enables	TFA Articles
Decentralized data storage	• Secure data storage/ transfer • Each partner owns and has visibility of data • No central party holds all the data	Art. 1: Availability of information
Consensus	• Simplification of verification • No need for reconciliation	Art. 8: Border cooperation Art. 10: Formalities Art. 12: Customs cooperation
Immutability	• Risk mitigation • Transparency of transaction • Auditability	Art. 6: Fees and charges Art. 7: Release and clearance Art. 9: Movement
Privacy*	• Sharing of confidential data in a secure way	

Source: Authors' assessment. Note: Privacy is a feature of permissioned blockchains only (e.g., Corda); public blockchains do not share this feature (e.g., Bitcoin, Ethereum). This is an approximate assessment of the Trade Facilitation Agreement Section 1 Articles and does not account for sub-articles that may fall into other categories.

blockchain's characteristics make it particularly relevant to international commerce, where trust is proxied through the use of several intermediaries including banks, customs brokers, online exchanges, and more.

International trade requires the exchange of data and information on the buyer, the seller, the product, as well as where and how the product was made. Other important information for the trade to complete includes shipping and payment information – whether it has been shipped, to whom it is being sent, when payment will be made, and so on.

The two main friction points for data exchange in the trade process are intermediaries and scaling solutions to conduct transactions across a large number of various institutions.

First, consider the role of intermediaries in the exchange of data and information, which enables trade to occur at all. Documented intermediation in trade goes back at least as far as the eleventh century, as Greif (1993) details the role of intermediaries among Maghribi traders. Today, a web of intermediaries has emerged to facilitate a vast expansion of global trade.

Intermediaries have facilitated trade over years by enabling data exchange, transferring liability, and mitigating risk. Intermediation is critical to facilitate activities in markets that are difficult to navigate (Ahn, Khandelwal, and Wei 2011) or where there is a need to ensure credibility and honest behaviour (Olsen 2010). As international commerce expanded across the globe, the role of intermediaries has become embedded.

Intermediaries centralize data and information and enable cross border exchange. Yet many of the trade frictions that persist in modern trade are traced back to the costs and inefficiencies of these intermediaries.

Blockchain architecture removes the need for much existing intermediation by allowing counterparties to know that the data that they see is the same as the data other parties see. As a result, there is a lesser need for multiple parties' verification and checking of documents. Rather than exchange data between entities, each of whom imports that data into their own system, blockchain offers a shared data point visible by multiple parties – i.e., what you are seeing is what I am seeing, and vice versa.

A second friction point in the chain of trade is rooted in the sheer number of counterparties involved in each step of a trade transaction, and the resulting time and costs involved in verification and compliance. Measures such as the WTO Trade Facilitation Agreement have been initiated to overcome these frictions and help traders conduct large numbers of transactions in less costly ways. Existing trade facilitation measures, however, are centralized, and all parties that use that system must undertake an onboarding process to familiarize themselves with each new regime. Further, in cross border transactions, it is unlikely that all parties from end to end (banks, suppliers, the buyer, logistics firms, customs agents, and regulators) will be using the same platform. Indeed, the lack of a single platform has historically been a significant stumbling block for digital innovation. As a result, such innovations to date have been sporadic and largely disjointed, giving rise to the term "digital islands."[5]

---

[5] Blockchain technology was first invented to facilitate transactions between parties that did not necessarily know or trust each other, and one of its first applications – and what most people still commonly confuse it with – was cryptocurrencies, such as Bitcoin. Blockchain technology's most basic function, however, is to facilitate exchanges between untrusting parties and provide a permanent record of the transactions.

Blockchain, by virtue of being a decentralized solution, does not require all parties to be on the platform. This is a key differentiator of blockchain from existing digital solutions in trade. By enabling a departure from centralized solutions, blockchain-based trade applications hold the promise of connecting the digital islands that now dot the landscape.

Removing the central data repository still leaves two issues that need to be resolved: storing data and tracking transactions. On the technical set up behind the issue of data storage, blockchains are data structures where entries, usually transactions, are written to a database in bundles called blocks. Each block refers to a previous block by a unique identifier known as its hash, which is determined by its contents. This forms a chain of blocks, which increases the security of the data.

On the issue of transaction tracking, the ledger is broadcast in a peer-to-peer fashion between participants on the blockchain network. Predetermined network and consensus rules determine what is acceptable as a transaction and a block, and participants to a blockchain network each validate transactions and blocks according to these rules, resulting in each participant holding identical copies of the ledger.

In a blockchain, multiple parties also write entries that must be agreed upon through a set of rules. The various classifications of blockchains are based on network design differences. Specifically, the terms public[6] and permissioned[7] refer to the underlying set up of the blockchain with regards to which parties are allowed to participate in the network and how transaction data are handled.

In summary, blockchain has the potential to solve problems regarding trust and verification of information and make the transfer of data safer. This is particularly valuable when there are multiple parties involved in a transaction. The following are four segments of the trade process where blockchain can apply[8]:

---

[6] In a public blockchain, anyone can run a node and download the full history of the ledger. While the identities of the parties on the ledger are abstracted by combinations of numbers and letters called addresses, the transaction details are publicly accessible.

[7] Permissioned blockchain is a term often used interchangeably with private blockchain. They require that potential participants undergo a vetting process so that legal entities can be associated with the transactions. While an entire blockchain can be permissioned, sometimes just specific business networks within the ledger will be permissioned.

[8] For more detailed information on blockchain in trade, see DiCaprio and Jessel (2017) and DiCaprio and Malaket (2018). For a discussion from a non-technical perspective see WTO (2018a). Further benefits can be gained by linking in data analytics and other technologies such as artificial intelligence and the Internet of Things.

- Blockchain can enable multiple participants to reach consensus over a shared set of facts. For example, small business owners who want to start exporting their goods must first fulfil export documentation by proving exactly where all their inputs came from. Blockchain would serve them well in this capacity.
- Blockchain is useful where participants control the evolution of shared facts. In such a system, both the buyer and the seller would need to agree to any changes in the price of goods – for example, in the event of a new tariff.
- Lastly, blockchain can slot in when there is a need for an industry-workflow tool without a single actor that coordinates or knows everything. This is the case where a centralized source of data is creating vulnerability or where market-sensitive data are being shared.

8.2.2   Blockchain, Trade, and SDGs

Trade is an important part of the toolkit for achieving each of the SDGs. As Helbe and Shepherd (2017) note, "Given that trade is not an end in itself, there is no specific SDG goal for trade, but it is recognized as an important means of implementation."

Our interest in understanding the potential impacts of blockchain on SDGs comes from the expectation that it will yield outsized benefits for populations that struggle to achieve gains from trade, namely developing countries, least developed countries, and small and medium-sized businesses across the world economy.

To the extent that blockchain can reduce trade frictions and free up assets, the argument for blockchain technology in helping achieve the SDGs is straightforward. But, in this chapter, we have chosen to focus on the indirect impacts of blockchain in trade by detailing three channels through which blockchain technology can smooth trade frictions – trade finance gaps, low-preference utilization, and cumbersome custom processes.

As Hoekman argued, technology's role is to "operationalize" trade to facilitate SDG attainment (Hoekman 2017). By smoothing the trade process through reducing costs and removing frictions at the border, increased trade can provide opportunities for small business to grow, and for consumers to attain lower prices goods. In short, the ecosystem for trade is tightly tied to the ecosystem for development.

Next, we consider each of the three trade friction areas in detail and detail the role of blockchain technology in terms of trade facilitation and the subsequent impact on achieving the SDGs.

8.3   Customs and Border Measures

Blockchain technology can streamline customs and border measures, in particular, documentation processes and compliance requirements. While the 2017 WTO Trade Facilitation Agreement is the first multilateral agreement to explicitly focus on customs and border measures, countries have highlighted the need for such measures for decades. For instance, the Office of the US Trade Representative prepares an annual report on significant barriers to US exports. For example, in 1986, the first year the report was prepared and published, customs procedures as a barrier to US exports was mentioned dozens of times (USTR 1986).

Firms in developing and least developed countries are more vulnerable to inefficient customs procedures but firms in all countries – rich and poor alike – rely heavily on customs procedures to maintain smooth cross border operations. Even in one of the most advanced trading countries in the world, Great Britain, just the potential of a new customs process has spurred firms to implement second-best risk mitigation measures, such as storing inventory and reducing European Union (EU) inputs.[9] This refers to the UK's decision in a 23 June 2016 referendum to leave the EU (commonly referred to as Brexit). The prospective disruption of treatment of goods at the border could result in a customs capacity shortage that would hinder trade flows.

Increased integration and the ICT revolution have given rise to global supply chains, which are highly dependent on customs for smooth operations. Growth in intermediate goods trade has outpaced growth in final goods trade since the early 1990s (Nicita et al. 2013). The World Bank's World Development Report 2020 describes how firms in developing countries that were part of a global value chain were more likely to grow, be more productive, hire more employees, and have higher performance compared to their domestic counterparts that did not participate in global value chains.

Smoothing customs frictions is also important for both governments and the private sector.[10] For some governments, trade taxes account for

---

[9] UK Daily Express (2019).

[10] The customs process embodies all of the rules and regulations related to transporting merchandise across a national border and hence is an integral component of any successful international trade transaction. There are several separate steps for merchandise to clear customs and be ready for import or export. The import and export licenses, customs declaration paperwork, and cargo declaration paperwork must all be confirmed and verified, and sometimes separately by different people. Trade security procedures must also be completed and verified.

up to 50 percent of state revenue (Cantens and Raballand 2017). For firms, documentation and customs compliance can increase transactions costs by as much as 24 percent (Moise and LeBris 2013). Additionally, there is a wide literature showing the key role of exports in accelerating economic growth more broadly underscoring the importance of facilitating customs (Hausmann and Rodrik 2003).

Recent initiatives to improve and simplify the customs process have focused on electronic documentation. Automation, self-certification, and the so-called electronic single window (e.g., a single access point for traders and businesses within a country that is connected to various government agencies) have helped to streamline the process. However, to realize the benefits of most customs innovations, cooperation and interoperability across customs authorities and regulators from all participating jurisdictions is required and hence progress remains slow.

By offering a safe and efficient way to keep and share digital documents, blockchain has the ability to improve many of these customs challenges. In the text that follows, we detail how blockchain technology can simplify documentation and compliance. Features such as decentralized data storage, consensus, and immutability offer new solutions to the frictions experienced today. Additionally, numerous blockchain pilots in customs agencies are emerging around the world, and while many countries' existing legal and regulatory requirements still require paper documentation to be stamped or signed, numerous regulatory bottlenecks are being revisited as a result of blockchain. The blockchain-based pilots to date have demonstrated the ability to facilitate both customs processing and the required changes by industry and government.[11] We now turn to the first challenge of customs: documentation.

8.3.1   The Difficulty of Documentation

The rise of e-commerce over the past decade illuminated the potential of digital trade. While the retail part of process is electronic, many exporters are still dealing with a paper-based system for getting goods across the border.

Digital documentation has been pursued to different degrees by various actors in the trade process. Yet, even as shipping companies and banks have introduced digital documentation, as soon as a container arrives at the port, printed documents are a necessity. This is

---

[11] See McDaniel and Norberg (2019).

a combination of creaky customs infrastructure and outdated legal and regulatory requirements.

The sheer resulting volume of documents is a challenge for small and medium-sized businesses, which tend to lack the administrative resources and expertise for customs processing (see Table 8.2). There are steep learning costs to finding the right agencies and acquiring

Table 8.2 *Sample List of Documents Required to Import (US)*

Customs Bond	This is required for all customs entries into the US. Bonds can be obtained in two forms: single and continuous. A single bond is valid for only one entry and is recommended for shippers who don't import goods on a frequent basis. A continuous bond is ideal for shippers who are constantly importing goods via CBP, as it is often the cheapest, most convenient option.
Importer Security Filing (ISF)	This is required for shipping via ocean shipment. An ISF needs to be filed at least two days before cargo sails from its origin location in order to avoid penalties and fees from CBP.
Shipping documents	This may include but is not limited to: • Commercial invoice • Bill of lading or airway bill • Certificate of origin • Packing list
Government certifications	If you are importing goods that need to be cleared or are regulated by a partner government agency (such as the FDA, DOT, FTC, etc.), additional permits and certifications may be required for customs clearance.

Source: Authors' compilations of information from US Customs and Border Protection (CBP).

updated documents, while ensuring that they are filled out and submitted properly is yet another hurdle.

Many countries' governments have benefited from moving registries and documents into an online format. For instance, once Tonga put their business registry online, the time required to register a business fell from weeks to hours (ADB 2015). Such benefits, however, can be undone by other parties using different processing systems. Unless all related parties are on the same system, a business will often have to deal with documents that have changed hands multiple times and have gone through multiple systems, and someone eventually will need to print the document to make it accessible and verifiable to a particular entity. This accessibility of official documentation is one of the primary concerns of the WTO Trade Facilitation Agreement.

Paper documents are "sticky" and slow down the trade process even when technology can accommodate it. For instance, laws often require a physical stamp or signature; hence if different systems are not inter-operable and cannot accept a digital-format stamp, then the process will grind to a halt. Port systems, customs systems, and enterprise resource planning systems of the buyer or supplier must all be interoperable for the benefits of a digital infrastructure to be realized.

A common misnomer in trade facilitation discussions is that digital documentation alone can facilitate international trade. In fact, the individual actors in trade that have digitized documentation have been able to do so only within their own supply chain. When documents are transferred between entities, they need to be printed or re-keyed, which limits the benefits of electronic documentation.[12]

Blockchain technology can do three things that electronic documents alone cannot. First, it can link up existing electronic documents into a single transport layer. The usage of blockchain does not require replacing each entity's system but rather integrating existing systems. Second, blockchain enables different actors to receive digital assets without verifying or re-keying information. In other words, it allows digital documentation to address different jurisdictions' origin requirements. For example, under the current system, NAFTA origin is based on tariff shift and regional value content (RVC), whereas the African Growth and Opportunity Act (AGOA) origin is a substantial transformation "plus,"

---

[12] DiCaprio and Malaket (2018) introduce a network model of technology diffusion and examine the condition under which blockchain and connectivity could progress in the trade finance space.

meaning that the backup documentation of the certificate of origin is also different. However, if the goods were tracked on blockchain, the same data could be used to fulfil both.

Third, blockchain has the ability to limit lobbying tendencies and the influence of special interest groups. This is a functionality that electronic documents alone cannot deliver. According to UNCITRAL (1999), the Model Law on Electronic Commerce "was the first legislative text to adopt the fundamental principles of non-discrimination, technological neutrality and functional equivalence" of paper-based and paperless trading. UNCITRAL model laws have been around for many years, but digital progress has been limited mainly to e-commerce and regional trade agreements (Wu 2017). Under the current system, special interests lobby their respective governments for preferential treatment in local or foreign content rules, tariff waivers, or special classifications that confer benefits. In a blockchain environment, however, these terms of trade would be more transparent. The added transparency could work to limit ad hoc special and preferential treatment politicians grant to any one industry over another.

8.3.2   Compliance Requirements and Delays

Two major costs that exporters and importers incur are the administrative costs and delays related to customs and border compliance and documentation requirements. The World Trade Organization estimates that these costs are significant and hence it is not surprising that improving customs and border procedures are a large component of the WTO's Trade Facilitation Agreement.

Analysis by the Organisation for Economic Co-operation and Development (OECD) illustrates the potential magnitude of these costs. Customs officials typically select containers for inspection based on how they were produced, where they were transformed, and how they were packed. There are numerous steps required to demonstrate compliance with customs criteria. The OECD estimates that by streamlining these compliance checks, and facilitating the verification of compliance, the WTO Trade Facilitation Agreement could reduce trade cost by 16.5 percent for low-income countries, 17.4 percent for lower middle-income countries, 14.6 percent for upper middle-income countries, and 11.8 percent for OECD countries (OECD 2015a, 2009).

The application of blockchain technology has potential to reduce customs delays particularly when the delays stem from the exchange and verification of documentation. The costs savings are amplified when the traded goods are perishable goods or part of a supply chain. This is reflected in the higher ad valorem equivalent for a day in transit for such types of goods (Hummels and Schaur 2013).

As an illustrative example, Liu and Yue (2013) examined lettuce and apple imports in 183 countries, determining that reducing delays from the median two days to only one day would increase lettuce imports in those countries by around 35 percent, or 504,714 tons, and world consumer welfare by $2.1 billion. By the same measure, the authors found apple imports would increase by 15 percent, or 731,937 tons, and the consumer welfare would increase by roughly $1.1 billion (Liu and Yue 2013). The implications for the SDGs are straightforward, since not only are agricultural products a significant part of developing countries' trade, but also the fact that, according to the Food and Agriculture Organization of the United Nations, around a third of global food production is lost or wasted annually (United Nations 2011).

8.4   Trade Finance

Trade finance is another area where the use of blockchain technology can have an impact on international trade. We provide a brief description in the text that follows of where we see blockchain technology addressing some of the inclusion problems in this area. Trade finance is not modelled in the present chapter but left for future quantification.

Trade finance facilitates trade by reducing the risk of the transaction (banks are less risky than a firm), and by improving capital flow for both the buyer (who can pay later) and the supplier (who gets paid earlier). The demand for trade finance exceeds supply and the Asian Development Bank (ADB) has estimated the trade finance gap to be $1.5 trillion (ADB 2017). Surveys of the private sector show corporates consistently putting "lack of finance" at the top of their list of obstacles to increasing trade volumes (WTO 2016). A recent survey of 1,336 firms indicated that 60 percent of rejected applications cases resulted in no trade transaction being executed (ADB 2017). These figures suggest that foregone trade due to the trade finance gap could be roughly $900 billion.

Some of this discrepancy has been traced back to inefficiencies, including information asymmetries. In the text that follows, we will discuss how blockchain technology can be instrumental in narrowing the gap between supply and demand.

8.4.1   The Inclusion Problem in Trade Finance

The gap between supply and demand in trade finance is greatest for small- and medium-sized traders worldwide; and for firms in countries with less-developed financial markets. Small and medium-sized firms exhibit some of the highest rejection rates (Figure 8.1). These firms face constraints that include the high price of capital and the inability to meet bank requirements. In countries with less developed financial markets, trade finance constraints are exacerbated by low or non-existent country risk ratings, weak banking systems, lack of credit information, and regulatory requirements.

Bank-intermediated trade finance typically covers an estimated 36 percent of international trade (IMF 2009). Smaller firms and traders in high-risk countries, however, are more dependent on credit to support their exports than large corporates and multinational corporations (Auboin and DiCaprio 2016).

8.4.2   How Blockchain Can Reduce Trade Finance Gaps

A study by the Asian Development Bank (2016) found four main reasons banks reject trade finance applications with the following shares of rejections by category: (1) know your customer concerns: 29 percent; (2) the need for more collateral and information: 21 percent; (3) low profitability: 15 percent; and (4) not suitable for financing: 20 percent.

The need for collateral or information for a trade finance transaction can be a heavy burden in areas where asset ownership or land titles are difficult to ascertain or where recording methods of transactions may be

Figure 8.1   Proposed and rejected applications for trade finance, by firm size.
Source: Asian Development Bank, Trade Finance gaps, Growth and Jobs Survey (2016).

time consuming or untrustworthy. It is precisely this lack of reliable information that makes it difficult for trade finance lenders and other stakeholders to accurately measure risk, a problem that is compounded for developing countries, least developed countries, and smaller firms. Hence, the 21 percent of rejections that are due to collateral or information-related issues can be solved at the firm-level. For instance, taking the $900 billion in foregone trade, then this would suggest that blockchain technology has the potential to capture $189 billion of global trade currently foregone due to inefficiencies in the trade finance process. Evidence from further pilots will enable more comprehensive analysis in the future.

8.5   Preference Utilization Rates

The final piece of the puzzle is preference utilization rates, which are typically defined as the share of trade that takes place under preferences as a share of the total value of trade that is eligible for preferences (Swedish Board of Trade 2018a). Trade liberalization is important for development and so for developing countries that do not have a free trade agreement (FTA) in place, the EU and the United States offer easier access to their market by offering preferential market access.

The EU, United States, Canada, and other industrialized countries offer preferential tariffs rates to developing countries and least developed countries.[13] In negotiations, developing countries typically give concessions in exchange for these preferences.[14] For instance, the eligibility criteria for sub-Saharan African countries to participate in AGOA included improving labor rights and implementing reforms toward a market-based economy.

---

[13] For instance, the European Commission's General Scheme of Preferences 'allows vulnerable developing countries to pay fewer or no duties on exports to the EU, giving them vital access to the EU market and contributing to their growth'. The US Generalized System of Preferences 'promotes economic development by eliminating duties on thousands of products when imported from one of 120 designated beneficiary countries and territories' and 'provides opportunities for many of the world's poorest countries to use trade to grow their economies and climb out of poverty'. Canada's General Preferential Tariff aims to encourage imports from developing countries to increase their export earnings and promote their economic growth. While these types of preferences are aimed to promote economic development and eliminate poverty, many other preferential rates are provided in FTAs, many of which are between developed countries.

[14] The average length of time from launch of negotiations to signing for US FTAs is two and a half years. The length of time from launch to implementation is nearly four years, with the additional time reflecting government passage. Some negotiations can get lengthy – the US-Panama FTA took 8½ years from launch to implementation.

When preferences are not fully utilized, the benefits of increased trade foregone and the concessions become for naught. While the reforms are arguably beneficial regardless of the preferences, recipient countries still undergo the domestic political and legislative process necessary for compliance and eligibility. Ex post analysis of detailed data on preference utilization rates indicates that many market access wins stay on the table, unused, or underutilized (e.g., Francois et al. 2005).

In the aggregate, utilization rates for preferences in EU and US FTAs and preference programs appear to be fairly high, 75 percent and up.[15] But the aggregate figure obscures heterogeneity across sectors and countries. Utilization rates hover around 40 percent for some entire sectors, such as transportation equipment, paddy rice, and machinery and equipment (Figure 8.2). Preference utilization rates are under 40 percent for transportation equipment and electronic equipment, 42 percent for paddy rice (in contrast to 98 percent for processed rice for the EU preferences). Some developing countries are also better at taking advantage of tariff preferences than others.

Low preference utilization rates at the country and sector level reflect a combination of low preferential margins, excessive compliance costs, and exporters unaware of the preferences. Nilsson (2011) for example, finds that low utilization is primarily in low-value goods. Least developed countries have some of the lowest utilization rates (DiCaprio and Trommer 2010). At the firm level, utilization rates are positively correlated to the size of shipment and the size of the trading firm – i.e., the bigger the firm or shipment, the higher the utilization rates (Nilsson 2016).

The share of US and EU imports eligible for preferences but not claimed is rather low (Figures 8.3 and 8.4, respectively), which indicates the foregone tariff revenue would likely be low as well. These aggregate figures obscure sector-specific outliers; for instance, preference utilization rates have been found to be as low as 50 percent in some garment sectors for AGOA exporters to the United States (Brenton and Ikezuki 2004).

8.5.1 Effort and Cost

It takes time to for an exporter to understand what preferences are available and which forms to fill out, and some exporters simply are

---

[15] Swedish Board of Trade (2018a); Keck and Lendle (2012).

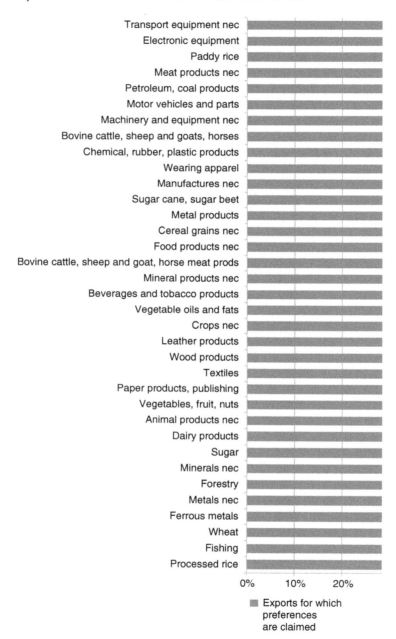

Figure 8.2 Utilization rate of preferences for exports to the EU, by sector.
Source: Mimouni et al. (2015).

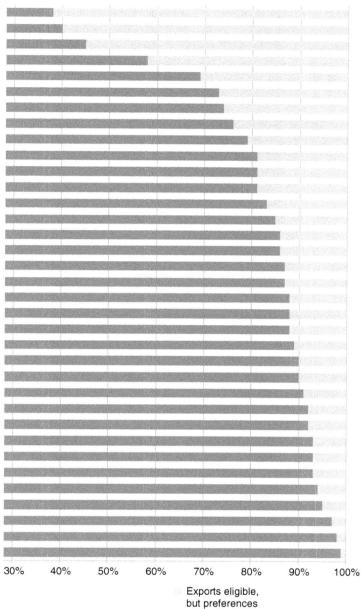

Exports eligible,
but preferences
not claimed

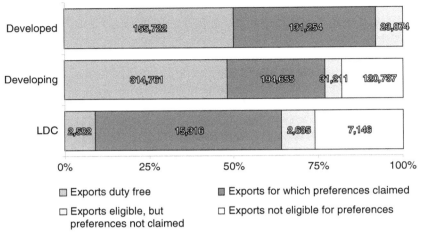

Figure 8.3   US imports by tariff treatments and category of development ($ millions).
Source: Mimouni et al. (2015).

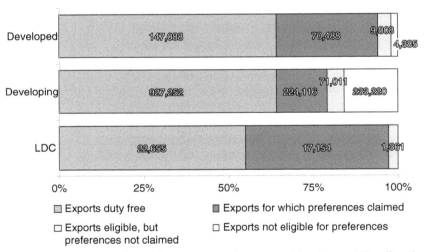

Figure 8.4   EU imports by tariff treatments and category of development ($ millions).
Source: Mimouni et al. (2015).

unaware that there are preferences available to them at all. The application of a preferential rate at the border requires proper certification and
documentation. Firms in the developing world often lack the resources

required to successfully file the required certification documents, even for goods that are relatively easy to certify. Firms aiming to participate in global value chains can face even greater compliance costs. Cadot et al. (2002) note that "the combination of bookkeeping costs with rules of origin-induced constraints on international sourcing can be particularly penalizing for companies operating globally integrated supply chains, which is now the norm in many manufacturing sectors."

Brenton (2011) examined the EU's Everything but Arms Agreement, which offers duty-free access for all products for least developed countries. While nearly all of Cambodia's exports to the EU were eligible for zero duty preferences in 2001, only 36 percent of those exports obtained duty-free access. That figure was estimated to translate into a 7.7 percent ad valorem tariff equivalent (AVE) on the total value of Cambodia's exports to the EU. Brenton reports that the rules of origin were the main contributing factor for the underutilization of trade preferences.

More recent empirical work finds tariff equivalents of rules of origin to be of similar magnitude: Francois et al. (2005) found 4 percent; Cadot and Ing (2017) estimated the average AVE to be 3.5 percent and trade-weighted to be 2.1 percent. The implication of these findings is that preferences matter only if the effective margin is greater than the cost of satisfying the rules of origin. Further, Keck and Lendle (2012) found that utilization costs involve an important fixed cost element, which appear to be in the range of $14 to $1,500 per transaction, which suggests that as compliance costs decline, new exporters will enter the marketplace.

8.5.2   Blockchain Can Increase Preference Utilization Rates

The information on any shipment, such as proof of purchase, a clearance form, a bill of lading, or insurance, can be made part of the block, a transparent chain of custody, and be accessible to suppliers, transporters, buyers, regulators, and auditors.[16] Customs would be able to see the necessary and accurate data from all actors in the transaction to prove rules or origin and the preference eligibility of the shipment. This greater visibility on the part of customs would facilitate a better-informed and more data-driven customs function in terms of its day-to-day operations. With the blockchain technology, Customs administrations and

---

[16] Botton (2018) and Okazaki (2018) provide detail on the use of blockchain technology from a Custom's perspective.

other border agencies would significantly improve their capacity for risk analysis and targeting, thus contributing to improved trade facilitation.

8.5.3 Authorized Economic Operator

The Authorized Economic Operator (AEO) programs are a potential vessel for blockchain. These programs create customs-to-business partnerships in which the participating businesses go through a relatively extensive approval process and incorporate various security measures. Once preapproved, businesses are recognized as low-risk and are less likely to experience customs delays.

Some countries are exploring the use of putting the AEO on the blockchain to reduce compliance costs for preference programs, and eliminate inconsistent and incorrect data (Inter-American Development Bank, 2019).

The World Customs Organization adopted an international AEO standard in 2005, and programs have been built into the WTO Trade Facilitation Agreement. Still, there is a long lead time to certification and the uptake for AEOs has been particularly low.

One of the main challenges of AEO programs is that countries must recognize each other's programs, which often requires a bilateral agreement. Such agreements can be slow and costly to negotiate and finalize, and the negotiators often (unknowingly) share spreadsheets with incorrect or quickly outdated information. Even once negotiated, the agreement can quickly become outdated.

8.6 Potential Economic Effects

In the previous sections, we described the channels through which the adoption of blockchain technology can enhance trade facilitation measures. In this section, we go further and set out to estimate the potential economic effects of blockchain on trade. Economic models such as these are helpful tools to consider how the economy of today may look in the future as a consequence of a specified set of policy changes. We use a standard applied general equilibrium model in conjunction with some stylized examples to provide a basis for estimating the impact of blockchain on trade. Our analytical approach is widely used in the field of international trade, and has been utilized by others, including the WTO, the OECD, and the European Commission. We focus our analysis on two specific examples: narrowing the preference utilization gap and reducing customs costs through trade facilitation.

8.6.1   Using GTAP to Estimate Trade Facilitation Benefits of Blockchain

As noted earlier, we use a computable general equilibrium (CGE) model to estimate the potential magnitude of the economic effects of using blockchain to narrow the preference utilization gap and reduce customs costs. We use the well-known and widely used GTAP model of global world trade (see Box 8.1). By employing global data on a wide range of issues such as trade, production, and income, CGE modelling can help to provide economy-wide assessments and sectoral-level results of various changes in border taxes, trade frictions, and other economic variables that may be affected by a change in trade policy.

These models help us answer *what-if* questions by simulating the price, income, and substitution effects in equilibrium on markets under different assumptions. Here, the economic outcomes of the baseline scenario, with no policy effects, are compared to the different scenarios with changes in trade policy. The baseline for the model is the equilibrium before the policy change, and the scenario is the equilibrium after the policy change. The effect of the policy change can then be quantified as the difference between the two.

BOX 8.1 TECHNICAL NOTES ON THE GTAP MODEL AND OUR APPROACH

We use GTAP version 10 Data Base, with a base year of 2014, containing 65 sectors and 141 countries/regions. We aggregate the 141 regions into 4 broad categories of regions: United States, Canada, EU-28, and rest of the world (all other countries, predominantly developing countries).

We employ the standard comparative static GTAP model (Hertel 1997) with neoclassical closure, involving generic assumptions such as perfect competition, constant returns to scale, and full employment of all factors. While explaining the model in its entirety is beyond the scope of this chapter, we shall focus on the trade aspect. Let the set SECT denote sectors (indexed by k) and REG denote regions (indexed by r in most cases and if the region is the source of exports/imports but by s if the region is destination of exports/imports).

The change in imports of each region from each of the others is determined by three factors: (1) substitution among different sources, based on the differential between import prices from specific sources and the sum of import-augmented technical change and aggregate import prices $pimk_{k,s}$, multiplied by the elasticity of substitution of imports between the sources $\sigma_{M,k}$, using the Armington elasticity for the sector as in the GTAP Data Base; (2) import-augmenting technical change, $amsk_{k,r,s}$, that lowers the effective price of a good in the destination market; and (3) the import penetration as captured by the change in composite

BOX 8.1 Cont.

imports of subsector commodity k, $qimk_{k,s}$. Note that the substitution effect for a particular flow (k,r,s) increases in divergence of import tariff for good k from regions r to s, from the weighted-average tariff of s. Since a higher weight means lower divergence, this effect decreases in import-shares of region r in the total imports by region s of the good k.

For all sectors k in SECT, regions r and s in REG:

$$qxsk_{k,r,s} = \ - amsk_{k,r,s} + \ qimk_{k,s} - \sigma_{M,k}$$
$$* \ [pmsk_{k,r,s} - \ amsk_{k,r,s} - \ pimk_{k,s}] \tag{8.1}$$

Global transport margins are treated in the same manner as in the standard GTAP model, with the quantity of international trade, transport, and insurance services required being a fixed proportion of the volume of goods shipped. Technical change in this sector is represented with the variable $atmfsdkk_{r,s}$ and is obtained by adding up the changes at different levels, which are directly translated from the aggregate changes in the corresponding variables. Trade and transport services are provided at a common price, pt, which represents a Cobb-Douglas aggregation of trade and transport services exports from all regions in the model. Deducting the rate of technical progress from this price change gives the percentage change in the commodity and route-specific transport margin, $ptransk_{k,r,s}$. The price linkages in the model also include export taxes, $txsk_{k,r,s}$, export *fob* prices $pfobk_{k,r,s}$, and import *cif* prices $pcifk_{k,r,s}$. Changes in import tariff and export taxes are the policy variables here.

There are three broad categories of consumption of products and services manufactured in a country: private households, government, and firms. In addition, each of these categories of agents also consume imports that are aggregated across exporters. For private households, GTAP assumes a Constant Difference Elasticity (CDE) functional form, which is flexible enough to handle Linearized Expenditure Systems (LES) and Constant Elasticity of Substitution (CES) as special cases. For government to consume different products and for firms to consume different intermediate inputs, the CES functional form is used. There is also a nested CES function between domestic and imported products for each of these agents.

Production functions in GTAP involve three levels of nests: (1) There is a Leontief function on the topmost part of production system, wherein intermediate inputs are a composite single input and primary factors as another composite single input are complements. (2) Within the intermediate inputs, there is a CES function. (3) Within the primary factor inputs, there is a CES function. Except for land and natural resources, which can move only within agricultural and extraction sectors respectively. Other factors are mobile across sectors. Trade, consumption, and production sub-modules of the GTAP model, which are explained in the preceding text, are linked with each other through general equilibrium conditions.

For a detailed discussion of the GTAP model and data base, see Walmsley et al. (2012).

8.6.2   Narrowing the Preference Utilization Rate Gap by Half

As shown earlier, the utilization rate for tariff preferences is below 100 percent, and this gap is most prominent for developing countries. Research has shown that burdensome compliance procedures can explain at least some of the gap, and, as discussed earlier, blockchain technology could facilitate traceability and reduce compliance burdens.

As a stylized experiment to gauge the economic impact of blockchain in this space, we base the analysis on the stylized assumption that blockchain technology could narrow this gap by half. For example, suppose the tariff rate is 10 percent, the preferential tariff rate is 0 percent, and the utilization rate is 60 percent; that is, 40 percent of imports are not utilizing the preference. The shock is to decrease the gap by half, which would be increasing the utilization rate to 80 percent (the utilization rate gap decreases from 40 percent to 20 percent). We use the GTAP import tariff variable *tms* to capture a change in the preference utilization rate.

To estimate the degree of underutilization of preference rates by sector and country, we employ an aggregated version of a novel dataset developed by the International Trade Centre in Geneva on utilization rates of preferences documented in Mimouni et al. (2015). This dataset has shipment transaction level data on tariffs actually applied on goods from all countries in the world to EU countries, the United States, and Canada. It also contains the tariff line code of the commodities traded and the International Trade Centre (ITC) has data on preferential and Most-Favoured Nation (MFN) tariffs for each of them. Based on the differences between actual applied and preferential tariffs, we compute the shocks in tariffs that would be needed for bringing down the existing tariff to a tariff level that's midway between the two. We implement these tariff shocks in the model.

Underutilization is most prominent among developed countries as importers and rest of the world as exporters although there are instances in which developed countries are not fully utilizing preference. Yet overall it is a small share of trade where preference utilization is relatively low. As such, we would expect the economic effects of closing the preference utilization gap to be of slight magnitude, and the effects of closing the gap by half to be even less.

8.6.3   Streamlining Customs Procedures

To estimate the increased trade facilitation as a result of using blockchain technology, we capture the reduction in trade frictions in a way that is tariff revenue neutral. Using the GTAP model, we adopt the *ams* approach – detailed in Section 8.6.3.1 – to estimate the potential economic effects of trade facilitation as a result of using blockchain technology. This allows us to capture import augmented technological change for a given commodity, exporter, and importer.

8.6.3.1   Our Modeling Choices

To explain our modelling choices with respect to using the *ams* variable to consider trade facilitation as a result of using blockchain technology, we consider the state of play in the economic modelling community in this broader area. Gravity-based estimation methods have mostly followed Kee et al. (2009). The authors estimate AVEs of trade restrictiveness as a whole based on the gravity equation. These AVEs are then used as the base nontariff measure data in CGE modelling and shocked for their changes as if they were tariffs. The limitation of treating nontariff measures as tariffs, however, is that they would be assigned revenue changes that are not practical.

To avoid this issue, several CGE papers have employed a non-tariff barrier variable, namely the *ams* variable in GTAP, which captures the effect of an unknown policy on prices, without any revenue implication. The *ams* variable is technically labelled as import-augmented technological change. A shock to *ams* results in a change in sourcing of imports from a particular exporter relative to the others. Several studies have used this approach for studying preferential trade agreements such as the Trans-Pacific Partnership (Petri et al. 2012), the Transatlantic Trade and Investment Partnership (Egger et al. 2015), other EU FTAs (Francois et al. 2012), etc. Studies such as Narayanan et al. (2016) and Minor and Tsigas (2008) use a reduction in *ams* to model trade facilitation.

Walmsley and Minor (2015) offer a new approach to model AVEs of reduced customs delays. The authors focus on altering preferences, specifically demand side changes in the willingness of consumer to pay in response to changes in nontariff measures.

The trade, welfare, and GDP implications of this method are shown to be slightly higher than our chosen method of iceberg costs, particularly for the low-income countries. Larger differences lie in the detailed mechanism of welfare decomposition. That is, the willingness-to-pay approach enables a more detailed analysis and decomposition of the welfare results. We did not adopt this approach because the efforts needed to modify the model to incorporate these changes are not commensurate with the payoffs in terms of better insight or dramatically improved results. We acknowledge that our results may be on the conservative side in comparison with the alternative willingness-to-pay approach.

A reduction in time spent on export and import compliance mirrors how we foresee blockchain technology facilitating customs procedures. We incorporate this into the analysis using the estimates from the World Bank Doing Business database on the AVEs of the time spent in compliance for exports and imports, by region. Compliance includes both border and documentary compliance for shipment of goods. For instance, in South Asia (includes Bangladesh, India, and Pakistan) compliance takes exporters on average 136.4 hours and importers 218 hours. It is worth noting that import compliance tends to be more burdensome than export compliance in nearly all regions. The estimated AVE from Hummels and Schaur (2013) for each additional day in transit is between 0.6 and 2.1 percent. For South Asia, that translates into 3.4 to 11.9 percent for exports, and 5.5 to 19.2 percent for imports.

To operationalize these AVEs in the model, we take the average of the export and import and apply that to each region in terms of a reduction of importing.

Table 8.3 reports the time spent in compliance for exports and imports, by region, and the AVEs. For instance, for overall trade, the range of reduction potential for South Asia is between 4.4 and 15.5 percent. Assuming that blockchain holds the potential to reduce this time by 50 percent, our results stems from the calculation in which we reduce these costs by half of the estimated spectrum. In other words, the shock for South Asia is a reduction of the trading costs 2.2 percent (low), 5.0 percent (medium), and 7.75 percent (high).

In addition to the direct effects, reducing the costs of importing for one country also corresponds to reducing the exporting costs of other countries that export to that country. In other words, decreasing everyone's import costs is also decreasing everyone's export costs.

To estimate the streamlining of customs procedures, again, we capture the reduction in trade frictions in a way that is tariff revenue neutral. In technical terms, this implies that, an increase in the GTAP variable *ams* reduces the effective price of the trade flow, without any direct implication for tariff revenue. In contrast, tariff reductions would have direct revenue implications, and cannot be carried out more than the degree of initial tariffs, which are usually far lower than the time costs of trade.

Table 8.3 *Time Spent in Compliance and Ad Valorem Equivalents*

Country or region	Time spent in compliance for exports (hours)	Time spent in compliance for imports (hours)	Ad Valorem Equivalent Cost of Each Additional Day in Transit (%)								
			Exports			Imports			Overall Trade		
			Low	Medium	High	Low	Medium	High	Low	Medium	High
East Asia and the Pacific	124.1	136.1	3.1	7.0	10.9	3.4	7.7	11.9	3.3	7.3	11.4
Europe and Central Asia	55.9	53.2	1.4	3.1	4.9	1.3	3.0	4.7	1.4	3.1	4.8
Latin America and Caribbean	115.9	144.3	2.9	6.5	10.1	3.6	8.1	12.6	3.3	7.3	11.4
Middle East and North Africa	136.9	206.8	3.4	7.7	12.0	5.2	11.6	18.1	4.3	9.7	15.0
OECD high-income countries	15.1	12.2	0.4	0.8	1.3	0.3	0.7	1.1	0.3	0.8	1.2
South Asia	136.4	218.9	3.4	7.7	11.9	5.5	12.3	19.2	4.4	10.0	15.5
Sub-Saharan Africa	197.9	239.4	4.9	11.1	17.3	6.0	13.5	20.9	5.5	12.3	19.1

Sources: Time spent in compliance is from table c1 of the World Trade Report 2018, World Trade Organization. Note: Those figures are from the World Bank Doing Business database, and compliance includes both border and documentary compliance for shipment of goods. Ad valorem equivalents are from David Hummels and Georg Schaur (2013), "Time as a Trade Barrier," *American Economic Review*, vol. 103, no. 7. The low end is 0.6 percent for each additional day; mid-range is 1.35 percent, and high end is 2.1 percent.

We use the AVEs to shock *ams,* because we want to capture the tariff-equivalent effect without directly affecting the tariff revenues. A change in the variable *ams,* therefore, is well suited for our analysis of reductions in customs procedures.

8.6.4   Summary of Results

The economic logic behind interpreting the results of reducing the preference utilization gap and customs costs are straightforward and as can be described as follows. As the customs cost decrease and developing countries take advantage of preferences, trade flows increase, developing countries export more, countries with initially relatively high trade costs experience relatively greater boosts in trade, incomes rise, consumption rises, and countries are better off from a more efficient allocation of resources.

In terms of magnitude, reducing the preference utilization gap alone is estimated to yield negligible economic results. Welfare, imports, exports, and GDP change by 0.01, 0.1, 0.1, and 0.002 percent, respectively. Complete elimination of the preference utilization rate gap yields results double that magnitude although the magnitude is still negligible.

Reducing customs costs, on the other hand, is shown to have has much larger payoffs. In the text that follows we present the combined results of implementing blockchain-based technology to reduce the preference utilization gap and customs costs. As noted earlier, we take a conservative approach and assume blockchain technology could reduce the preference utilization gap and trade costs by half.

8.6.4.1   Welfare Effects

The estimates suggest that all countries are better off from reducing customs costs and the preference utilization gap. Table 8.4 reports the estimated effects on welfare from reducing customs costs and preference utilization gaps by half. (The PUR results are negligible compared to the customs streamlining effects. We report the combined effects of reducing the customs costs through the *ams* variable and reducing the preference utilization gap by half through the *tms* variable.) For instance, the economic welfare in South Asia's economies could increase by between 1.06 and 3.50 percent, with a mid-range estimate of 2.31 percent. In dollar figures, these welfare effects translate into $27.3 billion to $90.4 billion, with a mid-range estimate of $59.6 billion.

The largest payoff in dollar terms is in the East Asia Pacific (includes China, Hong Kong, Japan, South Korea, and Taiwan) region. This reflects the large size of those economies and the moderately high initial trade costs. In terms of the effects relative to the size of the economies, however, Southeast Asia (includes Indonesia, Malaysia, Philippines, Singapore, Thailand, and Vietnam) gains the most as it has some of the largest trade costs. Traders in Indonesia spend 53.3 hours to import and 61.3 hours to export, compared to traders in OECD countries that spend 12.5 and 2.4 hours, respectively.

8.6.4.2   Trade Effects

Next, we turn to the aggregate global effects of the implementation of blockchain to reduce customs costs and increase preference utilization. The trade effects for each region are reported in Table 8.5, and the mid-range total increase in world trade (the total increase in world exports plus world imports) is estimated at be $1.3 trillion (the sum of the mid-range column).

Looking at the geographic division of these results shows that all regions are expected to experience a resulting increase in exports. Meanwhile, most regions are expected to increase imports as well. The rich OECD countries and EU-28, however, are expected to experience a slight decline in goods imports. These changes in trade patterns reflect the a priori differences in trade costs. That is, trade costs in developing countries decrease more than in developed countries and hence imports in these countries increase to a greater degree. Furthermore, since the initial value of trade flows is less in developing countries the percentage change will be greater. As these changes in trade costs occur, trade is diverted away from developed countries and towards developing countries. A proportionate reduction in costs in developing countries is thus shown to yield a greater effect on trade than in developed countries.

A more disaggregate look at the expected increase in exports reveals that at mid-range, the increase is 0.2 percent for the EU-28, 3.6 percent for rich OECD countries, 5.1 percent for Latin America, and 6.3 percent for Middle East and North Africa. In accordance with the foregoing analysis, we also find that the estimated increase in imports is larger for many countries (6–10 percent for most regions), although rich OECD countries and the EU-28 experience a decrease in imports of 1.2 and 1.4 percent, respectively.

Table 8.4 *Effects on Welfare from Reducing Customs Costs and Preference Utilization Gaps by Half*

	Low	Medium	High	Low	Medium	High
	in billions of dollars			as a percent of GDP (%)		
East Asia Pacific	169.5	374.8	573.8	0.98	2.16	3.31
Southeast Asia	50.7	112.4	172.3	2.02	4.48	6.87
South Asia	27.3	59.6	90.4	1.06	2.31	3.50
Other Rich OECD	31.0	69.3	107.2	0.15	0.33	0.52
Latin America	32.9	74.7	117.0	0.51	1.17	1.83
EU-28	54.1	119.9	184.0	0.29	0.65	0.99
Middle East North Africa	23.6	56.6	93.0	0.55	1.32	2.17
Sub-Sahara Africa	18.9	42.9	67.0	1.09	2.46	3.84
European Central Asia	1.8	6.3	13.1	0.04	0.16	0.32

Source: Authors' calculations. These results include the low end of potential effects, the medium range, and the high end.

8.6.4.3   GDP Effects

As a result of reducing time in customs and increasing the use of preferential trade agreements, our experiment shows that all regions experience an increase in the size of their economy (Table 8.6). This reflects the freeing up of resources towards more efficient uses. In terms of dollar value, East Asia Pacific experiences the largest gains of $275.2 billion. In terms of the percent of their economy though, Southeast Asia gains the most (3.2 percent). The economies of rich OECD countries and the EU-28 (large economies with low initial trade costs) grow in size but by relatively small amounts, 0.7 and 1.0 percent, respectively.

Table 8.5 *Effects on Exports and Imports from Reducing Customs Costs and Preference Utilization Gaps by Half, by Region*

Exports	Low	Medium	High	Low	Medium	High	Initial Values (bln$)
	in billions of dollars			in percentage change (%)			
East Asia Pacific	94.7	221.7	355.6	2.0	4.7	7.5	4,763.9
Southeast Asia	27.7	61.2	93.1	2.0	4.3	6.6	1,415.2
South Asia	5.3	13.8	23.9	1.0	2.6	4.6	522.2
Other rich OECD	45.4	99.8	151.6	1.6	3.6	5.4	2,794.4
Latin America	29.1	64.2	97.5	2.3	5.1	7.8	1,251.4
EU-28	8.1	17.4	25.8	0.1	0.2	0.4	7,121.3
Middle East North Africa	46.9	105.2	161.8	2.8	6.3	9.8	1,658.3
Sub-Sahara Africa	11.1	23.7	34.9	2.3	4.8	7.1	491.1
European Central Asia	26.3	58.1	88	1.8	4.0	6.1	1,447.6

Source: Authors' calculations. These results include the low end of potential effects, the medium range, and the high end.

Imports	in billions of dollars			in percentage change (%)			Initial Values (bln$)
	Low	Medium	High	Low	Medium	High	
East Asia Pacific	176.8	397.8	617.9	4.3	9.6	14.9	4,154.6
Southeast Asia	52.4	114.5	172.7	3.8	8.2	12.4	1,392.0
South Asia	18.5	41.7	64.9	2.8	6.3	9.9	657.2
Other rich OECD	−19.8	−42.9	−64.5	−0.5	−1.2	−1.8	3,633.0
Latin America	44.0	98.6	152.2	3.3	7.3	11.3	1,351.9
EU-28	−46.4	−102.7	−157.2	−0.7	−1.4	−2.2	7,129.4
Middle East North Africa	39.8	91.9	145.0	2.8	6.5	10.2	1,417.1
Sub-Sahara Africa	20.6	45.6	69.3	4.2	9.2	14.0	493.6
European Central Asia	8.9	21.1	34.3	0.7	1.7	2.8	1,236.6

Source: Authors' calculations. These results include the low end of potential effects, the medium range, and the high end.

8.7   Policy Challenges and Concluding Remarks

The allure of applying blockchain technology in the international trade space stems from why it was developed in the first place: to help strangers share information and validate accountability in a trustworthy and efficient manner; these aspects relate directly to the core of most trade frictions.

In this chapter, we have explored the potential of blockchain technology to facilitate international trade, and in turn, contribute to achieving the Sustainable Development Goals. Blockchain can be used in nearly every step of sourcing and production and consumption. The technology can be used to trace labor and verify production meets International Labour Organization (ILO) standards; to instantly verify for customs agencies that the contents of a container satisfy rules of origin; to manage land and other asset ownership and provide verification of collateral in trade finance; and to empowering consumers that seek information other than price to make more informed choices.

In the foregoing we have detailed the channels through which blockchain technology can smooth three stubborn friction areas in trade, namely, increase the access to trade finance, narrow the preference utilization gap, and streamline customs processes. Small and medium-sized exporters and importers in developing and least developed countries stand to gain the most, since these entities bear the largest brunt of the trade frictions.

We find blockchain technology could eliminate the inefficiencies in information sharing and collateral management in trade finance and has the potential to close the trade finance gap by $189 billion. We also find that the adoption of blockchain technology in customs could achieve lower trade costs and narrow the preference utilization gap, which could increase world trade by $1.3 trillion.

Blockchain technology is in a nascent stage of development and these are only laboratory results. The estimates provided in this chapter are based on the calculation of easing a few specific bottlenecks, and a subset of those bottlenecks at that. The estimates should not be taken as an overall definitive implication of the potential of blockchain technology in trade, but rather among the first estimates in this research area. The potential is likely far greater once scalability and interoperability are achieved.

We hope this work spurs more research in this area. The pilots to date shed light on blockchain technology's potential regarding individual

Table 8.6 *Effects on GDP from Reducing Customs Costs and Preference Utilization Gaps by Half, by Region*

	Low	Medium	High	Low	Medium	High	Initial Values (bln$)
		in billions of dollars			in percentage change (%)		
East Asia Pacific	122.8	275.2	426.6	0.7	1.6	2.5	17,333
Southeast Asia	36.1	80.5	124.0	1.4	3.2	4.9	2,507
South Asia	19.5	43.3	66.5	0.8	1.7	2.6	2,584
Other rich OECD	68.9	154.0	238.0	0.3	0.7	1.1	20,795
Latin America	24.9	56.3	88.2	0.4	0.9	1.4	6,397
EU-28	81.6	182.4	281.9	0.4	1.0	1.5	18,533
Middle East North Africa	29.0	66.2	104.3	0.7	1.5	2.4	4,278
Sub-Sahara Africa	13.7	30.9	48.1	0.8	1.8	2.8	1,744
European Central Asia	14.2	32.0	50.1	0.3	0.8	1.2	4,058

Source: Authors' calculations. These results include the low end of potential effects, the medium range, and the high end.

cases or transactions, highlighting the need for more to be learned about the required regulatory changes needed to achieve wide scale adoption. For instance, blockchain cannot be scaled up for a broader impact on trade facilitation without the active engagement of regulators, customs agencies, food safety authorities, and central banks. Nonetheless, pilots have been instrumental in introducing a number of potential improvements to today's trade facilitation measures.

Full-scale global deployment will require policymakers to engage with economic operators across the international trade landscape. For governments that are seeking to achieve the full benefits of blockchain, we highlight four helpful actions.

First, engagement is essential. Most trade practitioners have heard of blockchain, but it will take effort to understand how the current regulatory environment can adapt to allowing users to take advantage of the technology. Policymakers must engage with private sector developers, civil society, academics, regulators, users, customs officials, and policymakers in other countries. Pilots will likely continue, and some governments appear to be moving much faster than others (e.g., WEF 2018). This engagement can happen through regulatory or government sponsored pilots, or participation in existing projects in other countries. The EU Blockchain Roundtable is one example of how a governmental agency is bringing all stakeholders to the table to discuss how to create the ecosystem for safe and secure blockchain technology in trade.

Second, review the domestic legal environment around electronic documentation. Users cannot fully benefit from blockchain without electronic documentation, yet the degree to which governments accept electronic document varies across countries, and even across regional and local governments within a country. In the United States and EU, negotiable instruments – defined as written and signed customs documents – often require stamps and physical signatures. Requiring physical adjustment of documentation limits digitization, and by extension will slow the scale of blockchain solutions (Shearman and Sterling et al. 2018). Another option would be to use existing legislation targeted towards finance and trade sectors, and then simply allow these regulations to be met using the new technology.

Third, participate in and support standards initiatives such as the Universal Trade Network and the International Organization for Standardization (ISO). The development of a common taxonomy, with respect to a standardization of terminology, data formats, communication protocols, and identity frameworks would enable blockchain applications to scale up. Currently, the same service across difference blockchain platforms can have different names (e.g., an Oracle on Corda is the same thing as an Ordering Service on Fabric). These types of inconsistencies make it difficult for the general public to understand the technology, and even for those familiar with one terminology and its corresponding systems to understand and communicate with those associated with another system that uses different terminology.

These issues may appear easily solvable at first glance, but multilateral efforts around standards for paperless trade like UNCITRAL have existed for decades with little progress to date. Bilateral efforts have made more progress. According to Monteiro and Teh (2017), there are forty-seven regional trade agreements that have paperless trade provisions although evidence on adoption is scarce.

Fourth, adjust regulatory regimes to allow for international adoption and international collaboration in technology. A wholly top-down approach, in which only governments decide on the uses of blockchain technology across the trade landscape, is not necessarily optimal. On the other hand, a wholly bottom-up approach may yield various digital islands that do not seamlessly interact. For the chain to work end-to-end, the incorporated systems need to be coherent with cross border cooperation, collaboration, and regulation across all the countries through which the product passes. The EU's blockchain initiative to support the technology and encourage work across member states could be an example to follow. Keeping the conversation going and offering a forum for the different parts of the chain to highlight challenges and explore solutions is an important role for the public sector.

In closing, this chapter illustrates that blockchain has the potential to facilitate existing trade and open up new avenues for cross border exchange for buyers and sellers in developing and least developed countries, thereby helping to fulfil many of the 2030 Agenda for Sustainable Development's Sustainable Development goals, as well as to promote global growth and employment in general. For policymakers focused on trade as a vehicle for achieving these goals, supporting the development of blockchain technology across the international trade landscape is a good place to start.

References

ADB (Asian Development Bank). (2015). *Aid for Trade in Asia and the Pacific-Thinking Forward About Trade Costs and the Digital Economy*. Mandaluyong City, Philippines: Asian Development Bank,

ADB (Asian Development Bank). (2016). "2016 Trade Finance Gaps, Growth, and Jobs Survey." ADB Briefs, No. 64, August.

ADB (Asian Development Bank). (2017). "2017 Trade Finance Gaps, Growth, and Jobs Survey." ADB Briefs, No. 83, September.

Ahn, JaeBin, Khandelwal, Amit K. and Wei, Sh.-J. (2011). "The Role of Intermediaries in Facilitating Trade." *Journal of International Economics* 84: 73–85.

Auboin, M. and DiCaprio, A. (2016). "Why Do Trade Finance Gaps Persist: Does It Matter for Trade and Development?" WTO Working Paper no. ERSD 201701.

BAFT, R3 and Shearman and Sterling LLP. (2018). "Code Is Note Law: The Legal Background for Trade Finance Using Blockchain." R3 Research Paper, July.

Baldwin, R. (2016). *The Great Convergence*. Harvard University Press.

Botton, N. (2018). *Blockchain and Trade: Not a Fix for Brexit, but Could Revolutionise Global Value Chains (If Governments Let It)*. ECIPE Policy Brief No 1/2018. Brussels.

Brenton, P. (2011). *Preferential Rules of Origin: Preferential Trade Agreement Policies for Development: A Handbook*. Washington, DC: World Bank.

Brenton, P. and Ikezuki, T. (2004). "The Initial and Potential Impact of Preferential Access to the U.S. Market Under the African Growth and Opportunity Act." World Bank Policy Research Working Paper No. 3262.

Cadot, O., de Melo, J., Estevadeordal, A. and Tumurchudur, B. (2002). *Assessing the Effect of NAFTA's Rules of Origin*. Washington, DC: World Bank.

Cadot, O and Ing, L. Y. (2017). "Facilitating ASEAN Trade in Goods. Working Paper No. DP-2016–20." Economic Research Institute for ASEAN and East Asia, ERIA.

Cantens, T. and Raballand, G. (2017). "Cross-Border Trade, Insecurity and the Role of Customs: Some Lessons from Six Field Studies in (Post) Conflict Regions." ICTD Working Paper 67, August.

DiCaprio, A and Jessel, B. (2017). "Can Blockchain Make Trade Finance More Inclusive?" R3 Research.

DiCaprio, A. and Malaket, A. (2018). "Digital Islands in Trade Finance: Can a Decentralized System Solve the Network Problem?" R3 Research.

Di Caprio, A. and Trommer, S. (2010). "Bilateral Graduation: The Impact of EPAs on LDC Trade Space." *The Journal of Development Studies* 46: 1607–1627.

Egger, P., Francois, J., Manchin, M. and Nelson, D. (2015). "Non-tariff Barriers, Integration and the Transatlantic Economy." *Economic Policy* 30: 539–584.

Francois, J. F., Hoekman, B. and Manchin, M. (2005). "Preference Erosion and Multilateral Trade Liberalization." World Bank Policy Research Working Paper No. 3730, October 2005.

Francois, J., Narayanan, B., Norberg, H., Porto, G. and Walmsley, T. (2012). Assessing the Economic Impact of the Trade Agreement between the European Union and Signatory Countries of the Andean Community. Project Report published by the Directorate General of Trade, European Commission under Framework Contract TRADE10/A2/A16 and Centre for Economic Policy Research, London.

Greif, A. (1993). "Contract Enforceability and Economic Institutions in Early Trade: The Maghribi Traders Coalition." *American Economic Review* 83: 525–548.

Hausmann, R. and Rodrik, D. (2003). "Economic Development as Self-Discovery." *Journal of Development Economics* 72: 603–633.

Head, K. and Mayer, T. (2013). "Gravity Equations: Workhorse, Toolkit, and Cookbook." CEPII Working Paper, September 2013.

Helb, M. and Shepherd, B. (2017). *Win-Win: How International Trade Can Help Meet the Sustainable Development Goals.* Tokyo, Japan: ADB Institute.

Hertel, T. (1997). *Global Trade Analysis: Modelling and Applications.* Cambridge University Press.

Hoekman, B. (2017) *Trade and the Post-2015 Development Agenda in Win-Win: How International Trade Can Help Meet the Sustainable Development Goals.* Tokyo, Japan: ADB Institute.

Hummels, D. L. and Schaur, G. (2013). "Time as a Trade Barrier." *American Economic Review* 103: 2935–2959.

IMF (International Monetary Fund). (2009). *World Economic Outlook, Crisis and Recovery,* Washington, DC: International Monetary Fund.

Inter-American Development Bank. (2019). "Beyond Borders: How Blockchain Can Make Trade Safer. Available at https://blogs.iadb.org/integration-trade/en/blockchain-trade-safer/.

Keck, A. and Lendle, A. (2012). "New Evidence on Preference Utilization." Staff Working Paper ERSD-2012, 12. Geneva, Switzerland: World Trade Organization, Economic Research and Statistics Division.

Kee, H., Nicita, A. and Olarreaga, M. (2009). "Estimating Trade Restrictiveness Indices." *The Economic Journal* 119: 172–199.

Liu, L. and Yue, C. (2013). "Investigating Impact of Time Delays on Trade." *Food Policy* 39: 108–114.

McDaniel, C. and Norberg, H. (2019). Can Blockchain Technology Facilitate International Trade? Arlington, VA: Mercatus Research, Mercatus Center at George Mason University.

Mimouni, M., Pichot X. and Narayanan, B. (2015). "Utilization of Preferential Tariffs." GTAP Conference Paper, presented at the 18th Annual Conference on Global Economic Analysis, Melbourne, Australia.

Minor, P. and Tsigas M. (2008). "Impacts of Better Trade Facilitation in Developing Countries." GTAP 11th Annual Conference, Helsinki, Finland.

Moïse, E. and LeBris, F. (2013). "Trade Costs: What Have We Learned? A Synthesis Report." OECD Trade Committee Working Paper, Paris.

Monteiro, J. and Teh, R. (2017). "Provisions on Electronic Commerce in Regional Trade Agreements." WTO Working Paper No. ERSD-2017–11.

Narayanan, B., Sharma, S. and Razzaque, M. (2016). "Trade Facilitation in the Commonwealth: An Economic Analysis Margin." *The Journal of Applied Economic Research* 10: 305–336.

Nicita, A., Ognivtsev, V., and Shirotori, M. (2013). "Global Supply Chains: Trade and Economic Policies for Developing Countries." UNCTAD Policy Issues in International Trade and Commodities Study Series No. 55.

Nilsson, L. (2011). "Small Trade Flows and Preference Utilization: The Case of the EU," *South African Journal of Economics* 79: 392–410.

Nilsson, L. (2016). "EU Exports and Uptake of Preferences – a First Analysis." *Journal of World Trade* 50: 219–252.

OECD (Organisation for Economic Co-operation and Development). (2009). *Overcoming Border Bottlenecks: The Costs and Benefits of Trade Facilitation.* Paris: OECD Trade Policy Studies, OECD Publishing,

OECD (Organisation for Economic Co-operation and Development). (2015). "Implementation of the WTO Trade Facilitation Agreement: The Potential Impact on Trade Costs." Policy Brief, June 2015.

Okazaki, Y. (2018). "Unveiling the Potential of Blockchain for Customs." Research Paper No. 45. World Customs Organization, Brussels.

Olsen, M. (2010). "Banks in International Trade: Incomplete International Contract Enforcement and Reputation." Harvard University mimeo.

Petri, P., Plummer, M. and Zai, F. (2012). "The Trans-Pacific Partnership and Asia-Pacific Integration: A Quantitative Assessment." Washington, DC: Peterson Institute for International Economics.

Swedish National Board of Trade. (2018a). "The Use of the EU's Free Trade Agreements," 3rd ed. National Board of Trade Sweden, Stockholm, November 2018 – Third Edition.

UK Daily Express. (2019). "No Deal Brexit Ready: UK Firms Automatically Enrolled in Customs System for Post-EU Future." Available at www.express.co.uk/news/politics/1168626/brexit-latest-news-uk-no-deal-brexit-boris-johnson-automatic-enrolment-customs-EROI-number.

UNCITRAL (United Nations Commission on International Trade Law). (1999). "UNCITRAL Model Law on Electronic Commerce with Guide to Enactment 1996 with Additional Article 5 bis as Adopted in 1998." United Nations Publications, New York.

UNECE (United Nations Economic Commission for Europe). (2006). *A Roadmap towards Paperless Trade*. United Nations Economic Commission for Europe, ECE/Trade/ 371. New York and Geneva: United Nations.

United Nations. (2011). *Global Food Losses and Food Waste – Extent, Causes and Prevention*. Rome: The Food and Agriculture Organization of the United Nations,

United Nations. (2017). "Trade Facilitation and Paperless Trade Implementation: Global Report." Geneva, Switzerland.

USTR (United States Trade Representative). (1986). Annual Report 1986. United States International Trade Commission, USITC Publication 1935. Washington, DC.

Walmsley, T., Aguiar, A. and Narayanan, B. (2012). "Introduction to the Global Trade Analysis Project and the GTAP Data Base." GTAP Working Paper No. 67. Purdue University, West Lafayette, IN: Global Trade Analysis Project (GTAP).

Walmsley, T. and Minor, P. (2015). "Willingness to Pay in CGE Models." GTAP Working Paper.

WEF (World Economic Forum). (2018). "Trade Tech – A New Age for Trade and Supply Chain Finance," January. Report. World Economic Forum. Geneva, Switzerland: World Economic Forum.

World Bank. (2019). "World Bank World Development Report 2020. Trading for Development in the Age of Global Value Chains." Washington, DC: World Bank.

WTO (World Trade Organization). (2015). World Trade Report, Speeding Up Trade: Benefits and Challenges of Implementing the WTO Trade Facilitation Agreement." Geneva, Switzerland: World Trade Organization.

WTO (World Trade Organization). (2016). *Trade Finance and SMEs Bridging the Gaps in Provision*. Geneva, Switzerland: World Trade Organization.

WTO (World Trade Organization). (2018a). *Can Blockchain Revolutionize International Trade?* Geneva, Switzerland: World Trade Organization.

WTO (World Trade Organization). (2018b). *Mainstreaming Trade to Attain the Sustainable Development Goals*. Geneva, Switzerland: World Trade Organization.

Wu, M. (2017). "Digital Trade-Related Provisions in Regional Trade Agreements: Existing Models and Lessons for the Multilateral Trade System, RTA Exchange." International Centre for Trade and Sustainable Development (ICTSD) and the Inter-American Development Bank, Geneva, Switzerland.

9

The Effects of Environmental Costs on Public Support for Foreign Direct Investment

Differences Between the United States and India

HYE-SUNG KIM AND YOUNGCHAE LEE

9.1 Introduction

The growth in foreign direct investment (FDI) around the world has been exponential in recent decades. In 1990, the annual global flow of FDI was approximately US$200 billion, and this figure grew to about US$1.52 trillion by 2017. Many countries continue to engage in strong competition to attract FDI to their economies. This is primarily due to the economic benefits that are associated with FDI. These advantages include economic growth, job creation, and transfer of technological and managerial expertise to domestic firms in the economy (Chen et al. 1995; Barry and Bradley 1997; Blomström and Sjöholm 1999; Li and Liu 2005; Waldkirch et al. 2009).

However, FDI and the economic benefits it generates often come with a significant (if not necessarily inevitable) downside: environmental damage. These negative environmental effects can assume many forms, including carbon and sulfur dioxide emissions, oil spillage, soil erosion, chloride contamination of the water supply, and threats to biodiversity (Grimes and Kentor 2003; Acharyya 2009; Kingston 2011; Jiang 2015;

This research was supported by the Hayek Fund for Scholars granted by the Institute for Humane Studies. It was approved by the Institutional Review Board at Winthrop University. We would like to extend our sincerest thanks to the editors, Cosimo Beverelli, Damian Raess, and Jürgen Kurtz, and the participants of the World Trade Forum 2018, hosted by the European University Institute. We also appreciate the feedback provided by Jessica O'Reilly, Jonas Gamso, and the rest of the participants at the Innovations in International Climate Development Workshop, hosted by the School of Global and International Studies at Indiana University Bloomington.

Lleras and Leal 2017). Environmental concerns have at times been significant enough to mobilize protests against FDI, such as the decade-long popular resistance in County Mayo, Ireland against a gas pipeline project scheduled by the oil and gas company Royal Dutch Shell (Siggins 2017).

This tension between the economic benefits and environmental costs of FDI is not a newly observed phenomenon. In 1999, at the opening address for the Organisation for Economic Co-operation and Development (OECD)'s "Conference on FDI and the Environment" held at the Hague, the Dutch Minister for Foreign Trade remarked, "In our globalising society, it would appear that the environment and the economy are involved in some kind of trench warfare. A trench warfare between two sworn enemies, in which ground gained by one side inevitably means ground lost by the other side" (OECD 1999). This observation conveys the wide-ranging influence that FDI has on Sustainable Development Goals (SDGs), affecting not only those related directly to investment itself, but also those that relate to economic growth and the environment.

Broadly, our study speaks to the ongoing concerns surrounding the economic and environmental consequences of FDI on sustainable development. In particular, we focus on public opinion regarding the trade-off between the economic and environmental effects of FDI and examine whether there is a difference in public opinion between residents from developed and developing countries. We conduct online survey experiments in one developing country (India) and one developed country (the United States) to examine how environmental costs and economic benefits affect people's support of FDI, and how this differs between the United States and India. Our data analysis finds that among residents of the United States, being informed of the environmental costs of economically beneficial FDI decreases support of this FDI; however, this pattern, although observed, is much weaker among residents of India. We also explore whether people's concern for the environmental consequences of FDI depends on how immediate the damage is to themselves. People in the United States show more concern for environmental damage in their immediate surroundings compared to damage in a distant location, while residents of India are indifferent to the location of environmental damage caused by FDI.

Our study contributes to several bodies of literature. The first is the literature examining public opinion on environmental issues. We gather new data through a survey experiment, which reduces the difficulty of making causal inferences that is inherent in observational studies using survey data. Our survey also addresses several additional problems that we notice in previous surveys, such as social desirability bias and issue priming. The second is the literature on the political economy of FDI, particularly that of the public opinion of FDI. Previous literature has not focused on how people's support of FDI is influenced by its environmental consequences, which is a gap addressed by this study. The third is the literature that examines whether development is a prerequisite for environmental quality and protection.

In the following section, we present the existing literature. We then discuss our theory and the survey experiment that we use to test our hypotheses. After presenting our findings, we discuss the implication of our findings on sustainable development.

9.2   Existing Literature

9.2.1   Existing Public Opinion Surveys on Environmental Issues

We build on and address a significant body of existing literature that investigates the differences in opinion between residents of developed and developing countries on environmental issues. Until the late 1980s, the prevailing presumption was that residents of developing countries would be relatively unconcerned about environmental problems compared to residents of developed countries, and that they would prioritize economic growth and security over environmental protection. This was long accepted as common wisdom, especially prior to the advent of widespread survey implementation in developing countries.

This situation changed in the early 1990s when polling organizations started extending their coverage to developing countries (Dunlap et al. 1993; Inglehart 1995). New data gathered from these surveys led to a divide between scholars who think that wealth and affluence lead to a higher level of environmental concern and those who argue that citizens of developing nations are more concerned about the environment owing to their vulnerability to climate change and generally lower levels of environmental quality. One of the earliest studies to clearly delineate this tension was Inglehart (1995), which analyzed the 1990–1993 World Values Survey (WVS) carried out in forty-three countries. Its main analysis is based on an index that reflects responses to four questions concerning environmental protection, and it yielded two (somewhat contradictory) findings. The first is that "mass support for environmental protection tends to be greatest in countries that have relatively severe objective problems (as indicated by levels of air pollution and water pollution)" (p. 57), implying that residents of developing countries have the strongest incentives to demand environmental protection. The second finding is that "countries that have relatively post-materialistic publics, rank relatively high in their readiness to make financial sacrifices for the sake of environmental protection" (p. 57), suggesting that residents of developed countries will highly value environmental protection. As Inglehart points out, these two findings are at odds with each other, making it unclear whether developing countries will prioritize environmental problems more than developed countries. He declines to decide whether one factor might be decisively important over the other, saying that "the available evidence indicates that both of these factors are about equally important" (p. 57).

While the 1990–1993 WVS analyzed in Inglehart (1995) was a significant grassroots attempt to collect worldwide data that includes developing countries, there were concerns about its comparability and consistency across nations. Dunlap and York (2008, p. 538) identified the main problems as voluntary participation causing temporal discrepancies between nations, inconsistent implementation of the questions due to cost issues, and lack of information on sampling procedures in each nation.

The "Health of the Planet" (HOP) survey administered in 1992 by the George H. Gallup International Institute (Dunlap et al. 1993) also gathered survey data from developing countries but sidestepped many of the WVS' shortcomings. Specifically, each Gallup affiliate translated the questionnaire into the local language, and then the Gallup institute "back-translated" them into English to ensure consistency. Problems of literacy were minimized by conducting in-home interviews in person. All the surveys were completed between January and April 1992, which reduced discrepancies due to time lags.

Gallup's own analysis of the HOP data became the first of many studies to argue that citizens of developing countries had a strong interest in environmental protection, often exceeding that of people in developed countries. This study asked questions such as "How concerned are you personally about environmental problems – would you say a great deal, a fair amount, not very much, or not at all?" and gave the percentage of respondents who gave a particular answer (such as "a great deal") for each country. The answers suggested that people in developing countries showed a level of concern for the environment that paralleled, and at times surpassed, that of people in developed countries.

Since then, many additional studies have supported the conclusions of the HOP survey (Bloom 1995; Dunlap and Mertig 1995; Leiserowitz 2007; Sandvik 2008). Overall, these authors suggest that their findings strongly refute previous assumptions about the preferences of people in developing countries. Dunlap and Mertig (1995), for example, say, "The idea that environmental quality is a luxury affordable only by those who have enough economic security to pursue quality-of-life goals is inconsistent ... with the overall high levels of environmental concern found among residents of the low-income nations in the HOP" (p. 134).

Meanwhile, there are also a handful of studies that argue that residents of developing countries are less concerned about the environment than their counterparts in developed countries (Diekmann and Franzen 1999; Franzen 2003; Franzen and Meyer 2010). Still others find that the association between wealth and concern for the environment is empirically ambiguous (Dunlap and York 2008; Kvaløy et al. 2012). In Table 9.5 in the Appendix A, we present a more detailed description of these studies, including wording of the relevant questions and their methodological approaches.

9.2.2 Addressing Shortcomings of Previous Survey Research

As we have seen in the previous literature, there has been no shortage of public opinion surveys on environmental issues, and recent decades have seen coverage increasingly extended to developing countries. Methodologically, these surveys asked the same questions of all respondents in a non-experimental setting. When presenting the data, some of these studies show the percentage of respondents in a country that gave a particular response to a given question (Dunlap et al. 1993; Bloom 1995; Inglehart 1995; Leiserowitz 2007; Kull 2007; Ratter 2012). Others calculate correlation coefficients between responses and GDP per capita, or run linear regressions (Dunlap and Mertig 1995; Diekmann and Franzen 1999; Franzen 2003; Dunlap and York 2008; Sandvik 2008; Franzen and Meyer 2010; Kvaløy et al. 2012; Kim and Wolinsky-Nahmias 2014).

This study questions the robustness of the authors' inferences given the known problems of interpreting observational survey data. As Gaines et al. (2007) have pointed out, survey data are subject to "selection bias, spurious correlation, correlated measurement errors, censored data, the lack of true counterfactuals, and mutual causation ... As a result, statistical analyses of cross-sectional survey data are notoriously subject to misleading findings" (p. 2). We attempt to remedy these shortcomings by implementing an original survey experiment. Survey experiment research assigns respondents randomly to control and treatment conditions, which eliminates the confounders that affect both the treatment assignment and the study outcomes. By manipulating the independent variable, survey experiment data avoid many of the inferential problems associated with conventional panel survey data, providing us with "firmly grounded inferences about real-world political attitudes and behavior" (Gaines et al. 2007, p. 2).

Additionally, there are a number of additional problems in previous surveys that our survey addresses. One of these problems is "social desirability bias," which occurs when survey respondents feel the need to produce the socially desirable answer to a question in order to present a flattering image of themselves, rather than the honest answer (Kalton and Schuman 1982; Furnham 1986; Tourangeau and Yan 2007). This could be due to genuine self-deception, or a conscious decision to "fake" one's response in order to gain social approval (Huang et al. 1998; King and Bruner 2000; van de Mortel 2008). Survey respondents are, for example, likely to report having voted even when they have not, because voting is seen as the socially acceptable thing to do (Parry and Crossley 1950). This tendency will likely be amplified in face-to-face interviews, which unlike online surveys are not anonymous (Gallup's widely quoted "Health of the Planet" survey was conducted through face-to-face interviews). In our study, we ask online respondents to evaluate scenarios rather than asking them directly about the importance of environmental problems. Doing so alleviates social desirability bias by reducing the implicit pressure that respondents might feel to produce the "right" or socially acceptable answer.

Another problem we are concerned about is "issue priming," in which the questions that were asked earlier in a survey influence respondents' answers to questions that appear subsequently in the survey. Studies have shown that the ordering of questions, as well as the content of previous questions and items, can affect responses later in the survey (Strack 1992; Lasorsa 2003).[1] We are concerned that this "issue priming" may have

---

[1] As an example, consider the following survey, in which respondents were asked whether American reporters should be allowed access in Soviet countries, and vice versa:

Respondents are more likely to allow Communist reporters into the United States after having answered a question about allowing American reporters into Communist countries, and they are less likely to want American reporters admitted to Communist countries

been a significant problem that contaminated answers in previous environmental surveys. For example, in Gallup's 1992 "Health of the Planet" survey, one of the earlier questions is, "How concerned are you about environmental problems – would you say a great deal, a fair amount, not very much, or not at all?" By describing environmental issues as a "problem" early in the interaction, the survey designers could inadvertently have given respondents the impression that this is an issue over which it is socially correct to display concern. And having once stated concern about environmental issues, respondents would feel the need to produce consistent responses by answering that they would be willing to make economic sacrifices to protect the environment. In our research design, we avoid any discussion about the environment prior to the questions that address environmental issues, in an effort to avoid the problem of issue priming.

9.3   Hypotheses

To what extent do people support FDI that is likely to benefit their countries economically, but also cause environmental damage? Will residents of developing countries be more likely to support FDI for its economic benefits despite its environmental costs, when compared to residents of developed countries? To answer these questions, we generate several testable hypotheses by drawing from existing studies on public opinion on the environment, particularly the ones that address differences between developed and developing countries. As we have discussed, the previous literature is conflicted on whether residents of developing countries are as concerned about the environment as residents of developed countries. On one hand, some studies argue that residents of developed countries are more concerned about the environment than residents of developing countries. This is because economic prosperity leads to a rise in postmaterialist values, including greater concern for the environment. From this mechanism we derive the following hypothesis:

after answering the question on letting Communist reporters into the United States. The obvious interpretation is that when either question is asked first, many respondents answer in terms of pro-American or anti-Communist sentiments, but when the second question is asked a norm of reciprocity is immediately made salient and a substantial number of respondents feel bound to follow that norm and provide an answer that is consistent with their previous response (Schuman and Presser 1996, p. 28).

Hypothesis 1a: When provided with information about the environmental damage caused by FDI, residents of developed countries will be less likely to support FDI than residents of developing countries.

Meanwhile, many other studies argue that residents of developing countries will have stronger incentives to care about the environment, because environmental quality generally tends to be lower in developing countries, and developing countries are likely to bear the brunt of the environmental damage resulting from climate change. This gives us the following hypothesis:

Hypothesis 1b: When provided with information about the environmental damage caused by FDI, residents of developing countries will be less likely to support FDI than residents of developed countries.

We also predict that people's attitudes toward environmental problems in locations that are distant from their own city of residence will differ between developed and developing countries. A number of earlier studies have argued that people are more likely to care about the environment in their immediate surroundings than in distant locations. As deHaven Smith (1988) stated, "[Q]uestions dealing with a policy that affects people's immediate circumstances – their neighborhoods and the land directly around them – are most likely to tap the public's true environmental attitudes" (p. 279). Macnaghten (2003) later echoed this sentiment with the words, "Direct connections to the local and personal environment tended to 'hit home' and matter more" (p. 74). These statements imply that even among people who care about the environment, their concerns will be concentrated in their immediate surroundings, with distant locations relegated to a lower priority.[2]

We expect that the effect of distance on environmental attitudes will be more pronounced among people who display higher levels of environmental concern. Specifically, people who show higher levels of environmental concern will show a greater gap between their concern for the environment of their city of residence and concern for the environment of a distant location.

---

[2] One study investigated people's responses to environmental disasters with a survey of respondents based in Cardiff, with some respondents exposed to a map of rising sea levels around Cardiff, and others to a similar map of Rome. The respondents were then asked how they rated the severity of climate change and how they felt about climate change mitigation, with mixed results (Spance and Pidgeon 2010).

Meanwhile, people with lower levels of environmental concern will show a smaller gap. If Hypothesis 1a is confirmed through our empirical analysis, we will expect the following hypothesis to hold:

Hypothesis 2a: Residents of developed countries will be less likely to support environmentally damaging FDI in their city of residence compared to a city in a distant location. This pattern will be weaker among residents of developing countries.

On the other hand, if Hypothesis 1b is confirmed through our empirical analysis, we will expect the following hypothesis to hold:

Hypothesis 2b: Residents of developing countries will be less likely to support environmentally damaging FDI in their city of residence compared to a city in a distant location. This pattern will be weaker among residents of developed countries.

9.4   Empirical Analysis

We conducted survey experiments in one developed country (the United States) and one developing country (India). Our goal was to examine whether respondents in these two countries would support FDI, contingent on whether they were given information regarding the potential environmental damage that could be caused by FDI. The survey respondents were recruited through Amazon Mechanical Turk (also referred to as "MTurk"), a crowdsourcing Internet marketplace that enables individuals and businesses ("Requesters") to post short online tasks and pay respondents ("Workers") to complete them. We posted our online survey on MTurk, offered US$1 to US respondents who complete the survey, and $0.50 to Indian respondents who complete the survey. Surveys were completed by 447 respondents from the United States and 530 respondents from India. Aside from the requirement that they reside in either the United States or India, we did not impose any demographical restrictions on respondents. (All Workers are required by Amazon to be at least eighteen years old.) As our respondents are those who are registered as MTurk workers and self-select into participation, our samples are convenience samples. In other words, the average treatment effects (ATEs) we identify in our analysis should be understood as applying to the population represented by our sample, rather than to the general adult populations of the United States and India.

Our survey consisted of an informed consent page and two short experimental sections (the order of the experimental sections was randomized). We also included a few brief questions on demographic information such as age, gender, and income level, some of which are asked before the experimental sections, and the others following the experimental sections. The survey was administered in English. For the age and income variables, categorical answer choices were provided. When answer choices are available, respondents can easily click on the correct age and income bracket, rather than having to take time to type in the precise answer. This ease of entry increases the response rate.

We chose India as a survey location for several reasons. First, India receives a substantial flow of FDI; in 2017, the country received approximately US$45 billion in FDI, which was the third highest inflow among developing countries and tenth overall globally. Second, India has been suffering from high levels of environmental pollution in recent decades. For example, according to data reported by the World Health Organization in 2017, eleven of the twelve cities in the world with the highest levels of small particulate matter pollution were located in India (Irfan 2018). Third, English is one of the official languages of the central government of India, and widely spoken throughout the country. This allowed us to administer the survey in English, avoiding the need for translation and ensuring compatibility with the survey that we ran in the United States. (The two developing countries that received more FDI than India in 2017 – China and Brazil – do not use English as an official language.)

The United States was chosen for similar reasons. First, the United States is the largest recipient of FDI in the world, amounting to approximately US$311 billion in 2017. Second, the United States has been linked to high levels of environmental degradation. According to Bradshaw et al. (2010), the United States ranks second only to Brazil in terms of total global environmental impact, based on factors such as natural forest loss, habitat conversion, marine captures, fertilizer use, water pollution, carbon emissions, and species threat. Third, while the US government does not designate an official language, English is the lingua franca of the country. Overall, choosing the United States and India as our survey locations gave us the ease and flexibility of administering the survey in English, in countries that receive large amounts of FDI and also experience significant environmental problems.

9.4.1   Survey Experiment Design

For the respondents who consented to participate in our survey, two experiments are presented. To avoid confusion, we refer to one of the experiments as the "first experiment" and the other as the "second experiment," but the actual order of presentation was randomized between respondents. Table 9.1 summarizes our experimental design.

The first experiment tests which of Hypothesis 1a and Hypothesis 1b is supported.

Respondents are presented with one of two descriptions of FDI, where the information provided is randomly varied. Respondents assigned to the control condition are given information only about the economic benefits expected from FDI, while respondents assigned to the treatment condition are given information about both the economic benefits and the environmental costs expected from FDI. The descriptions presented to the respondents were as follows:

> **Control condition:** When foreign companies invest in your country, there are many economic benefits. The investments create local jobs and improve technology in your country. Foreign companies are requesting permission from your government to initiate their investments in [respondent's city of residence].

Table 9.1 *Experimental design*

	First Experiment (Support of FDI in city of residence)	Second Experiment (Support of FDI in distant city)
Control condition	Positive economic effects of FDI	Positive economic effects of FDI and negative environmental effects of FDI (details omitted)
Treatment condition	Positive economic effects of FDI and Negative environmental effects of FDI	Positive economic effects of FDI and negative environmental effects of FDI

Note: The order of the first and second experiments are randomized in the survey.

Treatment condition: When foreign companies invest in your country, there are many economic benefits. The investments create local jobs and improve technology in your country. However, environmental damage can result from foreign investments. Problems such as greenhouse gas emissions, air pollution, and water pollution are some of these concerns. Foreign companies are requesting permission from your government to initiate their investments in [respondent's city of residence].

After being given a description of FDI, the respondents are asked the following question: Do you support foreign investment in [respondent's city of residence], or do you oppose it? Our dependent (outcome) variable codes the respondents' answers to this question. The answers are coded as "Yes, I support it," "No, I don't support it," and "I don't know." For the data analysis, we included responses where the respondents answered "Yes, I support it" or "No, I don't support it," making our dependent variable a binary variable.

Our second experiment differs from the first experiment in two aspects. First, all respondents are informed of the environmental costs of FDI; however, the amount of information they are given regarding these environmental costs varies between the control and treatment conditions. We did this to verify that small variations in the volume of information provided would not substantially alter the survey responses, since the sensitivity of responses is a concern when gathering survey data. Second, rather than asking respondents whether they would support FDI in their city of residence, we asked them whether they would support FDI in a distant location. For US respondents, this location was Houston, Texas, and for Indian respondents the location was Bhopal, Madhya Pradesh. (We also implement a robustness check excluding respondents from Texas and Madhya Pradesh.) Since the only difference between the treatment conditions of the first and second experiments are in the location of FDI, this data allows us to test Hypothesis 2a and Hypothesis 2b, namely that the effect of distance on environmental attitudes will differ between residents in developed countries and those in developing countries.

The descriptions of FDI in the second experiment were as follows:

Control condition: When foreign companies invest in your country, there are many economic benefits. The investments create local jobs and improve technology in your country. However, environmental damage can result from foreign investments. Foreign companies are requesting permission from your government to initiate their investments in Houston, Texas (Bhopal, Madhya Pradesh).

Treatment condition: When foreign companies invest in your country, there are many economic benefits. The investments create local jobs and improve technology in your country. However, environmental damage can result from foreign investments. Problems such as greenhouse gas emissions, air pollution, and water pollution are some of these concerns. Foreign companies are requesting permission from your government to initiate their investments in Houston, Texas (Bhopal, Madhya Pradesh).

After being given one of these descriptions, the respondents are asked the following question: Do you support foreign investment in Houston, Texas (Bhopal, Madhya Pradesh) or do you oppose it? As in the first experiment, our dependent variable codes the respondents' answers to this question. The answers are coded as "Yes, I support it," "No, I don't support it," and "I don't know." For the purposes of data analysis, we used responses where the respondents answered "Yes, I support it" or "No, I don't support it."

9.4.2 Sample Description

Five hundred and twenty-nine residents of India and 447 residents of the United States completed our survey experiments. We excluded fifty-nine responses from India because we could not verify the locations of the respondents, leaving 470 responses from India. We also excluded three respondents from the United States and one resident from India, because they did not provide information on income, age, or gender.

To confirm our randomization process, we present the balance between the control and treatment conditions of the pretreatment variables (such as age, gender, and income level) for the United States and the India samples in Tables 9.6 and 9.7, respectively, in Appendix B in this chapter. We find that the balance between the control and treatment variables has been achieved, as chi-square tests for each pretreatment covariate suggest that the responses in the control conditions do not differ from ones in the treatment conditions (in both samples). However, each variable has certain categories that lack perfect balance, especially when the number of observations in the category is small. To check that this does not affect the analysis, we control for income,[3] age,[4] and gender in our regressions.

9.4.3 Results: Concern for the Environment

Table 9.2 shows the results of ordinary least squares estimation using the data from our first experiment. The binary outcome variable, Support of FDI, is coded 1 if the respondent supports FDI in his or her city of residence and 0 if he or she does not support it. This variable is regressed on the variable Environment, which is a treatment indicator that codes whether the respondent is assigned to the treatment condition or the control condition (assignment is random). Specifically, Environment is coded 1 if the respondent receives the treatment condition, which contains information about potential environmental damage caused by FDI, and 0 if the respondent receives the control condition, which does not include information about environmental damage.

The coefficient for Environment shows the average treatment effect of providing information about the environmental costs of FDI, on respondents' support of FDI in their city of residence. The first column of Table 9.2 shows the results from respondents in the United States, and the second column shows the results from respondents in India. The average treatment effect of Environment is negative in both samples, showing that respondents in both countries decreased support for FDI in their city of residence when informed about the environmental costs of FDI, despite the economic benefits associated with FDI. However, the decline in support was much larger in the US sample compared to the sample from India. We can see this by comparing the coefficients for

---

[3] For respondents from India, the income brackets are, in terms of the Indian Rupee: less than 10,000; 10,000–19,999; 20,000–29,999; 30,000–39,999; 40,000–49,999; 50,000–59,999; 60,000–69,999; 70,000–79,999; 80,000–89,999; 90,000–99,999; 100,000–109,999; 110,000–119,999; 120,000–129,999; 130,000–139,999; 140,000–149,999; and more than 150,000. For respondents from the United States, the income brackets are, in terms of the US Dollar: less than 10,000; 10,000–19,999; 20,000–29,999; 30,000–39,999; 40,000–49,999; 50,000–59,999; 60,000–69,999; 70,000–79,999; 80,000–89,999; 90,000–99,999; 100,000–149,999; and more than 150,000.

[4] The raw data is divided into six age brackets: 18–24; 25–34; 35–44; 45–54; 55–64; and 64 and above. However, for the sample from India, the 55–64 age bracket only had 1 respondent, and 65 and above also had 1 respondent. Not all treatment and control groups have respondents from these age categories, making the effects of these age groups difficult to estimate. Therefore, we combined the three eldest age brackets, resulting in one bracket: ages 45 and above. For consistency, we did this for both India and the United States sample.

Table 9.2 *Effects of information about environmental damage caused by FDI*

	(1) United States	(2) India	(3) Both (Pooled)
Environment	−0.164***	−0.086**	−0.079**
	(0.047)	(0.033)	(0.040)
United States			−0.237***
			(0.044)
Environment*United States			−0.085*
			(0.057)
Constant	0.616***	0.904***	0.869***
	(0.106)	(0.066)	(0.063)
Controls for income, age, gender	Included	Included	Included
N	444	469	913
Adjusted R^2	0.032	0.031	0.106

Note: Ordinary least squares regression. Standard errors in parentheses. *$p < 0.1$; **$p < 0.05$; ***$p < 0.01$. The dependent variable is *Support of FDI*. The variable *Environment* is coded 1 if the respondent receives information about potential environmental damage caused by FDI, and 0 otherwise. The variable United States is coded 1 if the respondent resides in the *United States*, and 0 if the respondent resides in India.

Environment between the United States and India: the average treatment effect of providing information about the environmental costs of FDI is almost twice as large among respondents from the United States than respondents from India. In other words, when respondents from the United States and India are given information about the environmental damage that could be caused by FDI, respondents from the United States are much more likely to disapprove of FDI in their city of residence when compared to respondents from India. To test whether the differences between the samples from the United States and India are statistically significant, we pooled the two samples. The variable United States is a country indicator that is coded 1 if a respondent is from the United States, and 0 if a respondent is from India. The coefficient for the interaction variable between United States and Environment gives us the average difference in the effects of providing environmental information between the two samples. The data analysis is presented in the third column of Table 9.2. The negative coefficient for the variable United States indicates that even when information about the environmental costs of FDI are not provided, respondents from the United States are less likely to approve of the project in their city when compared to respondents from India. Furthermore, the negative coefficient for the interaction variable between Environment and United States indicates that for respondents in the United States, receiving information about the environmental costs of FDI in their city will affect their responses more negatively when compared to respondents in India. Overall, these findings support Hypothesis 1a that residents of developed countries will be more likely to reduce support for FDI when informed of the environmental costs of FDI, compared to residents of developing countries.

Additionally, we examine the possibility that individual characteristics such as income, gender, and age may affect people's attitudes toward environmental protection. Figure 9.1 presents the marginal effects of the treatment assignment, Environment, conditional on the respondent's income bracket. Figure 9.2 presents the marginal effects of Environment conditional on gender. Figure 9.3 provides the marginal effects of Environment conditional on age bracket. We do not observe any linear or statistically significant effects of income, gender, or age on concern for the environment. Overall, the results show that concern for the environment does not vary with these individual characteristics. (We also find that removal of these control variables does not affect our results in any substantive way.)

9.4.4 Results: Effect of Distance on Concern for the Environment

We test Hypothesis 2a and Hypothesis 2b using the data from the treatment conditions (which provide information on the environmental costs of FDI) of our first and second experiments. The only difference between these two conditions is the location of FDI that is being requested for approval. Therefore, taking the difference in means of the outcome variable between the two conditions allows us to identify the average treatment effects of this locational difference, or "distance," on people's support of FDI. Specifically, we examined the difference between the proportion of respondents who do not support FDI in their city of residence and the proportion of respondents who do not support FDI in Houston, Texas (or Bhopal, Madhya Pradesh).

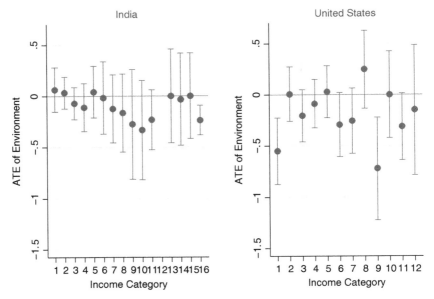

Figure 9.1 Average treatment effects of environment, contingent on income bracket. **Note**: This figure presents the point estimate and 95% confidence intervals of the average treatment effects. The dependent variable is Support of FDI. The variable Environment is coded 1 if the respondent receives information about potential environmental damage caused by FDI, and 0 otherwise. Income codes the respondent's income bracket, with larger numbers corresponding to higher levels of income.

The results are presented in the third column of Table 9.3, where "distance" is our treatment of interest in this case. This is obtained by calculating the difference between the proportion of respondents who do not support FDI in their city of residence and the proportion of respondents who do not support FDI in Houston, Texas (or Bhopal, Madhya Pradesh). Our results show that US respondents are less likely to support FDI when it is located in their city of residence: in the row United States, we can see that 37 percent of respondents answered they do not support FDI in their city of residence, but only 27 percent of respondents answered they do not support FDI in Houston, Texas. This is in contrast to the results from India: in the row India, we can see that 21 percent of Indian respondents did not support FDI in Bhopal, Madhya Pradesh, while only 16 percent did not support FDI in their city of residence (this difference was not statistically significant). These findings support Hypothesis 2a, which argues that people in developed countries will

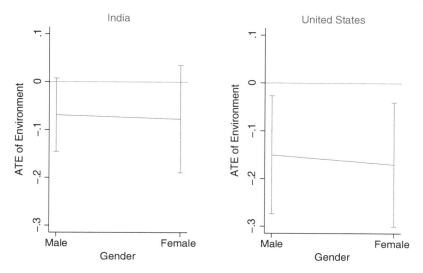

Figure 9.2 Average treatment effects of environment, contingent on gender.
Note: This figure presents the point estimate and 95% confidence intervals of the average treatment effects. The dependent variable is Support of FDI. The variable Environment is coded 1 if the respondent receives information about potential environmental damage caused by FDI, and 0 otherwise. Female is coded 1 if the respondent is female and 0 if the respondent is male.

show more concern about environmental problems in their city of residence than in a distant location, but that this pattern will be less observable in developing countries where environmental concern is weaker.

Our analysis is based on the assumption that people in the United States who do not reside in Houston consider that city to be a distant location, and also that people in India who do not reside in Bhopal consider that city to be a distant location. However, it is possible that people living in Texas may not consider Houston to be a distant location, even if they do not live in Houston itself (a similar logic applies to Madhya Pradesh and Bhopal). To address this possibility, we carry out a robustness check by excluding respondents living in Texas and Madhya Pradesh from the analysis and conducting a difference in means test. In the first experiment, there were nineteen respondents living in Texas who received the treatment condition, and in the second experiment, there were seventeen respondents living in Texas who received the treatment

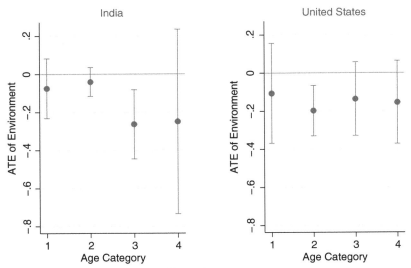

Figure 9.3   Average treatment effects of environment, contingent on age.
Note: This figure presents the point estimate and 95% confidence intervals of the average treatment effects. The dependent variable is Support of FDI. The variable Environment is coded 1 if the respondent receives information about potential environmental damage caused by FDI, and 0 otherwise. Age codes the age bracket of the respondent, with 1 indicating ages 18–24, 2 indicating ages 25–34, 3 indicating ages 35–44, and 4 indicating ages 45 and above.

condition (approximately 7 percent of the sample from the United States). The results after dropping these respondents are presented in the row United States (excluding Texas). We had one respondent who indicated they live in Madhya Pradesh (about 0.2 percent of the sample from India), and the results after dropping this respondent are presented in the row India (excluding Madhya Pradesh). We can see that the results are highly similar to those of the previous analysis.

These findings have interesting implications for the debate on whether people's preferences are driven by material self-interest or concern for the collective (national) interest. For example, Mansfield and Mutz (2009) have argued that individuals form their preferences based on collective-level information rather than personal considerations. On the other hand, Jamal and Milner (2019) showed that self-interest is a powerful influence on individual preference formation; similarly, Rho and Tomz (2017) showed that when people are more informed, the

Table 9.3 *Effect of distance on support of FDI*

	(1) Do Not Support FDI in City of Residence	(2) Do Not Support FDI in Houston (Bhopal)	(3) Difference
United States	Proportion = 0.367	Proportion = 0.265	0.102**
	$N = 229$	$N = 242$	(0.043)
India	Proportion = 0.162	Proportion = 0.209	−0.046
	$N = 234$	$N = 230$	(0.036)
United States (excluding Texas)	Proportion = 0.271	Proportion = 0.271	0.109**
	$N = 210$	$N = 225$	(0.045)
India (excluding Madhya Pradesh)	Proportion = 0.159	Proportion = 0.209	−0.050
	$N = 233$	$N = 230$	(0.036)

"selfish" nature of their responses becomes more evident. Our findings lend support to the latter perspective, by showing that people (at least in the United States) are less likely to support environmentally damaging FDI in their own city than a city at a distance. While this does not imply that people are devoid of concern for the collective interest, it does suggest that people have more concern for their immediate surroundings and the way they are affected by it.

9.4.5 Results: Survey Wording Effect

We also tested whether there were any significant differences between respondents who received the control condition and those who received the treatment condition in the second experiment. The results are presented in Table 9.4. The variable Detail is coded 1 if a respondent was presented with the treatment condition, which contained additional details about the environmental costs of FDI, and coded 0 if a respondent was presented with the control condition, which did not contain these details. The coefficient for Detail is insignificant, showing that there is no difference in the responses between respondents who

Table 9.4 *The effects of survey wording*

	(1) United States	(2) India
Detail	−0.038	−0.014
	(0.047)	(0.039)
Constant	0.571***	0.766
	(0.034)	(0.027)

were exposed to the control condition and those who were exposed to the treatment condition. This gives us some reassurance that slight variations in our survey wording would not substantially affect responses.

9.5   Discussion

Are people in developing countries less concerned about the environmental consequences of FDI compared to people in developed countries? Previous literature on whether economic development is a determinant of environmental protection has examined this question using public opinion research, but so far, no consensus has been reached. Some public opinion research studying mass attitudes toward environmental damage finds that residents of developing countries are deeply concerned about the environmental consequences of economic development (albeit with significant variation in the content and magnitude of that concern). Others have found that residents of developing countries are overall less concerned about environmental issues than people in developed countries.

We note several limitations in existing survey research. First, previous surveys do not directly address the relationship between environmental damage caused by FDI and public support of FDI. Second, problems of endogeneity in observational survey research make it difficult to make causal inferences from the data. Third, previous surveys are subject to social desirability bias and priming effects because they directly ask people (sometimes in an in-person interview) about their perception of environmental problems, rendering it difficult to accurately gauge the level of concern that people have about the environment.

These shortcomings are addressed in our study. We investigate how providing information about environmental damage caused by FDI affects people's support of FDI, and in particular how people's responses differ between developed and developing countries. This was done through an online survey experiment that we implemented in the United States and India. Our experiment provides respondents with information about FDI, where information regarding the environmental costs of FDI differs between the treatment and control conditions. This allows us to observe how respondents' support of FDI changes when they are given information about the environmental costs of FDI. We find that among residents of the United States, being presented with information about the environmental costs of FDI will sharply reduce support for FDI. Meanwhile, though residents of India also decrease their support for FDI when informed of possible environmental damage, the magnitude of this decrease is much smaller. This suggests that economic prosperity and wealth are important determinants of environmental concern.

We also examine whether the location of FDI (and any associated environmental damage) affects people's support of FDI, and whether this locational effect is stronger in the United States. Our findings suggest that residents of the United States are affected by the location of FDI, in that they are more likely to disapprove of environmentally damaging FDI in their own city than in a distant location. On the other hand, residents of India seemed to be less concerned with the locational aspect of environmentally damaging FDI: they were no less likely to approve of FDI in their own city compared to FDI in a distant location.

Our results open up other avenues of future research. Since our surveys were run in only one developing country (India) and one developed country (the United States), supplementary surveys in other developing and developed countries are necessary to generalize the results of our research. Additionally, a survey experiment that examines how the environmental costs of FDI affect people's support of environmental regulations would investigate the feasibility of enacting stricter environmental regulatory policies in developing countries. This research would contribute to our understanding of how to implement environmentally conscious and sustainable development policies.

9.5.1 Implications for Sustainable Development Goals

Our findings have important implications for sustainable development. FDI is an important driver of economic growth, and the creation of relatively high-paying jobs and the transfer of technologies to domestic firms are some of the benefits of FDI that contribute to economic development and growth in recipient countries. However, countries receiving FDI often sustain environmental damage caused by FDI. Our findings suggest that even in a country with extremely high pollution levels like India, residents on average prioritize economic development over environmental protection. This challenges the assumption of many previous studies that residents of areas with significant environmental damage will be willing to make economic sacrifices to preserve the environment. Our results might also imply that until developing countries grow large, relatively wealthy middle classes, their residents will on average prefer strategies that prioritize economic growth at the expense of environmental protection. One possible ramification of this is that residents of developing countries may oppose stringent environmental regulations if they are perceived as a barrier to attracting FDI. This could lead to lax environmental regulations in developing countries, making these countries vulnerable to foreign investors who seek to invest in locations that lack a strict regulatory regime. To address problems of sustainability and the environment, we need to recognize the possibility that the perceived urgency of these problems is low amongst citizens of developing countries, making it difficult to implement environmental policies that are desirable for long-term, sustainable development. Increasing awareness of the long-term consequences of environmental damage may be necessary for regulatory progress in the developing world.

References

Acharyya, J. (2009). "FDI, Growth and the Environment: Evidence from India on CO_2 Emission During the Last Two Decades." *Journal of Economic Development* 34: 43–58.

Barry, F. and Bradley J. (1997). "FDI and Trade: The Irish Host-Country Experience." *The Economic Journal* 107: 1798–1811.

Ratter, Beate M. W., Philipp, K. H. I. and von Storch, H. (2012). "Between Hype and Decline: Recent Trends in Public Perception of Climate Change." *Environmental Science and Policy* 18: 3–8.

Blomstrom, Magnus and Fredrik Sjöholm. (1999). "Technology Transfer and Spillovers: Does Local Participation with Multinationals Matter?" *European Economic Review* 43: 915–923.

Bloom, David. (1995). "International Public Opinion on the Environment." NBER Discussion Paper No. 732.

Bradshaw, Corey, J. A., Xingli Giam and Navjot S. Sodhi. 2010. "Evaluating the Relative Environmental Impact of Countries." *PLoS ONE* 5:1–16.

Chen, Ch., Chang, L. and Zhang, Y. (1995). "The Role of Foreign Direct Investment in China's Post-1978 Economic Development." *World Development* 23: 691–703.

deHaven Smith, L. (1988). "Environmental Belief Systems: Public Opinion on Land Use Regulation in Florida." *Environment and Behavior* 20: 276–299.

Diekmann, A. and Franzen A. (1999). "The Wealth of Nations and Environmental Concern." *Environment and Behavior* 31: 540–549.

Dunlap, R. E., Gallup Jr. G. H., and Gallup A. M. (1993). "Of Global Concern: Results of the Health of the Planet Survey." *Environment: Science and Policy for Sustainable Development* 35: 7–39.

Dunlap, R. E. and Mertig, A. G. (1995). "Global Concern for the Environment: Is Affluence a Prerequisite?" *Journal of Social Issues* 51: 121–137.

Dunlap, R. E. and York, R. (2008). "The Globalization of Environmental Concern and the Limits of the Postmaterialist Values Explanation: Evidence from Four Multinational Surveys." *The Sociological Quarterly* 49: 529–563.

Franzen, A. (2003). "Environmental Attitudes in International Comparison: An Analysis of the ISSP Surveys 1993 and 2000." *Social Science Quarterly* 84: 297–308.

Franzen, A. and Meyer, R. (2010). "Environmental Attitudes in Cross-National Perspective: A Multilevel Analysis of the ISSP 1993 and 2000." *European Sociological Review* 26: 219–234.

Furnham, A. (1986). "Response Bias, Social Desirability and Dissimulation." *Personality and Individual Differences* 7: 385–400.

Gaines, B. J., Kuklinski J. H. and Quirk, P. J. (2007). "The Logic of the Survey Experiment Reexamined." *Political Analysis* 15: 1–20.

Grimes, P. and Kentor, J. (2003). "Exporting the Greenhouse: Foreign Capital Penetration and CO2 Emissions 1980–1996." *Journal of World-Systems Research* 9: 261–275.

Huang, C., Liao H. and Chang, S.-H. (1998). "Social Desirability and the Clinical Self-Report Inventory: Methodological Reconsideration." *Journal of Clinical Psychology* 54: 517–528.

Inglehart, R. (1995). "Public Support for Environmental Protection." *Political Science and Politics* 28: 57–72.

Irfan, U. (2018). "Why India's Air Pollution Is So Horrendous." Available at www .vox.com/2018/5/8/17316978/india-pollution-levels-air-delhi-health.

Jamal, A. and Milner, H. V. (2019). "Economic Self-Interest, Information, and Trade Policy Preferences: Evidence from an Experiment in Tunisia." *Review of International Political Economy* 26: 545–572.

Jiang, Y. (2015). "Foreign Direct Investment, Pollution, and the Environmental Quality: A Model with Empirical Evidence from the Chinese Regions." *The International Trade Journal* 29: 212–227.

Kalton, G. and Schuman, H. (1982). "The Effect of the Question on Survey Responses: A Review." *Journal of the Royal Statistical Society: Series A (General)* 145: 42–73.

Kim, S. Y. and Wolinsky-Nahmias, Y. (2014). "Cross-National Public Opinion on Climate Change: The Effects of Affluence and Vulnerability." *Global Environmental Politics* 14: 79–106.

King, M. F. and Bruner, G. C. (2000). "Social Desirability Bias: A Neglected Aspect of Validity Testing." *Psychology and Marketing* 17: 79–103.

Kingston, K. G. (2011). "The Dilemma of Minerals Dependent Economy: The Case of Foreign Direct Investment and Pollution in Nigeria." *African Journal of Social Sciences* 1: 1–14.

Kull, Steven. 2007. "International Polling on Climate Change." Available at WorldPublicOpinion.org.

Kvaløy, B., Finseraas H. and Listhaug, O. (2012). "The Publics' Concern for Global Warming: A Cross-National Study of 47 Countries." *Journal of Peace Research* 49: 11–22.

Lasorsa, D. L. (2003). "Question-Order Effects in Surveys: The Case of Political Interest, News Attention, and Knowledge." *Journalism and Mass Communication Quarterly* 80: 499–512.

Leiserowitz, A. (2007). "International Public Opinion, Perception, and Understanding of Global Climate Change." United Nations Development Programme Human Development Report 2007/2008.

Li, X. and Liu, X. (2005). "Foreign Direct Investment and Economic Growth: An Increasingly Endogenous Relationship." *World Development* 33: 393–407.

Lleras, G. R. and Cabrera Leal, M. (2017). "Colombia and China: Social and Environmental Impacts of Trade and Foreign Direct Investment." In R. Ray, K. Gallagher, A. Lopez, and C. Sanborn (eds.), *China and Sustainable Development in Latin America: The Social and Environmental Dimension.* Anthem Press.

Macnaghten, P. (2003). "Embodying the Environment in Everyday Life Practices." *The Sociological Review* 51: 63–84.

Mansfield, E. D. and Mutz, D. C. (2009). "Support for Free Trade: Self-Interest, Sociotropic Politics, and Out-Group Anxiety." *International Organization* 63: 425–457.

OECD (Organisation for Economic Co-operation and Development). (1999). *Foreign Direct Investment and the Environment.* OECD Publishing.

Parry, H. J. and Crossley, H. M. (1950). "Validity of Responses to Survey Questions." *Public Opinion Quarterly* 14: 61–80.

Rho, S. and Tomz, M. (2017). "Why Don't Trade Preferences Reflect Economic Self-Interest?" *International Organization* 71: S85–S108.

Sandvik, H. (2008). "Public Concern Over Global Warming Correlates Negatively with National Wealth." *Climatic Change* 90: 333–341.

Schuman, H. and Presser, S. (1996). *Questions and Answers in Attitude Surveys: Experiments on Question Form, Wording, and Context.* Sage Publications.

Siggins, L. (2017). "Corrib Gas Timeline: 20 Years of Protests and Controversy." *The Irish Times*, July 13, 2017. Available at www.irishtimes.com/news/ireland/irish-news/corrib-gas-timeline-20-years-of-protests.

Spance, A. and Pidgeon, N. (2010). "Framing and Communicating Climate Change: The Effects of Distance and Outcome Frame Manipulations." *Global Environmental Change* 20: 656–667.

Strack, F. (1992). *"Order Effects" in Survey Research: Activation and Information Functions of Preceding Questions.* Springer.

Tourangeau, R. and Yan, T. (2007). "Sensitive Questions in Surveys." *Psychological Bulletin* 133: 859–883.

van de Mortel, T. F. (2008). "Faking It: Social Desirability Response Bias in Self-Report Research." *Australian Journal of Advanced Nursing* 25: 40–48.

Waldkirch, A., Nunnenkamp, P. and Alatorre Bremont, J. E. (2009). "Employment Effects of FDI in Mexico's Non-Maquiladora Manufacturing." *The Journal of Development Studies* 45: 1165–1183.

APPENDIX A

Overview of Previous Surveys

Table 9.5 *Literature summary*

Authors and Surveys	Survey Questions	Methods and Findings
Inglehart (1995): World Values Survey 1990–1993	Respondents are classified as "high" on support for environmental protection if they "agree" or "strongly agree" that: (1) *"I would be willing to give part of my income if I were sure that the money would be used to prevent environmental pollution"* AND (2) *"I would agree to an increase in taxes if the extra money is used to prevent environmental pollution"*; AND who "disagree" or "strongly disagree" with these statements: (1) *"The government should reduce environmental pollution, but it should not cost me any money"*; and (2) *"Protecting the environment and fighting pollution is less urgent than often suggested."*	The author presents the percentages of respondents classified as "high" for the countries that were surveyed. On balance, he says that vulnerability to environmental damage and postmaterialism are both important to determining public attitudes on the environment, and that it is not clear whether developing countries are more (or less) concerned about the environment than developed countries.

Table 9.5 (*cont.*)

Authors and Surveys	Survey Questions	Methods and Findings
Dunlap et al. (1993): Gallup 1992 "Health of the Planet" (HOP)	*"What do you think is the most important problem facing our nation today?"* *"I'm going to read a list of issues and problems currently facing many countries. For each one, please tell me how serious a problem you consider it to be in our nation – very serious, somewhat serious, not very serious, or not at all serious?"* *"How concerned are you personally about environmental problems – would you say a great deal, a fair amount, not very much, or not at all?"* *"Overall, how would you rate the quality of the environment (a.) in our nation, (b.) here in your local community, (c.) of the world as a whole? Very good, fairly good, fairly bad, or very bad?"*	The authors present the percentage of respondents who give a particular answer to a given question. The results show considerable variation among countries, but overall, respondents in developing countries show significant concern for the environment.
Dunlap et al. (1993): Gallup 1992 "Health of the Planet" (HOP)		The authors present the

Table 9.5 (*cont.*)

Authors and Surveys	Survey Questions	Methods and Findings
		percentage of respondents
	"How much, if at all, do you	who give a particular answer to
	believe environmental problems	a given question. The results
	(a) now affect your health, (b)	show considerable variation
	affected your health in the past	among countries, but overall,
	– say 10 years ago, (c) will	respondents in developing
	affect the health of our children	countries show significant concern
	and grandchildren – say over the	for the environment.
	next 25 years? A great deal, a fair	
	amount, not very much, or not at	
	all?"	
	"With which of these statements	
	about the environment and the	
	economy do you most agree:	
	protecting the environment and	
	the economy do you most agree:	
	protecting the environment should	
	be given priority, even at the	
	risk of slowing down economic	

Table 9.5 (*cont.*)

Authors and Surveys	Survey Questions	Methods and Findings
	growth, [or] economic growth	
	should be given priority, even if	
	the environment suffers to some	
	extent?"	
	"Increased efforts by business	
	and industry to improve environmental quality might	
	lead to higher prices for the	
	things you buy. Would you be	
	willing to pay higher prices so	
	that industry could better protect	
	the environment or not?"	
	"Which one of these do you	
	believe should have the primary	
	responsibility for protecting the	
	environment in our nation –	
	the government, busi- ness, and	
	industry, or individual citizens	
	and citizens groups?"	
	"In your opinion, how much of an	

Table 9.5 (*cont.*)

Authors and Surveys	Survey Questions	Methods and Findings
	effect can individual citizens and citizens groups have on solving our environmental problems?”	
Dunlap and Mertig (1995): Gallup 1992 “Health of the Planet” (HOP)	See above.	The authors correlate responses with GDP per capita. They do this by creating “national-level aggregate scores for every nation by computing the national mean of all responses” for each of the fourteen questions in the survey. Then for each of these scores, the authors computed Pearson's correlation coefficients with per capita GDP. The results support those discussed in Dunlap et al. (1993).
Bloom (1995): Gallup 1992 “Health of the Planet” (HOP) Louis Harris and Associates 1988–1989 Survey	*“How would you rate the quality of the environment in this country?”* (Harris) *“Do you feel the environment where you live has become better or worse or stayed the same in the last 10 years?”* (Harris)	The author uses cross-country population weighted averages and compares the difference in percentages between developing and industrialized countries, for an answer to a given question. He writes, “First, people in both

Table 9.5 (cont.)

Authors and Surveys	Survey Questions	Methods and Findings
	See above for Gallup's HOP survey questions.	developing and industrial countries perceive that environmental quality has been and is continuing to worsen, and express substantial concern about environmental quality overall and about a range of specific environmental issues. Second, in assigning responsibility for the world's environmental problems, the data indicate a remarkable willingness to accept responsibility rather than exclusively to blame others. Finally, people generally recognize the government's natural role in addressing local and national environmental issues and the equally natural role of strong international agencies in addressing transnational issues." (pp. 12–13)
Leiserowitz (2007): GlobeScan 1998–2001 Surveys	*"How serious a problem do you consider climate change or global warming, due*	This study presented the percentage of respondents in each country that gave a particular answer to a given

Table 9.5 (*cont.*)

Authors and Surveys	Survey Questions	Methods and Findings
	to the greenhouse effect?" "*Climate change will pose a direct threat to me and my family over the next decade.*" "*Air emissions from richer countries have had the most impact on the Earth's climate, however, emissions are growing more quickly in poorer countries with large populations. As a result, there is a debate about when these poorer countries should join richer countries in taking significant action to reduce human impacts on climate. Do you think these poorer countries should . . . ?*"	question. Many developing countries viewed climate change as a more serious risk than most developed countries did, and respondents from developing countries were generally more convinced that climate change would be a direct threat, compared to respondents from developed countries. Furthermore, the majority of respondents in developing countries answered that "*poorer countries should be required to take significant action [to reduce human impact on climate] immediately along with richer countries.*"
Sandvik (2008): Nielsen Company 2007 online survey	" . . . respondents from 46 different countries were asked how serious a problem (on a scale from 1 to 5) they thought global warming was." (p. 334)	The author conducted analysis of covariance and found that GDP per capita was negatively associated with concern for global warming.
Diekmann and Franzen	"*How willing would you be to pay much higher prices in order to*"	In Franzen and Meyer (2010), the authors took the answers from

Table 9.5 (*cont.*)

Authors and Surveys	Survey Questions	Methods and Findings

(1999);
 	
Franzen
 	
(2003);
 	
Franzen
 	
and Meyer
 	
(2010):
International Social
  Survey
	protect the environment?"
	
	*"How willing would you
	  be to pay
	much higher taxes in
	  order to
	protect the environment?"*
	
	*"How willing would you
	  be to accept cuts in your
	  standard of living in
	  order to protect the
	  environment?"*
		nine questions in the
		  survey, each
		coded on a scale of 1–5
		  (with
		higher numbers
		  corresponding
		to higher levels of
		  concern),
		and constructed an
		  additive
		index for each individual.
		Results from a linear
		  regression show that
		  GDP per capita
		  (adjusted for purchas-
		  ing power) has
		  a statistically signifi-
		  cant positive effect on
		  concern for the
		  environment.

Programme
1993 and 2000
	*"I do what is right for the
	  environment, even
	  when it costs
	more money or takes
	  more time."*
	*"Modern science will
	  solve our
	environmental problems
	  with little
	change to our way of
	  living."*
	*"We worry too much
	  about the
	future of the environment
	  and not
	enough about prices and
	  jobs."*
	*"People worry too much
	  about*	

Table 9.5 (*cont.*)

Authors and Surveys	Survey Questions	Methods and Findings
	human progress harming the environment." "*In order to protect the environment the country needs economic growth."* "*It is just too difficult for someone like me to do much about the environment."*	
Dunlap and York (2008): World Values Survey 1995–1998	"*I would agree to an increase in taxes if the extra money were used to prevent environmental damage."* "*I would buy things at 20 percent higher than usual prices if it would help protect the environment."* "*Here are two statements people sometimes make when discussing the environment and economic growth. Which of them comes closer to your own point of view? (a) Protecting the environment should be given priority, even if it causes slower economic growth and loss of some jobs. (b) Economic growth and creating jobs should be given the top priority,*	Using correlation coefficients between GDP per capita and survey answers, the authors find no statistically significant relationship between the two.

Table 9.5 (*cont.*)

Authors and Surveys	Survey Questions	Methods and Findings
Kvaløy, Finseraas and Listhaug (2012): World Values Survey 2005	*even if the environment suffers to some extent."* "*Now let's consider the environmental problems in the world as a whole. Please tell me how serious you con- sider [global warming or the greenhouse effect] to be for the world as a whole. Is it very serious, somewhat serious, not very ser- ious, or not serious at all?"*	Using a multilevel linear regression, the authors find that GDP per capita does not have a statistically signifi- cant effect on survey responses.

APPENDIX B

Balance Between Control and Treatment Conditions

Table 9.6 *Balance between control and treatment conditions: United States sample*

Age	First Experiment		Second Experiment	
	Control	Treatment	Control	Treatment
18–24	29	25	20	34
	(13.3)	(10.92)	(9.43)	(14.05)
25–34	109	102	102	114
	(50)	(44.54)	(48.11)	(47.11)
35–44	41	63	47	58
	(18.81)	(27.51)	(22.17)	(23.97)
45–54	25	21	28	19
	(11.47)	(9.17)	(13.21)	(7.85)
55–64	8	15	10	13
	(3.67)	(6.55)	(4.72)	(5.37)
65–74	6	3	5	4
	(2.75)	(1.31)	(2.36)	(1.65)
Total	218	229	212	242
	(100)	(100)	(100)	(100)
Gender	Control	Treatment	Control	Treatment
Female	104	108	106	107
	(47.71)	(47.16)	(50)	(44.21)
Male	114	121	106	135
	(52.29)	(52.84)	(50)	(55.79)
Total	218	229	212	242
	(100)	(100)	(100)	(100)
Income (in US dollars)	Control	Treatment	Control	Treatment
Less than $10,000	15	20	19	16
	(6.94)	(8.77)	(9.09)	(6.61)

Table 9.6 (*cont.*)

Income (in US dollars)	Control	Treatment	Control	Treatment
$10,000–$19,999	21	32	20	33
	(9.72)	(14.04)	(9.57)	(13.64)
$20,000–$29,999	26	29	28	27
	(12.04)	(12.72)	(13.4)	(11.16)
$30,000–$39,999	38	28	36	31
	(17.59)	(12.28)	(17.22)	(12.81)
$40,000–$49,999	26	30	24	34
	(12.04)	(13.16)	(11.48)	(14.05)
$50,000–$59,999	23	15	21	19
	(10.65)	(6.58)	(10.05)	(7.85)
$60,000–$69,999	14	24	17	22
	(6.48)	(10.53)	(8.13)	(9.09)
$70,000–$79,999	14	11	12	13
	(6.48)	(4.82)	(5.74)	(5.37)
$80,000–$89,999	9	6	9	7
	(4.17)	(2.63)	(4.31)	(2.89)
$90,000–$99,999	10	10	7	13
	(4.63)	(4.39)	(3.35)	(5.37)
$100,000–$149,999	16	18	11	23
	(7.41)	(7.89)	(5.26)	(9.5)
More than $150,000	4	5	5	4
	(1.85)	(2.19)	(2.39)	(1.65)
Total	216	228	209	242
	(100)	(100)	(100)	(100)

Note: Percentages of responses in parentheses.

Table 9.7 *Balance between control and treatment conditions: India sample*

Age	First Experiment		Second Experiment	
	Control	Treatment	Control	Treatment
18–24	34	43	38	39
	(14.17)	(18.38)	(15.57)	(16.96)
25–34	162	165	169	158
	(67.50)	(70.51)	(69.26)	(68.70)
35–44	40	22	32	30
	(16.67)	(9.40)	(13.11)	(13.04)
45–54	3	3	5	1
	(1.25)	(1.28)	(2.05)	(0.43)
55–64	1	0	0	1
	(0.42)	(0.00)	(0.00)	(0.43)
65–74	0	1	0	1
	(0)	(0.43)	(0)	(0.43)
Total	240	234	244	230
	(100)	(100)	(100)	(100)
Gender	Control	Treatment	Control	Treatment
Female	74	76	88	62
	(30.96)	(32.48)	(36.07)	(27.07)
Male	165	158	156	167
	(69.04)	(67.52)	(63.93)	(72.93)
Total	239	234	244	229
	(100)	(100)	(100)	(100)
Income (in Indian rupees)	Control	Treatment	Control	Treatment
Less than ₹10,000	19	21	26	14
₹10,000–₹19,999	(7.98)	(9.05)	(10.74)	(6.14)
	37	41	37	41
₹20,000–₹29,999	(15.55)	(17.67)	(15.29)	(17.98)
	37	39	36	40
₹30,000–₹39,999	(15.55)	(16.81)	(14.88)	(17.54)
	16	18	19	15
₹40,000–₹49,999	(6.72)	(7.76)	(7.85)	(6.58)
	12	19	16	15
₹50,000–₹59,999	(5.04)	(8.19)	(6.61)	(6.58)
	8	7	9	6
₹60,000–₹69,999	(3.36)	(3.02)	(3.72)	(2.63)
	9	8	7	10

EFFECTS OF ENVIRONMENTAL COSTS ON SUPPORT FOR FDI 309

Table 9.7 (*cont.*)

Income (in Indian rupees)	Control	Treatment	Control	Treatment
₹70,000–₹70,000	(3.78)	(3.45)	(2.89)	(4.39)
	7	6	8	5
₹80,000–₹89,999	(2.94)	(2.59)	(3.31)	(2.19)
	9	2	6	5
₹90,000–₹99,999	(3.78)	(0.86)	(2.48)	(2.19)
	6	3	3	6
₹100,000–₹109,999	(2.52)	(1.29)	(1.24)	(2.63)
	10	12	11	11
₹110,000–₹119,999	(4.20)	(5.17)	(4.55)	(4.82)
	0	1	0	1
120,000–₹129,999	(0.00)	(0.43)	(0.00)	(0.44)
	4	5	2	7
₹130,000–₹139,999	(1.68)	(2.16)	(0.83)	(3.07)
	10	3	9	4
₹140,000–₹149,999	(4.20)	(1.29)	(3.72)	(1.75)
	8	4	8	4
More than ₹150,000	(3.36)	(1.72)	(3.31)	(1.75)
	46	43	45	44
	(19.33)	(18.53)	(18.60)	(19.30)
Total	238	232	242	228
	(100)	(100)	(100)	(100)

Note: Percentages of responses in parentheses.

Conclusion

COSIMO BEVERELLI, JÜRGEN KURTZ AND DAMIAN RAESS

The chapters in this volume have shown that international trade and foreign investment can contribute in different ways to achieving the Sustainable Development Goals (SDGs) at all levels, be it international, supranational, transnational, national or subnational.

Part I of this edited collection focused on international pathways for penetration and diffusion of the SDGs. Within that broad category, it seems likely that, alongside use of voluntary sustainable standards (VSS) in global supply chains, bilateral and regional trade agreements will comprise the dominant site of transmission for the immediate future. Chapter 1 by Adinolfi aptly charts the growing assertiveness of the European Union (EU) in harnessing preferential trade agreements (PTAs) to export European standards to select counterparties in the form of trade and sustainable development chapters. In the past, there was a de facto limit on the hard transfer of those broader ('WTO plus') standards. Faced with the possibility of a dispute, most states parties elected to pursue trade enforcement through the dispute settlement system of the World Trade Organization (WTO) which limits adjudication to its own 'covered agreements' under the Dispute Settlement Understanding (DSU). Generally speaking, states parties chose WTO dispute settlement over other fora (such as PTAs), as it had generated sizeable levels of state confidence and trust since inception in 1994. Yet WTO adjudicators were often forced to rule on charged political disputes engaging delicate questions of regulatory variance among its diverse member states. Chapter 3 by Espa reminds us of the remarkable sensitivity in which the WTO legal system confronted that formidable challenge, particularly in the environmental sphere.

WTO adjudication can no longer act as the default site for trade enforcement, given the current legal impossibility of exercising the right of appeal to the WTO Appellate Body reserved to members under the WTO DSU. States' parties will be forced therefore to activate PTA dispute settlement chapters when faced with non-compliance by a counterparty. In point of fact, the EU has already chosen to do so and crucially had begun to do so before the current stasis in WTO dispute settlement. Some of these claims promote simple (offensive) commercial interests without any direct engagement of the SDGs, such as the recent establishment of an arbitration panel under the EU–Ukraine Association Agreement on Ukraine's export ban on unprocessed wood. But others are squarely reflective of the underlying socio-political values that animate certain parts of the SDGs. Consider in this respect the July 2019 establishment of a panel under the EU–South Korea Free Trade Agreement by the EU to require implementation by South Korea of the labour obligations under that FTA.

Chapter 2 by Basedow explored the political economy drivers behind select inclusions on SDG-related treaty text in EU international investment agreements. Importantly, he found that politicisation and aggregation of member state preferences primarily fuelled policy changes while external legal obligations played no significant role. From a theoretical perspective, Basedow's chapter lends support to rational choice institutionalism, which suggests that institutional changes affect policy substance. With this analysis in mind, one can foresee the growing possibility of deeper levels of EU projection of SDG values, both through treaty text and enforcement choices. Environmental issues are particularly likely to comprise a terrain of contestation for the EU. Environmentalism has a strong role in the European Parliament, measured not only by the increased growth of dedicated environmental parties in the recent parliamentary elections. For many European governments and policymakers, the task of saving the world's forests and halting global warming has been elevated to the moral imperative of a climate emergency. Yet translating these European ideals into trade and investment policy evokes, for many developing countries as counterparties to PTAs, long-standing concerns of possible hidden protectionism.

The SDGs can also be diffused by different actors (to states) using non-legal pathways to PTAs. In fact, key contributions in Parts II and III of this edited collection show that there are significant SDG-related gains that can be realised by promoting trade and investment flows. In Chapter 7 Jackson and Balema, focusing on VSS in Côte d'Ivoire, show that the adoption of sustainable development practices – such as water conservation, soil management, integrated waste management and ecosystem conservation – significantly increased when farmers joined a certification program. In addition, the price premia received by certified farmers' organisations can be used to finance public goods such as health care, education and clean water. And there are also other benefits of working with certification in the case of cocoa producers from Côte d'Ivoire, such as training and capacity building which can lead to higher yields and better quality of cocoa products. These results confirm that the public good dimension of VSS identified by Fiorini et al. in Chapter 6 can have positive effects on a variety of SDGs without implying associated trade-offs. DiCaprio et al., in Chapter 8 on blockchain technology, show qualitatively that such technology has the potential to greatly reduce trade frictions in the areas of trade finance, customs and border procedures, and tariff preferences' utilization. They also provide quantitative evidence on the potential trade and welfare gains of lower trade costs and the ability of blockchain technology in customs to narrow the preference utilization gap. The authors offer the imposing possibility that these mechanisms might increase world trade by $1.7 trillion, and world gross domestic product by $0.92 trillion.

A major theme emerging from several contributions to this volume is, however, the existence of trade-offs in the simultaneous realisation of social, environmental and economic goals. Put directly, the challenge centres on the capacity of societies to manage growth in a sustainable and inclusive manner. This requires policymakers and other actors to balance economic growth with key social and environmental objectives without further accentuating within- and between-country inequalities. Fiorini et al. argue that, more than any other channel they identify in their analysis, the production channel of VSS (i.e. VSS-induced changes in production technology) can be associated with trade-offs in terms of the impact of VSS on different dimensions of sustainable development. For instance, technology requirements designed to protect biodiversity might come with high implementation costs, excluding the poorest producers from the use of associated VSS and potentially increasing income inequality. As argued by Di Caprio et al., blockchain technology could reduce trade frictions, bringing about increases in trade and in welfare. But this technology is also highly energy-intensive. The Cambridge Bitcoin Electricity Consumption Index (CBECI, cbeci.org) estimates that the global Bitcoin network (for which blockchain acts as ledger) consumes more energy than a country like Switzerland in one year (64 terawatt hours versus 58 terawatt hours).

The main tension running through several contributions pertains to the trade-off between environmental and economic dimensions, particularly unhindered trade and foreign direct investment (FDI) flows. These economic modalities are not considered simple ends in themselves in the 2030 Agenda but, as engines of economic growth, they are a means to support the achievement of the SDGs. This finding is consistent with the latest 'assessment of assessments' based on the review of 65 global assessments (e.g., UN flagship reports, international scientific assessments) and 112 scientific articles published since 2015 with explicit reference to the SDGs (Independent Group of Scientists appointed by the Secretary-General 2019). The UN-mandated report finds significant trade-offs in the interactions between Goal 8 (Economic Growth), on the one hand, and Goal 13 (Climate Action), Goal 12 (Responsible Consumption and Production) which deals with the management of natural resources, Goal 6 (Clean Water and Sanitation) and Goal 14 (Life Below Water), on the other hand (Independent Group of Scientists appointed by the Secretary-General 2019: Box 1–2).

Against this backdrop of trade-offs, in Chapter 4 Berger et al., corroborating the 'protectionism in disguise' claim, find that inclusion of more environmental provisions in PTAs reduces trade flows among trade partners and that this effect is entirely driven by a decrease in developing country exports to developed countries. Kim and Lee's survey experiments show that the presentation of information about the environmental costs of FDI sharply reduces support for FDI among developed country residents (American citizens) while a significant weaker effect is observed among developing country residents (Indian citizens). This suggests that citizens in high pollution environments – which are often found in developing countries (such as India) – seem less willing to forgo economic advantage to preserve the environment. In Chapter 5 Bauerle Danzman and Gertz show that investment promotion agencies (IPAs) integrated within government behave differently from autonomous IPAs, with the former being less inclined to spend resources to attract large foreign firms while devoting more on cultivating joint ventures between foreign and domestic firms. Integrated IPAs also promote greater domestic linkage activities, including educational linkages, than do autonomous agencies. On the economy–environment nexus more specifically, they present suggestive evidence that integrated IPAs are more disposed to evaluating investment projects for their environmental (and social) impact. Taken together, these results suggest that developing country governments in particular are facing hard choices. The 2030

Agenda, embodied in mottos such as 'Each country must respond to its own conditions and priorities, while breaking away from current practices of growing first and cleaning up later' (Independent Group of Scientists appointed by the Secretary-General 2019: xx), sets out a clear roadmap for decisions.

A comparison between the trade flows effect of labour and environmental provisions in PTAs further suggests that the trade-offs might be particularly pronounced with respect to the environment. Research finds that while the introduction of labour clauses in PTAs does not, on average, impact bilateral trade flows, the effect on exports from developing to developed countries is nil or even positive (International Labour Organisation 2016; Carrère et al. 2017). One possible explanation for the differentiated effect on South–North trade flows may have to do with the fact that – while a demand-side mechanism (i.e., increased consumer demand for goods produced under higher labour/environmental standards) *and* a supply-side mechanism (i.e., decent work may increase labour productivity) might offset increased production costs associated with more stringent labour market (or environmental) regulation – only the former mechanism is likely to operate in the case of environmental provisions. Further research is required to understand how variation in types and stringency of environmental provisions in PTAs might differently affect bilateral trade flows.

The latest round of multilateral talks on climate change in Madrid (December 2019), known as COP25, ended up in failure due to a lack of accord on new rules for a global carbon trading market. It has become commonplace to put the onus of inaction on world leaders, particularly those from the world's two biggest emitters (the US and China) and from large developing countries (Brazil and India). As Nat Keohane, senior vice-president at Environmental Defense Fund put it, 'COP25 showed that the yawning gap between what citizens are demanding on climate action, and what the UN negotiations are delivering, is wider than ever' (cited in Hook 2019). Yet, the growing wave of youth climate activism ('Generation Greta') is predominantly a developed country phenomenon. Lee and Kim's findings are a powerful reminder that what residents in developing countries demand on climate action and what their governments deliver is more aligned than what one tends to think. Raising public awareness regarding the long-term consequences of environmental damage may be necessary condition for regulatory progress in the developing world.

References

Carrère, C., Olarreaga, M. and Raess, D. (2017). 'Labor Clauses in Trade Agreements: Worker Protection or Protectionism?' CEPR DP12251, Centre for Economic Policy Research.

Hook, L. (2019). 'Climate Talks Undone by "Ghost from Past"'. *Financial Times*, 16 December.

Independent Group of Scientists appointed by the Secretary-General. (2019). *Global Sustainable Development Report 2019: The Future Is Now – Science for Achieving Sustainable Development.* New York: United Nations.

International Labour Organization. (2016). *Assessment of Labour Provisions in Trade and Investment Agreements.* Geneva, Switzerland: ILO.

INDEX

3D printing, 8
Aarhus Convention on Access to
  Information, Public Participation
  in Decision-Making and Access to
  Justice in Environmental Matters
  (1998), 38
Agreement Establishing the African
  Continent Free Trade Area,
  27
ams approach, 254
arbitration, 32, 38, 41, 45, 63, 64, 65,
  94, 311
  ad hoc tribunal, purpose, 64
arbitrators
  diversity, 64
  qualifications, 64
Argentina, 55
Article 3(1)(e) TFEU, 21
Article 3(5) TEU, 20
Article 11 TFEU, 20
Article 21 TEU, 21
Articles 191–193 TFEU, 21
Article 205 TFEU, 21
Article 207 TFEU, 21
Articles 208–211 TFEU, 21
Artificial Intelligence (AI), 8
Asian Development Bank (ADB), 243
Association of Southeast Asian Nations
  (ASEAN), 27
Authorized Economic Operator
  (AEO), 250
average treatment effects (ATEs), 278,
  283–288
AWG v. Argentina, 55
Bangladesh, 147, 255
Basel Convention on the Control of
  Transboundary Movements of
  Hazardous Wastes and their
  Disposal, 29

Belgium, 57
Bilateral Investment Treaties (BITs), 50
bilateral trade flows, 6, 119, 314
biodiversity, 19, 77, 81, 82, 99, 111, 118,
  181, 194, 196, 207, 270, 312
blockchain, 3, 8, 9, 228–238, 240–244,
  249–255, 257–258, 262,
  264–265, 312
Brazil, 145, 164, 279, 314
Brexit, 237
Brundtland Report, 76, 79
C.A.F.E. Practices, 182, 183
Canada, 18, 19, 26, 38, 62, 66, 244,
  251, 253
Canada–United States–Mexico
  Agreement (CUSMA), 26, 33
CARIFORUM States, 18, 19, 39
Cartagena Protocol to the Convention
  on Biological Diversity, 23
CETA, 23, 32, 33, 63, 65
  access to justice, 38
  dispute settlement, 39
  fair and equitable treatment standard
    (FET), 33, 62
  general exceptions clause, 23
  mutual supportiveness, 25
  right to regulate, 33
CGE modelling, 251, 254
Chile, 145, 164
China, 60, 66, 67, 91, 92, 258,
  279, 314
  export restrictions, 91, 92
China – Rare Earths, 91, 93
China – Raw Materials, 91, 93
China – Raw Materials II, 91
Chinese government. *See* China
climate change, 1, 4, 19, 34, 53, 83, 99,
  214, 272, 277, 314
Colombia, 19

For EU product safety concerns, contact us at Calle de José Abascal, 56–1°,
28003 Madrid, Spain or eugpsr@cambridge.org.